Assessment and Intervention Issues Across the Life Span

T0346630

Assessment and Intervention Issues Across the Life Span

Edited by

Stephanie M. Clancy Dollinger
Lisabeth F. DiLalla

Southern Illinois University at Carbondale

Routledge
Taylor & Francis Group

LONDON AND NEW YORK

First published 1997 by Lawrence Erlbaum Associates, Inc.

Published 2018 by Routledge
2 Park Square, Milton Park, Abingdon, Oxon OX14 4RN
52 Vanderbilt Avenue, New York, NY 10017

First issued in paperback 2018

Routledge is an imprint of the Taylor & Francis Group, an informa business

Library of Congress Cataloging-in-Publication Data

Assessment and intervention issues across the life span
/ edited by Stephanie M. Clancy Dollinger and Lisabeth
F. DiLalla.
    p. cm.
This volume is based on the second Life Span Development Conference held at Southern Illinois University Carbondale, Il, October 14–15, 1994.
Includes bibliographical references and index.
ISBN 0-8058-2164-3 (cloth : alk paper)
1. Neuropsychological tests–Congresses. 2. Clinical neuropsychology–Congresses. 3. Psychotherapy–Congresses. 4. Developmental psychology–Congresses. I. Dollinger, Stephanie M. Clancy. II. DiLalla, Lisabeth F. III. Life Span Development Conference (2nd : 1994 : Carbondale, Ill.)
    RC386.6.N48A84 1997
    616.07'5–dc20   96–27362
                                                            CIP

ISBN 13: 978-1-138-96401-3 (pbk)
ISBN 13: 978-0-8058-2164-2 (hbk)

Contents

Preface

This volume evolved from the second Life Span Development Conference held at Southern Illinois University at Carbondale, IL, October 14–15, 1994 entitled "Assessment and Intervention Issues across the Life Span." It consists of chapters based on the conference presentations, as well as additional chapters by experts in related specialty areas. Presentations focused on assessment and intervention issues across the life span spanning topic areas such as social ecology, cultural diversity, attitudes about aging, and attention, visual, and linguistic skills.

The format of the conference provided an exciting opportunity for students and researchers to interact with experts in the field in an informal setting. The conference was held at the Touch of Nature Environmental Center, Southern Illinois University. Participants were able to take advantage of the beautiful fall foliage and lake setting for informal lunches and walks. These informal exchanges led to many scholarly discussions among the participants and often resulted in a lively forum for sharing theoretical and research ideas. Overall, the conference successfully provided an opportunity for the presentation and exchange of research findings.

Eight chapters in this volume are by conference participants. Three additional individuals were invited to contribute to this volume on topics related to assessment and intervention: attachment theory, learning disabilities, and phonological processing. As reflected in the overview chapter by Molfese, this second conference was a continuation of the first conference and corresponding volume entitled, *Assessment of Biological Mechanisms Across the Life Span*. The second conference further considered critical developmental issues related to the areas of assessment and intervention relevant for the study of life-span development.

A wide range of topics is presented in this volume. Topics cover important interactions between assessment and intervention for each major developmental period. Several chapters emphasize the importance of early assessment and intervention. A common theme found throughout this volume is the critical connection between basic research and practice.

The role of environmental and social factors in infancy and early childhood are important themes in several chapters. Aylward's chapter opens with a discussion on models of outcome, specific environmental factors that affect outcome, and specific developmental processes. This is followed by a consideration of socioeconomic status, genetics, and the relation between biology and environmental risk. Research conducted by the author and his colleagues using the SES-Composite Index is summarized, indicating that environmental effects influence developmental outcome. Aylward concludes that a transactional model of environmental influences should guide intervention efforts.

Crittenden proposes the use of attachment theory to facilitate functional diagnosis of psychopathology following assessment and for the development of more effective treatment interventions. The chapter opens with a consideration of human information processing, followed by a discussion of attachment patterns and how they are reflected in developmental tasks across the life span. The importance of assessing the quality of attachment in psychotherapy is stressed especially with adults. Compulsive and obsessive patterns are considered as examples in the discussion of this perspective, and a summary of work conducted using the Adult Attachment Interview is presented. Finally, how clinicians can apply attachment theory to assessment and treatment is addressed.

The next three chapters focus on assessment and intervention issues specifically related to language skills in young children. Vandervelden and Siegel present a developmental theoretical framework to assess early phonological processing specific to learning to read and write. They address the conceptual and methodological challenges in assessing phonological processing skills. Basic phonological processing abilities and phonological processing in learning an alphabetic script are reviewed, including phonological recoding, phoneme awareness, task diversity, and letter knowledge. Examples of tasks that typify this developmental approach in the assessment of young children are presented. The need for early assessment is stressed as critical to provide relevant information needed to successfully design specific curriculums. A theoretically similar, but methodologically different, approach to the assessment of language skills in young children is taken by Molfese, Tan, Sarkari, and Gill. Research using electrophysiological measures obtained at birth to predict and assess language skills is presented. A review of phonological discrimination, phonological awareness, and orthographic skill development is presented. The mechanisms underlying the predictive power of evoked response potentials for later language assessment are considered. It is concluded that electrophysiological measures, as well as behavioral measures, are needed to identify children at risk for language problems and can serve as successful tools to monitor the progress of intervention training.

Language skills are also the focus of the chapter by Berninger and her colleagues. Models of brain–behavior relationships are presented, followed by an enlightening comparison of developmental neuropsychological and traditional approaches to intervention. A discussion of important measurement issues and innovations in treatment research is presented in the area of reading and writing disabilities based on a systems perspective. Current research on the treatment of reading and writing disabilities from the authors' own work, as well as that of others, is presented.

Vaughn and Sinagub also consider children with learning disabilities, but focus on the assessment of social competence in at-risk children. Models of social competence are presented and their application to research is considered. The role of interpersonal relationships as an indicator of social competence including peer acceptance, social status, friendship qualities, and the relation between social skills and maladapative behaviors are among the areas addressed. Observational techniques and the rating of social skills are also discussed.

Vaux discusses intervention strategies for violent behavior based on social ecology. The clinical and counseling psychology roots of current applied psychology are described in the opening sections of the chapter. Vaux proposes an interesting alternative paradigm—an applied psychology grounded in community psychology. The potential of community psychology for assessment and intervention especially in the area of violence is proposed. In the second section of the chapter he discusses demographics and incidence rates for specific antisocial behaviors including murder, rape, violence against children, and conduct disorders. In the final section, assessment and intervention for these areas of violence are considered on several levels based on Bronfenbrenner's ecological theory.

Mitchell's chapter addresses methodological and theoretical issues specific to conducting research and implementing intervention programs with ethnic minority groups. Individuals working in applied settings with culturally diverse populations will do well to pay attention to this chapter and learn from the author's rewarding personal experiences. Mitchell discusses her current project called VOICES (Voices of Indian Teen Project) being conducted in American Indian communities. The issues addressed include: measurement; common developmental tasks for all adolescents as well as those specific for the population; and community concerns including confidentiality, the need for respect, and communication styles.

The last two chapters address assessment and intervention issues specific to the middle and later part of the life span. Gannon reviews and critiques views of aging in women based on the contrasting feminist and medical paradigms. The paradigms are compared in their treatment of topics such as sexuality, depression, osteoporosis, and cardiovascular disorders. She argues that assessment and intervention techniques typically endorsed by the medical community are based on negative attitudes and stereotypes about aging and are best regarded as interference rather than helpful interventions.

Ball examines the relation between attention and driving in older drivers and presents research findings based on the Useful Field of View (UFOV) paradigm. The results of a validation study based on this new technique examining crash risk in older drivers is described. An especially notable finding was that the UFOV test proved to be more successful in the assessment of older drivers at risk for crashes as compared to traditional measures. Ball concludes with a discussion of attentional intervention training and the implications of the present findings for the assessment of driving skills in the older population.

As this volume reflects, the conference provided an overview and consideration of important directions for research in the areas of assessment and intervention. We hope that this book will prove useful to researchers and practictioners in related disciplines working with individuals of all ages.

ACKNOWLEDGMENTS

We gratefully acknowledge the cooperation and assistance of those who helped to make the conference a success. Financial support was in part provided by Southern Illinois University's School of Medicine and the Vice President's Office for Academic Affairs at Southern Illinois University at Carbondale (SIUC). We would also like to thank those who presented posters at the conference and contributed to many lively informal discussion sessions following the formal paper presentations. The poster presenters included: R. D. Allen, EG Bishop, J. S. Braddock, D. L. DiLalla, L. F. DiLalla, S. M. C. Dollinger, S. J. Dollinger, K. Fox, B. Gilbert, L. A. Gill, K. A. Gordon, A. N. Jiang, A. Karim, K. Klein, M. Le , T. W. Loboschefski, T. Martin, N. McArthur, C. McCallister, D. L. Molfese, V. J. Molfese, B. S. Molina, J. Monteiro, J. Morales, W. R. Nash, L. Nielson, C. L. Patrick, L. Pescara-Kovach, C. J. Peters, C. R. Reynolds, D. O. Ritzel, W. L. Rosse, S. Rubenzahl, R. R. Schmeck, P. G. Simos, J. F. Snyder, J. R. Stevens, A. Tan, A. Vaux, J. M. Vidic, T. Viviano, and T. R. Wolf. The assistance of many SIUC graduate students also contributed to the success of the conference. Finally, we wish to thank Christina Martin and Debbie Fields for the many hours of hard work they offered in helping us prepare for this conference and David and Leila Fisher for expert assistance in preparing this book.

1

When Worlds Collide:
Assessment Meets Intervention

Victoria J. Molfese
Shawn Acheson
Southern Illinois University at Carbondale

When originally conceived, this chapter was to be a recapitulation of the Second Life Span Developmental Psychology Conference. This was to be the chapter that summarized and put into perspective the sparkling new papers presented on the conference topic, "Assessment and Intervention: Issues Across the Life Span." However, due to unavoidable circumstances, the summary was actually presented as the first paper of the conference and the reordering in presentation serendipitously became an advantage. In the lead chapter, it is possible to present a retrospective of the status of assessment across the life span, followed by a discussion of how assessment could and should interface with intervention. The retrospective was shaped, in part, by the nine papers that were presented at the First Life-Span Developmental Psychology Conference, titled "Assessment of Biological Mechanisms Across the Life Span." The papers presented at the conference described a variety of different assessments useful for infants, children, and adults that were developed over many decades of work. Yet, as was clear from those papers, much remains to be learned about how the results obtained from the application of assessment techniques can be linked to appropriate intervention strategies. As the papers presented in the second conference revealed, many intervention strategies with demonstrated effectiveness for remediating a variety of developmental, social, and cognitive disabilities and different medical and physiological problems are not directly and individually linked to specific assessments. How to link the most effective assessments with the most effective interventions still remains to be determined.

1

In the book published from the first conference, entitled *Assessment of Biological Mechanisms Across The Life Span* (DiLalla & Dollinger, 1993), eight chapters detail a variety of assessment techniques useful for a diverse age range. To recapitulate, these chapters describe several visual, biomedical, behavior genetic, and brain processing mechanisms that were found to influence specific cognitive and social abilities. In the visual domain, novel techniques for assessing deficits in the visual pathway that influence contrast sensitivity and detection of spatial frequency were implicated in the deficits noted in children with reading disabilities and in vision problems in the elderly (Lehmkuhle, 1993) . A second paper provided a description of various techniques developed for assessing vision in infancy (Shea, 1993). The usefulness of assessments of perinatal risks in the detection of the developmental delay in later infancy and childhood is described in the third paper (V. Molfese, 1993). Examples were given in this paper of several ways in which perinatal risk conditions are used to predict performance on cognitive tests during the preschool years. Information on how behavior across the life span is affected by genetic influences was described in two papers along with details on how the often interactive effects of heredity and environment can be separated through twin studies (DiLalla & Falligant, 1993; McGue & Carmichael, 1993). The final three papers discussed biological approaches to assessment involving brain functioning (Clancy Dollinger, 1993; Molfese, Gill, Simos, & Tan, 1995; Ober & Shenaut, 1993). Assessments of memory functioning in patients with Alzheimer's disease using semantic priming, changes in cerebral asymmetry in adult subjects using visual half field methodology, and neuroelectrical responses in infants as predictors of cognitive abilities in childhood were discussed. In each case, clear evidence was presented showing that many different aspects of mental functioning can be detected using measures of biological mechanisms.

Together, the information presented in these papers from the first conference provided rich information on successful biological approaches to assessment that are useful with infant, child, and adult populations. It is clear from these papers that assessment is and has been a major focus of the research community. The result of all this research attention is the clear demonstration that many effective assessment techniques were developed.

With all the progress that was made, where does the assessment community need to direct its attention? If only the assessment side of the equation is known, what is lacking in our knowledge? The promising results obtained from the extensive assessment work has set the stage for making the transition to intervention, which is, after all, the intended link with assessment. Intervention typically receives little consideration in the various literatures that publish assessment research. This relative lack of attention is consistent with the observation that rarely in the development and implementation of new assessment techniques is there an explicit consideration of what specific intervention techniques are indicated in light of the assessment results. More typical are statements such as "if X can be assessed in the first few months of life, the targeted infants can be directed to appropriate interventions." The specifics as to what are the "appropriate interventions" are not often addressed.

Kaye (1986) argued that assessment and intervention must be considered together because both involve intersecting issues. Kaye points to several issues as showing this intersection. First, assessment and intervention both involve questions of costs and benefits. For assessment, the questions are, assessment of what conditions, and for what ends? In attempting to answer, we must identify assessments that can identify conditions leading to a poor prognosis if not treated (cost). The assessments must also be able to identify conditions for which an intervention exists that actually improves the prognosis (benefit). It makes little sense to assess individuals for risk conditions that are likely to lead to negative outcomes if treatability is unknown or if options for treatment are undeveloped or unavailable.

For intervention, the cost–benefit issue focuses on questions such as: intervention for what conditions? How successful is the intervention likely to be? If a variety of possible intervention techniques exist, the choice of which intervention strategy to apply would involve consideration of what the costs of the intervention will be in a particular case—in terms of applying the intervention and not applying it. In deciding between these choices, there must be a consideration of how much will be gained from applying the intervention and what will be lost from not applying the intervention. These decisions must include consideration of questions such as: what are the expectations that the intervention will actually succeed? and for what proportion of individuals to whom the intervention is applied will there be success? These questions address issues pertaining to estimates of the benefit side of the cost–benefit equation.

In considering the cost–benefit aspect of assessment and intervention, it is also important to determine whether or not intervention techniques exist that are appropriate for the age range in which the assessments are developed. For example, assessment techniques for children that identify conditions for which no interventions have yet been developed are not sufficient. Major efforts were made to develop assessment techniques for infants and preschool children under the belief that the earlier an intervention can be applied, the better the outcome. However, intervention techniques for infants and preschool children are not prevalent and are certainly less sophisticated than are the intervention techniques developed for school-age children. Clearly, the interface of assessment with intervention must be directed toward conditions for which complementary intervention techniques exist or can be developed, and for a condition that makes cost–benefit sense to treat with the age range within which the condition is prevalent.

Second, Kaye argued that the costs of the assessment and intervention techniques are often far too great to permit their use with large populations. Thus, decisions must be made as to who will be assessed and who will receive the intervention. These decisions are not easily done and are rarely addressed in these terms. Most frequently, assessment techniques are evaluated in terms of sensitivity and specificity, where sensitivity is the proportion of true positives (i.e., the identification of individuals who actually have the condition being screened for) and specificity is the proportion of true negatives (i.e., the identification of individuals who really do not have the condition). Ideally, the most efficient use of assessment techniques is to adjust their scoring criteria to maximize sensitivity so that the greatest possible benefits will be obtained for those individuals with the condition that the assessment technique was designed to identify. Attaining this goal of high sensitivity is difficult to achieve and usually involves the manipulation of assessment scores. Manipulation of scores tends to result in the overidentification of false positives (i.e., individuals identified as having the condition but who do not actually have it) and false negatives (i.e., individuals who are not identified as not having the condition but who actually have it). The usual assumption underlying the setting of assessment scores so that maximum identification of true positives is achieved is that missing true positive cases is far worse than identifying a few cases who do not actually have the condition being screened for. It is further assumed that in all cases the result of being "positively" identified and participating in a treatment program will do no harm to the individuals even if they do not actually have the condition being treated. Although arguments challenging these types of assumptions will continue, including concern about incorrectly labeling individuals and the costs of applying treatment where it is not needed, the seriousness of conditions being screened for often played a role in how issues of sensitivity and specificity are defined.

For intervention, cost is evaluated based on the attainment of specified outcome criteria by the individuals receiving the treatment. The effectiveness of the intervention technique is gauged by the outcomes achieved. Frequently, however, beneficial effects are only found for subgroups of individuals, and not for all the members of the group. Identifying which specific individuals or subgroups of individuals are most likely to benefit from the intervention has been as problematic to those developing effective intervention techniques as have the identification problems encountered by those developing assessment techniques. However, such identification issues are critical to overcome as important issues concerning the cost of treatment, and who will pay those costs is nationally debated.

Third, Kaye argued that decisions on administering assessments or providing interventions frequently involve the issue of what types of cases should have highest priority. Kaye argued that it makes little sense to develop and administer assessment and intervention techniques without knowing what their payoffs will be. Frequently, the payoff is not known with certainty. These payoffs can only be properly evaluated through the consideration of a variety of different issues. For example, school-age children are often targeted for interventions because their problems are readily apparent, especially in the school setting where assessments are applied on a weekly basis through classroom tests and at year intervals through the use of various mandated state and school district achievement tests. The presumption is that the payoff with school-age children will be great. However, complicating the payoff with regard to intervention effectiveness are the cognitive, social–environmental, personality, physiological, and other changes that come with developmental progressions in childhood. The intrinsic and extrinsic factors characterizing children's development can complicate the success of even the best intervention techniques. Yet, despite these complications, some people would wholeheartedly endorse the time and effort needed to develop, refine, and apply interventions for children. Considerably greater efforts might be made with children who have their whole lives ahead of them than efforts expended in developing intervention techniques for elderly populations in which the payoff might be seen as too short term. However, as the baby boomers age, the interest in assessments for screening and interventions for remediating conditions in order to assure healthy, cognitively intact adulthood years is growing rapidly! From an admittedly superficial observation, it appears that young infants and toddlers are about as unpopular as the elderly as targets for intervention strategies based on the availability of relatively few types of intervention techniques for both groups—possibly because neither group has enough of an advocacy force as yet.

A further difficulty in evaluating the payoff of interventions and, by implication, assessment is the ability to clearly specify what the outcomes of a particular case would be without intervention. The difficulty here, of course, is that naturally occurring cases are rarely available and those that are discovered are so unusual as to make generalizations difficult or impossible. For example, a California girl named Genie was discovered who was severely sensory deprived and without language after many years of abuse. Genie, who was in the middle childhood years when she was discovered, presented an opportunity for developmentalists to see how language might be acquired years after it would have naturally developed and after years of deprivation. Yet the extensive retardation across a variety of cognitive domains and Genie's uncertain prior developmental history made it clear that the intervention processes accompanying the complexities of language learning would be nearly impossible to study with Genie (Curtiss, 1977). There are also reports of situations in which an intervention technique was developed that was so successful that the researchers and practitioners were reluctant to establish a control group to use for comparison purposes because such a group would have been deprived of the benefits of the intervention (Gilkerson, 1995). In both of these examples, the effectiveness of intervention can only be inferred.

A closer linkage is needed between assessment and intervention techniques so that assessment results can be used in a prescriptive sense for identifying specific intervention programs. Kaye (1986) described this notion as using assessment techniques as placement tests for intervention programs. Then close study needs to be made of the relationship between the initial assessment performance and the influence of the intervention on subsequent assessment performance. Ideally, long term studies would be initiated in which assessment and intervention phases would be followed by phases of repeated assessment and intervention as long as these phases are needed to obtain the desired outcomes. We are using evoked brain potentials as a technique to identify children predicted to have problems in areas of language and cognitive development. We have now begun recording evoked potential and behavioral responses while the children are engaged in tasks involving phonological discrimination, phonological awareness, and orthographic skills—skills that are related to children's reading abilities. Intervention strategies are being developed to enable children with specific reading skill problems to incrementally master their problem areas. For example, children will be taught to use phonics in phonological awareness tasks and their performance will be compared over time to determine if resultant changes in reading skills can be shown. Following the application of the intervention strategies, reassessments using evoked brain potential and behavioral techniques will be applied to see if there are changes in brain and behavioral responses that reflect the benefits gained from the intervention. If there are changes, then intervention might proceed, but if there are no changes, then the type of intervention will be changed in an effort to effect a different result.

Another example of the successful demonstration of this assessment–intervention–assessment approach is a project by D. Molfese (1993) in which changes in brain responses to world geography knowledge was shown using a pretest–training–posttest approach. During the pretest, adolescents were asked to identify match–mismatch between names and shapes of fictional countries. Following a training session in which names and shapes of countries were learned, a posttest was given. Discrete regions of the evoked potential waveform obtained during the posttest were distinctly different from those obtained during the pretest. These differences were attributed to the effects of the training session. This approach offers a means for linking behavioral changes with neurological responses to obtain additional evidence of the effects of training beyond that which can be obtained from behavioral assessment alone.

The Next Steps

This book contains 10 chapters reporting on innovative and effective approaches to intervention across the life span. Each chapter focuses on what can be gained from assessment information that is helpful for considering intervention options. Two chapters describe environmental and social competence approaches to assessment and intervention with children who have disabilities (Glen Aylward; Sharon Vaughn & Jane Sinagub). Two chapters focus on the importance of biological and cognitive mechanisms in influencing both assessment and intervention in studies of cognitive and language development (Dennis Molfese & colleagues, Martha Vandervelden & Linda Siegel). One chapter describes successful approaches to treating children with reading and writing disabilities (Virginia Berninger et al.).

The role of social factors, such as attachment, social ecology, and culture, in interventions with specific populations is addressed in three chapters (Patricia Crittenden, Alan Vaux, and Christina Mitchell). Two chapters consider the needs of middle-aged and elderly people as factors in determining whether or not intervention is needed and how to intervene (Linda Gannon, and Karlene Ball). In each case, a multidimensional, multifactorial, or multisystem approach is taken in considering the types of intervention or approaches that are needed to address specific types of disabilities and dysfunctions. Such multiplicative approaches are consistent with findings from assessment research that most disabilities and dysfunctions are complex and multisystemic in nature. As more information is shared between assessment and intervention researchers and practitioners, and as more efforts are made to consider assessment and intervention from a life-span perspective, more areas affording opportunities for interface will be discovered, for the betterment of both fields.

REFERENCES

Clancy Dollinger, S. M. (1993). Assessment of cerebral asymmetry in aging: A review of the visual modality. In L. F. DiLalla & S. M. Clancy Dollinger (Eds.), *Assessment of biological mechanisms across the life span* (pp. 151–172). Hillsdale, NJ: Lawrence Erlbaum Associates.

Curtiss, S. (1977). *Genie: A psycholinguistic study of a modern-day "wild child."* New York: Academic Press.

DiLalla, L., & Clancy Dollinger, S. (1993). *Assessment of biological mechanisms across the life span.* Hillsdale, NJ: Lawrence Erlbaum Associates.

DiLalla, L., & Falligant, E. (1993). An environmental and behavioral genetic perspective on behavioral inhibition in toddlers. In L. F. DiLalla & S. M. Clancy Dollinger (Eds.), *Assessment of biological mechanisms across the life span* (pp.91–119). Hillsdale, NJ: Lawrence Erlbaum Associates.

Gilkerson, L. (1995, March). *An examination of the processes of implementation of developmentally supportive care in the NICU.* Paper presented at the Biennial Meeting of Society for Research In Child Development, Indianapolis, IN.

Kaye, K. (1986). A four-dimensional model of risk assessment and intervention. In D. Farrani & I. McKinney (Eds.), *Risk in intellectual and psychosocial development* (pp. 273–286). New York: Academic Press.

Lehmkuhle, S. (1993). Deficits in parallel visual processing in children with reading disabilities and in the elderly. In L. F. DiLalla & S. M. Clancy Dollinger (Eds.), *Assessment of biological mechanisms across the life span* (pp. 1–27). Hillsdale, NJ: Lawrence Erlbaum Associates.

McGue, M., & Carmichael, C. (1993). Life-span developmental psychology: A behavioral genetic perspective. In L. F. DiLalla & S. M. Clancy Dollinger (Eds.), *Assessment of biological mechanisms across the life span* (pp. 71–89). Hillsdale, NJ: Lawrence Erlbaum Associates.

Molfese, D., Gill, L., Simos, P., & Tan, A. (1996). Implications resulting from the use of biological techniques to assess development. In L. F. DiLalla & S. M. Clancy Dollinger (Eds.), *Assessment of biological mechanisms across the life span* (pp. 173–190). Hillsdale, NJ: Lawrence Erlbaum Associates.

Molfese, D. L. (1993). *World geography knowledge as measured through evoked potentials.* Poster presented at the Illinois Junior Academy of Science, Champaign, IL.

Molfese, V. (1993). Perinatal risks across infancy and early childhood: What are the lingering effects of high and low risk samples? In L. F. DiLalla & S. M. Clancy Dollinger (Eds.), *Assessement of biological mechanisms across the life span* (pp. 53–70). Hillsdale, NJ: Lawrence Erlbaum Associates.

Ober, B., & Shenaut, G. (1993). Theoretical and practical issues in semantic priming research with Alzheimer's disease subjects. In L. F. DiLalla & S. M. Clancy Dollinger (Eds.), *Assessment of biological mechanisms across the life span* (pp. 121–150). Hillsdale, NJ: Lawrence Erlbaum Associates.

Shea, S. (1993). From the lab to the clinic: Recent progress in the assessment of developing vision. In L. F. DiLalla & S. M. Clancy Dollinger (Eds.), *Assessment and intervention issues across the lifespan* (pp. 29–51). Hillsdale, NJ: Lawrence Erlbaum Associates.

2

Environmental Influences:
Considerations for Early Assessment and Intervention

Glen Aylward
Southern Illinois University at Springfield

In medical practice, prevention of cognitive delay has been traditionally defined primarily as prevention of biological abnormalities. (Weisglas-Kuperus, Baerts, Smrkovsky, & Sauer, 1993, p. 663)

Most of the mothers seemed so overwhelmed by the inadequacies of their social environments that no intervention short of massive environmental alteration was likely to have any lasting consequences. (Brown et al., 1980, p. 491)

These quotations underscore two issues encountered frequently by clinicians and researchers who work with infants and young children. First, cognitive delay is traditionally attributed to medical conditions such as asphyxia, seizures, or other central nervous system insults. Second, despite intensive, early intervention efforts, children from poor environments often demonstrate compromised developmental outcomes. The purpose of this chapter is to outline issues related to environmental influences on developmental outcome, and to relate these findings to intervention efforts.

Despite the continued emphasis on medical factors as causative agents, it now is assumed that environmental effects also play a critical role in developmental outcome, particularly for at-risk infants. Tjossem (1976) delineated three categories of risk: *established*, *environmental*, and *biologic*. Established risks are medical disorders of a known etiology whose developmental outcome is well-documented (e.g., Down syndrome). Environmental risks involve the quality of the mother–infant interaction, opportunities for stimulation, and health care. Biologic risks include exposure to potentially noxious prenatal, perinatal, or postnatal developmental events such as asphyxia, intraventricular hemorrhage, or low birth weight (LBW). Biologic and environmental risks often occur simultaneously, as children from poor socioeconomic circumstances and poverty are also exposed to medical risk factors such as poor prenatal care, LBW, environmental toxins, drugs, and limited access to medical care. This combination of risks is often referred to as "double jeopardy" (Parker, Greer, & Zuckerman, 1988), or "double hazard" (Escalona, 1982). In such cases, nonoptimal biologic and environmental factors work in a synergistic fashion to affect later outcome (Kopp & Kaler, 1989; Werner, 1986).

Although there is a mounting consensus that the environment exerts a significant effect on developmental outcome (Sameroff & Chandler, 1975), multiple questions persist regarding environmental influences (Aylward, 1990, 1992). It is well-established that children at environmental risk are overrepresented in special education classes (National Center for Children in Poverty, 1990), and that 75% of children with mild mental retardation come from lower socioeconomic status (SES) households. Moreover, four times as many children with intelligence quotients (IQ) less than 70 are born at birth weights greater than 2,500 g. Yet one cannot identify all children from low SES as being at risk for subnormal intelligence, because more of these children demonstrate normal than deficient intellectual development. Therefore, the dilemma faced by professionals working with children who are at risk for compromised outcome is how best to identify aspects of the environment that have deleterious influences, as well as those that are of a more protective nature. In addition, the relationship between environmental and biological issues needs further clarification. Such knowledge is critical when interventions are implemented. In a circular chain of causality, environmental factors will affect the findings of assessments, which, in turn, drive the focus of intervention. Often, the intervention focus will then be directed toward changing the environment.

Several issues will be addressed: models of effect on outcome; delineation of specific environmental factors that affect outcome; relationship between environmental factors and age; identification of the developmental processes that are most susceptible to environmental influences; the relationship between biologic and environmental risk; the role of genetics; discussion of the SES–Composite Index (Aylward, Dunteman, Hatcher, Gustafson, & Widmayer, 1985) with revisions for more contemporary samples, and implications for intervention.

MODELS OF EFFECT ON OUTCOME

An early model of effect is the *continuum of reproductive casualty* (Pasamanick & Knobloch, 1961). The basic assumption of this biologic risk-oriented model is that the severity of developmental disabilities (e.g., cerebral palsy, epilepsy, mental retardation, behavior disorders, and learning problems) is influenced by the degree of perinatal complications. A more serious condition such as cerebral palsy would be associated with more obstetric and perinatal complications than would a milder disorder such as a reading problem. Essentially, the basic tenet was the greater the degree of perinatal complications, the greater the later deviancy. However, studies such as the Kauai Longitudinal Project (Werner, Simonian, Bierman, & French, 1967) reported on in the late 1960s and early 1970s, did not support this model. Children with severe perinatal complications who grew up in middle-class homes had developmental quotients comparable to those without perinatal stress who lived in poor homes. Children who fared the worst were those from poor homes who also had severe perinatal complications (Werner, 1986).

The *interactional model* (Sameroff, 1975) assumes a two-dimensional array of constitution (biologic factors) and environment (e.g., good environment + good constitution = good outcome; good constitution + bad environment = medium outcome). This model did not account for mechanisms or processes by which biologic and environmental interaction evolve, and it held that environment and constitution are constant over time.

Perhaps the most popular model is the *transactional approach* (Sameroff & Chandler, 1975) in which a degree of plasticity is considered inherent in both the child (biologic component) and the environment. The child is constantly reorganizing and self-righting; a poorly stimulating environment would interfere with this self-righting, and the probability of a disrupted child–environment transaction increases. A more positive environment is assumed to enhance the child's resiliency. This environmentally driven model has led to coining of the phrase *continuum of caretaking casualty*. A variation of the transactional model is the *risk route concept* (Aylward & Kenny, 1979). It requires the assessment of a child at various times in three areas: medical–biologic, environmental–psychosocial, and behavioral–developmental. The degree of risk is additive across the three areas at each time of assessment and is cumulative over time (an interaction exists between previous effects and current risk indices). Most current data support these latter models (Aylward, 1992; Bee et al., 1982; Bradley, Caldwell, & Rock, 1988; Weisglas-Kuperus et al., 1993).

SPECIFIC ENVIRONMENTAL FACTORS THAT AFFECT OUTCOME

Identification of the specific, influential features of the environment, both positive and negative, has been elusive. Socioeconomic status is the environmental measure employed most frequently, and is typically represented by maternal education and occupational status. However, SES is not a pure measure. It contains considerable heterogeneity, particularly within middle- and lower class categories (Kopp & Kaler, 1989). Social support is even more difficult to operationalize, because social support includes *tangible* components (housing, financial assistance) as well as *intangible* components (attitudes, encouragement, guidance; Heitzmann & Kaplan, 1988). Moreover, one must consider both *process* and *status* features of the environment (Bradley, Caldwell, & Rock, 1988). Process environmental factors are those specific aspects that are experienced most directly (objects, persons, events), and status factors are broader and involve environmental aspects that are experienced more indirectly (social class, location of residence). Process factors can be considered more *proximal*, in that they involve the child and caretakers on a regular basis (e.g., mother–child interaction), whereas status factors are *distal*, meaning they are secondary and more peripheral (Aylward, 1992). These two environmental features do not have to be similar in terms of quality and this may help to explain why it is difficult to predict the outcome of children at environmental risk. For example, although a child may come from a low-SES household and live in the inner city, the quality of the mother–infant interaction could be exceptionally nurturing and supportive. This situation may buffer the child from the negative influences of broader disadvantages.

Isolated or single environmental factors have a small, incremental effect on later cognitive functioning, and the *accumulation* of risk factors is the major contributor to developmental morbidity. This point was demonstrated by Sameroff, Seifer, Barocas, Zax, and Greenspan (1987), who evaluated the relationship between macroscopic and microscopic risk factors in a sample of 215 4-year-old children enrolled in the Rochester Longitudinal Study. Applying multiple regression, SES (a distal or status variable) accounted for 35% of the variance in verbal IQ; however, inclusion of 10 other environmental risk variables (maternal mental health, mother–child interaction, anxiety, parental perspectives on child development, family support, life events, family size [proximal], and occupation, minority status, and education [distal]) produced a 50% increase in explained variance. As the number of risk factors increased, there was a corresponding decrease in verbal IQ. In children with four or more risk factors, 24% had IQs in the 50 to 84 range, whereas no children with one or no risk factors had IQs in this range.

A recent collaborative, six-site study involving more than 900 children also supports the need to look at process and status variables separately (Bradley et al., 1989). SES was determined using the Hollingshead Four-Factor Index (Hollingshead, 1975), and the Home Observation for Measurement of the Environment (HOME) Inventory (see Bradley & Caldwell, 1988) was employed to measure more specific, process environmental factors (Caldwell & Bradley, 1984). SES was not consistently related to quality of home environment or to developmental status during the 3-year follow-up; the relationship between HOME scores (which measured parental responsivity, acceptance of the child, organization of the environment, play materials, parental involvement, and variety of stimulation) and later developmental status was more consistent. However, there were some ethnic and SES differences in this relationship. For example, correlations between HOME scores and cognitive abilities in lower class children never exceeded $r = .34$; in the other SES groups, correlations approached .60.

Although both SES and total HOME scores predicted later mental test scores, the predictive contribution of SES was weaker than was continuous monitoring of more specific, process, environmental factors measured by the HOME scores. Addition of SES data to HOME data minimally improved prediction of 3-year outcome; in contrast, adding information about the home environment to a regression model that already contained SES information increased the amount of variability accounted for. Low HOME scores were associated with decreasing mental test scores in lower, lower middle, and middle-SES groups. Medium HOME scores were associated with decreasing scores in lower and lower-middle class households; high HOME scores were related to a slower rate of decline in cognitive test scores in lower-class children over the 3-year period.

Therefore, measurement of occupational status or other distal variables does not accurately reflect the type of parenting to which a child is exposed, nor does it provide appreciation of everyday stresses or day-to-day positive aspects of the environment that may serve to buffer the child from negative factors associated with global environmental risk, as measured by SES. Measurement of process factors is time intensive and costly; as a result, such measurement is often difficult to implement.

The concept of the environment is multidimensional and includes caregiver–child interaction, didactic activities (particularly those that encourage mastery of language skills), disciplinary techniques, the family social climate (birth order, spacing, size), and the family's beliefs and values regarding intellectual and educational endeavors (Wallace, 1988). Environment also contains physical properties, organization, regularity of experience, and provision of appropriate play materials. Along these lines, differences in childrearing practices between lower and middle-SES families were documented (Haskins, 1986). In contrast to lower SES families, middle-SES families provide more language that is responsive to the child, place emphasis on reasoning and positive reinforcement (vs. punitive discipline), and arrange the child's natural environment to promote learning.

Race and SES are often confounded in the United States, so that within a particular minority group, SES may not be a powerful predictor (Bradley et al., 1989). This may be due to few Black children living in high-SES home environments, as well as more extensive variation in the lower SES classes that include many minority group children (Kopp & Kaler, 1989). For example, in samples comprised of Black families, specific process-oriented variables (e.g., HOME Inventory) are more predictive of later cognitive development than are global SES measures. However, even the HOME scale is limited in its application to inner-city minority families because of the two decades since its development and changes facing contemporary families such as increased unemployment, violence, drugs, and single parenthood.

Although the HOME Inventory and other similar instruments do measure proximal variables, they are still deficient in their measurement of more subtle aspects of a child's microenvironment. Many factors influence parents' ability to meet their children's developmental needs; parenting is multiply determined. Child characteristics, parents' personal characteristics, situational factors, community characteristics, and broader sociocultural factors play a role (Belsky, 1984; Halpern, 1990). Because of the interrelatedness of these factors, each tends to mediate the other. The presence of poverty increases the likelihood that personal or situational determinants of parenting will become risk factors rather than protective factors in the child's life (Rutter, 1987). The chronic stress, material hardships, and personal debasement that result from poverty exert a negative potentiating influence on other determinants (Halpern, 1990) and magnify the effects of preexisting personal vulnerabilities. Although the effects of a single or even several risk factors can be mediated and lessened by the presence of protective factors in many environments, this is not the case in poverty. Thus, the chronic and pervasive influence of poverty increases the probability that the negative impact of early risk factors will accumulate and persist over time, and intensifies the strong draw toward poor outcome (Halpern, 1990). In essence, protective factors are minimized in these risk environments.

Therefore, in order to better determine potent, negative aspects of the environment, life events and daily coping characteristics (*microfactors*) need to be considered. Although major life events (moves, change in employment, death in the family) and the energy necessitated by readjustment are influential (Holmes & Rahe, 1967), the adaptational significance of relatively minor stresses and pleasures that characterize day-to-day living are probably underestimated. Moreover, the minor stresses and pleasures of daily living have proximal significance and a cumulative impact (Kanner, Coyne, Schaefer, & Lazarus, 1981). Thus, daily irritants may disrupt characteristic coping processes, and may also influence how a person's routine may be affected by major life changes or situations (including poverty). Conversely, to compound matters further, major life events could affect a person's patterns of daily stresses.

To date, approaches that consider daily *hassles* and *uplifts* (Kanner et al., 1981) were primarily limited to behavioral medicine; however, this line of reasoning is also important in identifying critical, environmental factors in developmental studies. Hassles are the irritating, frustrating, and distressing aspects of everyday transactions. They include troublesome neighbors, not having enough money for clothing or housing, personal use of drugs, being out of work, too much leisure time on one's hands, crime, excessive noise, planning meals, neighborhood deterioration, or demands of children (Kanner et al., 1981). Conversely, better insight into a family's adaptive capabilities also is afforded by identification of uplifts. Uplifts are positive experiences that include hearing good news, relating well with a spouse, getting enough sleep, having friendly neighbors, shopping, socializing, or engaging in recreational activities. Such positive experiences may serve as buffers for more proximal hassles and the broader stresses of poverty. As Rutter (1987) suggested, *stress* (unpleasant mental and emotional state) leads to *strain* (negative force), which in turn necessitates *adaptation* (how the family responds to changes or chronic environmental problems). The degree of adaptation determines *risk* (i.e., poor adaptation produces disequilibrium in response to environmental changes and the inability to control these changes).

Summary

No single environmental factor appears to be responsible for compromised developmental outcome (Aylward, 1992). Rather, the cumulative effects of multiple risk factors increase the probability of developmental morbidity. These risk factors are both process (proximal) and status (distal) types. Proximal measures such as the HOME Scale do add to the prediction of childhood IQ above the variance explained by SES (Johnson et al., 1993). However, the relationship between the two types of measures is not clear (Lotas, Penticuff, Medoff-Cooper, Brooken, & Brown, 1992), and the broader status variable of poverty probably has an effect on the parents' basic capacity to parent. Moreover, more constant, albeit minor, positive and negative aspects of day-to-day living and their resultant adaptational potentials must also be considered; these can determine whether the child will be buffered from, or exposed to, major negative life circumstances.

ENVIRONMENTAL FACTORS AND AGE

Generally, it is assumed that environmental effects act in a cumulative fashion from infancy through adolescence. As a result, children from poor or nonstimulating households tend to display a decline in cognitive performance over time. Escalona (1982, 1984) followed a cohort of 144 urban, LBW children from birth to age 3.5 years. The majority of these children were living in poverty. At 15 months, the mean developmental quotient was 99.8; however, by 28 months, it declined to 85.4. Although there was some improvement in the overall mean score at 40 months (89.3), at this age the mean score in children from the lowest SES group was 79.9 (vs. 102 in children from the top SES quartile). These data suggest that the negative effects of a poor environment become increasingly more evident in LBW children from approximately 2 years onward.

Similar findings were reported in the Louisville Twin Study (Wilson, 1985), where mental development scores were reported for biologically at-risk, LBW, and small-for-gestational age twins from 6 months to 6 years of age. Correlations between more distal (status) variables (such as parental education and family status), and IQ scores increased as the children became older, ranging from .06 at 6 months to .45 by 6 years. Interestingly, the reverse was true in regard to biologic variables, with correlations decreasing from .50 at 6 months to .15 by age 6 years. The slopes of the correlations between biologic and environmental variables and outcome crossed between 18 and 24 months, with maternal education and SES demonstrating dramatic correlational gains with IQ by age 24 months. Developmental indexes of children from the upper and lower SES groups were essentially parallel through the first 18 months, but then diverged sharply at 2 years. LBW children from high-SES families began to improve by 3 years of age and showed normal scores by age 6; LBW children from low-SES families continued to display depressed scores at 6 years. Again, there was evidence of increased environmental influences over time in terms of distal factors, with effects becoming more pronounced between 18 and 24 months.

In the National Heart, Lung, and Blood Institute's (NHLBI) Collaborative Antenatal Steroid Study (Collaborative Group on Antenatal Steroid Therapy, 1984) environmental effects were measured with the SES–Composite Index (SES–COMP; Aylward, Dunteman, Hatcher, Gustafson, & Widmayer, 1985), which consisted of six marker variables: maternal education, paternal education, family occupation, integration of an adult male into the family, availability of a car or phone, and freedom from public assistance. Cognitive, motor, and neurologic assessments were made at 9, 18, and 36 months. Outcome scores declined precipitously in cognitive function in the lowest SES–COMP quartile. A markedly lesser decline in cognitive function was found in the middle two SES quartile groupings, and no decrease was noted in the upper SES quartile. The decline was most dramatic between the 18-and 36-month assessments.

Cohen and Parmelee (1983) reported that developmental scores diverged among different ethnic groups of preterm infants by age 2, whereas Bradley et al. (1989) found an increasing relationship between SES and mental test scores from ages 1 to 3 years (.20 to .50). Seigel, Saigel, and Rosenbaum (1982) also found that SES and maternal education were predictive of 2-year developmental status in a biologically at-risk population. Children classified as developmentally at risk at 12 months, but whose developmental scores were in the average range by age 3 years, came from families with high scores on the HOME scale (a proximal measure); those not developmentally at risk initially but whose development was delayed at age 3, came from families having lower HOME scores (Siegel, 1982).

Summary

The effects of status environmental variables such as SES and maternal education become increasingly apparent between 18 and 36 months, with 24 months being an age that is frequently cited. However, environmental effects are apparent even during the first year (Aylward, Verhulst, & Bell, 1989), particularly when parent–infant interaction measures are combined with environmental quality (Bakeman & Brown, 1980; Bee et al., 1982). Proximal, process environmental variables (e.g., HOME scores, parent–child interactions) may be more predictive early on; generalized, distal measures (SES, social support) are more predictive later. Thus, although effects of a poor environment may become more apparent and measurable at approximately 2 years of age, these effects were probably influential throughout infancy.

The age range just cited is a critical transition period in cognitive development, during which skills in symbolic function, language, development, and early concept formation emerge. Moreover, these skills can be measured more accurately at this time, particularly because of the divergence of cognitive and motor function, and the fact that earlier sensorimotor function is strongly canalized. It is also possible that the age correction for prematurity may have some effect, as most of the studies involve preterm infants and correction is discontinued after 2 years. Given that the incidence of prematurity is greater in lower SES families, the age adjustment issue then may have a greater negative impact on children from disadvantaged households.

SPECIFIC DEVELOPMENTAL PROCESSES

Consistency in the diagnosis of cognitive, motor, and neurologic function from 9 to 36 months was studied in the NHLBI Collaborative Antenatal Steroid Study (Aylward, Gustafson, Verhulst, & Colliver, 1987). Motor function diagnoses were most stable over time, with diagnoses of cognitive function being least stable. For example, 25% of infants with normal cognitive function at 9 months had developmental problems by 36 months; the major shift occurred between 18 and 36 months. In contrast, 9 of 10 infants who displayed normal 9-month motor or neurologic function continued to do so. Further analysis revealed that clinical center, child's race, and the SES–COMP were related to cognitive outcome, but only gender influenced later motor function.

In a related study, 14 maternal–prenatal, 24 perinatal, and 12 asphyxia-related variables were correlated with outcome in a subset of this population at term conceptional age, and at 9, 18, and 36 months (Aylward, Verhulst, & Bell, 1989). Correlations between medical–biologic variables and outcome were weak. Three-year neurologic function was influenced more by medical–biologic variables, whereas cognitive function was associated with environmental influences. The SES–COMP predicted 36-month cognitive outcome, particularly when combined with early neuropsychologic assessment. Significant correlations between the SES–COMP and cognitive function began to appear by 9 months.

However, caution must be exercised in dismissing the importance of biologic variables on developmental outcome. In another sample of 150 high-risk nursery graduates (Aylward, 1993), maternal–prenatal, perinatal–postnatal, and asphyxia-related variable arrays and the SES–COMP were correlated with 36-month outcome measures. The SES–COMP had modest, although consistent correlations with outcome. However, when variable arrays of biologic influences (ranging in number from 7 to 16 items) were employed, and when these variables measured change (e.g., initial and 6-hour pH), prediction of later outcome improved, although for specific areas of function (perceptual–performance, motor, and memory). Therefore, the type of outcome measure that is employed is critical.

Siegel (1982) reported that SES, maternal, and paternal education were the most significant variables in predicting 2-year Bayley Mental Developmental Index (MDI) and expressive language scores in a biologically at-risk population. At 5 years of age, environmental and demographic variables continued to contribute more than did medical–biologic variables to the prediction of language function; however, perinatal and reproductive variables were more predictive of perceptual–motor function (Siegel, 1983). These findings were confirmed in other studies as well (Bee et al., 1982; Pfeiffer & Aylward, 1990).

Summary

Available data overwhelmingly support the finding that environmental variables most strongly influence verbal and general cognitive outcome. Medical–biologic factors are more strongly related to neurologic and perceptual–performance function. Medical–biologic factors may influence cognitive scores if the tests include perceptual–performance and perhaps memory items (Aylward, 1993). Because of the relationship between intelligence tests at later ages and language function, environmental variables assume increasing importance in tests administered at that time.

RELATIONSHIP BETWEEN BIOLOGIC
AND ENVIRONMENTAL RISK

As mentioned previously, the continuum of reproductive casualty has not been supported by contemporary studies (Aylward, 1990). Reciprocally, the concepts of double jeopardy (Parker et al., 1988) or double hazard (Escalona, 1982) in which biologic and environmental risks co-occur, were substantiated. The Kauai Longitudinal Project (Werner, 1986; Werner et al., 1967) was the first study to clearly indicate the synergistic combination of biologic and environmental factors. In addition to the aforementioned findings of the worst-case scenario of severe perinatal stress and poor environment leading to compromised development in infancy, similar results were noted when the children reached 10 years of age. Children with and without severe perinatal stress who grew up in middle-class homes achieved IQ scores that were above average; however, scores were significantly lower in children from low-SES households, particularly if they had experienced severe perinatal stress. The synergistic effect of combined biologic and environmental stress was apparent, with innate, biologic factors and environmental influences interacting to adversely affect outcome. By age 18 years, adolescents who lived in poverty were 10 times more likely to have serious learning and behavioral problems than were those who had survived severe perinatal stress but who were not living in poverty.

   In a LBW sample, Drillien (1964; Drillien, Thompson, & Burgoyne, 1980) demonstrated that cognitive deficits in LBW (< 2,500g) infants decreased between the ages of 6 months and 4 years in higher SES classes; however, in the lowest SES class, the deficits increased. In general, there were more children with mental handicaps in poor homes, regardless of birth weight. Moreover, LBW children had a 27% rate of dysfunction (IQ < 90), but the rate in those born at term was 14%; however, no difference in rate of dysfunction between preterm or full-term children was found in the upper two SES groupings. Similarly, in the UCLA Longitudinal Project (Cohen, Parmelee, Beckwith, & Sigman, 1986; Sigman, Cohen, & Forsythe, 1981), path analyses indicated that relationships between perinatal complications and cognitive development at 9 and 24 months were mediated by caregiver–infant interaction. Postnatal complications were not directly related to 9- or 24-month outcome but were indirectly related to 2-year scores through caregiver–infant interaction. These findings again indicate that the effects of biologic risk were influential early on but that this influence decreased by 2 years of age. The environmental path appeared to be most critical in determining outcome, mediating the effects of biologic variables.

Perhaps some of the most persuasive data suggesting interactive effects of environmental and biologic risk are derived from an 8-year longitudinal follow-up of 108 LBW infants (Hunt, Cooper, & Tooley, 1988). Ratings of neonatal illness and parent education influenced outcome at age 8. However, when these environmental and biologic ratings were dichotomized (low vs. high neonatal illness; low vs. high parent education), level of neonatal illness primarily influenced the likelihood of normal outcome; level of parental education influenced the severity or degree of disability. Low parent education plus high neonatal illness yielded almost a 55% rate of moderate to severe problems; in contrast, approximately 9% of children with high parental education and high neonatal illness displayed problems of the same magnitude. Environmental factors had a tempering effect on the degree of abnormality but did not determine whether or not the abnormality occurred.

Summary

Biologic and environmental factors work in tandem to influence environmental outcome. Moreover, these factors are highly interrelated, and the relationship becomes highly complex considering the fact that low-SES children also have more biologic risks such as perinatal complications and LBW (Gould & LeRoy, 1988; Gray, Dean, & Lowrie, 1988). Nonetheless, compromised outcome appears to be due to a combination of these factors. Biologic risk factors tend to be associated with severe mental retardation and multiple handicaps, and when biologic risk is severe, the mediating influence of the environment is minimized. Environmental (and perhaps genetic) factors are assumed to be the underlying cause of mild mental retardation, because biologic factors other than genetics cannot be identified, and most mildly mentally retarded children live in lower SES households (Haskins, 1986; Shonkoff, 1982). Biologic factors determine whether or not a given dysfunction or deficit will occur; environmental factors have a tempering effect and determine the severity (except in cases of severe biologic risk). Vis-à-vis the transactional or risk route approaches (Aylward & Kenny, 1979; Sameroff & Chandler, 1975) a positive environment seems to facilitate the self-righting tendencies of the child, thereby enhancing the child's resiliency to biologic stresses.

ROLE OF GENETICS

Genetic studies added a provocative aspect to the biologic and environment interaction issue by questioning whether it is the environment that exerts a cumulative effect on later outcome, or whether declines in later functioning are the manifestations of an insidious genetic influence. Loehlin, Horn, and Willerman (1989), using data from the Texas Adoption Project, questioned the widespread view that genetic effects are fixed at birth, with environmental effects changing. Using path analyses, environmental effects, although influential early in childhood, were found to have a decreasing influence on IQ as the children grew older. Reciprocally, changes in genetic expression continued into late adolescence or early adulthood. Heritability values between parent and offspring were in the 40% to 50% range. These investigators interpreted the decline in IQ scores over time in children from at-risk environments as reflecting the emergence of previously latent constitutional factors, rather than the cumulative, negative aspects of the environment.

In a related study (Loehlin, 1989), estimates of IQ heritability using direct methods (correlations between identical twins or other relatives reared apart) tended to be higher than heritability estimates obtained by indirect methods (comparison of identical and fraternal twins, or biological and adoptive siblings). The heritability of IQ from direct equations was .58; from indirect equations, .47. Because direct methods involve comparison of individuals who were not reared together in the same families, and indirect methods involve comparisons among individuals who were reared together, these data were interpreted to suggest that some aspects of the family interaction (proximal factors) may have attenuated genetic effects in creating resemblance among family members (Loehlin, 1989). Other authors reported reduced estimates of the contribution of shared family environments once subjects reach adolescence or early adulthood (Scarr & Weinberg, 1977; Wilson, 1983).

Capron and Duyme (1989), using a French sample, reported on a full cross-fostering design that included children born to biologic parents from the most highly contrasting SES environments, and adopted by parents with equally divergent SES. A 2 × 2 factorial design (high–low SES biologic parents; high–low SES adoptive parents) revealed that children adopted by high-SES parents had higher IQs than did children adopted by low-SES parents; children born to high-SES parents scored better than children born to low-SES parents. Most surprising, however, was the lack of evidence for an interaction; the mean IQ in children from high adoptive and high biologic parents was 119.50; the IQ in children from low-SES adoptive and biologic parents was 92.40. There was no IQ difference in children from high adoptive, low biologic parent SES (103.60) and low adoptive, high biologic parent SES (107.50). These data suggest that both genetics and environment influence subsequent IQ. However, here the subjects again had reached adolescence, where a diminution of environmental influences may occur.

Further complicating the nature–nurture issue is the emerging speculation that prenatal stressors that confront the mother may affect fetal brain development (Lou et al., 1994). This so-called *fetal stress syndrome* (Lou, 1993) is characterized by decreased fetal growth, short gestation, and a disturbance of neural development. Using a sample of 70 stressed mothers and 50 controls, Lou et al. (1994) found that psychosocial factors have adverse effects on both gestational age and birth weight. In addition, fetal head growth and neurological optimality scores were also affected by psychosocial factors. Therefore, what may be interpreted as genetic influences on outcome could feasibly be due to other biologic influences (e.g., glucocorticoids). Such influences also may provide an underlying basis for temperament as well.

Summary

Both genetics and environment influence developmental outcome. However, the issue of genetics is confounded by prenatal factors, lack of consideration of schooling, and differences in methodology (which can produce different results). Genotypes account for approximately one half of observed differences in IQs between individuals (.40 to .60), yet there is alterability of IQ. However, a ceiling exists, which is produced by genetic and more severe biological limiting factors. In such cases, environmental effects are minimized. Moreover, genetic makeup also can influence how environmental factors might affect the child. Scarr and McCartney (1983) suggested that genetic–constitutional factors drive development by influencing the child's early responses to the environment in terms of eliciting interaction and seeking experiences. In addition, some children simply may have constitutional (genetic) resiliency and therefore be less affected than are others by negative environmental factors.

SES–COMP

Environmental effects influence developmental outcome. However, what remains unanswered is the pragmatic issue of how best to accurately measure these environmental effects. Entwisle and Astone (1994) provided practical guidelines for measuring race–ethnicity and SES. These authors indicated that the traditional procedure of using the characteristics of a father or father figure as the primary indicator of SES when a male is present, and the mother or mother figure otherwise, can be problematic. For example, women are concentrated in occupations that are relatively prestigious, yet these occupations pay relatively poorly (e.g., teacher, social worker); as a result, occupational prestige is a less valid indicator of financial resources for women than for men (Entwisle & Astone, 1994). Moreover, children in single-parent and stepparent families may be more affected by the SES of the "breadwinner" of the family in which they live, rather than by that of their biological father. Conversely, some children in otherwise poor stepfamilies receive support from a more affluent biological father. Thus, the traditional method of measuring SES may be limited to White, middle-class, two-parent families.

Coleman (1988) suggested that there are three types of capital that facilitate optimal development: *financial capital* (money to buy food, clothing, and other necessities), *human capital* (nonmaterial resources that are indexed by parental education, such as helping with homework or language development), and *social capital* (social connection networks that are shared with children). Therefore, financial capital measures should include total income of all persons who live in the same household as the child, plus any other money or services such as WIC, MEDICAID, or Aid to Families with Dependent Children (AFDC). In terms of human capital, the highest educational degree of the mother and the highest grade completed should be recorded. Finally, social capital measurements include the number of birth parents in the home, presence of a stepparent, and an indicator of whether or not there is a grandparent in the home. These recommendations are not without criticism, however (Hauser, 1994). Some investigators suggested that rather than focusing on father's or mother's characteristics, it is better to detail the characteristics of one adult in the household; namely, the head of household, householder, or principal earner (Hauser, 1994). Moreover, questions regarding the cost of housing, housing tenure, and family size are recommended (Entwisle & Astone, 1994; Hauser, 1994).

The SES–COMP (Aylward et al., 1985) is a 6-item instrument that was designed to provide a gross indicator of SES and social support. Items included:

1. Mother's education (scores ranging from 0 [< 10 years of schooling] to 4 [> / = 16]).
2. Father's education (same scoring and range).
3. Family occupation (1 [unskilled] to 4 [professional, technical, managers]).
4. Integration of male in family (0–5, e.g., did baby's father attend childbirth classes with mother, have meals with family > 3 times per week, or help or play with children in family > 3 times per week?).
5. Availability of car or phone (0–2).
6. Freedom from public assistance (0–1; 0 if mother receives any assistance such as housing benefits, unemployment benefits, AFDC, etc.).

Although this instrument proved quite useful in earlier studies (e.g., Collaborative Group on Antenatal Steroid Therapy, 1984) it was developed in the late 1970s, and probably does not accurately measure factors that are more instrumental in today's socioeconomic circumstances. S. P. Berger (personal communication, 1995) indicated several points that need further consideration: (a) levels of occupation did not always match jobs that were encountered, (b) part-time work was not considered, (c) benefits (e.g., insurance) were not addressed, (d) the person living in the home on a regular basis with the highest educational level should be considered (e.g., mother not working, yet has a college degree), (e) because higher education has changed since the original SES–COMP was developed, other educational attainments such as trade school, AA (2–year) degrees, and more than 2 years of college but no degree, need to be considered. Housing (owning, renting, neither), supplemental income, and possible deletion of the integration of male item (because of birth order, no contact with the father whatsoever yet a different significant household member did provide support, etc.) were also suggested. Moreover, Berger (1995) found the integration of male item to not be a useful item, because only 39% of her sample included fathers in the home.

In response, SES–COMP data for a total of 458 families from a more contemporary sample were reviewed. These families participated in the St. John's Hospital–Southern Illinois University School of Medicine Developmental Continuity Clinic. This clinic was designed for follow-up of infants who graduated from the High Risk Nursery (NICU) who met any of the following specific selection criteria: 5-minute Apgar < 5, birth weight < 1,250 g, prolonged mechanical ventilation, intraventricular hemorrhage, seizures, or persistent fetal circulation (see Aylward, Verhulst, & Bell, 1994). Children were evaluated at 6, 12, and 24 months conceptional age, and 36 months chronological age. The Bayley Scales of Infant Development and the Early Neuropsychologic Optimality Rating Scales (Aylward et al., 1994) were administered on the first three occasions; the McCarthy Scales were given at 36 months. In addition, the SES–COMP was obtained at the 6-month follow-up appointment.

In our sample, the modal value for both maternal and paternal education was 12th grade (50% and 52%, respectively). Many parents were employed in unskilled positions in regard to family occupation (41%); the male (father) was most frequently involved in 3 (31%) or 4 (32%) activities with the family; fully 86% of the families had a car and phone available. Freedom from public assistance was almost evenly split (46% having some form of assistance, 54% having none).

The six items from the SES–COMP were then intercorrelated ($p < .05$; see Table 2.1). The strongest intercorrelations were found with SES–related variables (maternal education, paternal education, family occupation), whereas integration of male and availability of car or phone (social support variables) had weaker associations with other remaining variables.

The same six items were then correlated with the 24-month Bayley Scales of Infant Development Mental Developmental Index (MDI) and the Psychomotor Developmental Index (PDI). First, none of the SES–COMP variables correlated significantly with the PDI–24 (including the SES–COMP total score). Second, more proximal (status) variables did not have strong correlations with the MDI–24, nor did the social support variables (integration of male, availability of car or phone) (see Table 2.2). In terms of associations with 36-month outcome, four out of six SES–COMP variables were significantly correlated, whereas the two social support variables were not.

TABLE 2.1
Intercorrelations of SES–Composite Index Items

	Maternal Education	Paternal Education	Family Occupation	Integration of Male	Availability Car/Phone	Freedom From Public Assistance
Maternal Education	—	—	—	—	—	—
Paternal Education	.59*	—	—	—	—	—
Family Occupation	.56*	.63*	—	—	—	—
Integration of male	.31*	.23*	.31*	—	—	—
Availability of car/phone	.26*	.25*	.24*	.20*	—	—
Freedom from public assistance	.34*	.15**	.34*	.34*	ns	—

*$p < .0001$. **$p < .001$.

Because of the lack of predictive utility of the integration of male item coupled with previous findings reported by Berger (1995), it was deleted in the SES–COMP2 (see Table 2.3). There was a modest increase in the magnitude of correlations between the SES–COMP2 score and 36-month outcome. The Pearson correlation between the original SES–COMP and the SES–COMP2 was significant ($r = .87$). Next, the availability of car or phone item was also deleted; the correlation between this third SES version (SES–COMP3) and outcome was essentially unchanged, and the revised SES–COMP3 was still significantly associated with the original, six-item SES–COMP ($r = .86$).

In this more contemporary sample, the predictive power of several of the social support items lessened. In response to the current findings and in conjunction with new data (S. P. Berger, personal communication, 1995), several alterations in the SES–COMP are proposed. First, in order to better define occupation than by using the four levels in the SES–COMP, the Socioeconomic Index for All Detailed Categories found in Entwisle and Astone's (1994) Appendix B could be utilized, placing occupations in eight levels (no job = 0, occupations receiving 20–29 points [e.g., housekeepers, agricultural sorters] = 1, 30–39 points [short-order cooks, bellhops] = 2, etc.). Berger also suggested inclusion of a labor force status multiplier based on the number of hours per week of employment (no employment = 0, 1–8 hours per week = .25, 9–19 hours per week = .50, 20–31 hours per week = .75, and ≥ 32 hours per week = 1.0). The occupational level could be multiplied by this number to produce a better estimate of financial capital. Education ("human capital") measurement should also be expanded, measured on the person who lives in the house a substantial amount of time who has the highest educational level. Although the SES–COMP ranged from 0 to 4 points on this item, Berger suggested this be expanded to eight levels of .5 increments (e.g., < = ninth grade = .5, grade 10–11 = 1.0, high school graduation = 1.5, etc.). The most dramatic change here would include trade

TABLE 2.2
Correlations Between SES–Composite Index Items and Later Outcome

	36-Month McCarthy Scales						Bayley Scales	
	GCI	Verbal	Perceptual–Performance	Quantitative	Memory	Motor	MDI–24	PDI–24
Maternal education	.28 (.0001)[a]	.24 (.001)	.29 (.0001)	.24 (.001)	.20 (.006)	.28 (.0001)	.17 (.008)	—
Paternal education	.26 (.0001)	.24 (.001)	.26 (.0001)	.23 (.002)	.23 (.002)	.26 (.001)	—	—
Family occupation	.25 (.0001)	.22 (.003)	.25 (.0001)	.21 (.004)	.17 (.02)	.25 (.002)	—	—
Integration of male	.15 (.04)	—	—	—	—	—	—	—
Availability of car/phone	.14 (.05)	.19 (.01)	—	—	—	—	.13 (.04)	—
Freedom from public assistance	.19 (.009)	.22 (.003)	.15 (.05)	.17 (.02)	.18 (.02)	.18 (.02)	.18 (.005)	—
SES–COMP Index	.29 (.0001)	.27 (.0001)	.24 (.001)	.25 (.001)	.23 (.002)	.25 (.001)	.16 (.01)	—

[a] p value

25

TABLE 2.3
Correlations Between Individual Items, 36-Month Outcome,
and Three SES–COMP Index Versions ($N = 458$)

	SES–COMP Index[a]	SES–COMP2[b]	SES–COMP3[c]
Maternal education	.69[*]	.81[*]	.82[*]
Paternal education	.76[*]	.80[*]	.81[*]
Family occupation	.73[*]	.84[*]	.81[*]
Integration of male	.66[*]	—	—
Availability of car/phone	.40[*]	.41[*]	—
Freedom from public assistance	.33[*]	.51[*]	.53[*]
SES–COMP index	—	.87[*]	.86[*]
MSCA GCI	.29[*]	.30[*]	.30[*]
MSCA verbal	.27[*]	.29[*]	.28[*]
MSCA percep–perf.	.24[*]	.28[*]	.28[*]
MSCA quantitative	.25[**]	.26[*]	.27[*]
MSCA memory	.23[**]	.23[**]	.23[**]
MSCA motor	.25[*]	.27[*]	.28[*]

[a]Original SES–COMP Index. [b]SES–COMP Index, deleting integration of male item.
[c]SES–COMP Index, deleting integration of male and availability of car/phone items.

[*]$p < .0001$. [**]$p < .002$.

school certificate, AA degrees, and several years of college with no actual degree. The SES–COMP item, availability of car or phone, would be subdivided and be more restrictive in terms of actually having each. Supplemental income from unemployment insurance, disability, child support, child support/alimony or other financial support should also be an item, as should housing tenure (2 points for owning a home, 1 point for renting, 0 points for simply staying with someone but not having a permanent residence). Finally, Berger suggested that a health insurance item be included (0 = no health insurance, 1 = health insurance). She also suggested that such alterations would add finer discrimination of families within a given SES status.

Therefore, scoring for the proposed SES–COMP–R (revised) would include the following:

Category	Scoring
Occupation × labor force multiplier	0–8 points
Education	0.5–4 points
Car	0–1 point
Phone	0–1 point
Public aid	0–1 point
Supplemental income	0–1 point
Housing tenure	0–2 points

Health insurance   0–1 point
Total possible points   0.5–19 points

A potential criticism of the SES–COMP–R is that it is geared to measure only more status or distal features of the environment, thereby missing process items such as those found on the HOME scale. Such a criticism may be justified, but utilization of the SES–COMP–R addresses two pragmatic issues: it is less costly and time consuming because parents can act as self-informants, and it lends more insight into social support characteristics in addition to SES. Moreover, because of its more detailed subdivisions of various items, the index allows better differentiation of environmental resources within a given SES grouping or neighborhood (Berger, 1995). In addition, the previously mentioned microfactors (life events and daily coping characteristics) also could be measured with the Daily Hassles and Uplifts Scales (Kanner et al., 1981). Therefore, although the proposed SES–COMP–R has shortcomings, it still affords clinicians and researchers the ability to easily measure environmental influences to an adequate degree by including measures of financial capital, human capital, and social capital, vis-à-vis Entwisle and Astone's (1994) recommendations.

IMPLICATIONS FOR INTERVENTION

The relationship between environmental influences and intervention is complex, and, to a degree, circular. Environmental influences affect assessment results, which in turn drive intervention efforts. Intervention efforts include addressing child and family factors, which in essence involve altering the environment. Simply extracting a child from his or her environment in order to provide intervention activities is not productive, and a more encompassing approach is more appropriate. Parry (1992) delineated three broad categories of children for whom early intervention efforts are directed: those at environmental risk, those at increased biological risk, and infants and children with established developmental delays, disabilities, or deviations. However, in many instances, such groupings are combined, particularly in the case of double jeopardy (Parker et al., 1988) or double hazard (Escalona, 1982) situations.

The eight-site Infant Health and Development Program (IHDP) involved LBW (< 2,500 g) infants whose mean maternal education was high school or less. The study included 985 families (Ramey et al., 1992) and utilized a biosocial systems approach to intervention. The basic assumption of this prototypal approach (based on the Abecedarian Project; Ramey & Campbell, 1991) is that there are four levels of influence on a given child's development: biological and social historical contexts of the child and caregivers; the current status of these biological and social factors; potential transactions among the child, caregivers, and their environments; and the developmental progress of the child and caregivers. Along these lines, pediatric, educational, and family support services were provided in the intervention model; the former two considered extrafamilial support mechanisms. Pediatric services included surveillance, developmental follow-up, and referrals for special interventions. Educational services included home visits, parent group meeting, and enrollment of the child in specific programs in child development centers. Family support was interwoven with these interventions, and included problem-solving training to increase parents' general adaptational and parent-specific skills. It is clear that intervention is geared to both the child and environment.

Provision of intervention may enhance development, or it may prevent decline. The IDHP data indicate that genetic and sociocultural contextual factors exert additive influences on cognitive development above and beyond early intervention efforts (Ramey et al., 1992). Therefore, it is likely that strong, negative biologic or genetic influences will limit the impact of any intervention efforts, and that a moderate or a minimal degree of negative biologic influences theoretically will yield moderate and good intervention effects, respectively. Similarly, if the environment is extremely negative, intervention will have some positive effect; however, this effect would be greater if the environment is minimally or moderately negative.

Although data from the IHDP indicated that children in the intervention group had higher 3-year IQ scores than did controls, and the frequency of problem behaviors decreased, many issues remain unanswered. Although many well-conceived intervention programs have been implemented, a given family's actual participation in the program may be a critical factor. Ramey et al. (1992) reported on a Family Participation Index that was developed for IHDP subjects. The index was a sum of frequencies of home visits, attendance at parent group meetings, and days of attendance at the child development center. Participation was related to 3-year IQ scores. Only 1.9% of families in the highest tercile of participation had children with IQs $\leq$ 70; 3.5% and 13% of children in the middle and lowest participation terciles, respectively, scored in the mentally retarded range. Similar findings were noted in regard to borderline mental retardation. Participation scores were not related to identifiable background variables (e.g., mother's ethnicity, age, education; infant's birth weight, health status). Therefore, although intensity of intervention appears to affect positive cognitive outcome, the determinants in variations in individual family participation remain unknown.

Intervention effects vary in terms of other variables. In the IHDP, at 3 years of age, the intervention group had higher mean IQ scores than the control group; however, the differences varied by birth weight. The mean difference in infants weighing 2,001 to 2,500 g was 13.2 points, whereas in the < 2,001 g group the mean difference was 6.6 IQ points (Infant Health and Development Program, 1990). There were no group differences at 12 months, whereas group differences (9.75 points) began to emerge by 24 months (Brooks-Gunn, Klebanov, Liaw, & Spiker, 1993). Also pertinent to previous arguments regarding age at which environmental effects become apparent, there was a decline in test scores over time for both intervention and control groups; however the drop was more pronounced between 12 and 24 months than between 24 and 36 months. Change over time was less pronounced in the interventionthanintheroutinefollow-upgroup(Brooks-Gunnetal.,1993).

At 5 years of age (Brooks-Gunn et al. 1994), the intervention group had IQ scores similar to those of controls. However, in the heavier LBW group, children in the intervention program had higher full-scale IQ scores (3.7 points) and higher verbal IQ scores (4.2 points) than did matched controls; in the LBW group, no differences were noted. Thus, intervention provided in the first 3 years had effects on heavier LBW premature infants' IQ and verbal performance at age 5 years that were not observed for lighter LBW babies. Moreover, the data suggest that overall, the intervention appeared to prevent decline (vs. enhance development).

Whether these data suggest that lighter LBW babies do not benefit from the services offered because of health and developmental problems, or that longer intervention is needed, is not clear. Effects are not apparent in the first year of life, perhaps suggesting that home-based interventions are not as intensive or cannot be controlled as adequately as can center-based programs that began during the second year. A mix of services over the first several years appears to be important. In addition, no accurate indicator of school performance was obtained, due to the children's ages.

In a subsequent analysis (Cluett & Ramey, 1995), both risk and protective factors were indicated to predict 3-year IQ. Regression analyses revealed that birth weight, maternal IQ, maternal education (risk factors), and intensive early intervention (protective factor) all contributed significantly to the model. Glick and Fewell (1995) evaluated a subsample of the IHDP infants at 30 months in free-play situations with their mothers. A play assessment scale was scored for each. Results indicated that the mean play score for children of mothers with postsecondary schooling was significantly higher than the means for the children of mothers who were either high school graduates or who did not complete high school. However, for mothers who did not complete high school, the mean play score for the intervention group was significantly higher than the score of the follow-up only group. Other studies (e.g., Olds, Henderson, & Kitzman, 1994) suggest that home visitation over the first 2 years may not influence IQ scores, but may have enduring effects on environmental variables such as parental caregiving, safety of the home, and decreased utilization of emergency rooms.

Summary

The IDHP studies were selected as representative of current intervention efforts primarily because of the combined biologic and environmental risk status of participating children. Other studies (e.g., Shonkoff, Hauser-Cram, Wyngaarden-Krauss, & Upshur, 1992) focused on infants with identified disabilities. However, the bulk of research on the value of early intervention focused primarily on infants and children at environmental risk (Parry, 1992).

From these studies, several generalizations can be made. First, for infants at environmental risk, intervention programs generally do not enhance early intellectual development to the above-average range; rather they appear to prevent the slow decline away from average. Moreover, individual risk factors are not related to deleterious outcome as strongly as are the number of risk factors present for a given child or family (Rutter, 1981). Second, interventions are more effective for children in lower SES circumstances who reside in communities where intervention resources are not routinely provided. Third, intervention programs should be multifaceted and include home visits, parent involvement, and provision of structured curricula that begins in the first or second year of life (i.e., process and status modifiers). This impression was also espoused by Bryant and Ramey (1987) who stated, ". . . intellectual development can potentially be influenced by systematic efforts aimed at a variety of nodes in the social-interactional system of infants and their caregivers" (p. 75). Finally, in addition to evaluating gains in IQ or academic achievement, one must consider improvement in social competence, family functioning, and parental empowerment that result from intervention services.

CONCLUSIONS

Relating back to major points contained within this chapter, one should consider the transactional model of environmental influence as providing the framework for intervention efforts; moreover, intervention should be grounded in developmental theory (Olds, 1992). The child's age will determine the most effective mode of intervention: Early on, efforts should be directed toward enhancing caretaker–infant interaction, parental understanding of development, and provision of stimulation within the home (e.g., Shonkoff, 1993). This would address the more proximal or process factors. Efforts should also be directed toward helping the family deal with microfactors encountered in day-to-day living, by means of group problem solving, and assistance in securing community resources. While maintaining these proximal interventions, the scope in the second year should expand to include the addition of structured out-of-home programs, particularly in light of the precipitous decline in cognitive abilities between 18 and 24 months of age in children from poor environments. Interventions should be frequent and longitudinal, with the objective being to establish a therapeutic alliance between caretakers and interventionists. Emphasis should be placed on enhancement of verbal and cognitive functioning in particular, as these areas are most susceptible to negative environmental influences. Biologic risks cannot be discounted, as biologic risks will determine whether or not a given deficit will occur whereas the environment will influence the severity of the dysfunction. There is broad theoretical support for the notion that intrinsic developmental vulnerability can be moderated by the influence of extrinsic (i.e., environmental) protective factors that increase the probability of positive adaptation (Shonkoff, 1993). Genetic influences may also drive development by influencing the child's early responses to the environment in terms of the child eliciting interaction and seeking experiences; how the environment (caretakers) responds to these overtures from the infant or child may again be facilitated by interventions aimed at process variables. Unfortunately, it is virtually impossible to truly alter the more distal, status components of the environment via intervention efforts (i.e., SES). Nonetheless, parent involvement, empowerment, and provision of long-term, structured, center-based programs would be significant influences in that regard.

Development is a complex, interactive process that involves children, families, and the environment. Intervention programs that facilitate positive changes in the family, home, and environment are likely to continue to exert a positive influence on the child long after the intervention ends (Black, 1993).

REFERENCES

Aylward, G. P. (1990). Environmental influences on the developmental outcome of children at risk. *Infants and Young Children, 2,* 1–9.

Aylward, G. P. (1992). The relationship between environmental risk and developmental outcome. *Journal of Developmental and Behavioral Pediatrics, 13,* 222–229.

Aylward, G. P. (1993). Perinatal asphyxia: Effects of biologic and environmental risks. *Clinics in Perinatology, 20,* 433–449.

Aylward, G. P., Dunteman, G., Hatcher, R. P., Gustafson, N., & Widmayer, S. (1985). The SES-Composite Index: A tool for developmental outcome studies. *Psychological Documents, 15* (MS 2683).

Aylward, G. P., Gustafson, N., Verhulst, S. J., & Colliver, J. (1987). Consistency in diagnosis of cognitive, motor and neurologic function over the first three years. *Journal of Pediatric Psychology, 12,* 77–98.

Aylward, G. P., & Kenny, T. J. (1979). Developmental follow-up: Inherent problems and a conceptual model. *Journal of Pediatric Psychology, 4,* 331–343.

Aylward, G. P., Pfeiffer, S. J., Wright, A., & Verhulst, S. J. (1989). Outcome of low birth weight infants over the last decade: A metaanalysis. *Journal of Pediatrics, 115,* 515–520.

Aylward, G. P., Verhulst, S. J., & Bell, S. (1989). Correlation of asphyxia and other risk factors with outcome: A contemporary view. *Developmental Medicine and Child Neurology, 31,* 329–340.

Aylward, G. P., Verhulst, S. J., & Bell, S. (1994). Enhanced prediction of later normal outcome using infant neuropsychological assessment. *Developmental Neuropsychology, 10,* 377–393.

Bakeman, R., & Brown, J. V. (1980). Early interaction: Consequences for social and mental development at three years. *Child Development, 51,* 437–447.

Bee, H. L., Barnard, K. E., Eyres, S. J., Gray, C. A., Hammond, M. A., Spietz, A. L., Snyder, C., & Clark, B. (1982). Prediction of IQ and language skill from perinatal status, child performance, family characteristics, and mother-infant interaction. *Child Development, 53,* 1134–1156.

Belsky, J. (1984). The determinants of parenting. A process model. *Child Development, 55,* 83–96.

Berger, S. P. (1995, March). *Methods of assessing the relationship between personal and family characteristics in high-risk neighborhoods.* Paper presented at the biennial meeting of the Society for Research in Child Development, Indianapolis, IN.

Black, M. (1993). Strategies to promote healthy child development and parenting. *Child, Youth and Family Services Quarterly, 16,* 1–3.

Bradley, R. H., & Caldwell, B. M. (1988). Using the HOME Inventory to assess the family environment. *Pediatric Nursing, 14,* 97–102.

Bradley, R. H., Caldwell, B. M., & Rock, S. L. (1988). Home environment and school performance. A ten year follow-up and examination of three models of environmental action. *Child Development, 59,* 852–867.

Bradley, R. H., Caldwell, B. M., Rock, S. J., Ramey, C. T., Barnard, K. E., Gray, C., Hammond, M. A., Mitchell, S., Gottfried, A. W., Siegel, L., & Johnson, D. L. (1989). Home environment and cognitive development in the first 3 years of life: A collaborative study involving six sites and three ethnic groups in North America. *Developmental Psychology, 25*, 217–235.

Brooks-Gunn, J., Klebanov, P. K., Liaw, F., & Spiker, D. (1993). Enhancing the development of low-birthweight, premature infants: Changes in cognition and behavior over the first three years. *Child Development, 64*, 736–753.

Brooks-Gunn, J., McCarton, C. M., Casey, P. H., McCormick, M. C., Bauer, C. R., Bernbaum, J. C., Tyson, J., Swanson, M., Bennett, F. C., Scott, D. T., Tonascia, J., & Meinert, C. L. (1994). Early intervention in low-birth-weight premature infants. Results through age 5 years from the Infant Health and Development Program. *Journal of the American Medical Association, 272*, 1257–1262.

Brown, J., LaRossa, M., Aylward, G. P., Davis, D., Rutherford, P., & Bakeman, R. (1980). Nursery-based intervention with prematurely born babies and their mothers: Are there effects? *Journal of Pediatrics, 97*, 487–491.

Bryant, D. M., & Ramey, C. T. (1987). An analysis of the effectiveness of early intervention programs for environmentally at-risk children. In M. J. Guralnick & F. C. Bennett (Eds.), *The effectiveness of early intervention for at-risk and handicapped children* (pp. 33–78). New York: Academic Press.

Caldwell, B., & Bradley, R. H. (1984). *Home observation for measurement of the environment.* Unpublished manuscript, University of Arkansas at Little Rock.

Capron, C., & Duyme, M. (1989). Assessment of effects of socio-economic status on IQ in a full cross-fostering study. *Nature, 340*, 552–553.

Cluett, S. E., & Ramey, C. T. (1995, March). *Differential responsivity to a comprehensive early intervention program for low birth weight infants.* Paper presented at the biennial meeting of the Society for Research in Child Development, Indianapolis, IN.

Cohen, S. E., & Parmelee, A. H. (1983). Prediction of five-year Stanford-Binet scores in preterm infants. *Child Development, 54*, 1242–1253.

Cohen, S. E., Parmelee, A. H., Beckwith, L., & Sigman, M. (1986). Cognitive development in preterm infants: Birth to 8 years. *Journal of Developmental and Behavioral Pediatrics, 7*, 102–110.

Coleman, J. S. (1988). Social capital in the creation of human capital. *American Journal of Sociology, 94*, S95–S120.

Collaborative Group on Antenatal Steroid Therapy. (1984). Effect of antenatal dexamethasone administration on the infant: Long-term follow-up. *Journal of Pediatrics, 104*, 259–267.

Drillien, C. M. (1964). *The growth and development of the prematurely born infant.* Baltimore, MD: Williams & Wilkins.

Drillien, C. M., Thompson, A. J., & Burgoyne, K. (1980). Low birthweight children at early school age: A longitudinal study. *Developmental Medicine and Child Neurology, 22*, 26–47.

Entwisle, D. R., & Astone, N. M. (1994). Some practical guidelines for measuring youth's race/ethnicity and socioeconomic status. *Child Development, 65*, 1521–1540.

Escalona, S. K. (1982). Babies at double hazard: Early development of infants at biologic and social risk. *Pediatrics, 70*, 670–676.

Escalona, S. K. (1984). Social and other environmental influences on the cognitive and personality development of low birthweight infants. *American Journal of Mental Deficiency, 5*, 508–512.

Glick, M. P., & Fewell, R. R. (1995, March). *Play skills of low birthweight toddlers: Effects of intervention and maternal education.* Paper presented at the biennial meeting of the Society for Research in Child Development, Indianapolis, IN.

Gould, J. B., & LeRoy, S. (1988). Socioeconomic status and low birth weight: A racial comparison. *Pediatrics, 82*, 896–904.

Gray, J. W., Dean, R. S., & Lowrie, R. A. (1988). Relationship between socioeconomic status and perinatal complications. *Journal of Clinical Child Psychology, 17*, 352–358.

Halpern, R. (1990). Poverty and early childhood parenting: Toward a framework for intervention. *American Journal of Orthopsychiatry, 60*, 6–17.

Haskins, R. (1986). Social and cultural factors in risk assessment and mild mental retardation. In D. C. Farran & J. D. McKinney (Eds.), *Risk in intellectual and psychosocial development* (pp. 29–60). New York: Academic Press.

Hauser, R. M. (1994). Measuring socioeconomic status in studies of child development. *Child Development, 65,* 1541–1545.

Heitzmann, C. A., & Kaplan, R. M. (1988). Assessment of methods for measuring social support. *Health Psychology, 7,* 75–109.

Hollingshead, A. B. (1975). *Four-factor index of social status.* Unpublished manuscript. Holmes, T. H., & Rahe, R. H. (1967). The Social Readjustment Rating Scale. *Journal of Psychosomatic Research, 11,* 213–218.

Hunt, J. V., Cooper, B. A. B., & Tooley, W. H. (1988). Very low birth weight infants at 8 and 11 years of age: Role of neonatal illness and family status. *Pediatrics, 82,* 596–603.

Infant Health and Development Program (1990). Enhancing the outcomes of low birth weight, premature infants: A multisite, randomized trial. *Journal of the American Medical Association, 263,* 3035–3042.

Johnson, D. L., Swank, P., Howie, V. M., Baldwin, C. D., Owen, M., & Luttman, D. (1993). Does HOME add to the prediction of child intelligence over and above SES? *Journal of Genetic Psychology, 154,* 33–40.

Kanner, A. D., Coyne, J. C., Schaefer, C., & Lazarus, R. S. (1981). Comparison of two modes of stress measurement: Daily hassles and uplifts versus major life events. *Journal of Behavioral Medicine, 4,* 1–37.

Kopp, C. B., & Kaler, S. R. (1989). Risk in infancy. *American Psychologist, 44,* 224–230.

Lazarus, R. S., Cohen, J. B., Folkman, S., Kanner, A., & Schaefer, C. (1980). Psychological stress and adaptation: Some unresolved issues. In H. Selye (Ed.), *Selye's guide to stress research* (Vol. 1, pp. 90–117). New York: Van Nostrand Reinhold.

Loehlin, J. C. (1989). Partitioning environmental and genetic contributions to behavioral development. *American Psychologist, 44,* 1285–1292.

Loehlin, J. C., Horn, J. M., & Willerman, L. (1989). Modeling IQ change: Evidence from the Texas Adoption Project. *Child Development, 60,* 993–1004.

Lotas, M., Penticuff, J., Medoff-Cooper, B., Brooken, D., & Brown, L. (1992). The HOME Scale: The influence of socioeconomic status on the evaluation of the home environment. *Nursing Research, 41,* 338–341.

Lou, H. C. (1993). Prenatal stressful events of human life affect fetal brain development. *Neuropediatrics, 24,* 180.

Lou, H. C., Hanson, D., Nordentoft, M., Pryds, O., Jensen, F., Nim, J., & Hemmingsen, R. (1994). Prenatal stressors of human life affect fetal brain development. *Developmental Medicine and Child Neurology, 36,* 826–832.

National Center for Children in Poverty. (1990). *Five million children.* New York: Author.

Olds, D. L. (1992). Home visitation for pregnant women and parents of young children. *American Journal of Diseases in Children, 146,* 704–708.

Olds, D. L., Henderson, C. R., & Kitzman, H. (1994). Does prenatal and infancy nurse home visitation have enduring effects on qualities of parental caregiving and child health at 25 to 50 months of life? *Pediatrics, 93,* 89–98.

Parker, S., Greer, S., & Zuckerman, B. (1988). Double jeopardy: The impact of poverty on early child development. *Pediatric Clinics of North America, 35,* 1227–1240.

Parry, T. S. (1992). The effectiveness of early intervention: A critical review. *Journal of Paediatrics and Child Health, 28,* 343–346.

Pasamanick, B., & Knobloch, H. (1961). Epidemiologic studies on the complications of pregnancy and the birth process. In G. Caplan (Ed.), *Prevention of mental disorders in children.* New York: Basic Books.

Pfeiffer, S. I., & Aylward, G. P. (1990). Outcome for preschoolers of very low birthweight: Sociocultural and environmental influences. *Perceptual and Motor Skills, 70,* 1367–1378.

Ramey, C. T., Bryant, D. M., Wasik, B. H., Sparling, J. J., Fendt, K. H., & LaVange, L. M. (1992). Infant health and development program for low birth weight, premature infants: Program elements, family participation, and child intelligence. *Pediatrics, 89,* 454–465.

Ramey, C., & Campbell, F. (1991). Poverty, early childhood education, and academic competence: The Abecedarian experiment. In A. Huston (Ed.), *Children in poverty* (pp. 190–221). Cambridge, MA: Cambridge University Press.

Rutter, M. (1981). Stress, coping, and development: Some issues and questions. *Journal of Child Psychology and Psychiatry, 22,* 323–356.

Rutter, M. (1987). Psychosocial resilience and protective mechanisms. *American Journal of Orthopsychiatry, 57,* 316–331.

Sameroff, A. J. (1975). Early influences on development: Fact or fancy? *Merrill-Palmer Quarterly, 21,* 267–294.

Sameroff, A. K., & Chandler, M. J. (1975). Reproductive risk and the continuum of caretaking casualty. In F. D. Horowitz (Ed.), *Review of child development research* (Vol. 4, pp. 157–243). Chicago: University of Chicago Press.

Sameroff, A. J., Seifer, R., Barocas, R., Zax, M., & Greenspan, S. (1987). Intelligence quotient scores of 4-year-old children: Social-environmental risk factors. *Pediatrics, 79,* 343–349.

Scarr, S., & McCartney, K. (1983). How people make their own environments: A theory of genotype-environmental effects. *Child Development, 54,* 424–435.

Scarr, S., & Weinberg, R. A. (1977). Intellectual similarities within families of both adopted and biological children. *Intelligence, 1,* 170–191.

Shonkoff, J. P. (1982). Biological and social factors contributing to mild mental retardation. In K. A. Heller, W. H. Holtzman, & S. Messick (Eds.), *Placing children in special education: A strategy for equity,* (pp. 133–181). Washington, DC: National Academic Press.

Shonkoff, J. P. (1993). Blending science and advocacy: Foundation for a rational policy for early childhood intervention. *Child, Youth and Family Services Quarterly, 16,* 11–13.

Shonkoff, J. P., Hauser-Cram, P., Wyngaarden-Krauss, M., & Upshur, C. (1992). Development of infants with disabilities and their families. *Monographs of the Society for Research in Child Development, 57,* (230).

Siegel, L. S. (1982). Reproductive, perinatal and environmental factors as predictors of the cognitive and language development of preterm and full-term infants. *Child Development, 53,* 963–973.

Siegel, L. S. (1983). The prediction of possible learning disabilities in preterm and full-term children. In T. Field & A. Sostek (Eds.), *Infants born at risk: Physiological, perceptual, and cognitive processes* (pp. 295–316). New York: Grune & Stratton.

Siegel, L. S., Saigal, S., & Rosenbaum, P. (1982). Predictors of development in preterm and full-term infants: A model for detecting the at risk child. *Journal of Pediatric Psychology, 7,* 135–147.

Sigman, M., Cohen, S. E., & Forsythe, A. B. (1981). The relation of early infant measures to later development. In S. L. Friedman & M. Sigman (Eds.), *Preterm birth and psychological development* (pp. 313–328). New York: Academic Press.

Tjossem, T. (1976). *Intervention strategies for high risk infants and young children.* Baltimore, MD: University Park Press.

Wallace, I. F. (1988). Socioenvironmental issues in longitudinal research of high-risk infants. In P. M. Vietz & H. G. Vaughan (Eds.), *Early identification of infants with developmental disabilities* (pp. 356–382). Philadelphia: Grune & Stratton.

Weisglas-Kuperus, N., Baerts, W., Smrkovsky, M., & Sauer, P. J. (1993). Effects of biological and social factors on the cognitive development of very low birth weight children. *Pediatrics, 92,* 658–665.

Werner, E. E. (1986). A longitudinal study of perinatal risk. In D. C. Farran & J. D. McKenney (Eds.), *Risk in intellectual and psychosocial development* (pp. 3–27). New York: Academic Press.

Werner, E., Simonian, B. S., Bierman, J. M., & French, F. E. (1967). Cumulative effect of perinatal complications and deprived environment on physical, intellectual, and social development of preschool children. *Pediatrics, 39,* 490–505.

Wilson, R. S. (1983). The Louisville Twin Study: Developmental synchronies in behavior. *Child Development, 54,* 298–316.

Wilson, R. S. (1985). Risk and resilience in early mental development. *Developmental Psychology, 21,* 795–805.

3

Truth, Error, Omission, Distortion, and Deception:
The Application of Attachment Theory to the Assessment and Treatment of Psychological Disorder

Patricia M. Crittenden
Family Relations Institute

Psychopathology is observed as maladaptive behavior. Underlying the behavior, however, are distortions of perception, attention, and attribution of meaning. These cause individuals to misconstrue the probable outcomes of their behavior or the nature of their situation. In either case, the result is behavior that is inappropriate for prevailing conditions. There are two important aspects to these assertions. First, behavior alone is not indicative of psychopathology; instead, behavior must be evaluated in terms of appropriateness, given its temporal and physical context. Second, behavior is the outcome of a mental process. This process evaluates conditions in terms of their implications for the self and, on the basis of that evaluation, a behavioral response is implemented. When information about what is "out there" is faulty or when information is not fully integrated, the evaluation is likely to result in both a distorted model of "reality" and maladaptive behavior. In this chapter, I apply an expansion of attachment theory to the processes of using information to model reality and of organizing behavioral strategies to change prevailing conditions. I focus specifically on behavioral strategies that promote survival and on mental processes that lead to true, erroneous, omitted, distorted, or deceptive information.

I address several issues: the developmental pathways leading to the disorder; the protective function of the disorder to the individual; and

35

various means of intervening to correct the disorder. In addition, I describe assessment procedures that make reliable distinctions between currently understood classes of functioning and provide a basis for identifying new and more meaningful distinctions. Theory should promote the description, explanation, diagnosis, and modification of maladaptive behavior. I use this perspective to consider the application of attachment theory and assessments of quality of attachment to psychotherapy, particularly with adults. I select attachment theory because it is already a life span, integrative theory (and, therefore, open to further integration with other theories) and because its roots in evolutionary biology focus attention on the adaptation of individuals to their contexts.

Because all human behavior is based on information, access to valid information is central to human adaptation. Therefore, I begin with a discussion of how the brain transforms sensory stimuli into meaningful information relevant to safety and reproduction.1 Then I reconceptualize Ainsworth's patterns of attachment in infancy and sketch their elaboration across the life span; tied to this is a discussion of procedures for assessing quality of attachment. Next, I consider the application of attachment theory to treatment. Finally, I close with clinical material drawn from adult attachment interviews; I interpret this material in light of theory regarding distortion of information for the purpose of protection.

MENTAL TRANSFORMATIONS OF INFORMATION THAT PROMOTE PROTECTION AND REPRODUCTION

I start with three simple notions. First, to survive, a species must have individuals capable of protecting themselves and their progeny and of reproducing (Tooby & Cosmides, 1990). These two functions, protection and reproduction, constitute the two central organizing functions of life. Second, because behavior is based on information, behavior can be no more adaptive than information is reliable and valid. The process of interpreting information is thus critical to mental health and is dependent on the characteristics of our evolved nervous system, particularly the brain.[2] Third, the ability of the brain to interpret information changes over the course of childhood, thus changing the adaptiveness of behavior.

Information

Privileged Information.   Not all sensory stimulation is equally important, and attending to all of it would overwhelm neurological functioning. Successful species are neurologically organized in ways that favor attention

---

[1]In combining these two functions, I attempt to draw together aspects of Freud's psychoanalytic theory and Bowlby's attachment theory.

[2]See Crittenden (in press-b) for a discussion of the neurological evidence supporting the psychological distinctions made later.

to important information; such attentional biases exclude information with low probabilities of being important and give *privileged* attention to information with high probabilities of being important to safety or reproduction (Gallistel, Brown, Carey, Gelman, & Keil, 1991). Infants attend to features typically found in human faces; adults attend to the sounds, especially the distress sounds, of infants (Bowlby, 1969/1982); adults are attentive to sexually arousing stimuli; and humans of all ages focus on information about danger. These biases promote protection and reproduction. Nevertheless, such innate, schematized perceptual and attentional biases do not identify all dangers, nor is everything that catches our attention important (i.e., we make Type I and Type II errors). Consequently, each individual must refine these innate biases on the basis of unique experience.

The Reptilian Mid-Brain And Cognitive Information.   Adaptive functioning requires transformations of sensory stimuli into meaningful information. The reptilian mid-brain transforms information on the basis of temporal order (Luria, 1973; MacLean, 1973, 1990; Ornstein & Thompson, 1984). That is, when an event is followed by desirable outcomes, the event is repeated. When it is followed by undesirable outcomes, it is not repeated. This is operant conditioning, as described by the principles of learning theory (Skinner, 1938). It enables organisms to modify their behavior on the basis of experience and to function as though prior events *caused* following events. I call information transformed on the basis of temporal order *cognitive information.*[3]

The attribution of causation is preconscious, inarticulate, and prone to particular kinds of error. Because not all preceding events cause subsequent events, misattributions of causation are possible. This is particularly likely if the outcome is dangerous, because, under dangerous conditions, organisms exert considerable effort to prevent the very repetition that could correct the attributional error (Garcia, 1981; Gustavson, Garcia, Hankins, & Rusiniak, 1974). Thus, under dangerous conditions, erroneous attributions are most likely to occur and to remain uncorrected.

Such errors create the potential for disorders of *inhibition* and *compulsion.* When a behavior is followed by punitive outcomes, the behavior is inhibited. When there is a causal relation, the inhibition is functional. If, however, the behavior did not, in fact, cause the punitive outcome or if inhibition is used in situations with different contingencies, the inhibition serves no function. Nevertheless, erroneous judgment of causality may maintain the inhibition indefinitely. On the other hand, if a punitive outcome is expected but does not occur, protective qualities may be attributed to the immediately preceding behavior. In this case, the protective behavior may be displayed whenever the danger is expected. When the "compelled" behavior is actually protective, the compulsion is functional. However, when there is no causal connection, display of the protective behavior will usually

---

[3]My usage of the word *cognitive* is limited to the concept of temporal contingency. I reserve the words *mental, think,* and *intelligent* for more sophisticated, cortical functioning.

be followed by the absence of the danger, thus irrationally reinforcing the response. When the danger does occur in spite of the protective action, the compelled behavior is likely to be displayed more frequently, more intensively, and with greater elaboration.

The Limbic System and Affective Information.   In more highly evolved mammalian species, certain contextual stimuli give rise to feelings (Lang, 1995). In humans, one set of these eliciting contextual stimuli includes darkness, entrapping conditions, unfamiliar surroundings, sudden and loud noises, and being alone (Bowlby, 1973; LeDoux, 1986; Seligman, 1971). Each of these elicits a generalized feeling of anxiety that prepares the individual to fight or flee (Selye, 1976) or to freeze (Lang, 1995). The presence of another person, especially a trusted attachment figure, adds a protective advantage and also reduces anxiety and elicits its opposite feeling, comfort (Bowlby, 1969/1982). Such feelings of anxiety and comfort are not based on experience with danger or safety; rather, they are unfocused feelings that alert us to contexts with changed probabilities of risk. They enable us to predict danger before experiencing risk. A second set of stimuli give rise to sexual desire; sexual desire alerts us to opportunities for reproduction. Its opposite is sexual satisfaction. Such contextual stimuli are generalized templates that include most dangerous contexts and appropriate objects of sexual activity; however, in order to be comprehensive, they necessarily create the Type II error of overinclusion. I call sensory information that is transformed into feeling states *affect.*

Like cognitive information, affect can be modified by experience. In particular, unique contextual stimuli associated with danger or sexuality can become conditioned elicitors of affect, that is, they are learned on the basis of the principles of classical conditioning (Pavlov, 1928). Furthermore, both unconditioned and conditioned elicitors of feelings can be in error. We can feel anxious when there is no danger and we can feel safe when there is imminent danger. Especially when there is no danger, it can be difficult to alleviate the feeling of anxiety, thus opening the way to disorders of anxiety. We can also feel sexual desire when there is, in fact, no opportunity for sexual behavior.

Prediction.   Both cognitive and affective information function to predict dangerous conditions and conditions suitable for reproduction, that is, they provide *true* predictive information on which individuals can organize their behavior. Furthermore, both can be *erroneous*, although the basis for cognitive and affective errors is different. Information can also be *discarded* or omitted from processing. When experience indicates that one or the other sort of information is misleading (e.g., signals of desire for comfort lead to angry rejection or feelings of comfort precede dangerous conditions), we learn to discard the useless or dangerous information.

In addition, both cognition and affect can be *distorted*. Cognition is distorted when causal prediction is treated as exact, rather than probabilistic. Affect is distorted when it is exaggerated, such that some feelings are acknowledged and displayed intensively, while other concurrently experienced feelings are inhibited. In both cases, the distortion reduces ambiguity. Information is most likely to be distorted when conditions are dangerous and when responses based on the distorted information are less dangerous than responses based on undistorted information. For example, the child of hostile parents may experience less danger of parental attack if he or she behaves as though punishment would always follow display of his or her negative feelings. Children of inconsistently available parents may experience less danger of abandonment if they behave as though all separations were traumatically distressing. Under changed circumstances, however, these learned distortions may interfere with accurate mental assessment of, and response to, new situations.

Finally, both sorts of information may be *falsified*. Affective information may be falsified by inhibiting displays of true feeling and exhibiting displays of false feelings. Usually, this is observed as an inhibition of negative feelings and false display of positive feelings. This transformation reduces the assistance we receive from others and misleads them regarding our underlying anger and fear. Because anger and fear are the basis of most violence, the falsification of display of affect misleads others regarding our dangerousness. Cognition is falsified when we behave in a manner that suggests one set of intentions when an incompatible set reflects our true intentions. Use of false cognition tricks others into feeling they are safe when, in fact, we plot aggression against them.

The Neomammalian Cortex. According to Lashley, thought and consciousness are cortical processes that are dependent on recognition of discrepancy (Lashley, 1958/1960). The cortex of the brain integrates information coming from the lower brain, including sensory stimuli and transformed cognitive and affective information. When all yield the same outcome (e.g., all signal danger or all signal no opportunity for reproduction), behavior proceeds unimpeded. When, however, there is discrepancy between the sources of information, the mind must first resolve the dilemma of which information is true (i.e., which is most likely to be accurately predictive), before action can be taken. Resolving this dilemma creates the opportunity for erroneous information to be corrected. It also creates opportunities for new and meaningful distinctions to be made. Because the cortex matures over the childhood of humans, our ability to identify and resolve discrepancies and to create distinctions increases with age.

Viewed from this perspective, mental health depends on comparisons that function to discern discrepancy, followed by integrative processes that resolve the discrepancy by correcting processing errors or identifying hierarchically more advanced continuities. In children, these processes are limited. Consequently, children are in need of protection. In addition, however, children experience paradoxical risks. That is, young children cannot yet display many forms of psychopathology, such as paranoia, promiscuity, or psychopathy, because these require distortions and falsifications of information beyond the capability of young children. On the other hand, uncorrected errors of interpreting stimuli that occur at very early ages can distort all functioning that follows. When such errors occur before consciousness and linguistic representation of information, they can be difficult to identify and correct.

Memory Systems

Basic and transformed information can be encoded and accessed in several different forms. Memory systems (Tulving, 1987) function to order information in ways that increase the efficiency with which the information can be used to guide behavior. The cost of organization is the loss of some information. The pattern of losses creates biases that are associated with each memory system. At several levels, transforming sensory information into meaningful and accessible information creates the possibility of error, omission, distortion, and falsification of information. Four memory systems are discussed here; there is, however, no reason to believe that these are the only memory systems or that these represent the only ways of clustering information.

Procedural Memory.   *Procedural memory* consists of integrations of sensory stimuli with motor responses; in Piagetian terms, it consists of sensorimotor schemata.[4] As such, it is an elaboration of cognitive information in which successful (i.e., reinforced) sequences are operantly learned and repeated until they become habitual. Schemata are also connected to other schemata to create more elaborate schemata. At heart, however, all are preconscious expressions of learned temporal sequences. Such sequences begin forming immediately after birth and are modified throughout life by changing contingencies, including (with age) increasingly subtle contingencies. Procedural memory regulates behavior under ordinary conditions, that is, most of the time throughout most of our lives.

Imaged Memory.   *Imaged memory* is an elaboration of affect. It consists of sensory information that became associated with feelings elicited by unconditioned (i.e., innate) stimuli (Crittenden, in press-a; Leventhal, 1984). In other words, it results from Pavlovian classical conditioning (Pavlov, 1928). It is retained as sensory images of the sight, sound, smell, feel, or taste of dangerous/safe and sexually frustrating/satisfying conditions. Beginning in infancy, it is the basis for modification and expansion of innate elicitors of affect to fit individuals' actual and unique experience. Images function to facilitate rapid identification of dangerous conditions or conditions suitable to sexual activity.

---

[4]Although I use Piaget's epigenetic framework, I also argue that the nervous system is innately organized and prepared to attend and attribute meaning to certain kinds of stimuli in preference to others (Gallistel et al., 1991; Karmiloff-Smith, 1991).

Semantic Memory. Semantic memory is a linguistic form of cognitive information. It consists of verbal statements of how things are and the conditions under which they can be expected to change. For example, the semantic statement *I am a good boy* implies that, therefore, I will do good things. Semantic statements in the if–then form indicate the conditions under which change can be expected. Both sorts of statements contain temporal predictions of a probabilistic sort. Semantic memory can, however, contain information about affect—for example, the statement, *When my mother is angry, you better stay out of her way*, gives the affective conditions used to predict mother's behavior. Unlike procedural and imaged memory, which represent actual experiences of interaction with other people, early semantic memory represents what others tell children about experience; later, children deduce their own semantic conclusions. Thus, it is biased toward others' (usually parents') perspectives (Bowlby, 1980). Semantic memory begins to be constructed toward the end of the second year of life as a result of the period of rapid neurological change associated with the preoperational shift. It is used to enable us to construct responses to new problems that cannot be resolved with existing procedures.

Episodic Memory. Episodic memory consists of the mental replays of events we usually call memories. It represents sophisticated integrations of affect with cognition such that sequentially organized images are recalled in multiple sensory modalities together with affects experienced during the event. Because the information necessary to mentally construct a recalled event is stored in many parts of the brain, integrating it to create an episode requires sophisticated cortical integration. As a consequence, few (if any) episodes are recalled prior to the third or fourth year of life. Like semantic memory, early episodic memory is a joint construction with important adults who, through their questions, tell children what is worth remembering, what is trivial, and what should not be remembered or spoken (Fivush & Hammond, 1990; Hudson, 1990; Pipe & Goodman, 1991). Adults highlight the important aspects of memories, and adults correct children's memories (Snow, 1990). All of these influences bias young children's memories toward adults' perspectives—either accurate or distorted (Bowlby, 1980). Because most events in life are not remembered, recalled episodes tend to reflect arousing incidents, especially events during which we felt unprotected or sexually frustrated. Retention of these is advantageous in that it permits us to recall the incident and to mentally construct alternative self-protective responses as we mature and become capable of more sophisticated functioning. Thus, recognition of, and adaptive response to, future dangers is promoted by retention in memory of previously unresolved problems. At the same time, however, there is the risk that feelings elicited by dangerous and sexually frustrating circumstances will elicit an episodic memory in which we felt similarly, thus promoting the repetition of the same failed response: regression.

PATTERNS OF ATTACHMENT AND ASSESSMENT
OF DEVELOPMENTAL PATHWAYS

Infancy

Ainsworth's three patterns of attachment reflect individual differences in how behavior with attachment figures is organized (Ainsworth, Blehar, Waters, & Wall, 1978) and, in information processing terms, three patterns for mentally integrating information about dangerous circumstances (Crittenden, 1994). In infancy, the patterns are labeled *avoidant (Type A)*, *secure (Type B)*, and *ambivalent (Type C)* and are limited to sensorimotor procedural functioning. Type A infants tend to have been predictably and negatively reinforced for display of negative affect. Thus, the Type A pattern of behavior is organized cognitively (to emphasize predictable outcomes) with inhibition of negative affect (because it leads predictably to undesirable outcomes). Inhibition of negative affect (i.e., attachment behavior) is made possible when infants *perceptually* avoid their attachment figure and focus their attention on less arousing aspects of the environment (such as toys). Type B infants tend to have been predictably positively reinforced for displaying their feelings clearly. The Type B pattern is organized around an integration of affect and cognition with clear communication of both feelings (affect) and intentions (cognition). As parents become better able to discern differences in infants' signals and to respond differentially to them, infants become better able to differentiate both their signals and the affective states underlying them. By approximately 9 months of age, anger, fear, and desire for comfort can be easily differentiated. Type C infants tend to have been on an unpredictable schedule of intermittent reinforcement of affective signals; this, of course, maintains displays of negative affect at high levels for long durations, and in spite of changed reinforcement patterns. As a consequence, the Type C pattern becomes organized around affect, particularly the intense display of mixed negative affects (anger, fear, and desire for comfort) in a context of inconsistent parental response (uncertain cognitive meaning). Thus, in infancy there are three types of procedural representational models of relationship (see Fig. 3.1).

Ainsworth's Strange Situation has become the best validated assessment of quality of attachment. The entire meaning of the procedure rests on the quality of mother–child interaction during the preceding year of life and on the prediction from this to developmental differences subsequent to the Strange Situation. In addition, the Strange Situation depends on a series of comparisons: between the infant's behavior with the mother and with the stranger, between his or her behavior before the mother's departure and on reunion, and between the infant's exploratory behavior when the infant is comfortable and when distressed. Discrepancies among these comparisons are critical to interpretation of the observations. Finally, it is important to note both that Ainsworth's original patterns have stood the test of time and varied samples and also that improved observational techniques, especially videotape, and an increasing range of samples to which the Strange Situ-

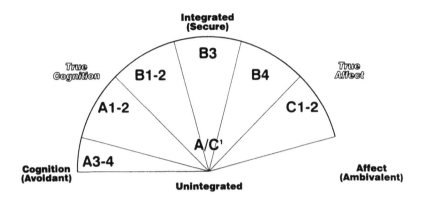

FIG. 3.1. Patterns of attachment in infancy as a function of type of information and degree of integration of information.
[1]Defended/Coercive

ation has been applied have led to an expansion of the patterns. This resulted from two processes, one beginning with theory and one with observation.

First, in samples of maltreated children, substantial numbers of securely attached infants were found (Crittenden, 1985; Gersten, Coster, Schneider-Rosen, Carlson, & Cicchetti, 1986; Egeland & Sroufe, 1981; Lyons-Ruth, Repacholi, McLeod, & Silva, 1991). This was highly discrepant with theory and led me to carefully review my videotapes of "securely" attached maltreated children. This led to the description of an A/C organization that was often misclassified as Type B when using a classificatory system limited to A, B, and C. The A/C pattern was often associated with the experience of both abuse and neglect (Crittenden, 1985). Second, in more normative samples, Main and Solomon (1986) noticed fleeting, but unusual, behaviors that did not fit the patterns described by Ainsworth. Further examination of these cases led to the description of a disorganized/disoriented category of attachment and its association with maternal loss (Main & Hesse, 1990). Thus, discrepancies between theory and careful observation led to important new insights (Lashley, 1958/1960). As noted earlier, the best assessments both accurately classify on the basis of current distinctions and also provide a means for generating more sophisticated distinctions. These are powerful attributes of Ainsworth's Strange Situation.

The Preschool Years

With the preoperational functioning of the preschool years, infant patterns are modified. The modifications reflect a greater use of language to represent meaning, especially including information about past and future behavior. In addition, preschool-age children use more sophisticated nonverbal communication; this includes new signals, new combinations of signals, and distortion of signals such as substitution of false displays of positive affect for true negative feelings and exaggeration of display of feelings. Furthermore, children begin to represent information semantically and episodically, although it is unlikely they are able to use this information in the preschool years to regulate their behavior. Finally, preoperational children are able to inhibit some behavior even when the eliciting stimuli are perceptually available—they are able to use *mental* inhibition of affective behavior.

The Type A pattern continues to be cognitively organized on the basis of predictable outcomes with inhibition of display of negative affect. As Cassidy and Marvin noted, this results in avoidant *behavior* becoming uncommon among Type A preschool-age children *because* it is considered rude by adults and, therefore, elicits adult anger (Cassidy & Marvin with the MacArthur Working Group on Attachment in the Preschool Years, 1992). Instead, preschool Type A children mentally inhibit display of negative affect (without having to turn their backs to their attachment figures) and, sometimes, cover its absence with positive affect (Crittenden, 1992a; Crittenden & DiLalla, 1987). Thus, the Type A behavioral pattern becomes one of inhibiting display of negative affect, displaying parentally desired affect, and doing as parents desire; in all cases, relationships are kept *psychologically* distant. In normative cases, the pattern includes mild psychological withdrawal, heightened "overbright" positive affect, and the over achievement associated with extensive exploration (Fig. 3.2, A1–2). In such normative cases, children are adequately protected by their parents; consequently, they learn not to attend to feelings of anxiety and to inhibit display of angry feelings that elicit parental anger.

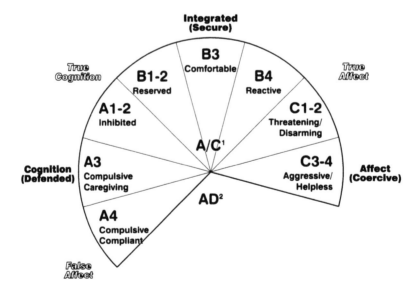

FIG. 3.2. Patterns of attachment in the preschool years as a function of type of information and degree of integration of information.
[1]Defended/Coercive   [2]Anxious/Depressed

Although they seemed to fit best in the Type A grouping, maltreated children did not entirely fit this pattern of behavior. Careful examination of the discrepancies led to the description of two new subcategories within Type A (Crittenden, 1992a, 1995). In cases of serious parental withdrawal (including neglect), Type A children displayed role-reversing, compulsive caregiving using false positive affect that functioned to attract the (protective) attention of psychologically unavailable caregivers (Fig. 3.2, A3). In cases of parental harshness (including abuse), the pattern became compulsive compliance in which negative affect was inhibited, the parent was observed with discreet vigilance, and the child did exactly as the parent desired (Fig. 3.2, A4). Unlike normative A1–2 preschoolers, both A3 and A4 children were very anxious, both with the attachment figure and especially when left alone; however, evidence of their distress was not displayed in the presence of attachment figures.

Mentally, all of the Type A subpatterns reflect the splitting of good and bad aspects of self and others such that the internal representational model of the parent is good and that of the self bad; thus, the "true" bad self is hidden by the displayed "false" good self (Winnicott, 1958). Because children's own behavior predictably determines parental behavior, Type A children tend to take full responsibility for dyadic outcomes. When these are undesirable, Type A children often feel shame.

The Type B pattern consists of accurate representation of feelings and intentions that are communicated to attachment figures both verbally and nonverbally. Preschool children become able to recognize that attachment figures may have feelings and intentions different from their own. With reciprocal communication, Type B children and their attachment figures are able to negotiate differences and use compromise to construct mutually acceptable plans; in Bowlby's terms, they construct a *goal-corrected partnership* with their attachment figures (Bowlby, 1969/1982). This promotes the construction of integrated internal representational models that are constantly being revised in a dynamic interaction of self, attachment figures, experience, and mental maturation. In a Type B relationship, there is mental integration of affect and cognition between partners and little distortion in the communication of these. Because Type B children are confident that the plans protect them, feelings are experienced within a moderate range. Responsibility for circumstances is experienced as shared between parent and child (Fig. 3.2, B1–4).

Type C children, whose parents are inconsistent, learn to use exaggerated angry demands (including overtly avoidant and aggressive behavior) to draw parental attention to themselves. When the attention received is angry, they use coy behavior (made up of nonverbal signals that terminate aggression and elicit nurturance[5]) to transform parental anger into caregiving. Thus, Type C children use a coercive strategy to capture, hold, and shape parental attention. Mentally, the strategy consists of splitting anger

---

[5]See Crittenden (1992a, 1995, in press-a) for full discussions of these signals and their use in the coercive strategy of Type C children and adults.

from fear and desire for comfort and displaying one set of feelings in an exaggerated form while inhibiting the other. In its mild form, the pattern alternates threatening and disarming behavior (Fig. 3.2, C1–2) whereas, in its more intense form, threats become aggression and disarming behavior escalates to feigned helplessness (Fig. 3.2, C3–4). Parents often feel trapped by this strategy and attempt to foil it by tricking their children with regard to their intentions. For example, a parent who intends to leave interests a child in a toy so as to be able to slip out of the room unnoticed. This teaches children not to let their attention be deflected from the relationship toward exploration and not to trust cognitive information about parents' probable intentions. Type C children learn that such information can be deceptive. In addition, the coercive strategy is a blaming strategy in which the other is held responsible for one's condition and the self is held blameless. Because such clear division of responsibility is rarely accurate, Type C children find themselves caught up in unresolvable struggles that, on the surface, look like endless fights, but function to maintain parental attention and availability and, thus, to promote safety.

In the context of evolved and maturing mental functioning and unique caregiver behavior, human children learn to use their minds to construct models of reality. Attachment figures operating in children's zone of proximal development provide the scaffold with which children learn to select information and construct meaning (Rieber & Carlton, 1987). On the basis of these models, children organize strategies for changing the probabilities of caregiver behavior. Under conditions of threat and danger, children learn to misconstrue, discard, or distort information. Although these mental functions promote the protection of children when conditions are dangerous, they increase the probability of maladaptation in other contexts, particularly contexts that are relatively safe (Crittenden, 1995). Finally, because functioning in the early years of life is largely preconscious and closely tied to caregiver functioning, intervention must necessarily emphasize caregiver behavior.[6] Therefore, I maintain the focus of this chapter on the developmental processes leading to adult functioning.

The School Years

There are two important developments in the ABC strategies in the school years. First, children learn to use the various memory systems to create more complete internal representational models and to regulate their behavior. For Type A children, this implies accessing parentally influenced semantic memory for information about what they ought to do and feel. Episodic memory, on the other hand, often includes desires and feelings in conflict with semantic "rules." In communication with caregivers, Type A children learn that they often recall episodes differently from their parents and that some things should not be recalled because they elicit unpleasant

---

[6]See Crittenden (1992b) for a discussion of the treatment of anxious attachment in young children.

responses, including uncomfortable feelings in oneself and anger in one's parents. On the whole, Type A children learn that they feel better and their parents are more supportive if they access borrowed parental semantic memory to explain their behavior and avoid direct recall of episodes, especially those that provide contradictory evidence. Type B children learn to access and integrate both sources of information. In particular, they learn to use each to correct the other and to use parents as a helpful resource in accomplishing this integration. The outcome is the ability to make an increasing range of distinctions and to integrate disparate sources of information to create increasingly accurate (i.e., predictive) internal representational models. Type C children are able to make little sense of parents' conflicting semantic guides (e.g., *You're a bad–good boy. Didn't I tell you to ask permission?–Can't you do anything for yourself?*). Exaggerated affect, however, is experienced as a reliable predictor of parental response. Consequently, Type C children tend to ignore semantic memory–models and to rely on procedural models guided by recall of unhappy images or episodes. Keeping past dangers and disappointments in mind keeps Type C children focused on relationships and their uncertainties and reduces their interest in exploration of the inanimate world. This may lead to hyperactivity, attentional problems, or learning difficulties.

The second important development in the school years is children's emerging ability to use false cognition to mislead others with regard to their intentions. Children become able to appear to focus their attention and behavior around one (overt) intention while carrying out (covertly) organized behavior to achieve another intention. Put another way, school-age children are able to mentally inhibit action they intend. Type C children, in particular, find that misleading information permits them to do as they desire with less obstruction from others (Fig. 2.3, C5–6). This permits them to get for themselves things they cannot count on inconsistent adults to provide, and to express their anger with relative impunity. Because safety is desired above all else, false cognition is used to make others believe that one is powerful (e.g., bullying behavior), to prevent others from deserting (e.g., the mutual complicity in crime and retribution for desertion of gangs), and to elicit protection from those who pretend to power (e.g., the right of the vanquished to be protected by the victor). Thus, like the Type A pattern, power is an issue, but, for those using the Type C strategy, it is feigned power and feigned helplessness (see Fig. 2.3).

Adolescence and Adulthood

Adolescence constitutes the last major period of rapid neurological increase in cortical functioning, the shift that permits formal (abstract) mental operations (Piaget, 1952). Concurrently, puberty results in sexual feelings and motivation. Access to formal mental operations initiates a period of reintegration of information about how to cope with other people and the constraints of reality, as well as more sophisticated ways of making mental distinctions. Together these become represented in complexly organized

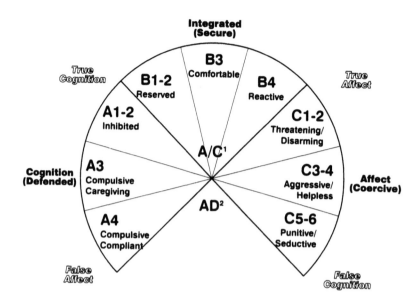

FIG. 3.3. Patterns of attachment in the school years as a function of type of information and degree of integration of information.
[1]Defended/Coercive   [2]Anxious/Depressed

internal representational models that are hierarchical and conditional. For example, in considering their two parents as well as the parents of friends, adolescents may construct models indicating that (hierarchically), *Most parents are well-intentioned, although my mother is more restrictive than my father,* and (conditionally), *My mother is most helpful when her work is completed and my father is impossible if he has been drinking.* Constructing such complex models involves repeated concatenations of the processes of perception, dichotomization, comparison, and integration that have been ongoing throughout childhood. In general, the more information an individual accesses in this integrative process, the more complex and representative of experience the resulting internal representational model will be. A particular achievement of adult mental functioning is the freeing of behavior from mental perception, intention, and attribution. That is, the perceptive adult may identify existing distortions of information and use this self-knowledge to select contextually appropriate behavior. For example, a Type A individual may recognize the nature of his or her underlying feelings of anger and fear, evaluate the potential of these feelings to predict future circumstances, and then choose when, how, and whether or not to maintain behavioral inhibition. Type C adults may recognize that they exaggerate their display of feelings and decide when it is advantageous to continue to do so and when it is not.

On the other hand, when some information has in the past been danger-
ously unreliable or invalid, it may continue to be discarded in the integrative
process. This may lead to models containing less complexity, requiring fewer
subtle distinctions, and entailing fewer integrations than more consciously
constructed models. In addition, such models will dichotomize reality as
compared to more fully integrated models. Finally, because all schematized
information is stripped of detail present in the original experience, there is
always some distortion of information, with greater distortion occurring
when access to the original (untransformed) information is obscured.

Sexuality becomes a major motivation in adolescence and with it adolescents experience the new affect of sexual desire. This affect and the intention
to find a reproductive partner must be integrated with the attachment
strategies for managing intimate relationships. Although fully exploring
this process is beyond the scope of this chapter, the integration of sexuality
and attachment is extremely relevant to adult adaptation. It is proposed
that, when erroneous, discarded, distorted, and false information is reflected in patterns of attachment, information about sexuality is likely to
become similarly distorted (e.g., A5–6, C5–6, C7–8, AC). The effect in
normative situations is likely to be the selection of partners who do not meet
one's expectations. In more severe situations, there is the risk of such
inappropriate selection of partners such that either the partner or the self
experiences physical or psychological danger.[7]

Type A adolescents are likely to construct internally consistent models of
what one ought (semantically) to do and to discard information about how
one feels and what others and the self have actually (episodically) done,
especially when these are inconsistent with semantic models. Frequently,
such models idealize the (powerful) parent and denigrate the (powerless)
self. Occasionally, however, the reverse process occurs: The parent is dero-
gated and the (empowered) self is idealized.[8] The more extreme this process, the less likely it is that individuals will be able to manage intimate
relationships (Fig. 3.4, A5). With the impetus of sexuality, however, the need
for physical closeness in the context of psychological distance may be
expressed as promiscuity with false positive sexual affect (Fig. 3.4, A6).

Type B adolescents are likely to have models in which there is considerable dichotomizing of the attributes of attachment figures and of attachment figures' attributes in oneself. Indeed, compared to adults' models,
adolescents' models appear less integrated and less stable over time (Jaeger,
Crittenden, Black, & McCartney, in press). The critical feature of Type B
models is not the completeness of the integration (which is yet to come) but
rather the access to all the information and the relative lack of distortion or
falsification of that information. In addition, most Type B adolescents are
assisted by supportive attachment figures who can accept their adolescents'

---

[7]See Crittenden (in press-a) for a fuller discussion of the integration of attachment and
sexuality.

[8]See Crittenden (1988) for an empirically based discussion of such split models based on
power and the range of behavior that can be displayed by a single individual across multiple
relationships that differ in the structure of power.

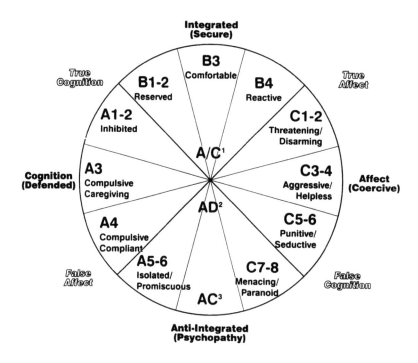

FIG. 3.4. Patterns of attachment in adolescence and adulthood as a function of type
of information and degree of integration of information.
[1]Defended/Coercive   [2]Anxious/Depressed   [3]Anti-Integrated AC

sometimes harsh judgments without anger, denial, or submission. Put
another way, such attachment figures provide a secure base of balanced
judgment and compassionate acceptance of their developing adolescent
from which the adolescent can safely explore and construct personal models. Where this experience is highly supportive, there may be little discrepancy and little need to contrast, correct, and integrate conflicting
information. As a consequence, the resulting internal representational
model may reflect a limited range of supportive reality in which there is
little threat, little false or erroneous information, and little need to engage
in the mental process of re-evaluating information. Such "naive" adolescents live in integrated contexts and are safe and happy. Nevertheless, they
are not necessarily mentally integrated (Crittenden, in press-a).

Type C adolescents are likely to have confused and unclear internal
representational models. Because semantic information proved unreliable
in the past, Type C adolescents are likely to focus on the details of imaged
and episodic recall and to engage in futile struggles with others over
retribution for past offenses or excessive nurturance (Fig. 3.3, C5–6). When
individuals have experienced very dangerous conditions, self-protection
may take the alternating forms of menacing threats (with covert intention
of harm) against others and paranoid beliefs that others pose such a threat
to oneself (Fig. 3.3, C7–8).

By adulthood, the A and C distortions of erroneous, discarded, distorted, and falsified information may combine in psychopathy, a condition in which no situations can be determined to be safe and no information is necessarily true (Fig. 3.4, AC). Psychopaths distort their behavior in order to mislead others with regard to both their feelings and their intentions and, at all times, behave so as to maximize their own safety and opportunity to reproduce and to destroy people perceived as threatening these.

Continuity Across Time

The previous developmental description may lead to the erroneous assumption that Types A, B, C, and A/C necessarily have continuity across time. This is not intended or implied. Development is conceptualized here using Bowlby's metaphor of *pathways* in which a given pathway may continue straight or may branch in ways that may lead to other pathways (Bowlby, 1979). The indeterminacy of pathways from their point of origin is an important aspect of the metaphor. This is in contrast to a similar term, *trajectory*, implying the predictability of outcomes from initial conditions.

There are several conditions that can modify behavioral and mental pathways. One is an unexpected, that is, random, change in conditions—for example, the death of a parent or the appearance of an alternate attachment figure. Another is a successful experience of therapy. It is generally accepted among attachment theorists that these two are relevant to changes in quality of attachment. But maturation itself plays an important role. By changing the ability of the mind to perceive discrepancies and to integrate information in ways that yield more complex representations than the sum of the bits of information (Sameroff, 1983), maturation itself creates the potential for both reorganizations within pattern (e.g., from A1–2 to A3 or A5–6) and also reorganizations that result in changes in pattern (e.g., from A1–2 to C1–2 or B1–2). Thus, evolution combined with maturation gives developing humans the potential for correction of error, omission, distortion, and falsification of information. Another source of change is the failure of attachment figures to adapt to children's development. When attachment figures are sensitive at one developmental stage, but do not modify their behavior in ways that fit their child's changing competencies, they can elicit both doubt and anger in their children. These can lead to shifts from Type B to Type A or C: Attachment figures operate in the zone of proximal development of the attached person (Rieber & Carlton, 1987). When maturation or experiential learning change that zone, attachment figures must modify their behavior. Failure to do so necessarily creates dyssynchrony. Conversely, however, an attachment figure who is out of synchrony at one time period may come to fit the more mature behavior of an older child. Thus, the uncomfortable and distant father of an infant may become the secure attachment figure of a school-age child. Moreover, this may occur just when the child's mother is becoming less supportive of her increasingly independent "baby."

I conclude this discussion of continuity with a perspective on probabilities. I propose that at any given moment, it is most probable (although not certain) that individuals will continue on their present pathway. Nevertheless, when external circumstances change or when maturation changes the individual, the probabilities are changed. Depending on the full set of circumstances (including innate capacities, past and current functioning) and new circumstances, some outcomes become more probable and others less probable. In this way, the probability of using a particular strategy is rather like the actual use of a strategy. The Type A, B, C, and A/C strategies do not guarantee protection. To the contrary, they only maximize the probability of it, given that future conditions are similar to past conditions. Such a probabilistic approach is systemic and dynamic (Sameroff, 1983). It also explains the value of the *integrated* Type B pattern; when one has access to all the information, including a recognition of others' use of distortion and deception, one is best able to select a protective behavioral strategy. Achievement of this status becomes possible in adulthood.

The Adult Attachment Interview

Just as the Strange Situation is the best assessment of quality of attachment in infancy and the preschool years, the Adult Attachment Interview (AAI) is the most accepted procedure for adulthood. Like the Strange Situation, it is based on comparisons and the search for discrepancy. In this case, however, the behavior is transcribed verbal discourse and the comparisons are based on Bowlby's notion that mentally healthy people integrate information from both semantic and episodic memory to create internal representational models of self and attachment figures. My work suggests that these models become integrated into more comprehensive models of *reality* (Crittenden, 1988, 1990). Because semantic and episodic memory are vulnerable to different types of error, mental integration of semantic and episodic information creates the opportunity to identify discrepancies between what is known semantically and what is known episodically. This creates the possibility of conscious reflection on the problem, correction of the erroneous information, and modification (i.e., reorganization) of internal representational models. The revised models permit the selection of behavior that is adaptive in its specific context (Bowlby, 1980). Maladaptation occurs when information is misconstrued and then used to construct internal representational models that are applied without modification to different contexts. I propose that, based on current work in cognitive psychology and neurology, Bowlby's perspective can be expanded to include basic transformations of cognitive and affective information as well as the organization of cognitive and affective information into at least *four* memory systems: procedural, imaged, semantic, and episodic memory. The AAI has the potential to take observers below the surface of the speaker's words to display where, how, and what is being distorted. Knowing this can enable clinicians to select treatment strategies that more effectively correct the identified distortion.

Although the AAI is usually spoken of as though it were one thing, it consists of four distinct components. The first component, the AAI itself (George, Kaplan, & Main, 1986), systematically accesses semantic and episodic memory and the speaker's ability to use integrative mental processes.[9] The questions move from simple probes of each memory system to integrative questions requiring access to varied sorts of information. It is, of course, in the integrative process that speakers may identify and correct the errors, omissions, distortions, and false information contained in the separate memory systems.

The second component, the *discourse analysis* (Main & Goldwyn, accepted for publication), focuses on aspects of the discourse indicative of discarded or distorted information. Based on the expansion of attachment theory that I have offered, I propose that the discourse analysis be extended to include identification of erroneous and false (deceptive) information. Furthermore, the analytic procedures can be applied to three memory systems: imaged, semantic, and episodic.[10] Thus, the AAI permits sophisticated analysis of the manner in which adults process information relevant to familial relationships. Specifically, it permits examination of the sources of information used by individuals as well as of the validity of that information—the extent to which the information is true, erroneous, discarded, distorted, or falsified. Finally, a major strength of George's interview and Main and Goldwyn's discourse analysis is that they promote exploration of organizations that were not identified at the time of the creation of the AAI. Thus, like the Strange Situation before it, the AAI holds the potential to expand understanding.

The third component of the AAI is the *classificatory system*. The one used by Main and Goldwyn for the AAI is the infant system (transformed to Ds, F, and E) with the addition of several empirically observed new classifications (Ds2, Ds4, F5, E3). Unresolved loss (U-loss) corresponds to Main and Solomon's (1990) infant disorganized/disoriented category; lack of resolution of abuse (U-abuse) is modeled on it. I propose that the expanded system of subpatterns displayed in Fig. 3.4 be used with the expectation that these will be of clinical importance.

---

[9]An abbreviated overview of the semistructured interview follows: The opening question is a simple integrative question: "Orient me to your family when you were a child." Follow-up questions flesh out who, when, and where details. Then another integrative question asks for a general description of the speaker's relationships with his or her parents in early childhood. This is followed by a probe of semantic memory in terms of five adjectives to describe the mother. Episodic probes follow in which an episode is sought for each semantic adjective. These are not direct probes of episodic memory, but rather retrieval strategies that use semantic memory. This semantic–episodic process is repeated for the father. There are then several direct probes of episodic memory: "What did you do when you were upset? Hurt? Separated from your parents?" An episode is requested for each. More difficult experiences are explored in terms of parental threats, including punishment and threats of abandonment. The interview concludes with a series of integrative probes: "Why do you think your parents behaved as they did? What is the effect on your personality? What have you learned from your experience?"

[10]Procedural memory is not accessed directly in the *AAI* although an assay can be made when speakers describe *scripts*, that is, verbalized procedures.

The final component of the AAI is a particular *version of attachment theory* in which the Ainsworth infant patterns form the basis for identifying patterns across the life span and in which patterns are thought to be quite stable from infancy even into future generations. Ironically, it is use of the AAI itself that provides evidence of the limitation of this version of attachment theory. Specifically, in van IJzendoorn's meta-analysis of 18 studies using the AAI, only 22% of the variance in parent and child classifications is accounted for by the continuity hypothesis (Van IJzendoorn, 1994), suggesting the critical importance of more complex hypotheses that account for change and discontinuity. Furthermore, as more studies focused on clinically interesting populations, the proportion of transcripts that could not be classified (CC) using the Main and Goldwyn system increased dramatically to include one half or more of risk samples. Again, this suggests the limitation of a classification system and theory that are based on the continuity of infant mental organization throughout the life span.

Alternative Approaches.   These four components have been used and modified separately. For example, with my colleagues, I used an interview based more on parenting experience than the George et al. (1986) interview, but classified with the Main and Goldwyn procedure into the D_s, E, F classificatory system (Crittenden, Partridge, & Claussen, 1991). Grossmann, Fremmer-Bombik, Rudolph, and Grossmann (1988) used a different type of analysis, but retained the George et al. interview and a reduced D_s and F classificatory system.

For clinical purposes, I suggest modification of both the discourse analysis and the classificatory system to fit more precisely the range of disorders seen in clinical practice. Without such modification, most clinical transcripts are assigned to a "Cannot Classify" (CC) category, forced into a not-quite-fitting normative D/E/F classification, or clustered without differentiation into E3 and the unresolved (U) categories (Hesse, 1996). This global approach to disorder is not particularly informative to clinicians.

USING ATTACHMENT THEORY IN TREATMENT

Attachment theory and assessment may be useful to mental health therapists in two ways: They may facilitate improved diagnosis and they may lead to more effective and efficient treatment. In terms of diagnosis, attachment theory focuses attention on the protective and reproductive functions of maladaptive behavior and provides a gradient of diagnoses or subpatterns (Fig. 3.4), that cluster symptoms in ways that are developmentally and clinically meaningful. Essential to using these diagnoses is recognition that they are part of a model that, like all other models, is stripped of unique detail and constructed to organize what is now understood. Models are always limited and should always be open to expansion. My interest in attachment theory as a therapeutic tool derives from its recognition of its own incompleteness and its power, through careful observation and description, to highlight new and clinically relevant discrepancies.

In terms of treatment, therapists function as attachment figures in the client's zone of proximal development. Thus, they provide a safe base from which the client can explore the threatening aspects of his or her experience in the expectation of support and protection from the therapist.

The theory I propose also suggests that systematic use of the various assessments of quality of attachment can permit therapists to assess the ways in which clients transform and attribute meaning to information, together with the state of their various internal representational models. Because enduring treatment of psychological disorder implies reorganizing each of the models to bring them into concordance, it is important to be able to assess each model.

Each of the major schools of therapy seems particularly suited to effecting transformations of a particular memory system. Behavioral therapies and family systems therapies focus on changing the contingencies on behavior and making procedural models conscious and, thus, available for examination and modification. Cognitive therapies focus on identifying and changing faulty semantic generalizations. Psychodynamic therapies often focus attention on forgotten episodes and assist clients to work through feelings that were elicited long ago and left unresolved. Therapies that use visualization and imagery address imaged memory in an effort to enable clients to free themselves from inappropriately preoccupying images and to facilitate use of comforting images to reduce anxiety. Finally, the various meditative therapies emphasize the need for distancing from active involvement in life tasks in order to achieve mental integration.

From this perspective, it becomes possible to think about constructing a purposeful eclecticism in which therapists assess the state of mind of clients and then plan the process of therapy to progress through (a) clients' recognition of discrepancy, (b) resolution of the discrepancy, (c) integration of corrected information with other information, and (d) reorganization of internal representational models and associated behavioral strategies. A particularly important discrepancy is the vulnerability of the child (who distorted information in self-protective ways) as compared to the relative competence of the adult (who may no longer need such distortions to be safe). One of the exciting features of this model is that, because most therapists already are eclectic, they have many of the necessary tools for effective therapy. The task is to organize their use in the most effective manner. Attachment theory, as I have represented it here, may offer a means of systematically organizing these tools.

The final and essential step is, of course, to teach clients how to implement this mental process for themselves. That is, like the attachment figures of infants, therapists should teach clients how to use their minds to derive relatively accurate representations of reality on which they can organize (and reorganize) their future behavior. Because models are never perfect and because the future always involves changed conditions, it is the process of reorganization that is critical to enduring mental health.

EXAMPLES OF TRANSFORMED INFORMATION

In the remainder of this chapter, I present examples of erroneous, discarded, distorted, and false information. These are drawn from the George et al. interview using an expansion of the the Main and Goldwyn discourse analysis that is tied to the expanded classificatory system described in Fig. 3.4.

Comparisons

Following Bowlby's notion of comparison of semantic and episodic memory to identify discordance and Lashley's notion that discrepancy creates the opportunity for conscious and integrative mental processes, examination of the AAI discourse can be accomplished through a series of comparisons:

1. Between what the speaker says about their attachment figures and childhood experience and what we, the readers, believe to be true.
2. Between what the speaker says semantically (globally, in general, and at a distance) and what they say episodically (specifically, in detail, and up close).
3. Between what they say about attachment figures and what they say about more distant relationships, for example, with grandparents, stepparents, teachers.
4. Between what they say and how they say it.

Managing these comparisons requires that we generally know what happened in the speakers' childhood. If information is erroneous, discarded, distorted, or falsified, the truth regarding their experience will not be openly revealed. Therefore, we must find evidence (of which they would not be consciously aware) of distorted processing of information. One way to accomplish this is through discourse analysis of the interview transcript.[11]

Discourse[12]

Main and Goldwyn's method of discourse analysis permits the careful reader to find the moments in spoken thought when information is modified. These moments are identified by dysfluencies, with different sorts of

---

[11]Other ways exist, including analysis of affect, physiological measures, and so on. These may be equally valid techniques, but they are not addressed here.
[12]The discourse features mentioned here are not a complete list, nor are they described sufficiently to be the basis for coding. A full manual with accompanying training is needed for reliable coding and valid classification.

dysfluencies being expected for Type A and C individuals.[13] Specifically, Type A (Dismissing) adults tend to idealize parents semantically and distort conflicting episodic memory by failing to recall incidents, normalizing unsupportive behavior, cutting off episodes prior to unpleasant outcomes, removing the self from episodes, or drawing positive conclusions from negative episodes. When negative experiences are acknowledged, the speaker usually takes responsibility for them (thus, protecting the model of attachment figures). Type C (Preoccupied) individuals tend to have limited access to semantic memory (expressed as oscillation of semantic judgment and refusal to come to semantic conclusions). In addition, Type C adults relate episodes that are confusing, trivial, strung together without apparent logic or temporal order, and infused with affectively arousing images and display a blurring of personal, temporal, or geographic contexts (e.g., confusion of pronouns for self and attachment figures, use of angry speech to or from attachment figures as though the attachment figure were present in the place of the interviewer, slips to the present tense for past events, respectively). Unlike Type A speakers, Type C speakers are blaming with regard to attachment figures and take little or no responsibility for their contribution to their experience. These discourse markers allow the careful reader to identify discrepancies between what is said at different points in the transcript and, by reading "between the lines," to make reasonable assumptions about the underlying true information. In the sections to follow, brief examples of the various distortions of information are presented in excerpts from AAI transcripts. Similar examples for younger people can be found in Crittenden (in press-a).

Type A Transformations of Information

Distortion of Cognitive Information and Omission of Affective Information (A1–2). Type A speakers regulate their mental functioning by *distorting cognition* to create greater semantic predictability than exists in reality and *omitting or refusing to integrate* affective information that, if acknowledged, might elicit parental rejection and feelings of anxiety about being unprotected.

During his childhood, Mark's father was often away from the family for long periods for work, but his mother was at home with the children. When asked to describe his early relationship with his parents, Mark said:

> There were very close relations, very good relations. I suppose in my early years, my mother naturally featured more as my principle carer and provider of meals. Undoubtedly, it is to her that I went on falling over and crying. I always remember both of them being there and supportive. I really have no reservations or criticisms at all about them as parents in the early years. My

---

[13]Main relabels the A, B, and C patterns as Ds, F, and E in adulthood. For clarity, the A, B, C nomenclature will be maintained here.

father, I suppose, became more influential as I grew older. But I think each has had a very marked influence upon my life and almost entirely for the better. And I really can't record any negative aspects of that relationship, although, of course, there were many, the usual adolescent conflicts.

Even in this introductory paragraph, there is evidence of distortion of semantic information. "Very close, very good" suggests semantic idealization—unless Mark can provide clear, supporting information. This positive semantic conclusion is repeated four times, but the last three each contain some qualifier: "no criticisms at all *in the early years*," "*almost* entirely for the better," "can't *now* record any negative aspects." At some point, Mark must clarify these negations of his positive judgment in a clear and conscious manner or we will have to determine that semantic information is being distorted by making it too positive. Furthermore, in this paragraph, we get no image of Mark's parents as unique people; indeed, they are spoken of impersonally ("there were") and as a unit ("them"). The use of "suppose" and "undoubtedly" suggest that Mark's recollections were being constructed on the basis of his semantic generalizations rather than actually being remembered; it will be important to see if this is maintained when episodes are probed directly. Mark described his mother in very distancing, impersonal terms as a "carer" and "provider of meals"; such language is more suitable to paid institutional caregivers than to loving mothers. Even Mark's reference to hurting himself is distanced; he referred to his behavior "on falling over and crying" rather than including himself as subject and using active verbs: "when I fell down and hurt myself or cried." At one point, Mark inadvertently described his strategy for keeping distressing information out of consciousness: "I really can't now record any negative aspects," that is, I have such experiences but refuse to recall them. There is normalizing ("naturally") and this was used a second time in the last sentence when Mark spoke of conflicts. In that case, he seemed to slip and almost said, *there were many conflicts*, but caught himself and normalized the statement by adding the words *the usual*.

Without doubt, this reading of a single paragraph cannot be substantiated from within the paragraph alone. If, however, the pattern of idealizing the parents and dismissing the self is maintained throughout the interview, we will have strong evidence that semantic memory is idealized and conflicting episodic information is discarded. Both processes reduce the probability of Mark's discovering the discrepancy between the memory systems and having to deal with the conclusion that his parents were sometimes not supportive. Because an occasional lack of support is not usually very threatening, we must wonder if his parents were quite rejecting or even threatening.

Our search for corroborating information is rewarded. The five semantic adjectives for his mother are *warm, loving, generous, forgiving,* and *indulgent*. For his father, "It is the same really. I cannot enlarge much about that." Mark's parents appear to be two saints who are so uniformly perfect that they cannot be differentiated. When asked for a memory of his mother being warm, Mark responded, "I don't think there are any special incidents. I think warmness is a characteristic which pervades and it's ongoing and constant. I remember both my parents being very open about their affect. There were, there were cuddles and kisses and . . . no embarrassment about that." Note the lack of recall of episodes (altogether in the transcript, Mark said he could not remember nine times). Mark reverted to generalized semantic memory, but failed to include any people (e.g., Who was warm? What did warmth pervade? Their affect to whom? Who gave and received the cuddles?). The mention of embarrassment is surprising, unless affection is embarrassing. For the next adjective (loving), Mark says, "Well, it's the same really. I cannot enlarge on that." For generous, he says, "Well, this is for both parents." Then he goes on to say that his parents were economically poor, but "generous in the sense of having things provided when . . . it may have been a sacrifice on the part of my mother to provide them." Again, there is the lack of an episode, the semantic rendition of the information, idealization of his parents, and the lack of self as a recipient of the provided "things". As with his mother, Mark could not remember any episodes for his father.

When asked directly about what he did when upset as a child, Mark said, "I think tears were very frequent, but I probably ran to my mother, but I am guessing but I cannot remember. I remember cutting my hand badly on a shard of glass and screaming my head off and running back home. [Running back home and going to your mom?] Possibly, I can't remember." In this case, Mark was endangered and he could not remember receiving care or comfort from his warm, loving, generous, and indulgent mother. This creates an important discrepancy. Later, we learn that during a major operation, Mark's parents never visited him and, juxtaposed against this is the statement that his father used "physical chastisement, nothing excessive."

Finally, when he was asked questions that required integration, Mark was unable to integrate semantic and episodic information or even to notice this failure. For example, he was asked, "Why do you think your parents behaved as they did during your childhood?" Mark answered, "Because they loved each other and they loved us." Similarly, when asked how his early experiences affected his adult personality and if any aspect of them was a setback, Mark responded, "Rather in the same way as authors express their gratitude for the contribution made by others to their book whilst acknowledging responsibility for its shortcomings themselves, I can only feel gratitude that my parents were an influence for the good and any sins that I have, and there are many, are my own devising." These responses display shallowness of thought, idealization of the parent, and denigration of self. Although the comparison to an author suggests an awareness of artificiality, Mark did not pursue this idea. To the contrary, he continued to use his strategy of distorting semantic information and discarding episodic information.

Using the discourse analysis as a guide, we find major discrepancies between what Mark said about his childhood and what we believe to be true and between semantic and episodic memory systems. Because his discourse is semantically organized with episodic information discarded, we classify him as Type A1 (Dismissing). In terms of treatment, there is no evidence Mark *needs* treatment because he poses no danger to himself or others. Nevertheless, he might choose to seek treatment, particularly for affective depression or failed relationships. If he were to seek treatment, Mark's AAI would alert the therapist that important episodic information was missing and that its content would probably indicate that his parents were rejecting of or threatening to Mark. This implies a need for therapeutic tools aimed at recovering currently inaccessible episodic memories. Further, the therapist would note that the idealized semantic statements containing distorted internal representational models of his parents need revision on the basis of the information held in missing imaged or episodic memory. This suggests the need for therapeutic tools that both promote reasonable cognitive conclusions and also foster creative, integrative thinking. Finally, the therapist would presume that this process of accessing episodic memory and integrating it with semantic memory had not been already undertaken by Mark because he learned that doing so elicited parental rejection or disapproval. Therefore, Mark's perceived vulnerability to actual or imagined (i.e., internalized) parental responses should be reduced. This requires addressing both generalizations about personal needs (e.g., I must have my parents' approval, exploration that ends in failure is not acceptable) and also accurately assessing Mark's current resources to cope with adversity.

This analysis suggests a purposeful eclectic process in which the therapist assesses memory systems and mental processes, identifies specific goals, selects tools for reaching these, and then chooses an order of implementation. For example, the therapist might decide not to address the missing memories until Mark felt less vulnerable. Therefore early efforts might be directed toward establishing an attachment relationship between Mark and his therapist, in which the therapist fosters exploration of relatively distant and nonthreatening topics. This might develop into an assessment of current resources (both external resources, including the therapist) and internal psychological resources for coping with threats. For example, the availability of the spouse and therapist as supports might be clarified. Psychological resources might include Mark's ability to implement familiar defensive procedural models of inhibition and redirection of attention in the event of threat. Finally, focusing Mark on his greater competence in adulthood (as compared to childhood) can facilitate willingness to examine childhood distortions. Based on this preliminary work, the therapist might address underlying generalizations that can easily be proven false for all people, for example, *parents are always right, I need my parents' approval for everything, we must always agree*. By doing this, the therapist is using a familiar psychological process, normalizing, to foster reconsideration of distorted information.

With this groundwork done, approaches that elicit episodic recall could be used. Realistically, this is opening Pandora's box with two particularly likely outcomes. Once Mark becomes convinced that there were a substantial number of occasions when his parents were unsupportive or even hostile or cruel, he may either reverse strategies and become angrily enmeshed or become as coolly derogating as he was coolly idealizing. The desired outcome (of a smooth transition from distorting information to accepting and integrating it in a balanced manner) is probably the least likely outcome. Nevertheless, having once regained the omitted information, therapeutic effort can be directed toward integrating episodic and semantic information. Thus, the therapist moves among Mark's internal representational models, attempting to change each a bit in ways that will create greater coherence and balance among all the models. A shaping process is undertaken that moves toward full integration of Mark's experience. As a final step, the therapist should ensure that Mark knows how to engage in the self-monitoring process of identifying discrepancy, exploring its meaning, correcting omissions and distortions, and reintegrating information to yield revised internal representational models and new patterns of behavior.

Erroneous Cognitive Information and False Affective Information (A3, 4, 5, 6). Individuals whose development occurred under certain types of dangerous circumstances often learn to organize their behavior on the basis of *erroneous cognitive conclusions* and to use *false displays of affect* to mislead others with regard to their true feelings. In both cases, these distortions occur because they reduce the probability of danger and increase the probability of safety in the childhood context of the individual. As noted earlier, the contexts that tend to produce extreme Type A patterns often contain harsh punishment of negative affect, reinforcement of positive affect (including false positive affect), and high levels of danger or threat of danger. Jane's mother was often drunk and comatose, periodically abandoned Jane (by leaving home for days and weeks at a time), and rejected her daughter's feelings of pain, fear, and anger. Jane's father was more stable, but often lived away from the family. In addition, her father was psychologically unavailable ("So even when he played with us, he was somewhere else") and unpredictably violent.

Jane's *AAI* began with the distortion of idealization: "We lived in a very nice house in a very nice town. Everything was small and close and very nice. I think it was a very nice area." After giving more details, Jane ended this opening paragraph by stating that the family moved from the neighborhood before she was born and that she grew up elsewhere: "So they have lived in another way before I was born. They have had their glory days there in the neighborhood before I came into this world." Jane then stated that her siblings were dispersed, with one being mentally ill and another having committed suicide in the 1970s: "You know how it was then" (as if that explained it). This resulted in false verbal affect: "I must laugh, it might seem cynical, but it is comical when you see the total. Ahhh . . . Then there is my nearest sister . . . . " Later, Jane referred again to her father's psychological absence even when physically present: "He was very interested, he played with us, we would do things with us, but in a short while he fell asleep. We had to wake him up. [So you remember that from when you were a child?] Yes. But that is something we all laughed about; it was not painful in any way. We took it for granted, that is the way it is." In addition to the false positive humor, note the omission of *in us* after "interested" and the substitution of "we" for *he* in "we would do things with us." Speaking of her father's impatience, Jane said, "Not allowed to be noisy because he could not stand it. [Laughter] He is very impatient." In this case, the false affect is Jane's laughter that substitutes for her (probable) true feeling of fear of her father's anger. Evidence of the ongoing fear is displayed in Jane's omission of herself as a subject of the verb "allowed" and even more strongly in her switch to the present tense when speaking of her father's impatience. Finally, Jane described scenes when her oldest sister returned home and berated their mother for neglecting Jane. Jane defended her mother and was angry with her sister for upsetting their mother. ". . . and she [her sister] was so fed up with this so she was just angry with mama and asked her to be quiet or, if she made dramatic scenes, or just vanished . . . so I was left sitting alone with her. I had a close relationship with mother so I was very sad when I saw she was sad so I, during the first years, I would climb up into her bed and try to comfort her and lie close to her and things like that. When I became older, I became quite cynical and just run off." As a child, Jane used false comforting affect in a role-reversing manner to soothe her mother (thus, making her available as a potential protective figure) and also to cover her own inhibited feelings of fear. Again, evidence of the fear leaked in when Jane left uncertainty as to who "just vanished" or "run away"; further, "run" is in the present tense showing the ongoing effect of her inhibited and transformed fear.

There is also evidence of Type A transformations of cognition. Some are accurate (true) causal attributions: "If we got our clothes muddy, he would become very angry while our mother would not react at all." With regard to her sister's anger at their mother, Jane said, "I was angry with her [sister] because she said those things. And I also remember that when mother was drinking and my sisters would reject her, I was angry with them. I felt they were being evil. One ought to be nice to mama. When she was sad." Her mother's affective state was the basis of Jane's "decision" to be nice—because being nice increased the probability that her mother would remain conscious and, thus, potentially available to function like a mother. In addition, Jane called her drinking mother "mother," whereas she called her sad and vulnerable mother "mama." Jane seemed to take a motherly role with regard to her mother who needed protection and, in that role, called her an affectionate name. In these examples of accurate cognitions, Jane took full responsibility for regulating her parents' behavior.

Other cognitive transformations indicate that Jane did not always know what caused dangerous conditions: "There was much drinking and what happened when she drank and was in a coma, well, it could continue for days actually." In this example, Jane spoke of the drinking as though "it" inexplicably happened and continued on the basis of some innate and inanimate volition.

Not knowing what makes frightening things happen is very distressing and Jane's mind discovered an erroneous causal explanation that was more comforting than being at the mercy of unknown forces. Therefore, Jane continued the statement in the following erroneous manner: "actually, so every time I woke up, she would drink more and then she would go to bed again." This conclusion erroneously and irrationally attributed the cause ("so") of the mother's continued drinking to Jane's waking up. Although it was erroneous, it at least gave Jane the appearance of being real in the sense of being a participant in her mother's life. The comfort, however, was limited by the unpredictability of her mother's behavior: "There were periods when she did not drink at all and I, of course, would hope that it was over, it was not going to come happen again, but it happened again and again all the time." In another instance, Jane said she was never hit, but "if I had hurt myself or something, I did not receive comfort. So that was my own fault." In all cases, Jane's erroneous cognitive attributions put the responsibility on herself. Indeed, she even spoke of her birth as though she had decided to come into the world.

When asked what she had learned from her childhood, Jane gave evidence of her continued but unsuccessful search for true cognitive predictors: "Almost everything that has happened has been important I think . . Mmmmm . . Because so much sad and bad has happened and also very nice . . . I think almost everything has been important. That I was loved, that I was good at school, that there was fighting at home. I think everything has been important." Jane continued to think that the causes lay somewhere in the complexity of what happened and that if she could just find them out, she would be safe. Because she did not know what was related or unrelated, everything became potentially important.

Jane's situation is more severe than Mark's. She experienced greater danger than did Mark and she also distorted information and her behavior more to adapt to her threatening conditions. Because her experience of danger was primarily through neglect, Jane was obliged to depend for her protection on a caregiver who was often psychologically and physically unavailable. Like other compulsive caregivers, her use of idealization is less directed at reframing past experience and attachment figures as perfect than it is at distorting the representation of attachment figures as innocent and worthy of caregiving and protection. Behaviorally, Jane discovered that caring for her mother increased her mother's attention to her (true cognition). As a consequence, Jane learned to inhibit her own negative affect (omitted affect), exhibit comforting affect to her mother (false affect), and do as her mother needed for her to do (true cognition). Further, Jane perceived any threat to her mother as a threat to herself (distorted cognition). At one level, she was accurate: She depended on her mother for protection. At another, she was mistaken: She had needs her mother failed to meet. Being unable, as a child, to manage the complexity of this situation, she distorted reality by making protection of her mother primary, and omitted from recall memories of her mother's failure to protect her and her own feelings of anger, fear, and desire for comfort. In terms of the model that I present, Jane is a compulsive caregiver (A3). In terms of treatment, it will be important for Jane to acknowledge that, as an adult, she is no longer dependent on her mother for protection. This, together with trust of her therapist as an alternate attachment figure, may enable her to acknowledge her actual feelings without fear of threatening consequences in current relationships. Again, however, there is the probability of overcorrection and the use of a Type C (or A/C) strategy of preoccupied effort to exact retribution from her parents. Because Jane has not learned over the course of childhood to regulate her feelings through the integration of information from several memory systems, when affect is first made conscious, it may dominate Jane's functioning. The therapist's role includes anticipatory guidance and moderation of this as well as the ultimate task of helping Jane to achieve integrated and balanced mental and behavioral functioning.

Type C Transformations of Information

Distortion of Affective Information and Omission of Cognitive Information (C1–4).   Children of inconsistent caregivers often learn that there is little temporal predictability, but that exaggerated affective displays can maintain caregivers' attention, whereas splitting and alternating displays of mixed feelings can regulate caregivers' behavior. By adulthood, this coercive behavioral pattern is reflected, in AAI discourse, *as limited access to semantic memory, extensive access to contextual imaged memory*, and a tendency to *reduce episodes to images that have little temporal order*. Two examples follow, one of a coercive disarming individual and one of a coercive threatening person.

The first, James, is a disarming C2 (Preoccupied); he has few coherent semantic conclusions about his parents (in the AAI this is referred to as *passive thought*) and often uses humor to avoid drawing obvious conclusions. James is the middle child among several girls. His earliest memory is of his father punishing him:

> If he was going to spank us, it was always called a discussion and we had to go to his office for a discussion and he, I remember I think I was only ever spanked by him on one occasion that I can remember. It was with a paddle and I was over his, uh over his knees and he, I remember him saying, explaining why he was gonna do it—even at the time realizing that he was trying to justify to himself why he was gonna do it and I was in tears before I was spanked because it was such a, ugh, you know, agonizing situation. At times he can be quite crazy and jokey but he's—um—I remember him being quite serious and worried about things.

Although this episode seems innocuous, it contains typical elements of coercive individuals; these grow pronounced as the interview develops. First, the father used false, misleading cognition by calling the punishment "a discussion." Second, James was attuned to images of physical context:

the office and his position over his father's knees. Third, the reason for the spanking was of concern to him, but appeared to be unclear to both son and father. Fourth, affect was emphasized (both his own and his father's) and seemed to take the place of temporal sequencing as an explanation for events. Finally, James suddenly shifted his attention away from the episode and generalized that his father was humorous, but very "serious and worried." Although the inconsistency of this conclusion seemed not to have caught James' notice, it reflected both a defensive measure and the splitting of mixed and incompatible affects typical of Type Cs and many of their parents.

Later, when asked for five adjectives to describe his relationship with his father, James offered:

> "... Demanding ... um ... serious, oh dear ... I am trying to think of [laughs] I am trying to think of a counter example ... ummm ... helping ... umm ... interesting ... um ... and I guess, what's the other word, ... let's see ... I don't know, I'm torn with two words. I've got conscious as one of them and the other would be uh, this is my fifth, is that right? Oh dear dear dear dear dear. I'll just scrub conscious and stick conscious in with serious ... and come up with ... [long pause] I'm trying to come up with an adjective that describes him ... Oh! ... The word I'm looking for has to do with, I don't know, I guess cross-purposes ... cross-purposes [laughs] which is a well-known word! [laugh]."

For all his effort, James succeeded in describing his father more than the relationship. Moreover, he actively sought words that were opposites, words that canceled each others' meaning. Finally, when he offered the negative word, "cross-purposes," James immediately disarmed it with a small joke.

James was next asked to provide an episode for "demanding":

> I'm being wicked here. I think we were both demanding. Ummm ... I have two memories. I've got one memory of um, him saying, "So help me if I find that paddle, if I look into the garage and find that paddle." I can't remember the second part of that sentence but I think that just about sums it up. It was like I really should have known where that paddle was. It's funny, I'm aware ... Oh, dear ... [laugh] aware of how much splitting there is because I guess that some of that I could equally well have said other things.

Note that James' use of "wicked" suggests that he was consciously distorting what he said. When he said he could not remember the second part of the sentence, he was stating that he could not remember cognitive contingencies. He became half-aware of this, but diverted his attention to the process of splitting, which he then diverted into other memories. He did not pursue his conscious awareness of discrepancy. This was, of course, an opportunity for a metacognition, a new integration, but James instead hid in psychobabble and told another (incomplete) story. Throughout his attempts to retrieve information from semantic memory or from episodic memory through the semantic retrieval strategy of using adjectives, James was affectively highly aroused, as his use of exclamations indicates. This was hard work that never really got done. Nevertheless, James was cooperative, engaging, and superficially seemed to have satisfied the interviewer's request.

Later, when James described himself as "sly" and "sneaky," especially in his dealings with his father, he seemed to have self-knowledge. Nevertheless, he failed to use this knowledge to modify his own behavior or to come to accurate conclusions about the protectiveness of his attachment figure. Indeed, when asked about the relationship now, he reported that he had expected his father to support him in the early years of his marriage. When his father refused to give him money, James coerced him into taking out a loan in the amount of the expected support. Years later, James admitted that he did not repay the loan and implied that he did not intend to do so. He wished that his father would now make a gift of it. He volunteered this self-evaluation: "Gee that's a dreadful thing to confess. That what I actually want from my Dad is some money. But if you were to say what is it—that's there. [laugh] Makes me feel like a bit of a heel." James continued, even in adulthood, to desire this physical evidence of paternal protection and, without it, held a grudge against his father for many years and deceived (and continues to deceive) his father about his willingness to repay borrowed money. In addition, he deceived himself about the nature of his complaint and was unable to come to an appropriate semantic conclusion about his father as an attachment figure. Without this, his self-insight is wasted as it cannot lead to change in his thinking, behavior, or relationship with his father.

Although James distorts some information, there is no evidence that treatment is needed. With only a little more self-reflection, James could resolve the problems himself. That is, his mind is essentially healthy, even though he prefers not to give up his old complaints to make peace with his father. As both James and his father grow older, James may decide to adapt in ways that will permit resolution before his father's death. If James were to seek counseling to deal with these issues, it would be particularly important for the therapist not to emphasize the retrieval of feelings. To the contrary, James (and other Type C children and adults) must emphasize feelings less, relive the past less, and learn to use cognitive/semantic thought to moderate and regulate intense feeling states.

The second case is more distorted and has Type C1–5 qualities. Ernest reported an "oppressive" childhood with a mother who was critical and smothering and a father who was deceptive. In the excerpt included here, Ernest was asked about separation from his parents. First he mentioned going to his aunt's as an adolescent, then, when asked about early childhood, he said: "Now I remember being abandoned . . . the school . . . The first day . . . when I was flung in the classroom and told: 'This is your classroom and those . . . do it by yourself, now we have to go!' . . . I didn't attend nursery school and I know why!" Note the emphasis on place (context) and his intense affective response to it; "flung" contains both violent aggression (from his parents) and his own fearful vulnerability. Moreover, even now, in adulthood, the issue of why (causal attributions) he was not sent to nursery school seems threatening and its resolution is left unarticulated.

Because Ernest's first answer to the separation question mentioned a vacation at his aunt's summer home, he was asked if that was similar to going to school: "It was different . . . She was my aunt and the environment was very nice; in the countryside . . . there were streams, frogs . . . water spiders . . . footpaths . . . woods . . . " Evidence that the visit was pleasant is contained entirely in contextual descriptors (and not in the behavior of people). After stating that during the month-long visit, his parents did not call, write, or visit, Ernest continued:

Then very soon I tired, I began to wish to go away by myself! Already when I was 13, I stomped . . . I got to stay with my friends for three days in N____ (city out of region); it was an incredible thing! The possibility to manage by yourself without anyone who breathes down your neck and tells you what you have to do or not do . . . not saying what you have to do! Someone that waits for something wrong, to assault you! To criticize you, to make you feel like a piece of sh . . . in short, you know? Ah, that freedom . . . if I go out, I feel very good! Home is oppressive, therefore, if I go away from home, and also if I go outside a house, in the open air, really in the open air , I live my freedom . . . full of self-control . . . etc . . . I've always been a responsible person . . . even too responsible, I never worried my parents to such a point that when I was 16 they allowed to me, for example, with three friends of mine and few pennies in my pocket . . . it was in 1964, even before hippies went around . . . we left like that with the tents on our shoulders, to get somewhere in that time with the means of transport that were terrible to R____ (religious pilgrimage place), because there we were to meet a school fellow; in fact his mother sent him to the sanctuary for giving thanks about the promotion he didn't merit! It was very beautiful experience, because there I had the possibility to know K____(a religious and charismatic personality). For me it was a moment of absolute freedom, which I still think of with great pleasure . . . that I appreciate . . . It amazes me that my parents sent me, because I would have expected: "My son, but where are you going, 16 years old, for God's sake!" This one was the refrain after I was 8! I, when I was 16, I was already an adult, but in my opinion I was it also before . . . this is another important reason . . . I always felt like an adult, the famous "little man," because I was the first born. I was too responsible: "Ah," they say, "You know, he's a clever poor boy! What a clever boy! What a good boy! Respectful!" They make you grow up with these values! So that you do believe them, unfortunately! I know that some sons don't believe it and do what they want, but I did . . . so I also felt deeply "swindled" . . . deceived, from the kind of false education they gave us! Because only after I realized where that kind of education drove; where did it drive? To "Don't bother me!" and that is, the good son is good because he doesn't bother us! If then he develops bad habits, the essential thing is that he doesn't tell us! Do you know? They say, "He does everything by himself!"

There are several informative aspects in this dialog. First, the three events of school, trip to the aunt's, and the trip with adolescent peers merged temporally such that the reader is confused as the discussion moves backward and forward in time. Second, the transitions between the events are affective. A question about separation first elicited the visit to the aunt and then the first day of school. School was associated with abandonment and this was denied with regard to the visit to the aunt. Then, the exhilarating freedom of separation from oppressive parents led to the adventure with peers. In this process, temporal order is obscured, whereas split and intense affects (freedom–joy and oppression–anger) are maintained. Although the visit to the aunt was associated with both feelings, only one feeling was acknowledged at a time and it was exaggerated. In this manner, the emphasis on contextual affect was maintained, but the affects were split, exaggerated, and alternated, and, thus, distorted. Evidence of this distortion can be seen when the discussion of the pleasure of going to the aunt's was transformed into an angry diatribe about the parents. Confusion among contexts is evident when this diatribe against the parents switched to the second person as though his parents were speaking directly to him and then when the present tense was used for past experiences. When these transforming dysfluencies occurred, Ernest had lost sight of his present context (a grown man in an interview about the past) and felt himself alive in the context of past abandonment and anger—anger, fear, and desire for comfort. These three affects dominated his discussion of past separations, even those he defined as freedom; they were expressed by distorted discourse and blurring of contextual boundaries. Temporal information was discarded.

Erroneous Affective Information and False Cognitive Information (C5–8). Ernest also provided examples of erroneous affect and false cognition. Ernest was asked if he was ever threatened by his parents:

> Eh . . . (whispering) I don't remember these words . . . but . . . I remember . . . however, wait! . . . Yes, yes . . . however! Yes, yes, I remember my mother . . . my father, no, never . . . Yes, yes, "I made you and I can eat you back again!" Or "I'll take you to the boarding school! I'll send you to boarding school!" There was a famous one (trying to remember) . . . something like that! Then perhaps something's wrong . . . pinches given . . . she didn't say to me, "Don't say these things." No, no! Pinches given without anyone noticing . . . and so you realize she's going to be angry, mom, naturally!

First there was oscillation (i.e., distortion of cognition) as to whether or not there were threats; Ernest seemed to be trying to escape from both the memories and the conclusion that his parents were threatening. When the memories finally were recalled, the threats are irrational (e.g., "I will eat you back again") or false (e.g., "I'll send you to boarding school"). Both mislead Ernest regarding his parents' future behavior. Both were also frightening. Thus, Ernest learned that fear does not always predict danger. Similarly, the absence of anxiety does not assure safety because, without explaining why, suddenly Ernest's mother pinched him. He said, "So you realize she's *going to be* angry," but, in fact, no prediction is needed because, *without warning,* suddenly she *is* already angry and aggressive. At this point, Ernest slipped into the present tense. Other examples of erroneous affect and false cognition are found in the earlier excerpt.

Ernest provides a different sort of challenge for a therapist than do Mark, Jane, or James. Although he may not seek treatment, the extent of Ernest's distortions and the substitution of false information for true information suggest a more serious situation. His means of handling anxiety become important. His lack of contextual permanence threatens his ability to ascertain accurately his present degree of danger. If he perceives it as very great but not tied to specific people or acts, he might self-medicate to calm himself. If, on the other hand, he finds a focus for his fear and anger, he could become dangerous. In particular, the therapist will need to be vigilant to ensure that he or she does not become the threatening focus of Ernest's past anxiety. An early focus on managing affective state through images and then through true cognitive understanding may create the possibility of sufficiently reducing Ernest's anxiety to begin to explore his manner of habitually distorting information.

In a final brief example, Harry described a coldly rigid and hostile father and a weak mother who could not protect him. When asked about physical injuries or illness in childhood, he reported many accidents that often required hospitalization. For a specific incident, he offered, "It was just that I had accidents. The only one I can really remember is when I jumped off a roof and I banged my head and my mother took me to the hospital." Throughout the interview, Harry returned to the theme of his many accidents and the pleasure and relief of being hospitalized. Nevertheless, the false causal relation between the accidents and the caregiving from his mother and hospital staff remained hidden to both Harry and his family.

Type A/C and Multiple Distortions of Information

In more disturbed cases, the speaker uses both false affect and false cognition to mislead others. For example, Margaret, who was abused as a child, had a history of short and promiscuous relationships with adults outside her family that began in childhood when she was repeatedly rejected by her parents. Her father discovered some of her "affairs" with teachers and other caretaking adults and severely punished her for these. In addition, there is half-revealed evidence that she may have abused younger children in her adolescence. In the *AAI*, Margaret used false cognition about her intentions toward others and also presumed false cognition with regard to others. When asked what she hoped her (imaginary) children might learn from being raised by her, she first spoke of self-confidence, then genuine popularity: "not for sort of standing around at bars or something but a pleasant person to be around so I've got a friend who's like that and he's just . . . he's so nice, unfortunately he's [laughs] married, umm, and I suppose I mean I wouldn't say that I love him and his wife and his children but . . . you know I'm very fond of them and I do care for them." Given her history, this shift from hopes for a child to discussion of love for a married man may disguise hopes for herself. Elsewhere, when asked how she would feel when separating from her imaginary child, she presumed false cognition on the interviewer's part: "Is this um . . . lay guilt on Margaret time? You know, put yourself in your mother's position. [Interviewer rephrases question to focus her on the hypothetical future.] Well, like most parents, devastated I should think." These excerpts contain both menacing and paranoid false cognition, as well as evidence of promiscuity (Type A6) and exaggerated affect (Type C).

Margaret's situation is quite severe. She is both a danger to herself and to others and, thus, cannot be entirely free to accept or reject treatment. In her childhood, her parents were unpredictably dangerous. To accommodate in self-protective ways, Margaret developed distortions of information that now make her a threat to others. Like Mark, she needs a trusting alliance with her therapist. Establishing this will, however, be more difficult. In order for Margaret to trust, the therapist will have to display support for her and also accurate interpretation of the truth. At a minimum, this will mean correctly identifying and limiting the threat that Margaret poses to others. If the therapist cannot discern Margaret's distortions of information and cannot protect others from her, Margaret cannot reasonably trust the therapist to protect her. Thereafter, the treatment becomes a variation of Mark's. First, Margaret's resources and strengths are made conscious to her. Then she is helped to see the importance of feelings for predicting danger and opportunities for sexual activity as well as the need to evaluate these because they can be in error. Later, attention should be shifted to semantic conclusions and the normal state of imperfection of humans. In addition, she should be helped to see that not everything that others do can be predicted or is tied to oneself. As she becomes more realistic about her semantic conclusions and expectations and more secure in her competence to face as an adult the threats her parents posed, she can be assisted to regain access to missing aspects of episodic memory. Finally, she should be assisted to explore her need for intimacy and her procedures for fulfilling this need. The therapist can teach aspects of this within the relationship (i.e., transference). Other aspects, including her promiscuous falsification of affect and sexual behavior, must be carefully kept out of the relationship with the therapist even when they are part of the verbal therapy. Having a male therapist might facilitate this.

CONCLUSION

After all this theory and these lengthy examples of transformed information, one might ask how a clinician can use this knowledge. I return to theory and to the two notions of assessment and treatment.

Theory

In this chapter and in other papers, I offer an expansion of attachment theory that borrows extensively from learning theory, cognitive theory,

theory of affect, evolutionary biology, neuropsychology,[14] and psychoanalytic theory. Although it is not possible to fully integrate these in a single chapter, nevertheless, I hope I demonstrated that, together, they can yield a perspective on human functioning that is simple in its precepts and complex in the infinite variety of human outcomes it yields. This theory places the fit of person to context at the center of adaptation and, thus, of mental health and illness. Moreover, the critical aspect of context is its dangerousness. When danger is unpredictable, difficult to discern, or deceptive in its presentation, it is most likely to lead to distortions of mind and the potential for extreme or atypical behavior. These become maladaptive or psychopathological when applied to relatively safe contexts, as though the risk of danger were unchanged.

In particular, I am interested in the compulsive (A3–6) and obsessive (C5–8) subpatterns. Individuals displaying these patterns learned to cope with dangerous circumstances by emphasizing and transforming some information and distorting some behavior in ways that reduce the probability of being harmed. These transformations become maladaptively compulsive and obsessive when applied to substantially less dangerous circumstances. In many cases, however, the reduction in danger is not external to the individual—that is, the removal of the danger—but is, instead, a maturational change in the individual's vulnerability. Children are vulnerable to dangers that do not threaten adults. Thus, a major issue with the compulsive and obsessive patterns is convincing individuals of their present, adult competence to discern and cope with threat.

When one is endangered, truth may be given up for the benefit of safety. Because knowledge of contexts depends on information, faulty information leads to maladaptive and endangering behavior. Therefore, information is modified in ways that maximize identification or prevention of danger and behavior is organized on the basis of these transformations to maximize safety. In the most dangerous environments, the deception is often both cognitive and affective, thus leading to the frequent co-occurrence of compulsive and obsessive patterns, with the ultimate integration of untrue information in the psychopath.

The process of becoming mentally disturbed, is, however, developmental. As young children, we first learn to interpret information and, later, discover the impact of our signals (i.e., information about our own feelings and intentions) on others. We come to recognize that others use this information to organize their behavior. In some cases this leads to clearer signals, whereas in others it leads to inhibited signals. With greater maturation, we learn to regulate and control the information we offer to others. Although I approach this from a developmental perspective, the distinction may also differentiate the mild, treatable disorders that harm the self, from more severe and intransigent disorders that endanger others. This developmental perspective suggests that we are not capable of either full integration or

---

[14]See Crittenden (in press-b) for a fuller discussion of the underlying neurology and its application to trauma.

full psychopathology until after the cortical maturation associated with puberty. This might explain the late onset of some of the more ominous sorts of mental illness.

Of course, I am well aware of the current interest in biological processes, particularly genetic processes, that may in part account for mental illness. The theory here is not in conflict with such findings. There are several "causes" of mental and behavioral disturbance: genetic, pharmacological, physical injury, and experience. What all have in common is that they alter the way humans process information. My focus here is on the *psychology* of mental illness and its treatment. That in no way precludes other processes leading to disturbance. To the contrary, both other processes and interactions of experience with these other factors are needed to account for cases of mental illness. Indeed, when there is more than one sort of risk, that is, when there is the potential for an interaction among risk factors, the probability of maladaptive behavior is highest.

Assessment

The diagnostic perspective of attachment theory has to do with mental processing of information and behavioral organizing of self-protective and reproductive strategies. That is, diagnosis as I am offering it through attachment theory is *functional diagnosis* as opposed to *symptom-based medical diagnosis*. The intent of such diagnosis is to facilitate an understanding of how distorted behavior is used in the present and of the context and process through which it developed. These, in turn, can promote an understanding of what needs to be changed in order to reduce mental distortion and maladaptive behavior.

Although assessment of distorted behavior is possible in many settings, one of the advantages of the attachment assessments is that they highlight the organization and function of maladaptive behavior around issues of protection (in childhood) and protection and reproduction (in adulthood.) The AAI offers an opportunity to consider directly the distortions of thought that underlie maladaptive behavior. Although such a perspective is not new (cf. Bandler & Grinder, 1975; Grinder & Bandler, 1975), the AAI operationalizes the process well and is consistent with recent developments in information processing and evolutionary biology.

The emphasis on organization around protection and reproduction permits a positive understanding of disturbance. That is, mental and behavioral disturbance are the result of adaptation to dangerous circumstances or circumstances in which sexual activity was jeopardized. Viewed from this perspective, many forms of mental illness can be construed as active attempts to protect the individual, given the person's circumstances. Maladaptive behavior can be reframed as coping behavior suited to a past environment. This positive reframing fosters attention to the potential for change in all humans.

In addition, the perspective offered here suggests that mental health is not a state. To the contrary, it is an ongoing, lifelong process, both mental and behavioral, in which individuals interact with their environment to generate strategic protective and reproductive behavior. The interaction is affected by both innate, evolved biases in the human central nervous system and also unique experiences and genetic variance: temperament.[15]

Treatment

Attachment theory emphasizes the importance of the therapeutic relationship, that is, of therapists functioning as attachment figures who facilitate clients' exploration of the unknown and threatening aspects of their past and current experience and of their mental processing of information about these. Second, attachment theory focuses therapists' attention on various types of information (affect and cognition), various transformations of these into true, erroneous, discarded, distorted, and false information, and the clustering of information in memory systems. In particular, attachment theory points to the function of these sources of information in daily lives and the importance of intergration of various sorts of information to create relatively accurate internal representational models of reality, and to identify and correct faulty information and revise or reorganize internal representational models and behavioral strategies on the basis of the best current information. Third, attachment theory offers an increasing range of assessment procedures to assess the behavioral and mental processes of clients. Fourth, by emphasizing the developmental process by which models and strategies are developed, attachment theory offers a means of showing clients in treatment that childhood disorders need not be carried into adulthood. Fifth, by emphasizing developmental histories and the protective function of the distortion of information, attachment theory can highlight the "rationality" of irrational or maladaptive behavior and mental processes and help therapists to organize their own behavior so as not to augment the distortion. Finally, by aligning each of the memory systems with particular sorts of therapy, attachment theory suggests a process through which to create a purposeful theory of eclecticism. This, in turn, could lead to the potential to evaluate eclectic therapies and to compare them with single theory therapies.

The theory offered here reflects a broad range of psychological and psychiatric research and theory. Although it exceeds the current database and is often speculative, nevertheless, I have tried to represent existing findings accurately while concurrently focussing attention on new distinctions. The integration of many specialized disciplines around protection and reproduction permits a new perspective on the meaning of information and function of maladaptive behavior. I hope that a comparison of the accuracy of details with the meaningfulness of the whole

---

[15] For a fuller discussion of the contribution of unique genetic variation to functioning, see Crittenden (1995, 1997, in press-a).

will suggest the usefulness of this line of thinking to both researchers and clinicians. In addition, I hope that the theory will lead to specific testable hypotheses that will further both the development of theory and improve treatment. However, to the extent that theory both promotes creative re-evaluation of what each of us knows and believes and also fosters reorganizations that improve diagnosis and treatment, theory is inherently true and useful in the process of human adaptation. In this chapter, I have referred often to true information. Truth, however, was not used to mean a "a true representation." Rather the focus has been on true prediction of safety and danger and on how behavior will affect these. It is in this sense of improving prediction that I hope the theory that I offer will be found to be true.

ACKNOWLEDGMENTS

I wish to thank Loretta Cellini, Eugenia Cockroft, Colin Davidson, Anne Thompson, and Rigmor Grette Moe for access to Adult Attachment Interviews and case histories that were informative to the theory discussed in this chapter.

All figures were originally published in Crittenden (1995).

REFERENCES

Ainsworth, M. D. S., Blehar, M., Waters, E., & Wall, S. (1978) *Patterns of attachment: A psychological study of the Strange Situation.* Hillsdale, NJ: Lawrence Erlbaum Associates.

Bandler, R., & Grinder, J. (1975). *The structure of Magic I.* Palo Alto, CA: Science and Behavior Books.

Bowlby, J. (1973). *Attachment and loss: Vol. II. Separation.* New York: Basic Books.

Bowlby, J. (1979). *The making and breaking of affectional bonds.* London: Tavistock Publications.

Bowlby, J. (1980). *Attachment and loss: Vol. III. Loss.* New York: Basic Books.

Bowlby, J. (1982). *Attachment and loss: Vol. I. Attachment.* New York: Basic Books. (Original work published 1969)

Cassidy, J., & Marvin, R. S., with the Working Group of the John D. and Catherine T. MacArthur Foundation on the Transition from Infancy to Early Childhood. (1992). *Attachment organization in three- and four-year olds: Coding guidelines.* Unpublished manuscript, University of Virginia, Charlottesville.

Crittenden, P. M. (1985). Maltreated infants: Vulnerability and resilience. *Journal of Child Psychology and Psychiatry, 26,* 85–96.

Crittenden, P. M. (1988). Relationships at risk. In J. Belsky & T. Nezworski (Eds.), *Clinical implications of attachment* (pp. 136–174). Hillsdale, NJ: Lawrence Erlbaum Associates.

Crittenden, P. M. (1990). Internal representational models of attachment relationships. *Infant Mental Health Journal, 11,* 259–277.

Crittenden, P. M. (1992a). Quality of attachment in the preschool years. *Development and Psychopathology, 4,* 209–241.

Crittenden, P. M. (1992b). Treatment of anxious attachment in infancy and early childhood. *Development & Psychopathology, 4,* 575–602.

Crittenden, P. M. (1994). Peering into the black box: An exploratory treatise on the development of self in young children. In D. Cicchetti & S. Toth (Eds.), *Rochester Symposium on Developmental Psychopathology: Vol. 5. The self and its disorders* (pp. 79–148). Rochester, NY: University of Rochester Press.

Crittenden, P. M. (1995). Attachment and psychopathology. In S. Goldberg, R. Muir, & J. Kerr (Eds.), *Attachment theory: Social, developmental, and clinical perspectives* (pp. 367–406). Hillsdale, NJ: The Analytic Press.

Crittenden, P. M. (1997). The effect of early relationship experiences on relationships in adulthood. In Duck (Ed.), *Handbook of personal relationships* (2nd ed.). Chichester, England: Wiley. (pp. 99–119)

Crittenden, P. M. (1996). Language, attachment, and behavior disorders. In N. J. Cohen, J. H. Beitchman, R. Tannock, & M. Konstantareous (Eds.), *Language, learning, and behavior disorders: Emerging perspectives* (pp. 119–160). New York: Cambridge University Press.

Crittenden, P. M. (in press-a). Patterns of attachment and sexual behavior: Risk of dysfunction versus opportunity for creative integration. In L. Atkinson & K. J. Zuckerman (Eds.), *Attachment and psychopathology*. New York: Guilford Press.

Crittenden, P. M. (in press-b). Toward an integrative theory of trauma: A dynamic-maturation approach. In D. Cicchetti & S. Toth (Eds.), *The Rochester Symposium on Developmental Psycho-pathology: Trauma*. Rochester, NY: University of Rochester Press.

Crittenden, P. M., & DiLalla, D. (1988). Compulsive compliance: The development of an inhibitory coping strategy in infancy. *Journal of Abnormal Child Psychology, 16*, 585–599.

Crittenden, P. M., Partridge, M. F., & Claussen, A. H. (1991). Family patterns of relationship in normative and dysfunctional families. *Development and Psychopathology, 3*, 491–512.

Egeland, B., & Sroufe, L. A. (1981). Attachment and early maltreatment. *Child Development, 52*, 44–52.

Fivush, R., & Hammond, N. R. (1990). Autobiographical memory across the preschool years: Toward reconceptualizing childhood amnesia. In R. Fivush & J. A. Hudson (Eds.), *Knowing and remembering in young children* (pp. 223–248). New York: Cambridge University Press.

Gallistel, C. R., Brown, A. L., Carey, S., Gelman, R., & Keil, F. C. (1991). Lessons from animal learning for the study of cognitive development. In S. Carey & R. Gelman (Eds.), *The epigenesis of mind: Essays on biology and cognition* (pp. 3–36). Hillsdale, NJ: Lawrence Erlbaum Associates.

Garcia, J. (1981). The nature of learning explanations. *The Behavioral and Brain Sciences, 4*, 143–144.

George, C., Kaplan, N., & Main, M. (1985). *The Adult Attachment Interview*. Unpublished doctoral dissertation. University of California, Berkeley.

Gersten, M., Coster, W., Schneider-Rosen, K., Carlson, V., & Cicchetti, D. (1986). The social-emotional bases of communicative functioning: Quality of attachment, language development, and early maltreatment. In M. E. Lamb, A. L. Brown, & B. Rogoff (Eds.), *Advances in developmental psychology* (Vol. 4, pp. 105–151). Hillsdale, NJ: Lawrence Erlbaum Associates.

Grinder, J., & Bandler, R. (1975). *The structure of Magic II*. Palo Alto, CA: Science and Behavior Books.

Grossmann, K., Fremmer-Bombik, E., Rudolph, J., & Grossmann, K. A. (1988). Maternal attachment representations as related to patterns of infant–mother attachment and maternal care during the first year. In R. A. Hinde & J. Stevenson-Hinde (Eds.), *Relationships between relationships within families* (pp. 241–260). Oxford, England: Clarendon Press.

Gustavson, C., Garcia, J., Hankins, W., & Rusiniak, K. (1974). Coyote predation control by aversive stimulus. *Science, 184*, 581–583.

Hudson, J. A. (1990). The emergence of autobiographical memory in mother–child conversation. In R. Fivush & J. A. Hudson (Eds.), *Knowing and remembering in young children*. New York: Cambridge University Press.

Jaeger, L., Crittenden, P. M., Black, K., & McCartney, K. (in press). Attachment in adolescence. In P. Crittenden (Ed.), *The organization of attachment relationships: Maturation, context, and culture*. New York: Cambridge University Press.

Karmiloff-Smith, A. (1991). Beyond modularity: Innate constraints and developmental change. In S. Carey & R. Gelman (Eds.), *The epigenesis of mind: Essays on biology and cognition* (pp. 171–197). Hillsdale, NJ: Lawrence Erlbaum Associates.

Lang, P. (1995). The emotion probe: Studies in motivation and attention. *American Psychologist, 50*, 372–385.

Lashley, K. S. (1960). Cerebral organization and behavior. In F. A. Beach, D. O. Hebb, C. T. Morgan, & H. W. Nissen (Eds.), *The neuropsychology of Lashley* (pp. 529–543). New York: McGraw-Hill. (Original work published 1958)

LeDoux, J. E. (1986). The neurobiology of emotion. In J. E. LeDoux & W. Hirst (Eds.), *Mind and brain: Dialogues in cognitive neuroscience* (pp. 301–354). Cambridge, England: Cambridge University Press.

Leventhal, H. (1984). A perceptual-motor theory of emotion. In L. Berkowitz (Ed.), *Advances in experimental social psychology: Vol. 17. Theorizing in social psychology: Special topics* (pp. 117–182). New York: Academic Press.

Luria, A. R. (1973), *The working brain: An introduction to neuropsychology*. London: Penguin.

Lyons-Ruth, K., Repacholi, B., McLeod, S., & Silva, E. (1991). Disorganized attachment behavior in infancy: Short-term stability, maternal and infant correlates, and risk-related subtypes. *Development & Psychopathology, 3*, 377–396.

MacLean, P. D. (1973). *A triune concept of brain and behavior*. Toronto: University of Toronto Press.

MacLean, P. D. (1990). *The triune brain in evolution: Role in paleocerebral functions*. New York: Plenum.

Main, M., & Goldwyn, R. (in press). Adult attachment classification system. In M. Main (Ed.), *A topology of human attachment organization: Assessed in discourse, drawing, and interviews.* Cambridge, England: Cambridge University Press.

Main., M., & Hesse, P. (1990). Lack of resolution of mourning in adulthood and its relationship to infant disorganization: Some speculations regarding causal mechanisms. In M. Greenberg, D. Cicchetti, & E. M. Cummings (Eds.), *Attachment in the preschool years* (pp. 161–182). Chicago: University of Chicago Press.

Main, M., & Solomon, J. (1986). Discovery of an insecure disorganized/disoriented attachment pattern: Procedures, findings, and implications for the classification of behavior. In M. Yogman & T. B. Brazelton (Eds.), *Affective development in infancy* (pp. 121–160). Norwood, NJ: Ablex.

Ornstein, R., & Thompson, R. F. (1984). *The amazing brain*. New York: Houghton Mifflin.

Neisser, U. (1991). Two perceptually given aspects of the self and their development. *Developmental Review, 11*, 197–209.

Pavlov, I. P. (1928). *Lectures on conditioned reflexes: The higher nervous activity of animals.* (Vol. I, H. Ganett, Trans.) London: Lawrence & Wishart.

Piaget, J. (1952). *The origins of intelligence*. New York: International Universities Press.

Pipe, M. E., & Goodman, G. S. (1991). Elements of secrecy: Implications for children's testimony. *Behavioral Sciences and the Law, 9*, 33–41.

Rieber, R. W. & Carlton, A. S. (Eds.). (1987). *The collected works of L. S. Vygotskii.* (N. Minick, Trans.). New York: Plenum.

Sameroff, A. (1983). Developmental systems: Context and evolution. In W. Kessen (Ed.), *Mussen's handbook of child psychology: Vol. 1* (4th ed.). New York: Wiley.

Seligman, M. (1971). Preparedness and phobias. *Behavior Therapy, 2*, 307–320.

Selye, H. (1976). *The stress of life*. New York: McGraw-Hill.

Skinner, B. F. (1938). *The behavior of organisms*. New York: Appelton-Century-Crofts.

Snow, K. (1990). Building memories: The ontogeny of autobiography. In D. Cicchetti & M. Beeghly (Eds.), *The self in transition: Infancy to childhood* (pp. 213–242). Chicago: University of Chicago Press.

Tooby, J., & Cosmides, L. (1990). On the universality of human nature and the uniqueness of the individual: The role of genetics and adaptation. *Journal of Personality, 58*, 17–67.

Tulving, E. (1987), Multiple memory systems and consciousness. *Human Neurobiology, 6*, 67–80.

Winnicott, D. W. (1958). Psychoses and childcare. In *Collected papers: From pediatrics to psychoanalysis* (pp. 219–228). London: Tavistock.

van IJzendoorn, M. (1995). Adult attachment representations, parental responsiveness, and infant attachment: A meta-analysis on the predictive validity of the Adult Attachment Interview. *Psychological Bulletin, 117*, 387–403.

4

The Assessment of Phonological Processing in Early Literacy: A Developmental Approach

Margaretha C. Vandervelden
Linda S. Siegel
University of British Columbia

Research indicates an important role for phonological processing in the acquisition and use of written English (for reviews, see Liberman, 1983; Siegel, 1985, 1992; Stanovich, 1982, 1986a; Vandervelden & Siegel, 1995; Wagner & Torgesen, 1987). In their review of this research, Wagner and Torgesen (1987) defined phonological processing as "the use of phonological information (i.e., the sounds of one's language) in processing written and oral language" (p. 197).

Our purpose in this chapter is to present a theoretical framework for an approach to the assessment of early phonological processing specific to learning to read and write an alphabetic script. First, based on a similar distinction made by Share (1994), we differentiate between basic phonological processing that operates in all language processing and whose development is not contingent on literacy experience, and specific phonological processing whose development is primarily contingent on literacy experience. Next, we define the three phonological processing skills specific to reading and writing. In this section we also delineate the basic phonological processing abilities intrinsic to specific phonological processing or that may be confounding variables of various assessment tasks. Third, we address some of the conceptual and methodological problems in the assessment of skills that may need to be viewed as a continuum from simple to advanced. The relationship of these developing phonological processing skills to early reading and spelling is also discussed. In this section, we review empirical evidence in support of gradual and reciprocal development for specific phonological processing skills. Furthermore, we provide examples of tasks that exemplify a developmental approach to the assessment of specific phonological processing. These tasks are intended for use with children from senior kindergarten until the end of Grade 2, or for use with older students who have reading or spelling problems.

BASIC PHONOLOGICAL PROCESSING ABILITIES

Phonological processing basic to all language functioning pertains to the articulatory and acoustic characteristics of language and the limited set of linguistic units, or *phonemes*, that are the basis for constructing the vocabulary of a language (e.g., Liberman, Rubin, Duques, & Carlisle, 1985; Liberman & Shankweiler, 1985). The research indicates that early individual differences in basic phonological processing are related to later individual differences in learning to read and write. For example, a large body of research indicates a relationship between speed in naming common concepts (e.g., colors, digits, pictures depicting common concepts, or letters) and reading progress. Naming tasks include the retrieval of pronunciations (also referred to as *verbal or phonological codes* or *labels*). Evidence for the relationship between individual differences in naming and reading ability has been most conclusive for continuous naming tasks that assess the rate of repeatedly naming a small set of stimuli (e.g., Wolf, 1991). However, there is evidence that at least some reading-disabled older children may be less accurate than normal readers in naming pictures depicting relatively advanced vocabulary (e.g., Liberman & Shankweiler, 1985; Wagner & Torgesen, 1987). Scarborough (1989) found that children who later developed reading difficulties differed at 30 months of age in pronunciation accuracy. At age 5, weaknesses in object naming remained one of their characteristics. In a review of the literature, Wolf (1991) concluded that even though the evidence points to a changing relationship between naming and reading across development, the relationship endured "weaker but consistent across time" (p. 134).

There is also considerable evidence that use of verbal coding is used to facilitate short-term memory (e.g., Baddeley, 1979, 1982; Jorm, 1983) and that younger normal and older disabled readers show less efficiency in making use of verbal coding to facilitate short-term memory processing (e.g., Mann & Liberman, 1984; Shankweiler, Liberman, Mark, Fowler, & Fisher, 1979; Siegel & Linder, 1984; Siegel & Ryan, 1988). Another body of research that investigated the relationship between basic phonological processing and reading reported a link between impairments in speech perception and reading disability (e.g., Godfrey, Syrdal-Lasky, Millay, & Knox, 1981; Steffens, Eilers, Gross-Glenn, & Jallad, 1992) or with specific spelling problems (Marcel, 1980).

Share (1994) emphasized that the nature of the relationship between performance differences on basic phonological processing tasks and performance differences on reading tasks has not yet been resolved. However, as we discuss in the next section, basic phonological processing ability may be a component of specific phonological processing skill and thus an intrinsic requirement for the performance of tasks assessing specific phonological processing skill. As we also discuss, rather than being an intrinsic component, basic phonological processing ability may also be an extrinsic requirement (i.e., a confounding variable) of selective tasks frequently included in the assessment of specific phonological processing skills.

PHONOLOGICAL PROCESSING IN LEARNING AN ALPHABETIC SCRIPT

Individual differences in phonological processing skills specific to the acquisition of a first written vocabulary have been found well before children begin formal instruction in reading (e.g., Bradley & Bryant, 1988; Stanovich, 1986a, 1986b; Vandervelden & Siegel, 1995; Wallach & Wallach, 1976). In this section, we define these phonological processing skills. We begin with a discussion of *phonological recoding*. This chapter uses phonological recoding as a superordinate term for a set of gradually developing skills in making use of the systematic relationship between letters and phonemes in learning to read and write an alphabetic script. Such skill includes, but is not restricted to, the ability to read pseudowords. Next, we discuss *phoneme awareness*, which is a component of phonological recoding. Phoneme awareness (also often referred to as phonological awareness), is defined as the ability to analyze spoken words and syllables into their constituent phonemes. Finally, we also briefly discuss some problems related to the assessment of letter–phoneme correspondences, which, like phoneme awareness, is a component of phonological recoding.

Phonological Recoding

The role of phonological processing specific to the acquisition of a written vocabulary derives from the systematic relationship that exists between how words sound and how these words are written in alphabetic scripts. Making use of this systematic relationship between the sounds (phonemes) in spoken words and the letters of printed words (what we called phonological recoding) allows the learner to predict with varying degrees of accuracy how words are read or spelled and this facilitates written word learning. Phonological recoding may therefore function as a strategy for reading unknown printed words. This, together with the use of semantic and syntactic strategies, becomes a self-teaching device in the acquisition of a written vocabulary (Share, 1994). The role of phonological recoding in early literacy is further delineated in *amalgamation theory* (Ehri, 1978, 1980, 1984). In amalgamation theory, Ehri proposed that learning to read involves the acquisition of an orthographic form for words alongside already stored phonological and semantic and grammatical information. Once the orthographic form of a word is acquired, direct visual access becomes possible. However, the orthographic form is acquired in conjunction with the phonological form by using letters as symbols for the phonemes in words.

Evidence for a relationship between skill in using systematic relationships between letters and phonemes and the acquisition of a reading vocabulary comes from a large number of studies (e.g., Perfetti, 1985; Rack, Snowling, & Olson, 1992; Siegel, 1985, 1993; Stanovich, 1982, 1986a; Vandervelden & Siegel, 1995). For example, research shows a strong relationship between skill in reading pseudowords and skill in word reading (see Rack et al., 1992, for an extensive review of this research). Pseudowords are pronounceable combinations of letters. Speed and accuracy of pseudoword reading is an index of skill in using the systematic relationship between the letters in printed words and the phonemes underlying spoken language in reading unknown words. In addition to phonological recoding, such skill has variously been called *phonological recoding in lexical access* (Wagner & Torgesen, 1987), *pre-lexical phonological recoding* (e.g., Jorm & Share, 1983; McCusker, Hillinger, & Bias, 1981), *cipher reading* (Gough & Hillinger, 1980), or *decoding* (Ehri & Wilce, 1987a).

Basic Phonological Processing and Phonological Recoding

Although there is a systematic relationship between how words sound and how they are written, printed language is not "speech written down" (e.g., Liberman, 1983; Liberman, Cooper, Shankweiler, & Studdert-Kennedy, 1967; Liberman, Liberman, Mattingly, & Shankweiler, 1980; Liberman, Rubin, Duques, & Carlisle, 1985). Rather, the letters in printed words relate to the sequence of phonemes underlying spoken language (e.g., the phoneme sequence /d/ /o/ /g/ underlying the spoken word /dog/.[1] The problem for the beginning reader and writer is that in speaking and hearing language, the phonemes within syllables overlap (i.e., articulatorily and acoustically the phonemes in spoken syllables are inseparable, or nonsegmented). This characteristic of spoken language obscures the underlying phoneme structure.

One consequence of the indirect relationship between speech and print is the need for closure. That is, regardless of skill level, use of phonological recoding as a retrieval strategy requires closing the gap between a sounded out phoneme sequence and the spoken word or pseudoword it specifies (e.g., from /d/ /o/ /g/ to /dog/ or /d/ /e/ /g/ to /deg/). Of course, evidence for use of analogy strategies in written word learning (e.g.,

---

[1]Slashes are used to indicate spoken words, syllables, or phonemes; italics are used to indicate written words, syllables, or letters.

Goswami, 1986, 1988, 1990; Goswami & Mead, 1992) indicates that syllable-level recoding may occur early in development and as soon as children acquire some written vocabulary. For example, the unknown word *fog* may be recoded as two segments /f/ and /og/ (referred to as the *onset* and *rime*) based on the learner's knowledge of *dog*. Even so, the need for closure between the onset and rime parts and the whole remains. An example of failed closure is when children mispronounce a word or pseudoword in spite of accuracy in sounding out. This may occur when children are not familiar with a pronunciation or, in cases of familiar words, fail to relate a specific phoneme sequence to the word it specifies.

Evidence for the role of closure in phonological recoding comes, for example, from findings of a *familiarity effect*, which refers to the substitution of familiar words for unfamiliar words or for pseudowords in reading or on oral blending tasks (Gough, Juel, & Roper-Schneider, 1983). In early reading, closure is often based on partial recoding of the printed form due to lack of skill and this leads to an inaccurate reading of the printed form (e.g., sounding of the letter *s* only in reading the word *summer* as /snake/).

Phoneme Awareness

Because the underlying phoneme structure is obscured in spoken language, phonological recoding also requires the ability to analyze words and syllables into their constituent phonemes. Many tasks are used to assess phoneme awareness. For example, in a seminal study with kindergarten children, Liberman, Shankweiler, Fisher, and Carter (1974) used a phoneme counting task to assess phoneme awareness. Children tapped out with a wooden dowel the number of phonemes in spoken syllables (ranging from one to four phonemes long). Tasks may also require children to indicate the presence or absence of a target phoneme in a spoken word: for example, *Listen for /m/, /sock/, /meat/. Which one has a /m/?* (Wallach, Wallach, Dozier, & Kaplan, 1977). Other tasks may require the segmentation of a specific phoneme (e.g., *What is the first sound in sock?*), or all phonemes (e.g., articulating /sock/ as /s/ /o/ /k/; Yopp, 1988). Another often used task involves deletion of a target phoneme (e.g., *Say /feet/. Say it again without the /f/*), or deletion and substitution (e.g., *Say /feet/. Now say it again but instead of /f/ say /m/*, Perceptual Skills Curriculum, Auditory-Motor Skills Training, Rosner, 1973. A review of the many tasks used in the assessment of phoneme awareness may be found in Lewkowicz (1980).

The findings of a large body of research indicate a strong relationship between reading and a wide variety of tasks used to assess phoneme awareness as early as preschool and kindergarten (e.g., Backman, 1983; Blachman, 1984; Bradley & Bryant, 1983, 1988; Calfee, Lindamood, & Lindamood, 1973; Fox & Routh, 1976, 1980, 1984; Juel, Griffith, & Cough, 1986; Liberman et al., 1974; Liberman, Shankweiler, Liberman, Fowler, & Fisher, 1977; Lie, 1992; Lundberg, Olofsson, & Wall, 1980; Share, Jorm, Maclean, & Mathews, 1984; Skelfjord, 1987; Stanovich, Cunningham, & Cramer, 1984; Torneus, 1984; Wagner & Torgesen, 1987, Yopp, 1988).

Basic Phonological Processing and Phoneme Awareness

The ability to recognize target phonemes or to correctly articulate one or more of the phonemes underlying a spoken word presupposes the ability to perceive phonemes as identical attributes of different words even though they may not be acoustically equivalent. This ability has been labeled *phoneme categorization* (e.g., Baron, Treiman, Wilf, & Kelman, 1980). For example, the spoken words /tuck/ and /truck/ start with the phoneme /t/, spelled as *t*. However, the articulatory and, hence, the acoustic features of the phoneme, /t/, in /tuck/, differ from those in /truck/: /t/ followed by /r/ is affricated, whereas /t/ followed by a vowel is not. The /t/ in /tuck/ and the /t/ in /truck/ are said to be *allophonic variations*; that is, although both are instances of the phoneme /t/, they differ in their respective phonetic feature sets. These differences in the phonetic feature set for instances of the phoneme /t/ are determined by the articulatory context (i.e., whether an /r/ or a vowel follows the phoneme /t/). The term *phoneme* refers therefore to a category of sounds that signals a difference in meaning (e.g., /mad/ versus /sad/), whereas the term *allophones* (e.g., /t/ with or without affrication) refers to sounds that are functionally equivalent (e.g., Liberman, 1983; Liberman et al. 1985).

Phoneme categorization is one of the earliest developments in language acquisition, because without it, comprehension and production of spoken language are not possible. As such, *phoneme categorization* refers to a basic phonological processing ability that has been investigated, for example, in research into the relationship between speech perception deficits and reading (e.g., Godfrey et al., 1981) or spelling disabilities (Marcel, 1980). Immaturity in phoneme categorization may persist for some time as part of normal development and may be inferred from errors shown in children's early attempts at spelling. For example, sensitivity to the acoustic–articulatory features of /t/ followed by /r/ may result in spelling the /t/ in /train/ as *ch* (e.g., Read, 1971, 1975; Treiman, 1985). Because residual immaturity in phoneme categorization may affect children's ability to recognize or segment phonemes in specific contexts (e.g., /t/ or /d/ followed by /r/), the inclusion of such phoneme sequences in spoken stimuli (e.g., /truck/ or /drum/) may need to be avoided in early assessment. Children may fail such items due to immaturity in phoneme categorization rather than lack of requisite phoneme awareness skill (e.g., they may have no problem in identifying /d/ in /doll/).

Task Diversity and Task Comparability

Diversity in tasks used to operationalize the concept of phoneme awareness raised the issue of task comparability. Stanovich, Cunningham, and Cramer (1984) addressed the issue of task comparability in a study with kindergartners and found intercorrelations of .40 to .74 for 7 of the 10 measures investigated (the exceptions were three rhyming tasks). Also, factor analysis revealed only one factor on which all of the seven measures loaded highly. Regression analysis, predicting first-grade reading ability for their kindergarten sample, confirmed the essential redundancy of the seven measures, all of which showed from moderate to high correlations with reading. In a study with kindergartners, Yopp (1988) also investigated the comparability of tasks. Based on factor analytic and regression analyses for a large number of measures, Yopp concluded that all measures seemed to tap a similar construct (no rhyming tasks were included).

Even so, the factor analytic results of the study found a two-factor solution with different loadings for the two deletion tasks included in the study. Yopp (1988) observed that predictive validity may nevertheless hide differences in task difficulty. It was further noted that the "use of a wide variety of tasks has made interpretation, consolidation, and comparison of research findings difficult" (p. 160).

Confounding variables may be one source of differences in task difficulty. For example, one question for research and for educational assessment is the independence of tasks specifically assessing phoneme awareness skill from measures of general cognitive ability (as measured on IQ tests) and of general language ability. Such independence was confirmed in a number of studies (e.g., Stanovich, Cunningham, & Feeman, 1984; Wagner & Torgesen, 1987). Nevertheless, tasks differ in the extent to which they involve basic phonological processing, such as short-term memory processing, in addition to skill in phoneme awareness. For example, Bradley and Bryant (1988), in their longitudinal study of phoneme awareness as a correlate of reading and spelling, used a series of tasks they called *Odd One Out*. On these tasks, the child is presented with a series of three (4-year-old) or four (5-year-old) words and is asked to indicate which one does not fit. Of the three tasks in the Odd One Out battery, two involve essentially the identification of the nonrhyming word, for example, /fan/, /cat/, /mat/, /hat/ (end sound), or /mop/, /hop/, /tap/, /lop/ (middle sound). The third task, which Bradley and Bryant called the *alliteration test* (e.g., rot, rod, rock, box), involved recognition of the initial phoneme in spoken words. This task was also used in a similar longitudinal study by Lundberg, Olofsson, and Wall (1980).

The Odd One Out series may be complex for reasons other than the phoneme awareness skill it is assumed to measure. Although the Odd One Out tasks assess relatively easy phoneme awareness skill (rhyme detection and initial phoneme recognition), the comparison of multiple stimuli that characterizes these tasks may place considerable demands on short-term memory processing. Moreover, these excessive demands on short-term memory processing may seem unrelated (i.e., extrinsic) to the phoneme awareness skill being tested; for example, tasks that present a single word stimuli for each trial (*Listen for /s/. Does /spoken word/ have a /s/?*) test the same phoneme awareness skill (partial phoneme recognition). To determine whether or not memory was a confounding variable, Bradley and Bryant (1988) also assessed the subjects' abilities to repeat the words and included these results in their analyses of the data. These authors concluded that memory was not a confounding variable. It may be noted, however, that the simple span test is an insufficient control for the memory demands in the Odd One Out tasks, which additionally require comparisons of the stimuli set held in short-term memory. As Wagner and Torgesen (1987) noted, performance on the Odd One Out tasks may be more affected by short-term memory processing than by phoneme awareness.

Because, as we noted earlier, short-term memory processing is still limited in young children, reducing the extrinsic short-term memory requirements of tasks assessing early phoneme awareness may seem necessary to permit an unambiguous interpretation of performance. For example, as we noted, stimulus presentation may be restricted to a single phoneme target and single stimulus word or to pairs in rhyme detection tasks.

Performance on rhyming tasks (which are often included in the assessment of early phoneme awareness), may be confounded by naming requirements. For example, one type of rhyming task requires a judgment on rhyme based on pictures. Shown a pair of pictures (e.g., for fire–tire or fire–door), the child is asked whether they rhyme or sound the same at the end. Deficits in the accurate retrieval of the pronunciations of known vocabulary, rather than lack of the requisite phoneme awareness skill, may affect performance on this type of rhyme judgment task for some children. Judgment on rhyme for pictures starts with the ability to pronounce the labels or, at least, hear words in the mind. That is, this kind of rhyming task starts with a basic phonological processing skill: the ability to retrieve the correct verbal label. Asking children with normal speech to name the pictures first will reveal problems in the accurate retrieval of stimulus words, reducing problems in interpreting performance differences.

The previous examples illustrate the problem of basic phonological processing abilities as confounding variables in tasks assessing phoneme awareness. The inclusion of blending tasks in the assessment of phoneme awareness raises a similar issue; that is, do tasks measure what they are assumed to measure? Chall, Rosswell, and Blumenthal (1963) defined *blending* as accessing the sound form of a syllable or word from its segmented sequence. Blending is assessed in tasks that require subjects to indicate the word or pseudoword represented by a segmented sequence. Tasks often include syllable blending (e.g., saying /lipstick/ after hearing /lip/ /stick/) as well as phoneme blending (e.g., saying /nut/ after hearing /n/ /u/ /t/. That is, blending involves retrieval of the whole (the word or syllable) from its parts (the segmented syllable or phoneme sequence). The relationship between blending and segmentation skill and between blending and reading was investigated in a number of studies (e.g., Fox & Routh, 1976, 1984; Liberman, Shankweiler, Liberman, Fowler, & Fisher, 1977; Marsh & Mineo, 1977; Yopp, 1988).

First, there seems to be a general consensus that a similar construct underlies both phoneme blending and segmentation, even though conceptually these skills may seem opposites; that is, as a language operation, segmentation involves analysis (whole to part), whereas blending involves synthesis (part to whole). On the other hand, as Fox and Routh (1976, 1984) noted, the ability to blend a sequence of sounds into a word requires, at a minimum, the understanding that words consist of sequences of phonemes;

that is, some phoneme awareness seems to be a minimum condition for blending ability. For example, Fox and Routh (1984) found that the effect of blending training on a pseudoword learning task seemed to depend on the presence of phoneme segmentation skill. Also, the development of phoneme segmentation may lead, eventually, to blending skill. In both of these studies by Fox and Routh, children who were found to be segmenters without explicit training had no problem with blending. Consequently, Fox and Routh (1984) revised their earlier conclusion (Fox & Routh, 1976) that training blending is easier than training segmentation.

Of particular interest to the concept of blending as an early phoneme awareness skill is the finding that blending of familiar stimuli is easier than blending of less familiar items and that transfer of blending training to untrained items (words and pseudowords) is difficult (Helfgott, 1976; Lewkowicz, 1980). Helfgott also concluded that training blending was easier than training segmentation. However, as Lewkowicz pointed out, the effects of the blending training in the study by Helgott remained restricted to the set of stimuli included during training and did not transfer to untrained stimuli.

In fact, as indicated in the definition of blending and suggested by empirical findings, blending may be as much, or even more so, a measure of closure (i.e., the retrieval of the whole word or syllable from its parts) than a test of phoneme awareness. As such, Lewkowicz (1980) characterized instruction in blending as "helping children to supply the missing bonds between sounds or how to induce that *flash of recognition* that blending requires" (p. 696).

Letter Knowledge

As we noted, in addition to phoneme awareness, knowledge of letter–phoneme correspondences is also a component skill of phonological recoding and thus is a skill specific to learning written language. As a phonological processing skill, knowledge of letter–phoneme correspondences includes the recognition (e.g., which letter is /s/) as well as the pronunciation (sounding) of the phoneme represented by a letter or letter digraph. Assessment of letter knowledge in early reading is often restricted to letter naming accuracy or speed of naming. Ehri and Wilce (1985) noted that letter names are usually learned first and are useful because they provide children with nameable referents for the sounds represented by letters. The letter's sound is included in the letter's name in many cases (the letter *h* seems a notable exception). However, in spite of the relationship between letter names and sounds (e.g., /bee/ and /b/), the name and the corresponding phoneme associated with consonant letters represent two different phonological codes. Because letter names are usually learned first, the acquisition of the second code (the phoneme) for a letter may present a problem for children who have problems in the acquisition or retrieval of verbal labels. Letter name knowledge without a concurrent acquisition of letter–phoneme correspondences may obscure the relationship between letters and phonemes in words (e.g., /b/ but not /bee/ is the first segment in /book/).

Samuels (1971), as well as Tunmer, Herriman, and Nesdale (1988), noted that findings of predictive validity for letter naming rate should not lead to the conclusion that letter name knowledge alone predicts progress in reading. We suggest that in order to detect any possible discrepancies between letter name and letter–sound knowledge, early assessment may need to include the assessment of both letter names and letter–phoneme correspondences.

Summary

In this section, we defined phonological recoding and phoneme awareness that, together with knowledge of letter–phoneme correspondences, are skills specific to learning to read and write an alphabetic script. For phonological recoding, we delineated the inclusion of basic phonological processing abilities as intrinsic to the skill being tested. For example, we noted how the use of phonological recoding to retrieve the pronunciation of an unknown printed string requires closure. In the assessment of phoneme awareness, we focused on the need to select tasks that may seem relatively "pure" measures of phoneme awareness. We discussed the relative dependence of specific tasks (e.g., the Odd One Out series) on basic phonological processing abilities such as short-term memory. We also discussed the ambiguous status of blending, often included in phoneme awareness assessment, and concluded that blending may seem a measure of linguistic closure as well as of phoneme awareness. For letter assessment, we noted the need to include measures that specifically assess letter–phoneme correspondences.

A DEVELOPMENTAL APPROACH TO ASSESSMENT

Another problem for assessment in basic and applied research is that different tasks may assess different levels of skill in phonological recoding and phoneme awareness. This kind of task difference may affect not only relative difficulty but also relevance for different phases in reading or spelling development along a continuum from early to advanced skill. In this section, we discuss support for a developmental approach to assessment of phonological recoding and phoneme awareness and include examples of assessment in each of these areas, based on our own research (Vandervelden & Siegel, 1995).

Phonological Recoding

One of the findings that emerges from the research is that phonological recoding is not an all or none phenomenon, but a set of skills that develops over time which may include most of the elementary grades, even for normal readers (Siegel & Faux, 1989). Of particular importance for early assessment is the finding that the reading of simple (consonant vowel consonant) pseudowords is not fully developed until well after children acquire their first reading vocabulary (Siegel & Faux, 1989; Vandervelden & Siegel, 1995). For example, Siegel and Faux found that even at reading grade level 2, average readers attained only a score of 60% correct for reading a set of simple monosyllable pseudowords. Ehri and Wilce (1985) suggested that the finding that children may acquire a relatively large reading vocabulary even though they cannot read pseudowords led to the hypothesis of a first stage in which word learning is not supported by making use of the systematic relationship between letters and phonemes (e.g., Gough & Hillinger, 1980; Mason, 1980). However, from their studies of early development in phonological recoding, Ehri and Wilce (1985, 1987a, 1987b) concluded that the accurate use of sounding out and blending to retrieve the spoken form of unknown printed strings may be a separate and relatively advanced stage in the development of reading, and is preceded by a more rudimentary stage, phonetic cue reading. In *phonetic cue reading,* children use only some of the letters as cues to retrieve the spoken form. Ehri and Wilce (1985) found evidence that some form of phonetic cue reading is involved in the acquisition of a reading vocabulary from the outset.

The findings of Ehri and Wilce (1985) also indicate that phonetic cue reading refers to a complex of developing skills that may play a changing role in reading. For example, these authors suggested that phonological recoding may start with partial recognition of the letter–phoneme match when children hear and see words simultaneously. Furthermore, a study by Ehri and Wilce (1987a) also confirmed the findings of earlier research (e.g., Chomsky, 1979) in which children made use of phonological recoding to spell unknown words before they were able to do so in reading. The authors also found evidence for a developmental link between early spelling and early word reading.

We designed a study to investigate the role and development of phonological recoding in early reading prior to the ability to accurately read one-syllable, one-vowel pseudowords (Vandervelden & Siegel, 1995). Using a developmental approach, the measurement of phonological recoding was not confined to reading pseudowords, but also included a speech-to-print matching task to differentiate between recognition and retrieval in phonological recoding, as well as a spelling task. The following is a brief description of each task.

Speech-to-Print Matching.   Following presentation of a spoken word, the child indicated its match in a set of three printed words. Printed word sets were ordered to assess phonological recoding from partial to complete: for example *(mask) dress boat* (initial consonant difference); *meat (mask) mould.* (last consonant difference) *milk monk (mask)* (non initial–final consonant difference); *big (bug) bag* (vowel difference only).

Spelling.   This spelling dictation task included a set of one-syllable words and pseudowords (*bat mit puck sock dig top feet dime mif fak pim*). A picture illustrating the word was also presented as the examiner pronounced the word. The writing of letters was facilitated by placing, in view, a letter strip. Divided into squares, each square contained an upper- and lower-case letter, in alphabetical order, for all of the phonemes included in the spellings. Scoring on this task was based not on spelling accuracy but on the number of phonemes represented in the spelling, with a maximum score of 3 for each stimulus. For example, the spelling *s, sc* or *sk, soc, sok* or *sock* for /sock/ would be scored, respectively as 1, 2, and 3.

Pseudoword Reading.   Each pseudoword was printed on a card and presented one at a time for reading. The set of one syllable consonant vowel consonant (CVC) pseudowords included: *sup, mif, fak, tok, bes, kus, pof, dep, hib, gam.* In addition to measuring accuracy in simple pseudoword reading, partial accuracy measured the number of letters recoded correctly for each pseudoword across the set, with a maximum score of 3 for each three letter–phoneme pseudoword.

On the **speech-to-print matching task**, the target word (e.g., /frog/) was pronounced before children selected its match in a set of three printed words (e.g., *sad, mitt, frog*). On this task, phonological recoding is not required for pronouncing the printed string, but need only be used to recognize the match between a spoken stimulus (presented first) and its printed equivalent; that is, on this task, phonological recoding is redundant for retrieval of the spoken label. For purposes of investigating developmental progression in phonological recoding, *redundancy* was defined as the availability and ability to make use of information other than print to resolve problems of reading. In contrast, on the **pseudoword reading task**, recoding of part (e.g., *sup* read as /sock/) or all of the letters in the printed string precedes pronunciation and phonological recoding is never completely redundant for retrieval of the pronunciation (i.e., reading) of a printed string. The **spelling task** measured the child's ability to use phonological recoding in spelling. We used the terms *recognition, retrieval,* and *spelling,* to designate what we called the functions of phonological recoding operationalized in the speech-to-print matching, pseudoword reading, and spelling tasks, respectively.

On each of these three tasks, phonological recoding was measured from partial correctness, starting with correct first consonant recoding, to full correctness. That is, on the pseudoword reading and spelling tasks, it was also of interest how many letter–phoneme matches were correct and what their position was in substitutes. For example, reading /sock/ for *sup* or spelling /bat/ as *b* would indicate single letter–phoneme recoding of the initial consonant; reading /soup/ for *sup* or spelling /bat/ as *bt* would indicate two letter–phoneme recoding for initial and last consonants. Thus, even though reading *sup* as /sock/ or spelling /bat/ as *b* is inaccurate, partial use of phonological recoding has contributed to these substitutions. On the speech-to-print matching task, it was of interest to what degree correct selection could be made based on the overlap and position of letters in the printed word set. For example, correct selection of *sit* from the set *sit, milk, frog* or *sap, sink, sit* would indicate at least partial recoding skill, even though children may still be unable to select correctly from the set *sit sat sot*.

First, like Ehri and Wilce (1985), we found evidence that phonetic cue reading underlies written word learning from the outset. For example, all children who did not show at least some skill on the speech-to-print matching task failed to attain criterion on a simple word-learning task. The word-learning task, which was adapted from Ehri and Wilce (1985), included six one-syllable, thematically related words, each starting with a different initial consonant: *soup, milk, fork, bread, toast, glass.* Following pretesting for reading of the set, children were familiarized with the set of pictures and their labels. Using a paired associate approach, children were taught to read the set of words over a maximum of 10 trials. We also found that children who read more than five words correctly on an easy (high frequency, one syllable) word-reading task always showed skill in phonetic cue reading, including partial accuracy in pseudoword reading in most cases.

Second, regular progression in phonetic cue reading was identified as follows. Use of phonological recoding (recognition) on the speech-to-print matching task developed before use of phonological recoding (retrieval) on the pseudoword reading task at each level of analysis. For example, the initial consonant was recoded first on the speech-to-print matching task before children showed evidence of initial consonant recoding skill on the pseudoword reading task (or in word reading). In most cases, a two-letter level of recoding (i.e., first and last) on the speech-to-print matching task coincided with initial consonant recoding on the pseudoword task. Some children, however, showed a two-consonant level of recoding on the speech-to-print matching task and still did not indicate any skill in initial consonant recoding in pseudoword or word reading. Comparisons between uses of phonological recoding on the speech-to-print matching and spelling tasks showed that recognition of the letter–phoneme match for the initial consonant and medial vowel developed before spelling of these phonemes in equivalent positions, but that last consonant recoding on these two tasks developed simultaneously. Comparisons between spelling and pseudoword reading showed that spelling of the initial and final consonant developed before correctly recoding these consonants in reading. On both of these tasks, accuracy in recoding the vowel developed relatively late. Furthermore, development from partial to full recoding was similar across the three tasks: Initial consonant recoding developed first, followed by last consonant recoding, with medial vowel recoding developing last.

Third, although accuracy in reading simple pseudowords was found to be a relatively late developing skill, skills assessed on the early measures of phonological recoding (i.e., speech-to-print matching and partial accuracy in spelling and pseudoword reading) were found to be strongly related to skill on the word-learning task and on the easy (high frequency, predominantly one-syllable words) word-reading task. We concluded that the identification of a recognition level in phonological recoding that precedes even partial accuracy in pseudoword reading may explain how children start to notice the systematic relationship between spoken and printed words as they hear and see words simultaneously.

In conclusion, findings of a developmental progression in phonological recoding as well as strong relationships between early levels of skill and early reading indicate the need to measure phonological recoding along a developmental continuum. To tap early phases, assessment may need to include measures of the precursors of accuracy in pseudoword reading; that is, speech-to-print matching, and partial accuracy in spelling and pseudoword reading.

In the next section, we discuss that, like phonological recoding, phoneme awareness also needs to be assessed along a continuum from early to relatively more advanced skill.

Phoneme Awareness

Commenting on the wide variety of tasks used in research on phoneme awareness, Nesdale, Herriman, and Tunmer (1984) warned that "considerable caution must be exercised in comparing the results of specific studies since the child's level of phonological awareness will depend greatly on the task" (p. 60). Because it may seem plausible to assume that developmental phases in phonological recoding must be explained in terms of component phonological processing skills, the suggestion that phoneme awareness tasks may differ in the level of phoneme awareness that they assess may seem of considerable interest. In fact, the finding that phonological recoding refers to a complex of skills, starting with recognition of the consonant phoneme–letter match for initial consonants on speech-to-print matching, indicates that phoneme awareness also refers to a complex of skills that develop gradually and reciprocally with early phases in phonological recoding and in the acquisition of a written vocabulary. Evidence that phoneme awareness develops gradually and reciprocally with learning to read and spell an alphabetic script has been found in several studies (e.g., Ehri & Wilce, 1980; Mann, 1986; Morais, Cary, Alegria, & Bertelson, 1979; Perin, 1983; Vandervelden & Siegel, 1995).

Gradual and reciprocal development suggests two critical questions for appropriate task selection in the assessment of phoneme awareness in early identification. First, what kinds of task differences may be related to differences in task difficulty as a function of the kind (level) of phoneme awareness skill being assessed? Second, what is the relevance of performance on specific tasks of phoneme awareness for performance on specific tasks that assess different levels of skill in phonological recoding, and in reading or spelling?

Backman (1983) studied the role of phoneme segmentation skill as a function of age and reading level. Using a 1.5 or more grade level criterion on the word identification subtest of the Woodcock Reading Mastery Test (Woodcock, 1973), Backman included three groups in her study: kindergarten nonreaders; kindergarten readers, and a reading level matched group of children in Grade 2. Two measures of phoneme segmentation were used. One of these was the phoneme counting task used by Liberman et al. (1974). The second measure was a deletion task, which was an adaptation of the

Bruce test (Bruce, 1964), and included the deletion of syllables as well as target phonemes (e.g., *Say harm; Now say the word again but don't say the /h/*). Although both reading groups performed significantly better than the nonreaders on the deletion test, both were unable to show phoneme awareness on the phoneme tapping test. That is, accuracy in phoneme counting was more difficult than the deletion test and seemed of lesser relevance to early reading in as much as readers were unable to do this task. In fact, phoneme counting seemed more related to spelling skill in the study by Backman.

Other phoneme segmentation skills have been found relatively difficult and more related to spelling knowledge than to reading skill. For example, Perin (1983), in a study with adults, found that performance on a task requiring judgment on number of phonemes (which is a different kind of phoneme counting task) often reflected spelling characteristics (e.g., /boat/ or /foat/ were incorrectly judged to have four phonemes). Also, good readers who were also good spellers were significantly better on a spoonerism task (e.g., Chuck Berry to Buck Cherry) than good readers who were poor spellers. Perin (1983) concluded that certain phoneme awareness skills such as those assessed by the tasks in her study may be an epiphenomenon of spelling, rather than of reading skill. Performance on some tasks may also be an epiphenomenon of specific instructional approaches in the literacy curriculum. Alegria, Pignot, and Morais (1982), in a study with French-speaking children, found that children in a curriculum that stressed phonics teaching performed significantly better on a phoneme reversal task (e.g., /os/ to /sceau/) than children in a curriculum that did not teach phonics explicitly.

Task Dimensions Related to Level of Phoneme Awareness

In the literature on phoneme awareness, it has been suggested that several dimensions may be related to the level of phoneme awareness assessed and to the relative difficulty of the tasks. For example, Golinkoff (1978) proposed *operation to be performed* and *number of elements contained in the unit to be analyzed* as two dimensions related to differences among tasks in skill level and difficulty. Referring to Golinkoff, Lewkowicz (1980) commented that number of elements is a factor in estimating relative task difficulty that may vary with type of operation. In tasks involving recognition or even deletion of the initial consonant, word or syllable (pseudoword) length may be of minor importance. For example, /many/ to /any/, /feet/ to /eat/, or /sip/ to /ip/ may seem to tap the same level of phoneme awareness skill. Even so, one-syllable stimuli seem to predominate in phoneme deletion tasks (e.g., Rosner, 1973).

Addressing the issue of differences in operations among tasks, Golinkoff (1978) suggested the following hierarchy of skill and task difficulty: (a) recognizing the presence or absence of a unit (e.g., "Do fish and food start with the same sound?" or "Does fish have a /s/?"), (b) performing a deletion (e.g., /feet/ to /eat/), and (c) performing a deletion and replacing the deleted element with another element (e.g., /feet/ to /meat/). Lewk-owicz (1980) noted that the list excludes, for example, segmentation. However, because deletion involves partial segmentation, Lewkowicz may possibly refer to partial segmentation (e.g., "Say the first sound in feet") or to full sequential segmentation (e.g., full sequential articulatory segmentation where the child is directed to articulate a word with clear pauses between each phoneme). Lewkowicz also points out that Golinkoff's ranking of operations ignores the factor of position of the target phoneme in the word or pseudoword. For example, Lewkowicz and Low (1979) found that segmentation of the initial consonant seemed easier than segmentation of consonants in any other position.

Type of phoneme to be segmented may also be related to task difficulty, depending on the position of the target phoneme. For example, Marsh and Mineo (1977) found that children recognized continuants more easily than stops on a phoneme recognition task (e.g., "Which one starts/ends with___?"), but that position may interact with type of phoneme. Continuants (/m/, /s/,/f/) seemed more easily recognized in initial than final position, but this did not seem to be the case for stop consonants (/b/, /p/, /d/, /t/). In addition, the results of the study by Lewkowicz and Low (1979) also indicate an interaction between type of phoneme and type of operation (recognition compared to segmentation of phonemes). These authors failed to find support for an effect for phoneme type in their study of the development of phoneme segmentation skill.

Partial compared to complete segmentation may seem an obvious dimension affecting task difficulty, because the difference in skill is quantitative. Helfgott (1976) and Lewkowicz and Low (1979) who investigated the development of segmentation skill, found that initial phoneme segmentation may be relatively easy, is attainable by kindergarten children, and precedes full segmentation of cvc words. Using sequential articulatory segmentation, in which subjects are directed to pronounce words with clear pauses between phonemes in words, both studies found a developmental sequence in which a two part segmentation (C VC and CV C as in /c/ /at/ and /ca/ /t/ respectively) preceded full segmentation ability (C V C or /c/ /a/ /t/).

Even so, findings of relative task difficulty in the study by Yopp (1988) indicate that the partial–complete dimension may interact with type of operation. Yopp's investigation of seven phoneme awareness included two deletion tasks (Bruce, 1964; Rosner, 1973) and two full sequential segmentation tasks. The deletion task based on Rosner included deletion of syllables (e.g., "Say sunshine. Now say it again without sun"). There is evidence that segmentation into syllables taps an earlier level of skill than segmentation into phonemes. For example, in the study by Liberman et al. (1974), only 17% of the kindergarten sample showed any skill in phoneme counting compared to 48% for syllable counting. For that reason, a comparison of the relative difficulty of phoneme deletion may seem valid only for the test based on Bruce, which did not seem to have included trials involving segmentation into syllables. This comparison shows the mean percentage correct score on the Bruce test of about 25% (7.89 out of 30) compared to a mean percentage correct score of about 50% for the two full sequential segmentation tasks (11.78 out of 22 and 8.58 out of 16).

Lewkowicz and Low (1979) also suggested a differentiation between segmentation, a term these authors reserved for "responding to a spoken stimulus word by pronouncing that word as a correctly ordered sequence of separately articulated phonemes" (p. 239) and the ability to perceive (i.e., recognize the absence or presence of target phonemes) without the requirement of overt articulation. Presumably, segmentation may seem the more difficult task: The ability to separately articulate a target phoneme implies the ability to recognize the phoneme in the spoken stimulus.

However, findings by Skelfjord (1976, 1987) indicate that performance on phoneme recognition tasks (i.e., tasks that do not require overt articulation) may be affected by position of the target phoneme. For example, Skelfjord (1976) observed that in training identification of phoneme location for position other than initial (e.g., "Is there a /m/ at the end of ———, in the middle of ————-?"), children seemed to make use of overt articulation of the phoneme sequence. Although this was not tested separately, the study seems to indicate that articulatory segmentation may well play a significant role in what are ostensibly phoneme recognition tasks only.

In summary, several task dimensions have been related to task difficulty as a function of the level of phoneme awareness skill being assessed. Support for a number of these dimensions has been found and seems most unequivocal for the position of target phonemes and for partial compared to full analysis. Although type of operation may be another dimension related to task difficulty, complex interactions among the various dimensions suggest the need for careful attention to what and how many task dimensions are included in a single task.

Task difficulty as a function of the level of phoneme awareness being assessed also raises the question of task relevance for early phases in phonological recoding and in reading. Task relevance as the second criterion for task selection in the assessment of phoneme awareness is briefly discussed next.

Task Differences and Task Relevance

To be developmentally appropriate, tasks must be selected not only for their relative difficulty but also for their relevance to early phases in phonological recoding and in reading and spelling. For example, segmentation of syllable-sized segments (e.g., Liberman et al., 1974; Mann & Liberman, 1984) and rhyming (e.g., Stanovich, Cunningham, & Cramer, 1984) are two of the earliest skills to develop. In rhyming tasks, segmentation skill is also based on syllable-sized segments (i.e., the rhyme) in one-syllable words or pseudowords.

However, because alphabetic scripts map at the level of the phoneme, and not the syllable, the relationship between analytical skill for syllable-sized segments and reading acquisition may be indirect. Both syllable segmentation and rhyming tasks show relatively low correlations with early reading. For example, in a study with kindergarten-aged children, Mann and Liberman (1984), noting the good syllable counting skill compared to phoneme counting skill reported by Liberman et al. (1974), used a syllable counting task. Although syllable counting was found to be predictive for reading in Grade 1, these authors also reported that the task was a less accurate predictor of reading success than was the analogous phoneme counting test. In the study with kindergarten aged children to which we referred earlier, Stanovich, Cunningham, and Cramer (1984) investigated the predictive validity of seven partial phoneme recognition–segmentation tasks and three rhyming tasks. In contrast to the other seven tasks, performance on the three rhyming tasks was at ceiling. However, intercorrelations for rhyming with the other tasks and with reading were comparatively low. In fact, Bryant et al. (1989) suggested that the importance of rhyme production lies in its effect on the development of phoneme awareness. This position also implies that rhyming skill is a precursor that has only indirect relevance for developmental phases in early reading and spelling.

Whereas rhyming and syllable-sized segmentation tasks may assess too low a level of analytical skill that may have no direct relevance for early phases in phonological recoding and written word learning, other tasks may assess skill in excess of what is required in early development. For example, the finding that only 17% of the subjects showed skill in phoneme counting led Liberman et al. (1974) to the conclusion that phoneme awareness skill may seem beyond the ability of most kindergarten children. However, a developmental perspective suggests that phoneme counting may not only be too difficult a task for young children, but also in excess of what is required for starting to read (e.g., Backman, 1983). For example, we noted earlier how phoneme counting skill may be related to spelling, rather than to early reading.

Developmental Phases and Task Relevance

To investigate developmental phases in phoneme awareness and their relevance to developmental phases in phonological recoding and in early reading, we used a series of tasks in which we attempted to assess phoneme awareness along a continuum from early to advanced skill (Vandervelden & Siegel, 1995). For this purpose, we selected tasks to differentiate among the following dimensions: recognition or segmentation; position (e.g., initial or final consonant); partial to complete segmentation (e.g., following presentation of the spoken word /meat/, separate articulation of the /m/ or /m/ /t/ only to complete segmentation into /m/ /e/ /t/); simple or complex skill (e.g., articulating the /m/ in /meat/ compared to deleting /m/ and pronouncing the remainder /eat/). The design and ordering of tasks was based on earlier findings of the relative difficulty of tasks as well as on our findings of early phases in the development of phonological recoding outlined earlier. For example, the dimension recognition and segmentation was assessed because speech-to-print matching, which was found to develop early, may seem to require minimally partial recognition but not necessarily partial segmentation of target phonemes. The partial to complete dimension was included because early phases in phonological recoding seemed characterized by partial skill in phoneme–letter recoding on speech-to-print matching, spelling, and pseudoword reading. Furthermore, these partial phonological recoding skills were strongly related to early reading skill. The positional dimension was included because performance patterns on all three measures of phonological recoding indicated that recoding the initial consonant of one-syllable word and pseudoword stimuli seemed easiest, followed by the last consonant, with recoding of consonants in blends and medial vowels developing last.

First, we administered three tasks to assess phoneme recognition. In addition to assessing initial and final phoneme recognition separately on the first two tasks, the third task combined these skills (i.e., recognition of the target phoneme in either position) as well as identification of position (first or last) for instances. An example for each of these three tasks follows.

Initial Phoneme Recognition (based on Wallach et al., 1977).   For test trials, say: "Listen for /s/, /fat/. Does /fat/ have an /s/?" Additional trials for /s/ were: /s/, /soup/; /s/, /sock/; /s/, /meat/ (yes or no response). In our research (Vandervelden & Siegel, 1995), sets of four trials were included for the same set of consonants represented in initial position in the measures of phonological recoding (b, d, f, g, h, k, m, p, s, t).

Final Phoneme Recognition.   In the practice trials, the examiner stressed the change in position of the target phoneme. For test trials, presentation was identical to initial phoneme recognition. Test trials for /s/ included: /s/ /miss/, /s/ /fat/, /s/ /hiss/, /s/ /meat/. Additional sets of four trials for each phoneme were included from the same consonant set as for initial consonant recoding, with the exception of /h/, which does not occur in word final position.

Complex Phoneme Recognition.   In the practice trials, the examiner emphasized the need to indicate, first or last, whenever the target phoneme was recognized. For the test trials, the examiner said: "/s/ /neck/: First, last, or no?" Additional trials were: /s/ /sun/, /s/ /class/, /s/ /grass/, /s/ /sick/, /s/ pen. Additional sets of six trials were included as for final phoneme recognition.

First, for most children, initial phoneme recognition was easier than final phoneme recognition and this finding is in further support of position as a task dimension affecting relative difficulty. Skill on the complex phoneme recognition task depended on mastery of initial and final phoneme segmentation on the two separate tasks. This finding indicates the need to attend to the number of dimensions included in tasks; that is, whether tasks assess a single, simple skill or a complex skill.

Two tasks were included to assess phoneme segmentation. First, we included what we called a *sequential segmentation task* based on the

Yopp–Singer task (Yopp, 1988). On this task, the child was presented with a word and a picture to illustrate the word, or a pseudoword. Following presentation of the spoken word or syllable, the child was asked to separately articulate as many of the phonemes as possible (three practice trials in which the examiner modeled articulatory segmentation preceded the testing trials).

We found no support for the recognition–segmentation dimension proposed by Lewkowicz and Low (1979). Although initial consonant recognition and segmentation developed first, in most cases there was no difference between the ability to recognize or segment a phoneme in the same word position. In earlier research it was suggested that, especially for phonemes in noninitial word position, articulation may play a role in phoneme awareness, even though tasks do not require the use of overt articulation (Skelfjord, 1976, 1987). In fact, we observed the use of overt articulation by many children even on the initial phoneme recognition task, especially when phoneme awareness seemed still at a beginning phase (Vandervelden & Siegel, 1995). We concluded that articulation seemed to play a role even on the initial phoneme recognition task. Even so, for some children either one of these two skills (partial recognition or segmentation) seemed easier, which is why we suggest the use of both tasks in the early assessment of phoneme awareness.

In addition to the sequential segmentation task, we also included a series of deletion and deletion and substitution trials as a measure of complex phoneme segmentation skill (e.g., Yopp, 1988). As we discussed earlier, Golinkoff's (1978) hierarchy for operations suggests that deletion is easier than deletion and substitution. This assumption is also reflected in the ordering of trials across Levels F, G, and H, included in Auditory–Motor Skills Training (*Perceptual Skills Training Curriculum*, Rosner, 1973) on which we based our task. However, we found no difference between deletion and deletion and substitution. Instead, level of difficulty seems related to the position of the consonant; that is, initial consonant deletion and deletion and substitution was easier than similar operations for the final consonant. Deletion and deletion and substitution of consonants in blends (both initial and final) was the most difficult.

In support of the simple or complex dimension operationalized across the two measures of phoneme segmentation (sequential segmentation and deletion and substitution), we found that children were always able to separately articulate an initial or final phoneme before they were able to delete or delete and substitute in comparable positions.

On the question of task relevance, we also found that phoneme awareness increased concurrently, or reciprocally, with development in phonological recoding and in reading and spelling. For example, initial phoneme recognition, which was the easiest of the three phoneme recognition tasks, was strongly related to early phases in phonological recoding; for example, to select /frog/ in the set /meat/, /boat/, /frog/ on the speech-to-print matching task. Moreover, both partial phoneme recognition and partial segmentation was most strongly related to, and increased commensurately with, early skill in phonological recoding (i.e., skill prior to accuracy in simple pseudoword reading), and reading (the word-learning and easy word-reading task). On the other hand, deletion and substitution was most strongly related to accuracy in pseudoword reading, to reading multisyllable and less common words, and to accuracy in spelling. We concluded that findings of a gradual development in phoneme awareness and a strong but changing relationship with the measures of phonological recoding, of reading, and of spelling along a continuum of skill indicate the need for multiple tasks and task selection that matches commensurate skill levels in early reading.

CONCLUSION

There is considerable evidence that use of the systematic relationship between phonemes in spoken words and letters in printed language, or phonological recoding, is strongly related to the acquisition of a written vocabulary. Skill in using this systematic relationship between how words sound and how they are written enables the novice reader to predict, with varying degrees of accuracy, how words are read and spelled. This predictive power of phonological recoding explains its role in early literacy development.

In presenting a theoretical framework for the assessment of early phonological processing, we differentiated between basic phonological processing and phonological processing specific to learning to read and write an alphabetic script. Our discussion of basic phonological processing included a brief review of studies in naming, short-term memory processing and speech perception, all of which show a relationship with reading. Next, we defined phonological processing skills specific to learning to read and write. We began with defining the role of phonological recoding in the acquisition of a written vocabulary and related the importance of phoneme awareness and knowledge of letter–sound correspondences to their status as component skills of phonological recoding. We defined phonological recoding and noted that closure is an intrinsic requirement of using phonological recoding for the retrieval of pronunciations. We also discussed basic phonological processing abilities as confounding variables in tasks assessing phoneme awareness. To avoid ambiguity in the interpretation of task performance, we emphasized the need for the selection of tasks that seem relatively pure measures of phoneme awareness. In the assessment of letter knowledge, we stressed the need to include measures that specifically measure letter–phoneme correspondences.

Finally, we discussed evidence in support of phonological recoding and phoneme awareness as complexes of skills that develop gradually and reciprocally with learning to read and write along a continuum from easy to advanced. We reviewed our own research into early developmental phases in phonological recoding prior to the ability to read simple pseudowords and included descriptions of the tasks we used. Based on a review of the results, we concluded that early assessment of phonological recoding must include speech-to-print matching and spelling as well as pseudoword reading. In addition, use of phonological recoding on each of these tasks should be measured from initial to full recoding. In the discussion of phoneme awareness, we started with the assumption that, as a component skill of phonological recoding, phoneme awareness must also refer to a complex of developing skills rather than a single skill. With this in mind, we addressed the issue of differences in task difficulty as this may be related to the level of phoneme awareness skill being assessed in specific tasks. We discussed the various task dimensions specific to phoneme awareness that may specify a task's relative difficulty. Making the point that appropriate task selection is not only a matter of relative difficulty but also of relevance for early phases in phonological recoding, we concluded with a discussion of our own research investigating relative task difficulty and relevance in early development. Descriptions of tasks used in this research were also provided.

Phonological processing skills play an important role in learning to read and write an alphabetic script. The large individual differences found well before children receive formal instruction in reading suggest that early assessment that provides detailed information of children's competence is essential to the design of curriculum that addresses the learning needs of all children.

REFERENCES

Alegria, J., Pignot, E., & Morais, J. (1982). Phonetic analysis of speech and memory codes in beginning readers. *Memory & Cognition, 10,* 451–456.

Backman, J. (1983). The role of psycholinguistic skills in acquisition: A look at early readers. *Reading Research Quarterly, 18,* 469–479.

Baddeley, A. D. (1979). Working memory and reading. In P. A. Kolers, M. E. Wrolstad, & H. Bouma (Eds.), *Processing of visible language* (Vol.1, pp. 355–370). New York: Plenum.

Baddeley, A. D. (1982). Reading and working memory. *Bulletin of the British Psychological Society, 35,* 414–417.

Baron, J., Treiman, R., Wilf, J. F., & Kellman, Ph. (1980). Spelling and reading by rules. In U. Frith (Ed.), *Cognitive processes in spelling* (pp. 159–193). London: Academic Press.

Blachman, B. (1984). Language analysis skills and early reading acquisition. In G.Wallach & K. Butler (Eds.), *Language learning disabilities in school-age children* (pp. 271–287). Baltimore: Williams & Wilkins.

Bradley, L., & Bryant, P. E. (1983). Categorizing sounds and learning to read: A Causal connection. *Nature, 30,* 419–421.

Bradley, L., & Bryant, P. (1988). *Rhyme and reason in reading and spelling.* Ann Arbor: University of Michigan Press.

Bruce, D. J. (1964). An analysis of word sounds by young children. *British Journal of Educational Psychology, 34,* 158–170.

Bryant, P. E., Bradley, L., Maclean, M., & Crossland, T. (1989). Nursery rhymes, phonological skills and reading. *Journal of Child Language, 16,* 407–428.

Calfee, R., Lindamood, P., & Lindamood, C. (1973). Acoustic-phonetic skill and reading-kindergarten through twelfth grade. *Journal of Educational Psychology, 64,* 293–298.

Chall, J., Rosswell, F. G., & Blumenthal, S. H. (1963). Auditory blending ability: A factor in success in early reading. *Reading Teacher, 17,* 113–118.

Chomsky, C. (1979). Approaching reading through invented spelling. In L. B. Resnick & P. A. Weaver (Eds.), *Theory and practice of early reading* (Vol. 2 pp. 43–66). Hillsdale, NJ: Lawrence Erlbaum Associates.

Ehri, L. C. (1978). Beginning reading from a psycholinguistic perspective: Amalgamation of word identities. In F. B. Murray (Ed.), *The development of the reading process* (International Reading Association Monograph No. 3, pp. 1–33). Newark, DE: International Reading Association.

Ehri, L. C. (1980). The Development of orthographic images. In U. Frith (Ed.), *Cognitive processes in spelling* (pp. 311–388). London: Academic Press

Ehri, L. C. (1984). How orthography alters spoken language competencies in children learning to read and spell. In J. Downing & R. Valtin (Eds.), *Language awareness and learning to read* (pp. 119–147). New York: Springer–Verlag.

Ehri, L. C., & Wilce, L. S. (1980). The influence of orthography on readers conceptualization of the phoneme structure of words. *Applied Psycholinguistics, 1,* 371–385.

Ehri, L. C., & Wilce, L. S. (1985). Movement into reading: Is the first stage of printed word learning visual or phonetic? *Reading Research Quarterly, 20,* 163–179.

Ehri, L., & Wilce, L. S. (1987a). Cipher versus cue reading: An experiment in decoding acquisition. *Journal of Educational Psychology, 79,* 3–13.

Ehri, L., & Wilce, L. S. (1987b). Does learning to spell help beginners to read words? *Reading Research Quarterly, 22,* 47–65.

Fox, B., & Routh, D. K. (1976). Phonemic analysis and synthesis as word attack skills. *Journal of Educational Psychology, 68,* 70–74.

Fox, B., & Routh, D. K. (1980). Phonemic analysis and severe reading disability in children. *Journal of Psycho-linguistic Research, 9,* 115–118.

Fox, B., & Routh, D. K. (1984). Phonemic analysis and synthesis as word-attack skills: Revisited. *Journal of Educational Psychology, 76,* 1059–1064.

Godfrey, J. J., Syrdal-Lasky, A. K., Millay, K. K., & Knox, C. M. (1981). Performance of dyslexic children on speech perception tests. *Journal of Experimental Child Psychology, 32,* 401–424.

Golinkoff, R. M. (1978). Critique: Phoneme awareness skills and reading achievement. In F. B. Murray & J. J. Pikulski (Eds.), *The acquisition of reading: Cognitive, linguistic, and perceptual prerequisites* (pp. 23–43). Baltimore, MD: University Park Press.

Goswami, U. (1986). Children's use of analogy in learning to read: A developmental study. *Journal of Experimental Child Psychology, 42,*73–83.

Goswami, U. (1988). Orthographic analogies and reading development. *Quarterly Journal of Experimental Psychology, 40,* 239–268.

Goswami, U. (1990). A special link between rhyming skills and the use of orthographic analogies by beginning readers. *Journal of Child Psychology and Psychiatry, 31,* 301–311.

Goswami, U., & Mead, F. (1992). Onset and rime awareness and analogies in reading. *Reading Research Quarterly, 27,* 153–162.

Gough, P. B., & Hillinger, M. L. (1980). Learning to read: An unnatural act. *Bulletin of the Orton Society, 30,* 179–205.

Gough, P. B., Juel, C., & Roper-Schneider, D. (1983). Code and cipher: A two-stage conception of intial reading acquisition. In J. A. Niles & L. A. Harris (Eds.), *Searches for meaning in reading/language processing and instruction: 32nd yearbook of the National Reading Conference* (pp. 207–211). Rochester, NY: National Reading Conference.

Helfgott, J. A. (1976). Phonemic segmentation and blending skills of kindergarten children: Implications for beginning reading acquisition. *Contemporary Educational Psychology 1,* 157–169.

Jorm, A. F. (1983). Specific reading retardation and working memory: A review. *British Journal of Psychology, 74,* 311–342.

Jorm, A. F., & Share, D. L. (1983). Phonological recoding and reading acquisition. *Applied Psycholinguistics, 4,* 103–147.

Juel, C., Griffith, P., & Gough, P. B. (1986). Acquisition of literacy: A longitudinal study of children in first and second grade. *Journal of Educational Psychology, 78,* 243–255.

Lewkowicz, N. (1980). Phonemic awareness training: What to teach and how to teach it. *Journal of Educational Psychology, 72,* 686–700.

Lewkowicz, N., & Low, L. Y. (1979). Effects of visual aids and word structure on phoneme segmentation. *Contemporary Educational Psychlogy, 4,* 238–253.

Liberman, I. Y. (1983). A language oriented view of reading and its disabilities. In H. Myklebust (Ed.), *Progress in learning disabilities* (Vol. 5, pp. 81–102). New York: Grune & Stratton.

Liberman, A. M., Cooper, F. S., Shankweiler D., & Studdert-Kennedy, M. (1967). Perception of the speech code. *Psychological Review, 74,* 431–461.

Liberman, I. Y., Liberman, A. M., Mattingly, I., & Shankweiler, D. (1980). Orthography and the beginning reader. In J. F. Kavanagh & R. L. Venezky (Eds.), *Orthography, reading, and dyslexia* (pp. 137–153). Baltimore: University Press.

Liberman, I. Y., Rubin, H., Duques, S., & Carlisle, J. (1985). Linguistic ability and spelling proficiency in kinder-garteners and adult poor spellers. In D. B. Gray & J. F. Kavanagh (Eds.), *Biobehavioral measures of dyslexia* (pp. 163–176). Parkton, MD: York Press.

Liberman, I. Y., & Shankweiler, D. (1985). Phonology and the problems of learning to read and write. *Remedial and Special Education, 6,* 8–17.

Liberman, I. Y., Shankweiler, D., Fisher, F. W., & Carter, B. (1974). Explicit syllable and phoneme segmentation in the young child. *Journal of Experimental Child Psychology, 18,* 201–210.

Liberman, I. Y., Shankweiler, D., Liberman, A. M., Fowler, C., & Fisher, F. W. (1977). Phonetic segmentation and recoding in the beginning reader. In A. S. Reber & D. L. Scarborough (Eds.), *Toward a psychology of reading* (pp. 207–225). Hillsdale, NJ: Lawrence Erlbaum Associates.

Lie, A. (1991). Effects of a training program for stimulating skills in word analysis in first-grade children. *Reading Research Quarterly, 26,* 234–250.

Lundberg, I., Olofsson, A., & Wall, S. (1980). Reading and spelling skill in the first school years predicted from phonemic awareness skills in kindergarten. *Scandinavian Journal of Psychology, 21,* 159–173.

Mann, V. A. (1986). Phonological awareness: The role of reading experience. *Cognition, 24,* 65–92.

Mann, V. A., & Liberman, I. Y. (1984). Phonological awareness and verbal short-term memory. *Journal of Learning Disabilities, 17,* 592–599.

Marcel, T. (1980). Phonological awareness and phonological representation: Investigation of a specific spelling problem. In U. Frith (Ed.), *Cognitive processes in spelling* (pp. 372–404). London: Academic Press.

Marsh, G., & Mineo, R. J. (1977). Training preschool children to recognize phonemes in words. *Journal of Educational Psychology, 69,* 748–753.

Mason, J. (1980). When do children begin to read: An exploration of four-year old children's letter and word reading competencies. *Reading Research Quarterly, 15,* 203–227.

McCusker, L. X., Hillinger, M. L., & Bias, R. G. (1981). Phonological recoding and reading. *Psychological Bulletin, 89,* 217–245.

Morais, J., Cary, L., Alegria, J., & Bertelson, P. (1979). Does awareness of speech as a sequence of phonemes arise spontaneously? *Cognition, 7,* 323–331.

Nesdale, A. R., Herriman, M. L., & Tunmer, W. E. (1984). Phonological awareness in children. In W. E. Tunmer, C. Pratt, & M. L. Herriman (Eds.), *Metalinguistic awareness in children* (pp. 56–72). New York: Springer–Verlag.

Perfetti, C. A. (1985). *Reading ability.* New York: Oxford University Press.

Perin, D. (1983). Phonemic segmentation and spelling. *British Journal of Psychology, 74,* 129–144.

Rack, J. P., Snowling, M. J., & Olson, R. K. (1992). The nonword reading deficit in developmental dyslexia: A review. *Reading Research Quarterly, 27,* 28–53.

Read, C. (1971). Preschool children's knowledge of English phonology. *Harvard Educational Review, 41,* 1–34.

Read, C. (1975). Children's categorization of speech in English. *NCTE Research Report 17,* Educational Resources Information Center.

Rosner, J. (1973). *Perceptual skills curriculum: Auditory motor skills training.* New York: Walker.

Samuels, S. J. (1971). Letter-name versus letter-sound knowledge in learning to read. *Reading Teacher, 24,* 604–608.

Scarborough, H. S. (1989). Prediction of reading disability from familial and individual differences. *Journal of Educational Psychology, 81,* 101–108.

Shankweiler, D., Liberman, I. Y., Mark, L. S. , Fowler, C. A., & Fisher, F. W. (1979). The speech code and learning to read. *Journal of Experimental Psychology: Human Learning and Memory, 5,* 531–545.

Share, D. (1994). Phonological recoding and self-teaching: Sine qua non of reading acquisition. *Cognition, 55,* 151–218.

Share, D. J., Jorm, A. F., Maclean, R., & Mathews, R. (1984). Sources of individual differences in reading achievement. *Journal of Educational Psychology, 76,* 466–477.

Siegel, L. S. (1985). Psycholinguistic aspects of reading disabilities. In L. S. Siegel & F. J. Morrison (Eds.), *Cognitive development in atypical children* (pp. 45–67). New York: Springer–Verlag.

Siegel, L. S. (1993). Phonological processing deficits as the basis of a reading disability. *Developmental Review, 13,* 246–257.

Siegel, L. S., & Faux, D. (1989). Acquisition of certain grapheme-phoneme correspondences in normally achieving and disabled readers. *Reading and Writing: An Interdisciplinary Journal, 1,* 37–52.

Siegel, L. S., & Linder, B. (1984). Short-term memory processes in children with reading and arithmetic disabilities. *Developmental Psychology, 20,* 200–207.

Siegel L. S., & Ryan, E. B. (1988). Development of grammatical sensitivity, phonological and short-term memory skills in normally achieving and learning disabled children. *Developmental Psychology, 24,* 28–37.

Skelfjord, V. J. (1976). Teaching children to segment syllables as an aid in learning to read. *Journal of Learning Disabilities, 9,* 39–48.

Skelfjord, V. J. (1987). Phoneme segmentation: An important subskill in learning to read: I. *Scandinavian Journal of Educational Research, 31,* 41–57.

Stanovich, K. E.(1982). Individual differences in the cognitive processes of reading: 1. Word decoding. *Journal of Learning Disabilities, 15,* 485–493.

Stanovich, K. E. (1986a). Explaining the variance in reading ability in terms of psychological processes: What have we learned? *Annals of Dyslexia, 35,* 67–96.

Stanovich, K. E. (1986b). Matthew effects in reading: Some consequences of individual differences in the acquisition of literacy. *Reading Research Quarterly, 21,* 360–407.

Stanovich, K. E., Cunningham, A. E., & Cramer, B. B. (1984). Assessing phonological awareness in kindergarten children: Issues of task comparability. *Journal of Experimental Child Psychology, 38,* 175–190.

Stanovich, K. E., Cunningham, A. E., & Feeman, D. J. (1984). Intelligence, cognitive skills, and early reading progress. *Reading Research Quarterly, 19,* 278–303.

Steffens, M. L., Eilers, R. E., Gross-Glenn, K., & Jallad, B. (1992). Speech perception in adult subjects with familial dyslexia. *Journal of Speech and Hearing Research, 35,* 192–200.

Torneus, M. (1984). Phonological awareness and reading: A chicken and egg problem? *Journal of Educational Psychology, 76,* 1346–1358.

Treiman, R. (1985). Onsets and rhymnes as units of spoken syllables: Evidence from children. *Journal of Experimental Child Psychology, 39,* 161–181.

Tunmer, W. E., Herriman, M. L. & Nesdale, A. R. (1988). Meta-linguistic abilities and beginning reading. *Reading Research Quarterly, 23,* 134–159.

Vandervelden, M. C., & Siegel, L. S. (1995). Phonological recoding and phoneme awareness in early literacy: A developmental approach. *Reading Research Quarterly, 30,* 854–875.

Wagner, R. K., & Torgesen, J. K. (1987). The nature of phonological processes and its causal role in the acquisition of reading skills. *Psychological Bulletin, 101,* 192–212.

Wallach, L., Wallach, M. A., Dozier, M. G., & Kaplan, N. E. (1977). Poor children learning to read do not have trouble with auditory discrimination but do have trouble with phoneme recognition. *Journal of Educational Psychology, 69,* 36–39.

Wallach, M. A., & Wallach, L. (1976). *Teaching all children to read.* Chicago, IL: University of Chicago Press.

Wolf, M. (1991). Naming speed and reading: The contribution of the cognitive neurosciences. *Reading Research Quarterly, 26,* 123–142.

Woodcock, R. W. (1973). *Woodcock reading mastery tests.* Circle Pines, MN: American Guidance Service.

Yopp, H. K.(1988). The validity and reliability of phonemic awareness tests. *Reading Research Quarterly, 23,* 159–178.

5

Prediction And Intervention Of School-Age Language Problems Using Electrophysiological Measures Obtained At Birth

Dennis L. Molfese
Arlene Tan
Shirin Sarkari
Leslie Gill
Southern Illinois University at Carbondale

INTRODUCTION

Since the mid-1970s, numerous studies have attempted to predict the performance of infants, preschoolers, and primary grade children on cognitive, language, and intelligence tests using measures obtained in the neonatal, infancy, and early childhood periods. The focus of this chapter is a review of the electrophysiological precursors of cognitive and language development, and a review of the adaptation of these techniques for the study and evaluation of intervention effectiveness. Studies reviewed include normal children as well as children born "at risk" but without extreme biomedical risks. Because normal children and children with less extreme risks are frequently also characterized by various biomedical, social, and environmental risks that influence performance on tests, and because these children represent the majority of births, studies focusing on these children are directed toward a broad population. This chapter is divided into four parts: (a) the use of event related potentials (ERP) to study the development of phonological discrimination, (b) the use of these measures to predict later language outcomes, (c) a discussion of the possible auditory mechanisms present at birth that influence later language development, and (d) a review of ERP techniques that, when used in tandem with the predictive procedures, could allow us to intervene during infancy to remediate children who would later develop poor reading and spelling skills.

THE DEVELOPMENT OF PHONOLOGICAL DISCRIMINATION, PHONOLOGICAL AWARENESS, AND ORTHOGRAPHIC SKILLS AS RELATED TO READING AND SPELLING ABILITIES

Considerable work was published on the roles of *phonological discrimination* and *phonological awareness* in the development of language and reading abilities. Phonological discrimination refers to the ability to discriminate phonetic contrasts and includes discrimination of speech sound and categorical perception (voice-onset-time, place of articulation). Phonological awareness refers to the ability to segment and manipulate phonemes. Some phonological skills that are important for analyzing the sound patterns in spoken words are present at or near birth, whereas others begin to develop in infancy. Young infants are able to discriminate between speech sounds that contain phonetic contrasts characteristic of their language environments and are also sensitive to phonetic contrasts characteristic of other languages (Eilers, 1977; Eilers, Wilson, & Moore, 1977; Eimas, Siqueland, Jusczyk, & Vigorito, 1971). There is a change in later infancy toward increasing sensitivity to contrasts only within their language environments, a change that appears to facilitate language acquisition. Preschool children develop the ability to segment spoken monosyllable words into onsets and rimes, and thus to play nursery rhyme games (Vellutino & Scanlon, 1987). Onsets are the first phoneme(s) in a word (e.g., b in book or bl in black). Rimes are the part of the syllable remaining when the onset is deleted (e.g., ook in book, ack in black). Children learn to segment polysyllabic words into syllables around kindergarten and monosyllabic words into phonemes around first grade (Liberman, Shankweiler, Fischer, & Carter, 1974). Since the mid-1980s, a consensus emerged among researchers that phonological awareness is the single most important variable in reading acquisition (Brady & Shankweiler, 1991).

It is not clear why the children who show normal reading achievement develop these abilities, whereas others who have reading problems do not, or develop the abilities to a lesser extent. Fowler (1991) argued that a minimum level of cognitive development is necessary for the beginning of reading skills. Cognitive skills such as short-term memory for words, digits, and other verbally coded material, early language abilities (including MLU, syntactic complexity, naming), and recognition vocabulary distinguish successful from poor readers (Fowler, 1991; Scarborough, 1990). Although necessary, cognitive development is not sufficient for reading success and level of intelligence is not a distinguishing characteristic of successful readers (Stanovich, 1988). Others pointed to differences in the types of rhyming and sound game activities characterizing middle- and upper SES homes compared to low-SES homes (Bradley & Bryant, 1983; Maclean, Bradley, & Bryant, 1987). Such differences could influence the development of phonological skills needed for reading. Recent work suggests that orthographic processes may also play a role in beginning reading acquisition (Berninger, Chen, & Abbott, 1988; Olson, Lorsberg, & Wise, 1994; Siegel & Faux, 1989; Stanovich, West, & Cunningham, 1991; Wagner & Barker, 1994).

If phonological awareness plays a significant role in later reading and language development, measures of related processes earlier in development could identify children with poor reading development. One such link may be between the infant's early phonetic discrimination skills and skills the child will utilize while learning more complex aspects of language. The ERP procedure offers a well-established means to measure such abilities early in life. Moreover, because the same technique can be used at each age, direct comparisons can be made across ages. Molfese and colleagues were the first to systematically explore the development of phonological and phonemic processing using ERP techniques, noting that differences in ERP patterns to speech and nonspeech sounds are present at birth. Molfese (1972; Molfese, Freeman, & Palermo, 1975) began by using consonant–vowel contrasts to study speech perception in infants, young children, and adults followed by studies of newborns, including preterm infants. ERPs showed that phonological discrimination was present at birth for some phonetic contrasts (e.g., place of articulation, Molfese & Molfese, 1979a, 1980, 1985) and by 2 months for others (e.g., voicing contrasts, Molfese & Molfese, 1979b). Subsequent studies showed that these patterns of discrimination stabilized by 3 to 4 years of age in lateralized responses to place and voicing differences in speech sounds (Molfese & Hess, 1978; Molfese & Molfese, 1988). An expansion of the sound stimuli used in subsequent studies included consonant–vowel contrasts differing in formant structure to create speechlike and nonspeechlike contrasts. ERP responses to these stimuli pointed to the sensitivity of even newborn infants to speech (Molfese & Molfese, 1985, 1993). Further studies revealed that components in the ERPs that discriminated phonological differences displayed different lateralized patterns from those that reflected other acoustic differences (Molfese & Molfese, 1979a, 1985). Importantly, these effects were independently replicated by other investigators using different analysis procedures as well as acoustically different yet phonetically identical stimuli (Gelfer, 1987; Segalowitz & Cohen, 1989). Furthermore, performance on language tasks at 3 and 5 years of age was strongly predicted by newborn ERPs (Molfese, 1989b; Molfese & Molfese, 1985, in press).

PREDICTIONS OF INTELLIGENCE AND SPECIFIC
COGNITIVE ABILITIES USING ERP AND BEHAVIORAL
AND ENVIRONMENTAL MEASURES

Numerous attempts were made to develop systems in which biomedical risk scores reflecting prenatal, intrapartum, and neonatal complications are used to predict later cognitive functioning (Molfese, 1989). Several researchers showed that biomedical risk scores are predictive of performance on developmental tests within the infancy period (e.g. Low et al., 1985; Molfese & Thomson, 1985; Ross, 1985). However, attempts to extend the predictive period to include early and middle childhood were not as successful. Researchers reported that biomedical risk scores were either not predictive of outcomes in preschool and school-age children (e.g., Cohen & Parmelee, 1983; Crisafi, Driscoll, Rey, & Adler, 1987) or scores were only weak correlates (e.g., Bee et al., 1982; Largo et al., 1989; Silva, McGee, & Williams, 1984). A different approach using individual risk scores rather than summed scores to classify children as normal or developmentally delayed was taken by Siegel (1982b, 1985), Smith, Flick, Ferriss, and Sellman (1972), and Molfese, DiLalla, and Lovelace (1996) and showed greater success. Accuracy in classifying at-risk and normal 3- to 7-year-olds ranged from 71% to 97%. An increase in classification accuracy was noted by Siegel and Smith et al. when 1-year Bayley Mental Development Index (MDI) scores were included. These studies provide more hopeful evidence that biomedical scores are useful for predicting early childhood scores and play a role in children's performance for extended time periods, even for children not characterized by extreme biomedical risks.

Alternatives to the strictly behavioral and medical approaches described previously focused on physiological responses as the bases for screening techniques and also provided predictive results. Some researchers used auditory brain-stem evoked response measures (BSER) to predict developmental outcomes in the first year of life (Barden & Peltzman, 1980; Cox, Hack, & Metz, 1984; Murray, 1988; Murray, Dolby, Nation, & Thomas, 1981). Although the BSER procedure has promise as an effective and relatively low-cost technique for the early identification of hearing impairments, the number of false positives and false negatives makes the BSER procedure an ineffective means for identifying infants at risk for later developmental problems. Further, efforts to extend the use of BSER procedures from assessments of hearing impairment into areas of cognitive and language functioning is not well established. Published reports successfully using neonatal BSERs as predictors of later developmental problems are scant. A different and more reliable result was obtained through the use of event related potentials (ERP). ERPs are usually represented as complex waveforms thought to reflect changes in brain activity via fluctuations in peak latency (delay from stimulus onset) or amplitude (height of the wave) at different points during the time course of the wave following some stimulus event (Callaway, Tueting, & Koslow, 1978). Because of this time-locked feature, ERPs can reflect both general and specific aspects of the evoking stimulus (Molfese, 1978a, 1978b) as well as the individual's perceptions and decisions regarding the stimulus (Molfese, 1983; Nelson & Salapatek, 1986; Ruchkin, Sutton, Munson, & Macar 1981).

Studies conducted since the mid-1970s to predict later development based on neonatal ERP measures varied in their effectiveness. In general, studies that restricted their analyses to a single early peak or peak latency in the brainwave (i.e., usually the N1 component) achieved some success up to 1 year of age, but failed to find a long-term relationship (Butler & Engel, 1969; Jensen & Engel, 1971). Studies that attempted to extend the period of predictability into the second year of life and beyond reported little success (Engel & Fay, 1972; Engle & Henderson, 1973; Ertl, 1969; Henderson & Engel, 1974). Although these findings may appear discouraging for the usefulness of ERPs as predictors of later functioning, more recent studies suggest that these relationships do exist (Molfese, 1972; Molfese & Molfese, 1985; Molfese & Searock, 1986).

The difference in success between studies reflects a number of differences in methodology and experimental design. First, Molfese and associates typically analyzed the entire ERP waveform, whereas other researchers typically confined their analysis to a single ERP component. One might suspect, however, that analysis of all the data collected instead of only a small subset would increase the likelihood of finding a relationship between early brain responses and later development. Second, the frequency range of the ERPs studied by Molfese includes a lower range of frequencies (below 2 Hz) than those employed by earlier investigators. Given that the brain wave frequencies characterizing the ERP of newborn and young infants are concentrated in the frequency range below 2 Hz, this strategy utilizes much more of the neonate's brainwave activity. Third, Molfese employed language-related speech sounds as the evoking stimuli rather than the photic flashes used by earlier investigators. The relevance of photic flashes to the types of cognitive processing thought to be reflected in intelligence tests is not known. However, given available evidence showing that young infants have elaborate speech perception abilities (Eimas et al., 1971), and the obvious link between speech perception skills and the acquisition of various language domains, speech perception abilities must be related to language development. Because predictors of successful performance are generally better if they measure predicted skills, the inclusion of more language relevant materials such as speech sounds as the evoking stimuli should increase the likelihood for predicting later language related skills. Such differences in measures and stimuli across studies could be responsible for the better success found in the Molfese et al. studies cited to follow in using auditory ERPs recorded at birth as predictors of later cognitive and language functioning.

Extensive research since the 1960s indicates that ERPs recorded in a variety of paradigms are sensitive to phonetic variations (Kraus et al., 1993; Molfese, 1978b; Molfese & Molfese, 1979a, 1979b, 1985, 1988; Molfese et al., 1975; Sharma, Kraus, McGee, Carrell, & Nicol, 1993). Using this information, Molfese and Molfese (1985) demonstrated that ERPs recorded from 16 newborn infants in response to a series of consonant–vowel speech syllables predicted McCarthy verbal scores obtained 3 years later. They recorded ERPs from scalp electrodes placed over the left and right temporal regions of 16 newborn infants to a series of consonant–vowel speech syllables and then recorded ERPs again at 6-month intervals through 3 years of age. The ERPs were averaged and then submitted to a principal components factor analysis (PCA) with varimax rotation. Seven factors (accounting for 79.9% of the total variance) were derived from the analysis on the newborn ERP data. At 3 years, the verbal subtest of the McCarthy Scales of Children's Abilities (McCarthy, 1972) was administered to these children. The average McCarthy verbal score for the children was 50.8 ($SD = 33.7$). The group was then subdivided into two groups: One group of children had verbal scores above 50 (mean score = 77.25, $SD = 15.5$), and the second group had verbal scores below 50 (mean score = 20.5, $SD = 12.6$). Although the groups differed in language scores, they did not differ on other factors such as pre- and postnatal status, infant health, Bayley MDI scores at 6 and 12 months of age, or SES measures (Bayley, 1969, 1993). An analysis of variance (ANOVA) comparing the two groups showed three components or waveform peaks of the newborn ERP to reflect differential sensitivity to specific consonant and consonant–vowel characteristics of the evoking stimulus. These ERP components discriminated between children with different levels of language skills 3 years later. We were the first to document a relationship between brain responses from birth and language performance 3 years later. When the children were grouped by above average (high) and below average (low) scores, a combination of lateralized and bilateralized ERP components from three regions of the ERP waveform differentiated the two groups.

Molfese (1989b), with a different sample of 32 infants who by age 3 performed within a narrower range of McCarthy scores (range: 32–69), developed a discriminant function to correctly classify all but 1 child of 16 in the low performing group ($M = 45$) and all but one in the high group ($M = 61$). Molfese and Molfese (1993) replicated these findings with an expanded sample of 54 infants. In both cases, analyses focused on the same regions of the ERPs utilized by the earlier report (Molfese & Molfese, 1985) to discriminate children who performed well or poorly.

A further replication of these early findings involved a larger group of children who are part of the present longitudinal study. ERPs to auditory stimuli identical to those used in the earlier study were obtained from 79 newborn infants (Molfese, Gill, Simos, & Tan, 1995). In this study, children were separated into three groups based on 5-year Stanford–Binet Verbal Reasoning (VIQ) scores that were 1 SD above the sample mean (high, VIQ: 116–130), 1 SD below the mean (low, VIQ: < 95) and within 1 SD around the mean (average, VIQ: 95–115). Factor scores from two regions of the ERP previously found by Molfese and Molfese (1985) to discriminate children with high versus low language scores were used in this analysis. This combination of factor scores obtained from 4,266 averaged ERPs successfully discriminated 81% of the sample in which there were 16 high, 47 average, and 16 low performing children at 5 years of age.

The group averaged ERPs from these three groups of infants are depicted in Fig. 5.1. The two regions of the auditory ERP that temporally overlapped with those previously reported by Molfese and Molfese (1985) are enclosed within the rectangles labeled "1" and "5" for Factors 1 and 5, respectively. Note that the late negative component of the ERP is markedly negative for the low group. The negativity for this region is greatly reduced for the

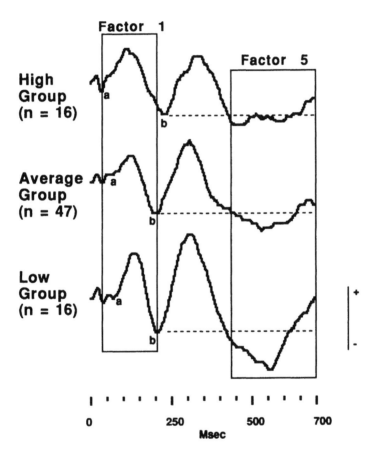

FIG. 5.1. The group averaged ERPs collapsed across six electrode sites and nine consonant–vowel syllables recorded from 16 newborn infants whose language performance at 5 years of age on the VIQ subtest score was 1 *SD* or more (range = 85–94) below the population mean (low group), the 47 infants who scored within 1 *SD* (range = 95–116) of the population mean (average group), and the 16 newborn infants who 5 years later scored 1 *SD* or more (range = 117–130) above the population mean (high group). The rectangle labeled "Factor 1" identifies the region of the ERP whose variability was reflected by Factor 1 of the principal components analysis. The region of variability characterized by Factor 5 is demarcated by the rectangle that frames the later portion of the ERPs.

average group. For the high group, the region generally shows a more flattened appearance before moving upward in a positive direction. In the early portion of the ERP waveform, the duration between the two points labeled "a" and "b" gradually increases as language performance increases. The two points are closest together for the low group, at an intermediate point for the average group, and more widely separated for the high group.

A subsequent study correctly classified 96% of the children when the ERPs were used in a discriminant function, discriminating between children at 5 years with verbal performance scores at or above 100 from those below 100 (Molfese & Molfese, in press). In this study, 3,834 averaged auditory evoked responses were recorded from six scalp electrodes placed on the heads of 71 children (39 females and 32 males). Using analysis procedures modeled after Molfese and Molfese (1985), a discriminant function was constructed using the factor scores selected from the first two ERP temporally occurring components identified by Molfese and Molfese to discriminate low from high later language performers (above and below 100). This discriminant function was significant, with χ^2 $(7, N = 71) = 42.93$, p < .00001, Wilks' Lambda = .5192, and correctly classified 96% of the sample (68 of 71 children). Nearly all of the low group (8 of 9 for 88.9%) were correctly classified along with 60 of 62 children (96.8%) belonging to the high group. The differences between the two groups of children are illustrated in Fig. 5.2 where the auditory ERPs are presented for the two groups, averaged across electrode sites and stimulus conditions. The rectangle labeled "2" encloses the portion of the ERPs characterized by Factor 2. As can be seen in the figure, the averaged ERP for the high group (dashed line) is more positive than that obtained for the low group (solid line). In addition, the overall amplitude of the large negative to positive shift within this window appears smaller for the high than the low group. Although not used in this analysis, the final large negative component also is more negative for the low performing group than for the higher performing one at 5 years of age. This is consistent with the findings of Molfese et al. (1995) as depicted in Fig. 5.1. These results demonstrate that predictive accuracy can extend to 5 years of age, 2 years beyond that first demonstrated by Molfese and Molfese (1985). Subsequent analyses of the current sample (n = 100) correctly classify 90% of the sample, including all 18 children with verbal performance scores below 100 at 5 years and 72 of 82 children with scores at or above 100. These data are unparalleled in their predictive accuracy and point to a major breakthrough in early screening accuracy.

Although neonatal brain responses were shown across studies to consistently discriminate between children who will later develop different levels of language skills, other studies investigated how ERPs at different ages following birth predict later outcomes. In the earliest work using ERPs recorded after the newborn period to predict later language developmental outcomes, Molfese and Searock (1986) reported an effect similar to Molfese and Molfese (1985), using ERPs recorded from 1-year-olds to predict 3-year McCarthy verbal performance. In this study, ERP components measuring discrimination of vowel sounds also discriminated between these children

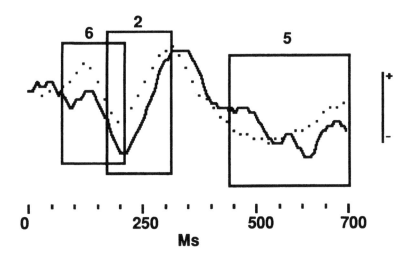

S-B Verbal < 100 ————
S-B Verbal => 100 ·········

FIG. 5.2. The newborn group averaged auditory ERPs for the nine children (solid line) who at 5 years of age scored below 100 on the VIQ and the 62 children (dotted line) who scored at or above 100 on that test. The time course is 700 ms with positivity up. The calibration marker is 5 microvolts.

at 3 years in terms of their McCarthy scores as the newborn ERPs had done. Using data obtained with the current longitudinal sample, a second set of analyses focused on the relationship between early brain responses and verbal performance at each of these ages. Across all analyses, variables were selected that reflect consonant and vowel discriminations in the regions of the ERPs identified by Molfese and Molfese (1985). Discriminant function procedures using newborn ERPs successfully discriminate between later differences in verbal skills at well above chance levels after 2 years of age (Molfese, 1989a, 1989b; Molfese & Molfese, 1985, in press). In addition, ERP measures at birth classify children at age 3 as well as did ERPs recorded at age 3. In a discriminant function procedure using eight variables, we successfully classified 81% (106) of the 131 newborn infants with χ^2 (8, N, = 131) = 50.38, p < .00001, Wilks' Lambda = .6683, who 3 years later either had VIQ at or above 100 (76 of 94) or below 100 (30 of 37). A similar procedure, which used ERPs obtained at 3 years to discriminate between 3-year-old children in language performance produced a similar level of classification accuracy—70.1%, χ^2 (5, N = 131) = 19.63, p < .0015, Wilks' Lambda = .8088. Using these same variables, accuracy using 3-year ERPs to classify 5-year VIQ was also high at 70.1%, χ^2 (5, N = 131) = 14.24, p < .014, Wilks' Lambda = .7933. Thus, ERPs obtained at later ages are at least as effective for discriminating later verbal performance measures as newborn obtained ERPs.

Although predictions from the neonatal period to the later childhood years were confirmed across a number of our studies, data from other laboratories show the high classification accuracy using ERPs extends into adolescence. For example, DeSonneville, Visser, and Njiokiktjien, (1989) used visual ERPs and reported a strong relationship between neurological optimality at birth and selective attention in 11- to 13-year-old children. These strong correlations between early physiological measures and later performance provides converging support for our findings that early ERP measures can predict later cognitive performance.

Other compelling evidence supporting the effectiveness of early measures for predicting later cognitive and intelligence scores involved measures of home environment and other variables that influence the intellectual level of the home environment (e.g., SES, parental IQ, parenting practices, family activities). In studies of normal and at-risk children, researchers reported strong correlations between markers for home environment quality and performance on intelligence tests in infancy and childhood (e.g., Aylward, in press; Bee et al., 1982; Bradley et al., 1993; Longstreth et al., 1981; Molfese et al., 1996; Sameroff, Seifer, Barocas, Zax, & Greenspan, 1987; Wallace, Escalona, McCarton-Daum, & Vaughan, 1982; Yeates, MacPhee, Campbell & Ramey, 1983). Although different types and numbers of these variables were used, social and environmental measures typically outperform other variables in the amount of variance accounted for in regression models predicting intelligence scores. Although the value of home environment variables in predictive modeling was demonstrated, there is not much guidance from previous studies in the optimal measure(s), number of measures, or optimal time in development (e.g., prenatally, at birth, in close proximity to the time at which other tests are administered) when measures of home environment should be taken to provide the most reliable information on the influence of home environment measures. There have also been differing views about the way in which the home environment affects intellectual development. Researchers argued either that the effects of home environment decline across childhood as children are exposed to more varied environments (Bradley et al., 1993; Schaimberg & Lee, 1991; Wilson, 1985), that they increase in influence between ages 2 and 4 years (Bee et al., 1982; Yeates et al., 1983), or that the role of home environment and biomedical conditions at birth interact to influence performance on intelligence tests and cognitive tasks in preschool children (Molfese & DiLalla, 1995; Molfese et al., 1993; Siegel, 1982a 1982b, 1985; Smith et al., 1972). These latter researchers reported that biomedical conditions play an important but possibly time-limited role in influencing development in infancy, especially in samples not characterized by extreme biomedical risk conditions, whereas the social environment plays an increasingly important role beginning in later infancy and throughout childhood. In addition, although the influences of social and environmental measures were studied extensively in infancy and early childhood, less work was with older children and there has been little work to measure the role of other dimensions of the home environment, such as parental IQ. The role of home environment as an influence on later outcomes needs further study as do issues of the development period (e.g., infancy, preschool, early childhood) when measures are taken, number of times measures are taken, and how parental IQ influences the predictive value of these measures.

MECHANISMS RESPONSIBLE FOR THE PREDICTIVE POWER OF ERPS FOR LATER LANGUAGE ASSESSMENT

The obvious question that arises from these results is why any type of behavioral or brain measure should discriminate developmental outcomes over a large age range with such high accuracy. Are human accomplishments predetermined from birth? Are genetic factors that potent that they all but force certain developmental outcomes despite the influence of any environmental factors? Rather, we hypothesize that these data reflect the state of an underlying perceptual mechanism on which some aspects of later developing and emerging verbal and cognitive processes are based. As a result of genetic and intrauterine factors, the developing organism develops a set of perceptual abilities responsive to variations in its environment. For most of us, these perceptual abilities are similar and readily enable us to discriminate elements within our environment in similar ways. For others, however, aspects of these perceptual skills may not respond to environmental elements in the same way. It is these fundamental differences in perceptual skills that set the stage for early detection of responses that influence verbal performance. This argument is developed more fully in the next few paragraphs using voice onset time (VOT) as an example.

VOT is a perceptual cue utilized to discriminate voiced from voiceless consonant sounds. American English speakers possess a perceptual boundary that allows them to normally discriminate voiced consonants (e.g., /b, d, g/) from voiceless consonants (e.g., /p, t, k/) (Liberman, Cooper, Shankweiler, & Studdert-Kennedy, 1967; Stevens & Klatt, 1974). Perception of this cue utilizes the temporal distance between laryngeal pulsing (i.e., vocal fold vibration) and the onset of consonant release (i.e., the passage of air through the vocal tract). Eimas, Siqueland, Jusczyk, and Vigorito (1971) demonstrated that young infants have this discrimination ability when they showed that 1- and 4-month-old infants discriminate voiced from voiceless consonants along boundary lines similar to those of adult language users. This ability to discriminate between speech sounds at certain temporal delays is not limited to humans. Kuhl and Miller (1975, 1978) reported that chinchillas also discriminated stop consonant speech sounds at approximately this boundary. Morse, Molfese, Laughlin, Linnville, and Wetzel (1987) reported a similar finding with infant and 1-year-old rhesus monkeys. Thus, it is possible that this skill may be a property of the mammalian auditory system. Furthermore, this ability to discriminate sounds based on temporal delays is not limited to speech sounds. Pisoni (1977) and Molfese (1980) presented behavioral and electrophysiological data, respectively, showing that adults discriminate between nonspeech multiformant tones in a similar fashion. These electrophysiological findings were later replicated in adults by Segalowitz and Cohen (1989) and with 3-year-old children (Molfese & Molfese, 1988). From this series of studies, it appears likely that humans are able to utilize an inherent auditory perceptual ability to make speech-relevant phonetic distinctions.

However, what happens if an infant possessed a different auditory boundary sensitivity? That is, what if the infant's auditory sensitivity to an acoustic boundary as VOT is shifted away from the usual boundary? A shift of only 30 ms would result in the infant hearing only one consonant sound across a range of sounds heard by listeners with normal auditory boundaries as two different consonant sounds. The voiced and voiceless bilabial stop consonants produced by the parent would only be heard as a single (voiced) consonant sound. Instead of hearing a difference between the word *big* spoken by the parent when pointing to a large object versus *pig*, the infant might hear the word, *big*. The objects or events co-occurring with the vocalizations would appear to the infant to have exactly the same label, *big*. Thus, there would be less invariance in the child's language environment and the infant's ability to map from sound differences to word meaning differences would be impaired. Because one half of the consonant sounds in American English are voiced, the potential exists that the infant could experience other voiced versus voiceless confusions as well. Although not all stop consonants have their voicing boundary at 30 ms, as in the case of the velar stops (e.g., /g/ vs. /k/), which have a boundary at approximately 40 ms, such a boundary shift could still affect other speech sound discriminations, lessening their distinctiveness.

Perhaps an even more difficult scenario is one in which the acoustic boundary is shifted just 10 ms. Thus, if the infant's boundary is at 40 ms instead of 30, the infant would most likely hear voiced consonants 75% of the time. Although the infant would have no difficulty in correctly identifying all of the voiced consonant exemplars (with VOT values at 20 ms), the voiceless tokens would be ambiguous and might force the infant to use a guessing strategy to classify the sound as voiced or voiceless. Such factors could contribute to delays in the child's acquisition of some words or, at the very least, make the task of mapping from phonetic contrasts to meaning differences a much more formidable one. In the meantime, infants with a more normally tuned auditory system would hear more readily the phonetic difference between the two words pronounced by the adult and would begin to develop the different semantic links that characterize different sounding words. Because the task for normally hearing infants is not as formidable because of their ability to more readily hear such voicing differences, these infants can use their resources to advance in other areas, which advantages them further over infants with perceptual boundary problems.

THE USE OF ERPS TO MONITOR INTERVENTIONS

With our ability to use ERP and behavioral data for early identification of children with predicted language delays and poor performance scores, it is time to move toward an investigation of possible intervention approaches. We explored two approaches involving ERPs as index measures of cognitive changes during training tasks. A preliminary study was conducted with 14-month-old infants (Molfese, Morse, & Peters, 1990). In this study, a group of 14 infants was pretested on a series of stimuli. Then, a 15-minute home training period (twice a day for 5 days) was begun, followed by a posttest session to evaluate changes. Auditory ERPs were recorded at both the pretest and posttest sessions. These ERP data were supplemented by parent ratings of their infant's knowledge of the trained material as well as by behavioral ratings on the posttest day. The test materials consisted of two consonant–vowel–consonant–vowel (CVCV) syllables and two wooden dowels of different colors and shapes. The training required parents to pair one specific dowel with one specific CVCV for one half of the morning and afternoon sessions and the remainder pairing the other CVCV and dowel. Parents were instructed to pair the items in a number of different situations, thereby providing the infant with multiple visual and tactile experiences with each pair. For example, a parent might say, "See the gibu. Hold the gibu. See the gibu float (in water). Put the gibu in this bottle." As part of the pretest and posttest sessions, the infant listened to the name of the object while looking and handling it. On one half of the trials, the object was paired with the name assigned it; on the other one half, with the name assigned to the other object. All infants were tested on both objects and names. Names were counterbalanced across objects across infants. During the pretest (see Fig. 5.3), no differences were found between auditory ERPs to the names when they were correctly paired versus not correctly paired with the objects. However, posttest results shown in Figure 5.3 indicate large differences between the ERPs on match versus mismatch trials in two regions of the ERP (indicated by the rectangles), as well as a change in the overall wave shape of the ERP. Although the pretest ERPs contained a single negative peak, posttest ERPs contained two negative peaks at different latencies. In addition, the overall magnitude of the ERPs nearly doubled on the posttest training trials. These ERP differences were distinctly different from those reported by Molfese (1989a) when familiarity but not training was manipulated. The ERP results, which were confirmed by the behavioral results as well, indicate that these infants had learned the correct labels for the two objects.

A subsequent study was undertaken with adolescents using a variation of this procedure (Molfese, 1993; Molfese & Molfese, 1996). The study involved three parts:

1. A pretraining session during which 6 male and 6 female right handed 16- to 17-year-olds viewed trials where a nonsense word appeared on a computer screen for 2 s, followed briefly by a blank screen, and then by a

PRETEST   **POSTTEST**

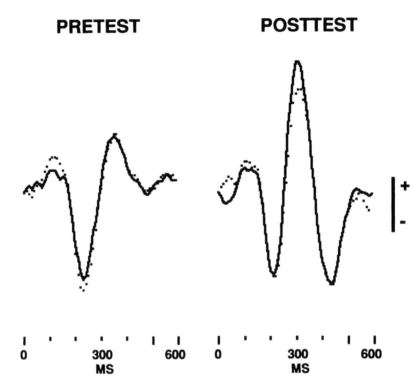

FIG. 5.3. Group averaged ERPs recorded from a group of 14-month-old infants during pretraining and posttraining trials. The solid line indicates ERPs collected on match trials and the dashed line indicates mismatch trials. The time course is 700 ms with positivity up. The calibration marker is 5 microvolts.

2-s display of a randomly generated shape. Subjects pressed one of two computer keys to indicate a match or mismatch between the name and shape. Twenty different nonsense CVCVC names and randomly generated shapes were used. All stimuli and response keys were counterbalanced across conditions and subjects.

2. A 15-minute training period for one half of the names and shapes.
3. A posttraining period that replicated the pretraining testing.

Visual ERPs were recorded to shapes during both the pre- and posttraining sessions from scalp electrodes over left and right frontal, central, and parietal areas referred to linked ear references. ANOVAs with Greenhouse–Geisser corrections evaluated the behavioral and ERP data. A significant Pre–Post × Learned–Not-Learned interaction, $F(1, 11) = 33.76, p < .0001$, indicated that performance improved for only the trained stimuli from pre- to posttraining, $F(1, 11) = 99.54, p < .0001$. After artifact rejection,

ERPs were averaged separately for the pre- and posttraining condition (2), for the learned and not learned stimulus sets (2), for the match and mismatch conditions (2), for three electrode sites (3) between hemispheres (2). Area under the curve measures of the ERPs were conducted on the 576 averaged visual ERPs between 350 ms and 850 ms following stimulus onset, an area corresponding to the P3 and late positive component (LPC) components thought to reflect cognitive processing. A Pre–Post × Learned–Not-Learned interaction, $F(2, 22) = 5.25, p < .043$, indicated that ERPs differed as a function of the training. Area increased significantly for the LPC when VERs were recorded to the learned materials during the posttraining situation over the response to these same materials during the pretraining session, $F(1, 22) = 8.76, p < .013$. No difference was noted for untrained materials. In addition, a Pre–Post × Learned–Not-Learned × Electrode interaction, $F(2, 22) = 3.479, p < .048$, indicated that ERPs recorded over frontal and parietal sites during the posttraining condition discriminated learned from not-learned stimuli. Shown in Fig. 5.4, ERPs reflected differences in familiarity (dotted line) versus learning (solid line). Marked in-

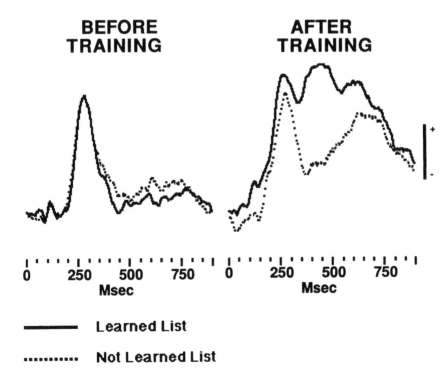

FIG. 5.4. Group averaged visual ERPs recorded to the same set of stimuli from a group of 12 adolescents during pretraining and during posttraining sessions. One half of the stimulus set was to be trained and one half was not. The time course is 700 ms with positivity up. The calibration marker is 5 microvolts.

creases in the area of the late occurring ERP regions characterize the learned versus unlearned material during the posttraining period.

Given these findings with both infants and adolescents, demonstrating changes in ERPs as a function of training, ERPs could be used to successfully monitor the progress of intervention training. This direction is clearly the next step to be taken. In the near future, both ERP and behavioral measures will be used to identify children who may be at risk for developmental delays in language areas and these same procedures could be used to evaluate the effectiveness of intervention programs designed to improve their later emerging performance on reading and spelling skills.

ACKNOWLEDGMENTS

Support for this work was provided by the National Institutes of Health (R01 HD17860), and a University Priorities and Interdisciplinary Initiatives grant (2–11221) obtained from the Office of Research Development and Administration, Southern Illinois University at Carbondale.

REFERENCES

Barden, T., & Peltzman, P. (1980). Newborn brain stem auditory evoked responses and perinatal clinical events. *American Journal of Obstetrics and Gynecology, 136,* 912–919.

Bayley, N. (1969). *The Bayley Scales of Infant Development: Manual.* San Antonio, TX: The Psychological Corporation.

Bayley, N. (1993). *Bayley Scales of Infant Development (2nd ed.): Manual.* San Antonio, TX: The Psychological Corporation.

Bee, H., Barnard, K., Eyres, S., Gray, C., Hammond, M., Spietz, A., Snyder, C., & Clark, B. (1982). Prediction of IQ and language skill for perinatal status, child performance, family characteristics, and mother–infant interaction. *Child Development, 53,* 1134–1156.

Berninger, V., Chen, A., & Abbott, R. (1988). A test of the multiple connections model of reading acquisition. *International Journal of Neuroscience, 42,* 283–295.

Bradley, L., & Bryant, P. (1983). Categorizing sounds and learning to read: A causal connection. *Nature, 30,* 419–421.

Bradley, R., Whiteside, L., Caldwell, B., Casey, P., Kelleher, K., Pope, S., Swanson, M., Barrett, K., & Cross, D. (1993). Maternal IQ, the home environment, and child IQ in low birthweight, premature children. *International Journal of Behavioral Development, 16,* 61–74.

Brady, S., & Shankweiler, D. (1991). Phonological processes in literacy. A tribute to Isabelle Y. Libereman. Hillsdale, NJ: Lawrence Erlbaum Associates.

Butler, B., & Engle, R. (1969). Mental and motor scores at 8 months in relation to neonatal photic responses. *Developmental Medicine and Child Neurology, 11,* 77–82

Callaway, C., Tueting, P., & Koslow, S. (1978). *Event-related brain potentials and behavior.* New York: Academic Press.

Cohen, S., & Parmelee, A. (1983). Prediction of five-year Stanford-Binet scores in preterm infants. *Child Development, 54,* 1242–1253.

Cox, L., Hack, M., & Metz, D. (1984). Auditory brain stem response abnormalities in the very low birthweight infant: Incidence and risk factors. *Ear and Hearing, 5,* 47–51.

Crisafi, M., Driscoll, J., Rey, H., & Adler, A. (1987, April). *A longitudinal study of intellectual performance of very low birthweight infants in the preschool years.* Paper presented at the Society for Research in Child Development, Baltimore, MD.

DeSonneville, L., Visser, S., & Njiokiktjien, C. (1989). Late sequelae of a non-optimal neonatal neurological condition in ERPs at the age of 11-13 years. *Journal of Electroencephalography and Clinical Neurophysiology, 72*, 491–498.

Eilers, R. (1977). Context-sensitive perception of naturally produced stop and fricative consonants by infants. *Journal of the Acoustical Society of America, 61*, 1321–1336.

Eilers, R., Wilson, W., & Moore, J. (1977). Developmental changes in speech discrimination in infants. *Journal of Speech and Hearing Research, 20*, 766–780.

Eimas, P., Siqueland, E., Jusczyk, P., & Vigorito, J. (1971). Speech perception in infants. *Science, 171*, 303–306.

Engel, R., & Fay, W. (1972). Visual evoked responses at birth, verbal scores at three years, and IQ at four years. *Developmental Medicine and Child Neurology, 14*, 283–289.

Engel, R., & Henderson, N. (1973). Visual evoked responses and IQ scores at school age. *Developmental Medicine and Child Neurology, 15*, 136–145.

Ertl, J. (1969). Brain response correlates of psychometric intelligence. *Nature, 223*, 421.

Fowler, A. (1991). How early phonological development might set the state for phoneme awareness. In S. Brady & D. Shankweiler (Eds.), *Phonological processes in literacy* (pp. 97–117). Hillsdale, NJ: Lawrence Erlbaum Associates.

Gelfer, M. (1987). An AER study of stop-consonant discrimination. *Perception & Psychophysics, 42*, 318–327.

Henderson, N., & Engel, R. (1974). Neonatal visual evoked potentials as predictors of psychoeducational testing at age seven. *Developmental Psychology, 10*, 269–276.

Jensen, D., & Engel, R. (1971). Statistical procedures for relating dichotomous responses to maturation and EEG measurements. *Electroencephalography and Clinical Neurophysiology, 30*, 437–443.

Kraus, N., McGee, T., Micco, A., Sharma, A., Carrell, T., & Nicol, T. (1993). Mismatch negativity in school-age children to speech stimuli that are just perceptually different. *Journal of Electroencephalography and Clinical Neurophysiology: Evoked Potentials, 88*, 123–130.

Kuhl, P. K., & Miller, J. D. (1975). Speech perception by the chinchilla: The voiced-voiceless distinction in alveolar plosive consonants. *Science, 190*, 69–72.

Kuhl, P. K. & Miller, J. D. (1978). Speech perception by the chinchilla: Identification functions for synthetic VOT stimuli. *Journal of the Acoustical Society of America, 63*, 905–917.

Largo, R., Pfister, D., Molinari, L., Kundu, S., Lipp, A., & Duc, G. (1989). Significance of prenatal, perinatal and postnatal factors on the development of AGA preterm infants are five to seven years. *Developmental Medicine and Child Neurology, 4*, 440–456.

Liberman, A. M., Cooper, F. S., Shankweiler, D., & Studdert-Kennedy, M. (1967). Perception of the speech code. *Psychological Review, 74*, 431–461.

Longstreth, L., Davis, B., Carter, L., Flint, D., Owen, J., Rickert, M., & Taylor, E. (1981). Separation of home intellectual environment and maternal IQ as determinants of child IQ. *Developmental Psychology, 17*, 532–541.

Low, J., Galbraith, R., Muir, D., Broekhoven, L., Wilkinson, J., & Karchmar, E. (1985). The contribution of fetal-newborn complications to motor and cognitive deficits. *Developmental Medicine and Child Neurology, 27*, 578–587.

Maclean, M., Bryant, P., & Bradley, L. (1987). Rhymes, nursery rhymes, and reading in early childhood. *Merrill-Palmer Quarterly, 33*, 255–281.

McCarthy, D. (1972). *Manual for the McCarthy scales of children's abilities*. New York: Psychological Corporation.

Molfese, D. (1972). *Cerebral asymmetry in infants, children and adults: Auditory evoked responses to speech and music stimuli*. Unpublished doctoral dissertation, The Pennsylvania State University, University Park.

Molfese, D. (1978a). Electrophysiological correlates of categorical speech perception in adults. *Brain and Language, 5*, 25–35.

Molfese, D. (1978b). Left and right hemisphere involvement in speech perception: Electrophysiological correlates. *Perception and Psychophysics, 23*, 237–243.

Molfese, D. (1980). The phoneme and the engram: Electrophysiological evidence for the acoustic invariant in stop consonants. *Brain and Language, 9*, 372–376.

Molfese, D. (1983). Event related potentials and language processes. In A. Gaillard & W. Ritter (Eds.), *Tutorials in ERP Research - Endogenous components* (pp. 345–368). Holland: Elsevier.

Molfese, D. (1989a). Electrophysiological correlates of word meanings in 14-month-old human infants. *Developmental Neuropsychology, 5,* 79–103.

Molfese, D. (1989b). The use of auditory evoked responses recorded from newborns to predict later language skills. In N. Paul (Ed.), *Research in infant assessment* (Vol. 25). White Plains, NY: March of Dimes.

Molfese, D. (1993). *World geography knowledge as measured through evoked potentials.* Champaign, IL: Illinois Junior Academy of Science.

Molfese, D., Freeman, R., & Palermo, D. (1975). The ontogeny of lateralization for speech and nonspeech stimuli. *Brain and Language, 2,* 356–368.

Molfese, D., Gill, L., Simos, P., & Tan, A. (1995). Implications resulting from the use of biological techniques to assess development. In L. DiLalla & S. Clancy-Dollinger (Eds.), *Assessment of biological mechanisms across the life span* (pp. 173–190). Hillsdale, NJ: Lawrence Erlbaum Associates.

Molfese, D., & Hess, T. (1978). Speech perception in nursery school age children: Sex and hemisphere differences. *Journal of Experimental Child Psychology, 26,* 71–84.

Molfese, D, & Molfese, V. (1996, February). Brain responses discriminate learning from familiarity in adolescents. Paper presented at the meeting of the International Neuropsychological Society, Chicago, IL.

Molfese, D., & Molfese, V. (1979a). Hemisphere and stimulus differences as reflected in the cortical responses of newborn infants to speech stimuli. *Developmental Psychology, 15,* 505–511.

Molfese, D., & Molfese, V. (1979b). Infant speech perception: Learned or innate? In H. Witaker & H. Witaker (Eds.), *Advances in neurolinguistics,* (Vol. 4, pp. 225–240). New York: Academic Press.

Molfese, D., & Molfese, V. (1980). Cortical responses of preterm infants to phonetic and nonphonetic speech stimuli. *Developmental Psychology, 16,* 574–581.

Molfese, D., & Molfese, V. (1985). Electrophysiological indices of auditory discrimination in newborn infants: The bases for predicting later language development. *Infant Behavior and Development, 8,* 197–211.

Molfese, D., & Molfese, V. (1988). Right hemisphere responses from preschool children to temporal cues contained in speech and nonspeech materials: Electrophysiological correlates. *Brain and Language, 33,* 245–259.

Molfese, D., & Molfese, V. (1993). Predicting long-term development from electrophysiological measures taken at birth. In G. Dawson & K. Fischer (Eds.), *Human behavior and brain development* (pp. 493–517). New York: Guilford.

Molfese, D., & Molfese, V. (in press). Discrimination of language skills at five years-of-age using event related potentials recorded at birth. *Developmental Neuropsychology.*

Molfese, D., Morse, P., & Peters, C. (1990). Auditory evoked responses from infants to names for different objects: Cross modal processing as a basis for early language acquisition. *Developmental Psychology, 26,* 780–795.

Molfese, D. L. & Searock, K. (1986). The use of auditory evoked responses at one year of age to predict language skills at 3 years. *Australian Journal of Communication Disorders, 14,* 35–46.

Molfese, V. (1989). *Perinatal risk and infant development: Assessment and prediction.* New York: Guilford.

Molfese, V., & DiLalla, L. (1995). Cost effective approaches to identifying developmental delay in 4- to 7-year-old children. *Early Education and Development, 6,* 265–277.

Molfese, V., DiLalla, L., & Lovelace, L. (1996). Perinatal, home environment, and infant measures as successful predictors of preschool cognitive and verbal abilities. *International Journal of Behavioral Development, 18,* 103–120.

Molfese, V., Helwig, S., & Holcomb, L. (1993). Standardized assessment of verbal intelligence in three year old children: A comparison of biomedical and psychoeducational data in a longitudinal sample. *Journal of Psychoeducational Assessment, 11,* 56–66.

Molfese, V., & Thomson, B. (1985). Optimality versus complications: Assessing predictive values of perinatal scales. *Child Development, 56,* 810–823.

Morse, P. A., Molfese, D. L., Laughlin, N. K., Linnville, S., & Wetzel, F. (1987). Categorical perception for voicing contrasts in normal and lead-treated macaques: Electrophysiological indices. *Brain and Language, 30,* 63–80.

Murray, A. (1988). Newborn auditory brainstem evoked responses (ABRs): Longitudinal correlates in the first year. *Child Development, 59,* 1542–1554.

Murray, A., Dolby, R., Nation, R., & Thomas, D. (1981). Effects of epidural anesthesia on newborn and their mothers. *Child Development, 52,* 71–82.

Nelson, C., & Salapatek, P. (1986). Electrophysiological correlates of infant recognition memory. *Child Development, 57,* 1483–1497.

Olson, R., Forsberg, H., & Wise, B. (1994). Genes, environment, and the development of orthographic skills. In V. Berninger (Ed.), *The varieties of orthographic knowledge I: Theoretical and developmental issues* (pp. 27–71). Dordrecht, The Netherlands: Kluwer Academic.

Pisoni, D. B. (1977). Identification and discrimination of the relative onset time of two component tones: Implications for voicing perception in stops. *Journal of the Acoustical Society of America, 61,* 1352–1361.

Ross, G. (1985). Use of the Bayley Scales to characterize abilities of premature infants. *Child Development, 56,* 835–842.

Ruchkin, D., Sutton, S., Munson, R., & Macar, F. (1981). P300 and feedback provided by the absence of the stimuli. *Psychophysiology, 18,* 271–282.

Sameroff, A., Seifer, R., Barocas, R., Zax, M., & Greenspan, S. (1987). Intelligence quotient scores of 4-year-old children: Social-environmental risk scores. *Pediatrics, 79,* 343–350.

Scarborough, H. (1990). Very early language deficits in dyslexic children. *Child Development, 61,* 1728–1743.

Schaimberg, L., & Lee, C. (1991, April). *Predictors of verbal intelligence and behavioral problems among four-year-old children.* Paper presented at the Society for Research in Child Development, Seattle, WA.

Segalowitz, S., & Cohen, H. (1989). Right hemisphere EEG sensitivity to speech. *Brain and Language, 37,* 220– 231.

Sharma, A., Kraus, N., McGee, T., Carrell, T., & Nicol, T. (1993). Acoustic versus phonetic representation of speech as reflected by the mismatch negativity event-related potential. *Journal of Electroencephalography and Clinical Neurophysiology: Evoked Potentials, 88,* 64–71.

Siegel, L. (1982a). Reproductive, perinatal and environmental factors as predictors of the cognitive and language developments of preterm and full term infants. *Child Development, 53,* 963–973.

Siegel, L. (1982b). Reproductive, perinatal and environmental variables as predictors of development of preterm (< 1500 grams) and full term infants at 5 years. *Seminars and Perinatology, 6,* 274–279.

Siegel, L. (1985). Biological and environmental variables as predictors of intellectual functioning at 6 years of age. In S. Harel & N. Anastasjow (Eds.), *The at risk infant: Psychosocial medical aspects.* Baltimore: Brooks.

Siegel, L., & Faux, D. (1989). Acquisition of certain grapheme-phoneme correspondences in normally achieving and disabled readers. *Reading and Writing: An Interdisciplinary Journal, 1,* 37–52.

Silva, P., McGee, R., & Williams, S. (1984). A seven year follow-up study of the cognitive development of children who experienced common perinatal problems. *Australian Pediatric Journal, 20,* 23–28.

Smith, A., Flick, G., Ferriss, G., & Sellmann, A. (1972). Prediction of developmental outcome at seven years from prenatal, perinatal and postnatal events. *Child Development, 43,* 495–507.

Stanovich, K. (1988). The right and wrong places to look for the cognitive focus of reading disability. *Annals of Dyslexia, 38,* 175–190.

Stanovich, K., West, R., & Cunningham, A. (1991). Beyond phonological processes: Print exposure and orthographic processing. In S. Brady & D. Shankweiler (Eds.), *Phonological processes in literacy* (p. 141). Hillsdale, NJ: Lawrence Erlbaum Associates.

Stevens, K. N., & Klatt, D. H. (1974). Role of formant transitions in the voiced-voiceless distinction for stops. *Journal of the Acoustical Society of America, 55,* 653–659.

Vellutino, F., & Scanlon, D. (1987). Phonological coding: Phonological awareness, and reading ability: Evidence from a longitudinal and experimental study. *Merrill-Palmer Quarterly, 33,* 321–363.

Wagner, R., & Barker, T. (1994). The development of orthographic processing ability. In V. Berninger (Ed.), *The varieties of orthographic knowledge: I. Theoretical and developmental issues* (pp. 243–276). Dordrecht, The Netherlands: Kluwer Academic.

Wallace, I., Escalona, S., McCarton-Daum, D., & Vaughan, V. (1982). Neonatal precursors of cognitive development in low birthweight children. *Seminars in Perinatology, 6*, 327–333.

Wilson, R. (1985). Risk and resilience in early mental development. *Developmental Psychology, 21*, 795–805.

Yeates, K., MacPhee, D., Campbell, F., & Ramey, C. (1983). Maternal IQ and home environment as determinants of early childhood intellectual competence: A developmental analysis. *Developmental Psychology, 19*, 731–739.

6

Directed Reading and Writing Activities:
Aiming Instruction to Working Brain Systems

Virginia W. Berninger
Sylvia P. Abbott
Karen Greep
Elizabeth Reed
Leihua Sylvester
Carol Hooven
Amanda Clinton
Jared Taylor
Robert D. Abbott
University of Washington

Neuropsychology and school psychology are both increasingly turning their attention from an exclusive focus on assessment to a broader focus on assessment–treatment links and treatment. The purpose of this chapter is therefore to examine assessment–treatment links and treatment issues for reading and writing acquisition from a developmental neuropsychological perspective, which is relevant both to basic research on learning and development and to practice in clinic and school settings. In this chapter, we generally use *treatment*, which is the term found in the medical literature, to include *intervention*, which is the term found in the psychological and educational literature. However, treatment is a broad concept that can include medical, psychological, and educational interventions. Our focus is mainly on treatment that involves instructional interventions.

We begin by examining alternative models of brain–behavior relationships and discussing the implications of these models for treatment involving reading and writing instruction. We then define the developmental neuropsychological perspective, which adopts a systems approach to the brain and to interactions between the brain and the instructional environment, and contrast this perspective with a more traditional perspective on treatment. Although we compare the developmental neuropsychological and traditional approaches to treatment within the context of reading and writing, we offer general principles that may apply to treatment in other domains, as well. Next, we discuss measurement issues and recent methodological innovations in treatment research and illustrate how we have taken these into account in our recent research on treatment of reading and writing disabilities. Finally, we provide a representative, although not comprehensive, review of other current research on the treatment of reading and writing disabilities and speculate on how the systems perspective to treatment might be applied across the life span.

ALTERNATIVE MODELS OF BRAIN–BEHAVIOR RELATIONSHIPS

Localization of Function

In this model, a specific brain function is tied to a specific brain site. This model contrasts with the outdated view of mass action according to which any brain tissue can assume any function. Much of what is known about localization of function is based on postmortem clinicopathological studies: Pathological behavioral changes prior to death are correlated with pathological neuroanatomical findings after death. A classic example of applying this method to localize function is the work of Broca who identified the area in the left frontal lobe that is correlated with speech and was named after him. (See Kolb & Whishaw, 1990, for further discussion of localization of function.)

Working Brain Systems

In this model, multiple brain sites participate in a functional system and different functional systems draw on common and unique brain sites in the working brain. For example, both oral reading and written spelling activate brain sites associated with orthographic, phonological, semantic, and morphological coding, but only oral reading also activates brain sites involved in speech and only written spelling also activates brain sites involved in handwriting. Luria (1973) pioneered the clinical inferential method to study working brain systems. He compared performance on tasks that were thought, based on postmortem clinicopathological studies, to draw on particular brain sites. He looked for patterns in which task performance was only impaired when a particular brain site was involved and performance was not impaired when that brain site was not involved. In this way the bottleneck (single brain site) in a functional system that may draw on multiple brain sites could be identified. Luria also emphasized that functional systems reorganize across development and may draw on different brain sites at different stages of development.

Orchestration of Mind

In this model, multiple local sites distributed throughout the brain are orchestrated to perform a single function. The metaphor of the orchestra captures this functional organization: Each instrument contributes at a local level but local contributions are coordinated at a global level by the conductor (Posner, Petersen, Fox, & Raichle, 1988). This model, which combines localization of function and a systems approach, received empirical support from the in vivo imaging of live adults performing tasks. For example, Posner et al. (1988) applied positron emission tomography (PET) to identify the distributed local brain sites that are activated during recognition of spoken and written words, and Petersen, Fox, Posner, Mintun, and Raichle (1989) applied PET to identify the distributed local brain sites that are activated during oral and silent reading. Different patterns of local activation, that is, unique signatures, occurred for exposure to oral and written words and for oral and silent reading.

Society of Mind

In this model, the orchestration of the distributed local activity is not accomplished by a homunculus or little man in the head. Rather, the orchestration is accomplished by complex managerial systems. Minsky (1986) proposed three possible managerial systems. In one kind of managerial system, sequences of layers are created in which the new brain layers or societies learn to exploit the capabilities of previous layers. In yet another kind of managerial system, agents are wired to send inhibitory signals to other agents to avoid uncontrollable spreading activation. In another kind of managerial system, conflicts resulting from imposing incompatible functions on the same agencies simultaneously are sent to a higher level administrative system.

Minsky (1986) applied methods of artificial intelligence to theorizing about these managerial systems. For example, to account for how the young child learns to build with blocks, he proposed that the mind is built from many small agents or processes, each mindless, but when they communicate within a mental society, they function intelligently. An agent, which is a simple process that switches on or off, does not know anything, but the agency of which an agent is a member knows its job. At any moment of time each agent is either in a quiet or active state. A total state of mind specifies which agents are active and which are quiet at a particular moment in time.

Mental processes are, therefore, not only the result of sequential neural transmission across synapses of interconnected neurons but also the result of the constellation of the neural networks that happen to be firing at a particular moment of time. Communication occurs within a heterarchical organization; that is, an organization of multiple hierarchies. Communication occurs laterally and vertically within hierarchies and between hierarchies. Communication among the societies increases across development but is always indirect in terms of models they construct of one another.

Implications for Assessment–Treatment
Links in Reading and Writing

The localization of function model contrasts with the other models of brain–behavior relationships in that it is not a systems model. The localization model is concerned with correlating a single function with a single brain site independent of the functional system(s) in which that component function may be activated. Consequently, assessment–treatment links based on localization of function are assumed to be *isomorphic*; that is, related in a simple fashion in which there is one-to-one correspondence between brain and behavior. For example, if assessment identifies a dysfunction in phonological awareness, which is the ability to analyze sound patterns in spoken words, then the treatment plan focuses on training phonological awareness (segmenting spoken words into component sound segments).

In contrast, the systems models, which include working brain systems, orchestration of mind, and society of mind, do not imply simple isomorphic assessment–treatment links. Rather, complex interrelationships among functions in a working system must be considered. That is, designing a treatment plan for reading begins with a task analysis of all the component functions involved in the working reading system and then plans instruction directed to all those component functions, with special attention to those component functions shown to be relatively weak or deficient in pretreatment assessment. Likewise, designing a treatment plan for writing begins with a task analysis of all the component functions involved in the working writing system and then plans instruction directed to all those component functions, with special attention to those component functions shown to be relatively weak or deficient in pretreatment assessment. For example, if assessment identifies dysfunctional phonological awareness, treatment will include more than phonological awareness training. The treatment plan will also specify instruction for all the other component processes that must be activated in a fully functional reading or writing system.

Of the systems models, Luria's working brain and Posner and colleagues' orchestration of mind do not make different predictions about instructional interventions. However, Minsky's society of mind, with its emphasis on heterarchical systems, implies that additional systems beyond those specifically involved in reading and writing should be considered in instructional planning. For example, systems underlying executive functions, motivation, and affect that support the functioning of the reading and writing system are relevant (Berninger & Abbott, 1994a).

In summary, localization and systems models differ in their implications for instructional intervention. Whereas the localization of function model leads to a "skills in isolation" approach to remediation, the systems models lead to a *"skills in functional context"* approach in which all component processes in a working system, both functional and dysfunctional, are trained. The process remediation approach, which a large research literature (see Arter & Jenkins, 1979, for a review) showed is ineffective in achieving transfer to academic skills, may be ineffective because it is a skills in isolation approach. A systems approach with its focus on skills in functional context may be more effective because instruction is aimed at both the strengths and the weaknesses of the learner in creating functional systems for academic skills.

COMPARISON OF THE DEVELOPMENTAL NEUROPSYCHOLOGICAL AND TRADITIONAL APPROACHES TO TREATMENT

Defining the Developmental Neuropsychological Perspective

Functional reading and writing systems are not modules preformed in the infant brain waiting to be elicited by a specific kind of environmental stimulation at a particular time in maturation (Ellis, 1985, 1987; Wolf, 1991). Like oral language, which is constructed from and draws on nonlinguistic systems, for example, attentional, perceptual, cognitive, and so on. (Bates, 1993), the reading and writing systems are constructed from and draw on other systems (Berninger, 1994/1996; Berninger, Cartwright, Yates, Swanson, & Abbott, 1994; Ellis, 1985, 1987; Wolf, 1991).

Both the systems from which reading and writing are constructed and the resulting reading and writing systems are characterized by *normal variation*; that is, diversity not related to pathology (Berninger, 1994/1996). The resulting interindividual differences occur prior to and in response to instructional intervention. Interindividual differences also emerge as a consequence of the constructive processes of learners who use instructional cues in varying ways (Berninger & Abbott, 1992). Intraindividual differences emerge as a consequence of developmental dissociations or unevenness in rate of development of components of functional systems; these developmental dissociations offer a unique methodological window for functionally disconnecting components of functional systems that are normally interconnected (Berninger & Hart, 1992). An example of the developmental dissociations we routinely see in children referred to the Clinical Training Laboratory at the University of Washington for evaluation of learning disability is a second grade girl whose skills spanned the

1st to 99th percentiles. Her standard scores on Word Identification (66) and Word Attack (59) on the Woodcock Reading Mastery Test–Revised fell below the 1st percentile. Her score on the Modified Rosner Test of Phonological Processing was average (grade appropriate), but her score on the University of Washington Orthographic Coding Test (Berninger, Yates, & Lester, 1991) was more than 3 *SD* below the mean. Her Verbal IQ on the WISC–III was 131 (more than 2 *SD* above the mean).

Redundancy is a design feature of functional systems that allows knowledge and procedures to be represented in multiple ways and guards against breakdown of the system if one component malfunctions. As a result of the normal variation, the constructive processes of the learner, and the redundancy, alternative pathways may be followed across development to the same learning outcome. Because of the normal variation and the alternative pathways, the unit of analysis is critical in analyzing research results and data should be analyzed at both the individual and group levels (Berninger & Abbott, 1992).

According to the developmental neuropsychological perspective, the brain is a dynamic system that contributes to learning and development and is changed structurally and functionally as a consequence of learning and development. Analyzing response to treatment may further our understanding of brain–behavior relationships. However, it is important to keep in mind the different levels at which brain structures and functions can be analyzed in drawing conclusions. In general, conclusions should be restricted to the level of analysis at which the data were collected unless the research design explicitly examines and permits conclusions about relationships between different levels of analysis (e.g., neuroanatomical, physiological, and cognitive). Furthermore, there may be a critical developmental period after which learning is more difficult, but not impossible. Conclusions about brain–behavior relationships based on treatment studies should take into account whether treatment occurs before or after a critical period for a particular functional system. For further discussion of the developmental neuropsychological perspective, see Berninger (1994/1996) and Berninger and Hart (1992).

Constraints Versus Causality

Considering the multiple levels at which brain structures and functions can be contributing to learning and development and the bidirectional influences of the brain on the learning environment and the learning environment on the brain, unidimensional, unidirectional, and linear causal mechanisms, as assumed by traditional treatment research, are probably not operating in learning to read or write. Rather, multiple variables, including but not restricted to learner characteristics, the constructive processes of the learner, and instructional variables, probably exert constraints that limit degrees of freedom on the learning process, but do not cause learning independent of each other. (See Berninger, 1994/1996, for further discussion of this issue.)

Nonisomorphic Relationship Between
Causality and Treatment

In searching for the most effective instructional interventions, we do not necessarily need to know the antecedent causes (constraining influences). There is not necessarily just one treatment for each causal mechanism, as has often been the unexamined presupposition of traditional instructional research based on the diagnostic–prescriptive, or process remediation, model. There may be multiple causes of the same syndrome and multiple effective treatments for the same syndrome. These general principles hold for many medical conditions as well as for complex behavioral disorders.

Cystic fibrosis is an example of a medical condition where treatment is often not linked to what is understood about its causality. The causal agent is genetic. Although gene therapy is in the experimental stages, treatment is generally directed to the symptoms related to lung infections and gastrointestinal malabsorption. Upper respiratory infection is another example of treatment not being linked to causal mechanisms. Upper respiratory infections are caused by hundreds of various germs and possibly associated with stress, poor diet, inadequate rest, chilling, and so on. Treatment is seldom linked to laboratory test results in which the responsible biological agents are cultured. Rather treatment is supportive and aimed at symptomatic relief, such as reducing fever and nasal congestion.

Diabetes provides an example of a medical condition in which there are multiple causes for the same symptomatology and the same symptoms respond to multiple treatments. Diabetes results when the pancreas does not provide insulin for any of multiple reasons, including genetic defects or viral infections of the pancreas. Regardless of the cause, the patient has high blood sugar, which may be reduced in multiple ways. Insulin or other medications that increase release of insulin from the pancreas may be used. Alternatively, insulin resistance may be decreased through weight loss and exercise programs. At the same time, treatment must consider secondary complications, such as atherosclerosis or pancreatitis, if they arise, and thus adopt a systems approach of taking into account treatment effects on multiple components of the system.

These general principles can also be illustrated in reference to reading acquisition. If assessment shows that an 8 year-old child has a phonological processing problem, we can recommend phonological awareness training without documenting the cause of the inadequate phonological processing problems. Potential causes will vary from child to child and include structural anomalies of the brain structures involved in phonological processing (for review, see Berninger, 1994/1996), lack of appropriate developmental activities during the preschool years (e.g., parents or nursery school teachers reading nursery rhymes to the child and playing rhyming games with the child), or lack of appropriate instructional activities in the formal reading program in first and second grade (e.g., explicit instruction in how phonological units are represented in the orthography of the language).

Furthermore, different children with the same pretreatment assessment profile may respond differently to the same kind of intervention, as the following two cases illustrate. We evaluated a 9 year and 1 month, third-grade girl who was found to have disabilities in orthographic coding of the letter patterns in written words and in phonological coding of the sound patterns in spoken words (more than 3 *SD* below the mean for grade). As a result, her word recognition was severely impaired (less than 1st percentile on the Word Identification subtest of the WRMT-R). We also evaluated an 8 year and 6 month, second-grade boy whose pretreatment assessment profile was exactly the same as the girl's. For both children, who had average IQs and were in whole language programs at school, we recommended the Lindamood Auditory Analysis in Depth Program as the first step of the treatment plan. Both children received intensive phonological training from qualified professionals who were appropriately trained in the Lindamood methods.

The girl was a *treatment responder*. At the beginning of fifth grade, her phonological coding skills on the University of Washington Clinical Assessment of Writing Skills (Berninger, Cartwright, Yates, Swanson, & Abbott, 1994) and her Word Attack skills on the WRMT-R (standard score of 102) were grade-appropriate. However, her sight word vocabulary (standard score of 79 on Word Identification of WRMT-R) and reading comprehension (standard score of 72 on Passage Comprehension of WRMT-R) were still delayed for grade. We recommended as a second step in the intervention plan a balanced program with instruction in sight vocabulary and reading comprehension as well as integrated reading–writing to capitalize on this girl's emerging strength in composition. When evaluated at the end of sixth grade, she had maintained her grade-appropriate phonological and decoding skills and was now instructional at the sixth grade level in sight vocabulary and reading comprehension. However, orthographic coding problems, which had not been the target of the intervention plan, remained (more than 2 SD below the mean on the Colorado Perceptual Speed Test, see Berninger et al., 1994); and although she had overcome accuracy problems, she seemed to have rate problems (see Lovett, 1987).

The boy, on the other hand, was a *treatment nonresponder*. Lindamood training had to be terminated after 6 months because he made no progress and was becoming increasingly upset at his inability to understand the task requirements in this training program. A year and a half later, he can only recognize his first name and is still working on his last name; he has no other sight vocabulary or decoding skill. He is truly dyslexic in the sense of having "word blindness" and has not responded yet to a variety of other instructional techniques. But we are not giving up and will continue to implement and evaluate alternative instructional interventions until one is effective.

Single Versus Multiple Dimensions of Instructional Interventions

Not only learners, but also teachers and instructional methods exhibit normal variation. Instructional methods are not unidimensional constructs as is often assumed in traditional instructional research. Rather, they are multidimensional constructs with multiple components. Thus, instructional research should investigate the multiple components of instructional methods and the combination of these components that is most effective, as we are doing in our research program. Rarely do teachers implement the same instructional methods in exactly the same way (teacher interindividual differences) or in the same way all the time or with all children (teacher intraindividual differences). Monitoring fidelity of treatment implementation is important in instructional research, but it is also important to systematically investigate how and why teachers modify instructional methods to meet the needs of individual learners, as we did informally in prior research and plan to do more systematically in future research.

Creative Tension Between Science and Art in Treatment Research

On the one hand, the goal of science is to answer questions about causal (or constraining) mechanisms by keeping the treatment constant for each individual within a treatment group. This goal is met by designing experiments to address whether or not (a) the treatment is effective based on the means of the treatment group(s) and treated or untreated control group(s) on outcome measures, or (b) one treatment is reliably more effective than another treatment based on the means of the two (or more) treatment groups on outcome measures. The advantage of this approach is that one can demonstrate the reliability of treatment effects for the group as a whole and draw inferences about causality. The disadvantage of this approach is that inferences cannot be drawn about the effectiveness of the treatment(s) for individuals and rarely is the achievement of all participants raised to expected levels.

On the other hand, the goal of clinical intervention as art is to change the level of function of each individual from a low level to the level expected based on age, grade, or IQ. Accomplishing this goal usually requires individualization of treatment. For this goal, research might address what components of a comprehensive treatment plan need to be in place for an individual to reach the expected level(s) of function. This kind of research is in keeping with Bronfenbrenner's (1979) admonition that to really understand a process, one must be able to show that one can change that process. It is also in keeping with Brown's (1992) design experiments, modeled on the procedures of design sciences such as aeronautics and artificial intelligence, where the goal is to orchestrate all aspects of an environment to accomplish a prescribed function. In Brown's work, the environment is a classroom system in which it is impossible to change one part of the system without creating perturbations in other aspects of the system. An advantage of clinical intervention as art is that one can potentially achieve full remediation for all individuals. The disadvantage of the clinical intervention approach is that one cannot make inferences about which components of the instructional system exerted causal or constraining influences.

In designing and carrying out our intervention studies over the past 3 years, we gave a great deal of thought as to how one might reconcile this creative tension between science and art. (Also see Brown, 1992, for a fascinating account of how she struggled with the same issues over the course of her research career.) At best, we concluded that we must deal with this tension in the same way that physicists deal with the Heidenberg uncertainty principle (i.e., one can know where a particle is or how fast it is going but not both simultaneously). Likewise, there are trade-offs between causal inferences and changing complex behaviors during learning. One can pursue either but not both of these goals in a pure fashion in the same study. So, the aim of one line of our instructional research is to exert tight control over manipulated variables in order to draw causal inferences about the effects of single instructional components or logical combinations of these instructional components. In contrast, the aim of a second line of instructional research, some of which is reported later in this chapter, was to maximize the achievement of the individual learner even if that means departing from strict standardization procedures.

We try to achieve the optimal combination of standardization and individualization in the second line of research in the following manner. We use a standard lesson frame for all individuals within the group (see samples for our writing and integrated reading–writing tutorials in the appendix). However, *scaffolding*—instructional assistance tailored to the individual—is permitted as long as the tutor documents in writing the nature of the individualized assistance provided. Examples of scaffolding include repeating, clarifying, modeling, or elaborating when necessary. Another feature of these studies is that treatment protocols are designed, in keeping with the systems models of brain–behavior relationships discussed earlier, to provide intervention for many of the relevant components of a functional system. For example, treatment for word recognition includes interventions aimed toward both orthographic and phonological processing; treatment for reading includes interventions aimed at low-level word recognition and high-level comprehension; and treatment for writing includes interventions aimed at low-level handwriting and spelling and high-level planning, translating, reviewing, and revising. The appendix contains sample scripted lessons for integrated writing tutorials and for integrated reading–writing tutorials, also referred to as directed reading and writing activities.

MEASUREMENT ISSUES AND INNOVATIONS IN TREATMENT RESEARCH

Difference in Status at Given Times Versus Growth Over Time

For years, the prevailing position was that difference scores (gains over time) had limited usefulness because they were more unreliable than the scores on which they were based (Lord, 1956). Cronbach and Furby (1970) therefore recommended that hypotheses be tested in terms of educational status at a single point in time rather than as growth over time. Recently, however, methodologists (Collins & Horn, 1991; Francis, Fletcher, Stuebing, Davidson, & Thompson, 1991; Willett, 1988) showed that these perceived problems are more apparent than real and can be resolved if one views change over time as a separate dimension from stability of measures at one point in time.

Group as the Unit of Analysis Versus Individual as Unit of Analysis

An emerging perspective in the measurement of change is that data should first be "formed up" (analyzed) at the individual level before analyzing it for multiple individuals (e.g., Berninger & Abbott, 1992; Bryk & Raudenbush, 1987; Francis et al., 1991; Rogosa & Willett, 1985; Rogosa, Brandt, & Zimowski, 1992; Willett, 1988). This approach is best exemplified in hierarchical linear modeling in which analyses focus on describing the individual's observed growth trajectory in terms of individual parameters and on using those parameters as outcome measures to be explained by characteristics of the individual or treatment at the group level of analysis. Bryk and Raudenbush (1987) and Burchinal and Applebaum (1991) were optimistic that change can be measured reliably and validly if (a) change is conceptualized as individual growth, (b) tests are constructed that are reliable and valid both for status (given points in time) and rate of change for individuals (multiple points in time), and (c) individuals are sampled at more than two time points. Parameters that might be used in modeling growth include asymptote (final level for individual), rate of change, and rate of growth (change over at least three time points).

Static Versus Dynamic Assessment

The traditional approach to defining learning disabilities is to evaluate whether or not there is a significant discrepancy between ability, as assessed by an individually administered IQ test, and achievement, as assessed by an individually administered standardized achievement test in reading, writing, or math. Berninger and Abbott (1994b) argued that this approach, which utilizes static measures of ability and achievement, does not take into account opportunity to learn. Many children may underachieve in reading, writing, or math because of lack of adequate opportunity to learn: They have not received explicit instruction in these skills (because current educational practice in many schools favors incidental learning of basic skills within a meaning-oriented curriculum) or instruction that is matched to their individual profile of strengths and weaknesses. (See Berninger, 1994/1996, chap. 3, for further discussion of the educational constraints on learning to read and write.) Berninger and Abbott (1994b) proposed dynamic assessment in which response to systematic, short-term instruction is evaluated as an alternative to static assessment. Children who are treatment responders (e.g., the girl described earlier) may not have had adequate, appropriate instruction in their classroom. Children who are treatment nonresponders (e.g., the boy described earlier) probably have constitutionally based learning disabilities.

APPLYING THESE RECENT METHODOLOGICAL DEVELOPMENTS TO OUR TREATMENT RESEARCH

Word Recognition and Spelling

In Hart's dissertation research (Hart, Berninger, & Abbott, in press), 12 reading-disabled children aged 7 to 10 were randomly assigned to each of two treatments. At pretreatment assessment, the sample was, overall, about 2 SD below the mean on Word Identification and Word Attack on the WRMT–R and WRAT–R Spelling. Each child participated in 16 30-minute individualized tutorials within a 4-week interval. The treatments contrasted different processes thought to create the working brain systems for word recognition (see Berninger, 1994/1996, chap. 4, or Berninger & Abbott, 1994a for the theoretical model based on multiple orthographic-phonological code connections of corresponding size). The combined coding and phonics group received four sessions of just orthographic and phonological coding activities for written or spoken words, respectively, followed by four sessions in which they received concurrent orthographic and phonological coding training and phonics (letter–phoneme or letter cluster–phoneme connections). The multiple strategies group received only training in orthographic–phonological connections at different unit sizes: phonics (letter–phoneme or letter cluster–phoneme connections), word families (letter cluster–rime connections), and sight words (whole written word–name code connections). The comparison of interest was Sessions 5 to 8 for the combined coding and phonics group and Sessions 1 to 4 for the multiple strategies treatment group when actual reading instruction was first provided.

Results were analyzed at both the group and individual levels of analysis for the standard battery (administered at pretest, midtest, and posttest) and the probes administered in each session for each skill taught. The only significant effect at the group level was for the pseudoword probe. Although group differences did not exist in initial pseudoword probes (i.e., at intercept), the multiple strategies treatment group showed significantly faster individual growth in reading pseudoword probes than did the combined coding and phonics group. When individual growth curves within treatment groups were analyzed across all 16 sessions (both groups got the multiple strategies treatment during the last eight sessions), the same pattern of results was found. These results suggest that when children are taught orthographic–phonological mapping of different unit sizes, they are able to transfer this knowledge more quickly to novel words than are children who are given training in orthographic coding (segmenting written words in component units) and phonological coding (segmenting spoken words into component units) and in orthographic–phonological connections of a single unit size.

At the individual level of analysis, treatment responders were identified whose slope was significantly different from zero. When all the measures in the standard battery and the probes were considered, all children were treatment responders on some measures and none were treatment responders on all measures. Treatment responding was not an all or none phenomenon and fell along a continuum of treatment responding. This result suggests children's constructive processes for using the same instructional cues in varying ways will result in individual differences in response to the same instruction in word recognition.

However, pretreatment word recognition skills on the WRMT–R also predicted the slope of the individual growth curves. Both Word Identification and Word Attack at pretest predicted the slope of individual growth curves for sight words, suggesting that both word-specific and rule-governed mechanisms (Carr & Pollatsek, 1985) play a role in word recognition. Word Identification at pretest predicted the slope of growth curves for pseudoword reading probes, suggesting that knowledge of letter–sound relationships in known words may facilitate learning of decoding strategies for novel, unknown words. Word Attack at pretest predicted the slope of individual growth curves for word family probes, suggesting that knowledge of letter–sound relationships plays a role in generating word analogies (e.g., save, gave). In addition, orthographic coding at pretest predicted the slope of growth curves for sight word, pseudoword, and word family probes, and phonological (phoneme) coding at pretest predicted the slope of growth curves for sight words. Thus, not only the constructive processes of the learner but also the preexisting coding and word recognition systems play a role in developing the word recognition system further. The vocabulary subtest of the WISC–R, which is highly correlated with verbal IQ, did not predict the slope of any growth curve.

Wagner, Torgesen, and Rashotte (1994) showed the importance of partialing out the effect of a variable at a prior time on the same variable at a later time. Past behavior is often the best predictor of future behavior and this phenomenon is an autoregressive effect. The finding that Word Identification at pretest predicted the analogous sight word probes is an example of the autoregressive effect. Although Word Attack at pretest did not predict the analogous pseudoword probes, it did predict an aspect of the functional word recognition system—generation of words sharing a common rime unit (a linguistic term for the part of the syllable remaining after the onset phoneme or phonemes). Likewise, Word Identification at pretest predicted reading of pseudoword probes, a related aspect of the functional word recognition system. Thus, the autoregressive effect may hold not only for the same component of a functional working brain system but also for a related component of a functional working brain system. These findings show that the components of a working system are not orthogonal to one another and may become highly interconnected in the course of skill acquisition.

Handwriting

In Rutberg's dissertation research (Rutberg, Abbott, & Berninger, in preparation), 14 first graders (12 boys, 2 girls) who scored at or below –1 *SD* on handwriting measures on the University of Washington Clinical Assessment of Writing Skills Battery (Berninger, 1994) were randomly assigned to one of two treatment conditions. The combined group received five sessions of neurodevelopmental treatment followed by five sessions of academic treatment. The academic only group received 10 sessions of academic treatment. The neurodevelopmental treatment consisted of *motor-free orthographic coding activities* (e.g., spelling orally a briefly displayed written word or a letter or letter group in a designated position in that briefly displayed written word) *and orthographic-free motor activities* to reduce low tone, strengthen fingers, and promote kinesthetic awareness, prehension pattern, eye–hand coordination, and motor planning. The academic treatment consisted of instruction in forming the 26 alphabet letters using verbal mediation (self-talk to guide forming of each stroke in sequence), and automatization (copying letters from models with nonverbal arrows) for direction and sequencing of strokes.

The combined neurodevelopmental and academic training resulted in significantly faster individual growth on the verbal mediation probe. Ironically, the group who received less verbal mediation training did better on the verbal mediation probe. This finding is consistent with other reports in the literature on the negative effects of verbal mediation training on handwriting (see Graham, Harris, MacArthur, & Schwartz, 1991). The combined training also resulted in marginally significant faster individual growth on the alphabet task (accuracy), which was not trained. In contrast to the combined treatment, which had beneficial effects on accuracy measures, the academic only treatment resulted in significantly faster individual growth on three probe measures (automaticity of letter speed, written language speed, and speed of writing alphabet from memory) and one standard battery measure (Woodcock Johnson Psychoeducational Battery–Revised Writing Fluency) involving speed. These results show that different treatments can have differential effects on components of a working system and on the accuracy versus speed of those components.

Handwriting, Spelling, and Composition

Berninger, Abbott, Whitaker, Sylvester, and Nolen (1995) investigated the effects of short-term treatment for writing disabilities in the summer between third and fourth grade. Thirty-nine children referred by their teachers for writing problems were randomly assigned to one of two treatment groups (*n* = 12 each) or an untreated control group (*n* = 15). The treatment was aimed at both low-level and high-level skills and integrating them within a systems approach. Both treatment groups received the following in each of 14 1-hour individual sessions: handwriting warm-up (10 min), spelling (15 min), and composition (20 min). (see appendix). The more composing treatment group also had extra practice in composition (15 min).

The coding treatment group also had training in orthographic and phonological coding (15 min).

Compared to the control group, individuals in the combined treatment groups showed faster individual growth on the alphabet task, phoneme task, and the compositional task (on both fluency and quality). When only those at risk for spelling (at or below –1 SD) were included, individuals in the combined treatment groups also showed faster individual growth than the control group on WRAT–R spelling. The treatment group who had extra practice in composition showed faster individual growth in speed of copying sentences than the treatment group who had coding training; but the treatment group who had coding training showed faster individual growth in the orthographic imaging strategy for spelling than did the more composing treatment group.

Treatment responding was also analyzed at the individual level. Individual treatment responding (slopes significantly different from zero) again fell along a continuum, as in the Hart et al. (in press) study on word recognition. No child was a treatment responder on all learning outcome measures but all were treatment responders on some learning outcome measures. The results show that individual differences occur in response to the same treatment, presumably because of the constructive processes of the learner. Children use the same instructional cues in varying ways to create functional systems. None of the measures in the standardized battery given at pretest, which included WISC–R verbal IQ, phonological coding, orthographic coding, the alphabet task, WRAT–R spelling, and compositional tasks, predicted growth curves for handwriting, spelling, or compositional probes for this short-term intervention. This finding provides additional support for the constructive processes of the learner, independent of preexisting skills, in the rate of constructing functional systems.

Orthographic and Phonological Coding Training, Word Recognition, Comprehension, Handwriting, Spelling, and Composition

Twenty children were referred by teachers at the end of first grade because they were struggling in reading. All were from first-grade instructional programs that were primarily whole language in orientation, although some were exposed to phonics in Chapter 1 pull-out programs. All were low functioning in reading on standardized tests (more than 1 SD below the mean on Word Identification or Word Attack on the WRMT–R) or were underachieving in reading (more than 1 SD between their score in Word Identification or Word Attack and their WISC–III verbal IQ). The mean verbal IQ was 106 (SD = 14). Their instructional level on the Qualitative Reading Inventory was preprimer (85%) or primer (15%), that is beginning or mid-first grade, respectively.

The 20 children participated in an average of 14.35 1-hour individual tutorials during the summer between first and second grade. Berninger wrote the standard, scripted lessons that included instruction in orthographic and phonological coding, phonics based on a connectionist framework, contextual reading to promote decoding and fluency, comprehension (question answering and story retell), handwriting automaticity, spelling (based on five orders of letter–sound predictability in Venezky's fluency metric, Venezky, 1995), and composition (see appendix). The rationale was that development of the functional reading system might benefit from development of the functional writing system. Children progressed through these lessons at their own rate. The individual tutoring was provided by the second through eighth authors. The goal of the tutoring was to provide a balance between decontextualized decoding skills and contextualized reading for meaning in order to help children achieve at grade level or their expected level based on verbal IQ. From a working brain systems perspective, instruction was directed to both the decoding and comprehension components of the functional reading system. Sixteen of the children continued to participate in the tutorial program 1 hour a week during second grade. The standard lessons during second grade introduced instruction in sight word and word families.

Here we report the results for (a) the pretreatment assessment, (b) treatment outcome for the summer and year-long tutorials based on traditional pretest–posttest comparisons and first one half of second grade based on growth curves, and (c) pretreatment assessment–treatment outcome links. The pretreatment assessment results support Wolf and Bower's double deficit hypothesis (e.g., Bowers & Wolf, 1993a) rather than the phonological core deficit hypothesis (Stanovich, 1988). Deficits were defined as performance at or below –1 SD on measures in the standard battery given prior to treatment. None of the children had a single deficit only in phonological coding as measured by a phoneme deletion task. Five had a *single deficit* (two in orthographic coding, using measures from Berninger, Yates, & Lester, 1991; three in rapid automatized naming, using measures from Wolf, Bally, & Morris, 1986). Eleven had a *double deficit* (10 in orthographic coding and rapid automatized naming; one in orthographic and phonological coding). Two had a *triple deficit* (in orthographic and phonological coding and rapid automatized naming). Two had no deficits in orthographic or phonological coding or rapid automatized naming, suggesting that learner characteristics are not the only source of reading failure.

Further research is needed to determine whether or not this pattern of deficits is related to whole language instruction; perhaps more phonological coding problems are found in children who fail in primarily phonics-oriented reading programs. In prior research in which our samples included more children from basic skills programs that emphasized phonics, we found more phonological coding problems and more cases of double deficits in orthographic and phonological coding (see Berninger & Abbott, 1994a).

Results also supported Bowers and Wolf's (1993b) contention that there is a relationship between orthographic coding and naming. Deficits in orthographic coding were more likely to be associated with deficits in rapid automatized naming (RAN) than were deficits in RAN to be associated with deficits in orthographic coding. If a deficit occurred in letter cluster coding ($n = 6$), the probability of a RAN deficit was .67; if a deficit occurred in whole printed word coding ($n = 8$), the probability of a RAN deficit was .75. However, if a deficit occurred in RAN ($n = 15$), the probability of a letter cluster deficit was .33 and the probability of a whole printed word deficit was .40.

The results also supported the multiple connections model (Berninger, 1994/1996) in that none of these poor readers had all three of the ortho-graphic–phonological code connections underlying beginning reading that we measured: eight had two; eight had one; and four had none. Of the 20 children, 19 had a dysfunctional whole printed word–whole spoken word connection, 9 had a dysfunctional letter–phoneme connection, and 8 had a dysfunctional letter cluster–syllable connection.

The double deficit and multiple connections models are not incompatible. Both predict that the name code for whole spoken words is important in learning to read. Wolf, Pfeil, Lotz, and Biddle (1994) emphasized that naming tasks tap temporal mechanisms involved in coordinating ortho-graphic and phonological codes. On a RAN task the phonological code a child has to activate is a whole word name code (segmental phones embedded in suprasegmental intonational contour) rather than component phonemes; that name code has to be mapped onto an orthographic code for a letter, number, or visual representation of a color. In reading a printed word, a whole word name code has to be mapped onto an orthographic code for a whole written word.

The speed and precision of this mapping process may depend on how well the other letter–sound connections (e.g., letter–phoneme, letter cluster–phoneme or rime) are represented in memory for specific words. Nevertheless we agree with Perfetti's (1992) position, which is supported by data reported in Berninger (1989): "The heart of lexical access is the activation of a phonologically referenced name code. Although this assumption does not appear to be universally shared, it should be without contention" (pp. 164–165).

Likewise, Ehri and Saltmarsh (1995) showed that disabled readers differ from normal readers in the quality of lexical-level representations in memory. It follows that reading involves more than discovering the alphabet principle of the relationship between letters and phonemes. It also involves access to name codes and coordination of name and other codes. Put another way, the oral language system must be coordinated at multiple levels of phonology with the reading system.

Comparison of scores before and after treatment, as in traditional data analysis, indicated that the reading–writing tutorial was effective, but moreso over a 1-year interval than 2-month interval. Growth curves over a 7-month interval also indicated that the reading tutorial was effective. To date, five kinds of data analyses have been performed.

First, a traditional approach was used to evaluate status before treatment at the end of first grade and then again at the end of summer after

TABLE 6.1
Pre- and Posttest Measures for 2-month Summer Tutorial ($N = 20$)

	End First Grade		Beginning Second Grade	
	M	SD	M	SD
Phoneme deletion	12.7	3.6	15.2	3.9
Whole word orthographic coding	76.2%	11.2	79.6%	9.9
Word identification	25.0	9.8	31.8	6.6
Word attack	7.0	4.0	14.6	4.9
QRI word recognition in isolation	0.4[a]	0.5	1.0[b]	0.9
QRI word recognition in context	0.1[a]	0.22	1.0[b]	1.0
Alphabet task	3.4	1.5	4.8	2.1

[a]preprimer (beginning 1st). [b]primer (mid 1st).

approximately 2 months of treatment. Correlated t tests were used because only two data points were available by then. The means and the standard deviations for the measures that improved are reported in Table 6.1.

Phoneme deletion improved from pretest to posttest, $t(19) = -2.494, p = .022$. Whole word orthographic coding improved marginally, $t(19) = -1.905$, $p = .072$; letter and letter cluster coding were not measured at the end of the summer because of time constraints. No improvement was found in the RAN tasks that were readministered (letters and numbers and letters only). Raw scores on the WRMT–R Word Identification, $t(19) = -15.115, p < .001$, and Word Attack, $t(19) = -7.673, p < .001$, improved. Instructional levels on the Qualitative Reading Inventory (coded 0 for preprimer, 1 for primer, and 2 for the end of first) improved for both word recognition in isolation, $t(19) = -3.584, p = .002$, and for oral reading in context, $t(19) = -4.414, p < .001$.

The number of letters produced in the first 15 seconds on the alphabet task, which is the best predictor of beginning handwriting and composition skills (Berninger, 1994/1996), improved, $t(19) = -2.964, p = .008$. These gains appeared to be related to improved retrieval of letter forms from memory rather than to improved motor production as there was no significant improvement on the copy task, a pure production task with no memory retrieval requirements. No significant improvement was found in WRAT–R spelling or compositional fluency (number of words produced in 5 min). Thus, with the exception of the alphabet task, children benefited most from the instruction in reading and less from the instruction in writing, a finding that raised the issue of how interconnected are the functional reading and writing systems initially or in readers of differing ability. Although the benefits of the integrated reading and writing instruction are generally touted, this educational practice may benefit normal readers more than disabled readers.

Second, changes on probes administered in instructional sessions were evaluated for the first six lessons completed by all students by the end of the summer. A repeated measures ANOVA on the phonological coding probes (sound games in the sample lesson in appendix) yielded a significant main effect, $F(5, 95) = 4.16$, $p < .0018$, $MSE = 478.42$; follow-up decomposition yielded a linear trend in the predicted direction, $F(1, 95) = 3.541$, $p < .0629$. It may have missed conventional significance, because 4 of the 20 subjects scored 0% on the fifth lesson resulting in a significant cubic component to the trend, $F(1, 95) = 12.50$, $p < .0006$. A repeated measures ANOVA indicated that the means on the orthographic probes (looking games in the sample lesson in appendix) were significantly different, $F(5, 95) = 9.141$, $p < .0001$, $MSE = 468.00$; follow-up decomposition yielded a significant linear trend, $F(1, 95) = 18.67$, $p < .001$. The comprehension checks seemed effective in inducing a set for meaning. Accuracy on the first frame (59.6%, $SD = 20.0$) was significantly below that on the subsequent four frames (range 83.2%–89.0%), $F(1, 76) = 75.573$, $p < .001$. Even though children were given assistance in word recognition to help them comprehend the passages, for some it was the first time they could read an entire passage and make sense of it. From a systems perspective, maintaining a set for meaning is important as children learn to map print onto sound to decode and recognize individual words.

Fluency was evaluated on the basis of change in accuracy or speed of probes for the first and second reading of the same passage; the means and standard deviations are reported in Table 6.2. The repeated readings had some effect on improved *accuracy* (passage 1, $t(19) = -.745$, ns; passage 2, $t(19) = -3.414$, $p = .003$; passage 3, $t(19) = -2.003$, $p = .06$) but consistent effect on improved *rate of words read per second* (passage 1, $t(19) = -2.477$, $p = .023$; passage 2, $t(19) = -3.414$, $p = .003$; passage 3, $t(19) = -3.574$, $p = .002$). Significant gains were found for spelling *order 0 words* (sounds map onto single letters and have conventional sounds associated with them) across practice trials: set 3 (mean number of words spelled correctly improved from 7.4 to 9.0), $t(19) = -3.310$, $p = .004$; set four (mean number of words spelled correctly improved from 6.9 to 8.2), $t(19) = -3.327$, $p = .004$) but not for spelling *order 1 words* (sounds map onto spelling units larger than a single letter, see Venezky, 1995).

Third, R. Abbott computed growth curves for the two measures (WRMT–R Word Identification and Word Attack) for which three data points were available at the middle of second grade. Table 6.3 describes the growth

TABLE 6.2
Accuracy (% Correct) and Words/Seconds for Rereadings of Same Passage

	First Reading		Second Reading	
	Accuracy	*Time*	*Accuracy*	*Time*
Passage 1	75.7	0.61	79.1	0.68
Passage 2	70.4	0.58	81.0	0.60
Passage 3	80.1	0.50	84.2	0.72

TABLE 6.3
Growth Curves (End 1st, Beginning 2nd, Mid 2nd) for Word Identification

Y' =	24.63 (mean of first testing) + 8.00 (time)	
SE	2.1638	1.2206
t	11.37	6.55
p	< .001	< .001
reliability	.877	.768

Note. Time was coded 0 (1st session), 1 (2nd session), and 2 (3rd session).

Treatment responders (b > or = 2.5 s.e.: 15 of 20)

Treatment nonresponders (b < 2.5 s.e.: 5 of 20)

Slope of Individual Growth Curves Predicted by		
	t	p
WISC–III Verbal IQ	2.218	< .04
WIAT listening comprehension	0.7742	< .295
RAN	1.742	< .089
Orthographic (whole word, letter, and letter cluster)	0.745	< .294
Phonological (phoneme deletion)	1.048	< .223

curve equation for Word Identification and Table 6.4 describes the growth curve equation for Word Attack based on the 20 children who participated in the summer tutorial and the 16 children who continued throughout second grade. These growth curves, which are both statistically significant (see t and p values in Tables 6.3 and 6.4), will be used in future tutorial studies to evaluate whether or not individual children are treatment responders or treatment nonresponders when adequate instruction in orthographic and phonological coding and multiple orthographic–phonological code connections is provided, as proposed by Berninger and Abbott (1994b).

Individual treatment responders (children whose slopes were significantly different from zero) were identified for the summer tutorial. Of the 20 children, 75% were treatment responders on Word Identification (see Table 6.3) and 80% were treatment responders on Word Attack (see Table 6.4). For both Word Identification and Word Attack, three of the treatment nonresponders included three of the four children who did not continue in the study during second grade. Had they continued, they may have been treatment responders. One child was a treatment responder for Word Identification but not for Word Attack and one child was a treatment responder for Word Attack but not for Word Identification.

Fourth, R. Abbott also examined the links between pretreatment assessment and response to treatment, as measured by the growth curves. As can be seen in Table 6.3, listening comprehension, RAN, orthographic coding, and phoneme coding did not predict the slope of growth curves for Word Identification from the end of first grade to the middle of second grade.

However, verbal IQ did, perhaps because verbal IQ is highly correlated with vocabulary knowledge, which may facilitate word-specific learning of written words. Only RAN was marginally significant, in keeping with the prediction that coordination of name codes and orthographic codes play a role in recognition of sight words. As can be seen in Table 6.4, none of the pretest measures predicted the slope of growth curves for WRMT–R Word Attack. Only phoneme coding is marginally significant, in keeping with the prediction that phonological segmentation is predictive of word attack skills for novel words.

Taken together, these results do not suggest that clinicians or reading researchers should eliminate from their batteries any of these measures, which have been validated for concurrent assessment of level of reading achievement in many studies over the years. Rather, these results suggest that these measures may predict level of achievement but do not predict rate of change or growth of the functional reading system over short intervals of time. Level of performance and rate of acquisition are different dimensions of functional systems.

These patterns of results may change when we consider individual growth from the end of first grade to the end of second grade. Functional systems reorganize over development and different patterns of relationships may emerge over a 12-month rather than a 7-month interval. Growth curve analyses for all dependent measures in the standard battery given at least three times and for all probes in each instructional session are in progress.

TABLE 6.4
Growth Curves (End 1st, Beginning 2nd, Mid 2nd) for Word Attack

$Y' =$	7.725 (mean of first testing) + 5.425 (time)	
SE	.9983	1.006
t	7.738	5.39
$p < .001$	< .001	< .001
reliability	.410	.652

Note. Time was coded 0 (1st session), 1 (2nd session), and 2 (3rd session).

Treatment Responders (b > or = 2.5 s.e.: 16 of 20)

Treatment Nonresponders (b < 2.5 s.e.: 4 of 20)

Slope of Individual Growth Curves Predicted By		
	t	p
WISC-III Verbal IQ	1.407	< .145
WIAT Listening Comprehension	0.963	< .243
RAN	0.767	< .289
Orthographic (whole word, letter, and letter cluster)	0.051	< .392
Phonological (phoneme deletion)	1.803	< .081

Finally, correlated t tests were used to evaluate change in status from the end of first grade prior to tutoring to the end of second grade at the termination of tutoring. Table 6.5 reports the means and standard deviations at pretest and posttest for the 16 children who remained in the study until it was completed and the t and p values. At completion of the study, all WRMT–R mean standard scores, which were in the low average range at pretest, were in the average range and QRI mean instructional levels for word recognition in isolation and in context, which were at a beginning first-grade level at pretest, were grade appropriate at the second-grade level.

All t tests were significant except for syllable deletion (for which there were ceiling effects at pretest) and the standard WRAT–R spelling scores. The findings that the age-corrected standard scores for both Word Identification and Word Attack statistically improved are important because they show that the learning outcome after tutoring was higher than expected solely on the basis of age-related maturation. Taken together, these findings show that a systems approach to instruction can lead to reliable improvement in level of achievement of nearly all relevant skills in a functional system. How the systems approach affects rate of growth awaits the results of the growth curve analyses over 12 months. However, further research using a control group is needed because we do not know how much of this improvement, achieved with a design experiment (Brown, 1992), is due to our instructional intervention, the classroom instruction children received during the regular school year, or regression to the mean.

This sample was below the mean on most pretest battery measures but not in the at-risk category (at or below –1 SD) except for rapid automatized naming (both letters and switching between letters and digits). By posttest 1 year later, the group as a whole was no longer in the at-risk category for rapid naming of letters (category constant) but was still in the at-risk category for RAN of letters and digits (category switches). This persisting problem in switching attention may explain why some individuals, even though their accuracy and speed improved dramatically, still sounded dysfluent at times, stumbling from word to word in connected text.

Although neither verbal IQ nor WIAT Listening Comprehension was correlated with any of the dependent measures in Table 6.5 at pretest, at posttest, verbal IQ was correlated with the Word Identification standard score ($p = .038$), the Word Attack standard score ($p = .012$), and the Word Attack raw score ($p = .034$). These findings coupled with the results of our other intervention studies suggest that verbal IQ is a better predictor of response to long-term than short-term intervention. Listening Comprehension does not appear to be a better measure than IQ for initial diagnosis of learning disability or for prediction of response to intervention.

REPRESENTATIVE TREATMENT STUDIES
IN PROGRESS IN OTHER RESEARCH GROUPS

Although other reading and writing researchers have not explicitly adopted a systems approach, their findings make sense within the context of the

TABLE 6.5
Pre- and Post-Test Measures for 12-month Tutorial (N = 16)

	End 1st		End 2nd			
	M	SD	M	SD	t	p
Word Identification						
Raw score	23.7	10.1	49.3	7.6	10.0	.001
Standard score	89.4	9.5	94.6	9.7	2.1	.054
Word attack						
Raw score	6.6	4.0	23.3	4.7	12.5	.001
Standard score	88.9	8.6	99.9	6.4	5.7	.001
Passage comprehension						
Raw score	8.7	5.6	28.3	5.4	18.2	.001
Standard score	84.9	8.1	97.6	9.3	7.6	.001
WRAT-R spelling						
Raw score	25.4	6.9	33.2	2.8	10.3	.001
Standard score	86.5	8.1	87.0	8.5	0.3	.778
QRI word recognition						
In isolation	0.3[a]	0.5	3.1[b]	1.1	11.0	.001
In context	0.1[a]	0.2	3.4[b]	1.1	13.2	.001
Rapid automatized Naming (sec.)						
Letters	52.1[c]	15.8	36.4	7.4	13.1	.001
Letters and numbers	64.1[c]	17.5	50.9[c]	13.6	13.8	.002
Phonological deletion						
Syllables	9.4	1.5	9.3	1.1	0.4	.684
Phonemes	12.2	3.3	17.0	2.6	5.5	.001
Phoneme localization	5.0	2.3	7.5	1.9	3.5	.003
Orthographic coding						
Whole word	75.6	10.6	92.9	6.4	7.4	.001
Letter in word	75.5	9.6	84.4	9.3	3.2	.006
Letter cluster in word	65.4	9.4	78.2	10.3	4.2	.001
Alphabet task						
First 15 sec.	3.1	1.4	8.1	2.7	8.4	.001
Total accuracy	19.8	6.2	24.9	1.7	3.5	.003
Total time (sec.)	121	48.4	64.3	22.2	3.9	.001
Composition						
Number words	18.8	7.7	31.0	11.9	4.2	.001

[a]preprimer (beginning first-grade level). [b]second-grade level. [c]at risk for grade.

Note. The sign of the *t* test was negative for all measures except RAN and alphabet task measures involving time.

systems perspective we discuss in this chapter. We provide a representative sampling of these findings.

Foorman, Francis, and Fletcher (1995) are conducting a number of large, school-based studies comparing alternative interventions for children with or at risk for developing reading disabilities. In one study, 108 second and third graders with reading disabilities received 1 hour a day of instruction from a special educator in a synthetic phonics program, a synthetic–analytic phonics program, or a sight word program. Individual growth curve analyses revealed superiority of sight word training over synthetic–analytic phonics in level of orthographic processing and word reading, and superiority of synthetic phonics over sight word training in level of phonological processing. Thus, different methods exerted beneficial effects on different components of the functional reading system.

Torgesen and Hecht (1996) reported results from a large-scale longitudinal study and a large intervention program (in schools and a clinic) conducted with their colleague, Wagner. Path analysis in the longitudinal study showed that only phonological analysis (e.g., phoneme segmentation) and word reading (an autoregression effect) in kindergarten had significant paths to word reading (based on WRMT–R Word Identification and Word Attack) in first grade; other predictor variables in the path analysis included home environment, phonological synthesis, teacher ratings, verbal intelligence, concepts of print, and letter knowledge. These findings suggest that the developing reading system draws on the existing reading system (autoregressive effect) and the related phonological system.

In the treatment study, kindergartners who were low in phonological skills were randomly assigned to four treatment conditions: (a) phonological awareness training plus synthetic phonics instruction (PASS); (b) phonological awareness training plus phonics instruction embedded in reading and spelling activities (EP); (c) instructional support to meet goals of the regular reading program (RCS); and (d) an untreated control condition. At mid-first grade, the PASS, EP, and RCS treatment groups did not differ in Word Identification (reading real words), but the PASS group was significantly better than the EP or RCS groups on Word Attack (reading pseudowords). The RCS, PASS, and EP groups were better on both Word Identification and Word Attack than the control group. In addition to these group effects, individual differences in response to these treatments were noted.

These treatment findings illustrate several aspects of a systems approach. First, because the resources of the system can be orchestrated in different ways to achieve the same goal, different methods may be equally effective, as was the case for PASS, EP, and RCS in improving the reading of real words. Second, different instructional methods may exert differential effects on components of a functional system, as was the case for synthetic phonics that exerted a relative advantage on reading novel pseudowords but not real words. Third, individual children may respond differently to the same treatment, probably because of the constructive processes of learners who use the same instructional cues in varying ways to construct or expand functional systems. Finally, the pattern of results may change as the investigators continue to follow these children during the ongoing intervention study. From a systems perspective, functional systems reorganize over the course of development.

Wise and Olson (e.g., 1995) have a systematic line of research in which they use talking computers to remediate the word recognition component of reading disabilities. Their program, Reading with Orthographic and Segmented Speech (ROSS), is designed to provide speech feedback and decoding assistance with unknown words children encounter while reading stories. When children signal they need assistance, the program highlights the written word as a whole, in syllables, or in subsyllabic segments and then pronounces the word at the corresponding whole word, syllable or subsyllable level. Their work showed that feedback improves word recognition, but the size of the segmentation unit does not exert an effect—whole word feedback does as well as segmented feedback. Levy and Lysynchuk (1995) reported a similar finding for noncomputerized teacher feedback during beginning reading instruction. These findings make sense in the context of a reading system that is designed to create orthographic–phonological links at different segment sizes (see Berninger, 1994/1996).

Recently Wise and Olson (1995) extended this work. They compared the performance of 45 children (PA group) who received phonological awareness training designed to improve awareness of the sound structure of words plus ROSS training with that of 58 children (RT group) who received Palinscar and Brown's (1984) reciprocal teaching designed to improve comprehension plus ROSS training. Children spanned the second to fifth grades and were on average 8.9 years old. The PA group gained more than the RT group on untimed tests of phoneme awareness, word recognition (accuracy), and pseudoword reading. The RT group gained more than the PA group on comprehension and on time-limited word recognition. Again, this finding makes sense in the context of a multicomponent reading system. Different instructional methods exert differential effects on different components of the functional reading system.

Vellutino and Scanlon's (1994) early intervention program to prevent reading problems is another example of a systems approach to reading instruction. Children who are struggling in the first-grade reading program are identified and one-to-one tutoring is begun in the middle of first grade and continued until the end of first grade. The tutorial includes the following components but the emphasis varies depending on the child, in keeping with a systems approach: (a) prereading of connected text; (b) recognition and production of alphabet letters, phonological awareness, letter–sound knowledge; and (c) reading connected text (decoding in context). Children who are remediation resistant (i.e., the treatment nonresponders) continue from the beginning to the middle of second grade. At the end of first grade, fewer children were below the 10th percentile (4%) and more were above the 40th percentile (47%) in the tutored group ($n = 76$) than in an untutored contrast group ($n = 42$; 17% below the 10th percentile; 40% above the 40th percentile). By the middle of second grade, none of the tutored children were below the 10th percentile in reading.

Henry (1989) compared three groups of third- and fifth-grade students: (a) controls (n = 97) who received traditional basal reading and spelling instruction; (b) Project READ (Calfee & Henry, 1985) (n = 182) who received supplementary training in vocabulary development and word and sentence structure including syllable patterns and morpheme patterns (prefixes, suffixes, and roots); and (c) Project READ PLUS (n = 164) who got READ plus letter–sound decoding instruction. In general, the READ PLUS group made the largest gains in tests of letter–sound knowledge, syllable and morpheme patterns, and reading–spelling, as would be predicted by a systems model because this group received the instruction directed to the most components of the functional reading system.

Lovett et al. (1994) compared three treatments for dyslexic children who on the average scored at the 3.7th percentile on the WRMT–R Word Identification subtest and at the 3.2nd percentile on the WRMT–R Word Attack subtest. These treatments included: (a) phonological analysis and blending and direct instruction in letter–sound correspondence; (b) four metacognitive strategies for word decoding (identifying words by analogy, seeking the known part of the word, attempting alternative vowel pronunciations, and removing prefixes and affixes in multisyllabic words); and (c) study skills training, which served as a contact control condition. The first treatment taps primarily rule-based learning, whereas the second treatment taps primarily instance or exemplar learning (see Lovett et al., 1994; also Carr & Pollatsek, 1985).

As predicted by a systems model, both training approaches resulted in positive effects because there is more than one way to utilize component processes to achieve a common function and each training approach exerted a differential effect because different methods affect different components of the system. Lovett et al. (1994) found that the phonological treatment exerted its greatest effect on phonological measures and that the multiple strategies treatment exerted its greatest effect on learning of real words. Likewise, Lovett et al. (1996) compared two comprehension treatments—remediation of deficient knowledge base and Palincsar and Brown's (1984) reciprocal teaching and found both were effective, but that each exerted differential effects on outcome measures.

Graham and Harris (1989) developed a research paradigm for writing intervention research that can also be applied to reading intervention research to tease apart the contribution of the multiple components of instructional interventions. First, an intervention is task analyzed into its multiple components. Then children are randomly assigned to experimental conditions that consist of a single component or of a combination of the single components. Results are analyzed to determine whether a single component or a combination of components is most effective. Just because components of a functional system are interconnected it does not mean that we cannot with carefully designed instructional experiments draw inferences about the mechanisms operating in the teaching–learning process.

A LIFE-SPAN APPROACH TO TREATMENT RESEARCH

Carr and Posner (1996) reviewed what is known about the neuroanatomical correlates of the functional reading system in adults and speculated on the implications of these for the learning process. They acknowledged the paucity of neurological evidence for children and the developing reading system. Yet, it is a step forward to begin to theorize about reading development across the life span.

Most of what we know about skilled reading is based on college educated adults who provide a ready population for researchers. Yet, adult reading cannot be equated with skilled reading. Position in the developmental life span and level of skill attainment are not synonymous concepts. Cutting-edge research in adult reading is no longer restricted to skilled readers who are highly educated. For example, through the National Center on Adult Literacy (NCAL) based at the University of Pennsylvania, adult literacy is being investigated in a broad spectrum of the population including manufacturing and assembly workers (e.g., Hart-Landsberg & Reder, 1993), women on welfare who are required as part of the welfare reform movement to go back to school (Wikelund, 1993), and adults attending basic literacy classes (e.g., Venezky, Bristow, & Sabatini, 1994).

Future research might compare the similarities and differences between young children who are struggling early in development to construct functional reading and writing systems and older adults who face the same task later in development. Such comparisons may shed light on the relative contribution of maturation and learning to the development of literacy skills (J. Sabatini, personal communication, April 1995). Fowler and Scarborough (1993) argued persuasively that there may not be meaningful differences in instructional needs between illiterate adults who have not had adequate educational opportunities and reading disabled adults who may have constitutionally based learning disabilities. Both groups probably need instruction aimed at improving their accuracy and fluency of low-level word recognition skills, which is not always a goal of adult literacy programs. Both adult groups probably share the same instructional needs as young children at comparable reading or writing achievement levels. Yet, beyond the applied issues of trying to improve their literacy skills, investigation of these populations alone and in contrast to one another may add to our basic science understandings of how functional reading and writing systems are constructed at different stages of development.

ACKNOWLEDGMENTS

The research reported in this chapter was supported by grants 25858–04, 25858–05, and 25858–06 from the National Institute of Child Health and Human Development.

REFERENCES

Arter, J., & Jenkins, J. (1979). Differential diagnostic prescriptive teaching: A critical appraisal. *Review of Educational Research, 49*, 517–555.

Bates, E. (1993, March). *Nature, nurture, and language.* Invited address, Society for Research in Child Development, New Orleans, LA.

Berninger, V. (1989). Orchestration of multiple codes in developing readers: An alternative model of lexical access. *International Journal of Neuroscience, 48*, 85–104.

Berninger, V. (1996). *Reading and writing acquisition. A developmental neuropsychological perspective.* Boulder, CO: Westview (Original work published 1994).

Berninger, V., & Abbott, R. (1992). The unit of analysis and constructive processes of the learner: Key concepts for educational neuropsychology. *Educational Psychologist, 27*, 223–242.

Berninger, V., & Abbott, R. (1994a). Multiple orthographic and phonological codes in reading and writing: An evolving research program. In V. W. Berninger (Ed.), *The varieties of orthographic knowledge: I. Theoretical and developmental issues* (pp. 277–317). Dordrecht, The Netherlands: Kluwer.

Berninger, V., & Abbott, R. (1994b). Redefining learning disabilities: Moving beyond aptitude-achievement discrepancies to failure to respond to validated treatment protocols. In G. Reid Lyon (Ed.), *Frames of reference for the assessment of learning disabilities. New views on measurement issues* (pp. 163–183). Baltimore, MD: Paul H. Brookes.

Berninger, V., Abbott, R., Whitaker, D., Sylvester, L., & Nolen, S. (1995). Integrating low-level and high-level skills in treatment protocols for writing disabilities. *Learning Disabilities Quarterly, 18*, 293–309.

Berninger, V., Cartwright, A., Yates, C., Swanson, L., & Abbott, R. (1994). Developmental skills related to writing and reading acquisition in the intermediate grades. *Reading and Writing Acquisition: An Interdisciplinary Journal, 6*, 161–196.

Berninger, V., & Hart, T. (1992). A developmental neuropsychological perspective for reading and writing acquisition. *Educational Psychologist, 27*, 415–434.

Berninger, V., Yates, C., & Lester, C. (1991). Multiple orthographic codes in reading and writing acquisition. *Reading and Writing Acquisition: An Interdisciplinary Journal, 3*, 115–149.

Bowers, P., & Wolf, M. (1993a, April). *A 'double-deficit hypothesis' for developmental reading disorders.* Paper presented at the Biennial meeting of the Society for Research on Child Development, New Orleans, LA.

Bowers, P., & Wolf, M. (1993b). Theoretical links among naming-speed, precise timing mechanisms, and orthographic skill in dyslexia. *Reading and Writing: An Interdisciplinary Journal, 5*, 69–85.

Bronfenbrenner, U. (1979). *The ecology of human development.* Cambridge, MA: Harvard University Press.

Brown, A. (1992). Design experiments: Theoretical and methodological challenges in creating complex interventions in classroom settings. *The Journal of the Learning Sciences, 2*, 141–178.

Bryk, A., & Raudenbush, S. (1987). Application of hierarchical linear models to assessing change. *Psychological Bulletin, 101*, 147–158.

Burchinal, M., & Applebaum, M. (1991). Estimating individual developmental functions: Methods and their assumptions. *Child Development, 62*, 23–43.

Calfee, R., & Henry, M. (1985). Project READ: An inservice model for training classroom teachers in effective reading instruction. In J. V. Hoffman (Ed.), *Effective teaching of reading: Research and practice* (pp. 199–229). Newark, DE: International Reading Association.

Carr, T., & Pollatsek, A. (1985). Recognizing printed words: A look at current models. In *Reading research: Advances in theory and practice* (Vol. 5, pp. 1–82). New York: Academic Press.

Carr, T., & Posner, M. (1996) The impact of learning to read on the functional anatomy of language processing. In B. de Gelder & J. Morais (Eds.), *Speech and Reading.* Hove, UK: Lawrence Erlbaum Associates LTD.

Collins, L., & Horn, J. (1991). *Best methods for the analysis of change. Recent advances, unanswered questions, future directions.* Washington, DC: American Psychological Association.

Cronbach, L., & Furby, L. (1970). How we should measure 'change'—or should we? *Psychological Bulletin, 47*, 68–80.

Ehri, L., & Saltmarsh, J. (1995). Beginning readers outperform older disabled readers in learning to read words by sight. *Reading and Writing: An Interdisciplinary Journal, 7*, 295–326.

Ellis, A. (1985). The cognitive neuropsychology of developmental (and acquired) dyslexia: A critical survey. *Cognitive Neuropsychology, 2*, 169–205.

Ellis, A. (1987). Review of problems in developing cognitively transmitted cognitive modules. *Mind & Language, 2*, 242–251.

Foorman, B., Francis, D., & Fletcher, J. (1995, April). *Early interventions for children with reading disabilities and at risk for developing reading disabilities.* Paper presented at the annual meeting of the American Educational Research Association, San Francisco, CA.

Fowler, A., & Scarborough, A. (1993, September). *Should reading-disabled adults be distinguished from other adults seeking literacy instruction? A review of theory and research* (Tech. Rep. No. TR93-7). Philadelphia: National Center on Adult Literacy, University of Pennsylvania.

Francis, D., Fletcher, J., Stuebing, K., Davidson, D., & Thompson, N. (1991). Analysis of change: Modeling individual growth. *Journal of Consulting and Clinical Psychology, 59*, 27–37.

Graham, S., & Harris, K. (1989). Component analysis of cognitive strategy instruction: Effects on learning disabled students' compositions and self-efficacy. *Journal of Educational Psychology, 8*, 353–361.

Graham, S, Harris, K., MacArthur, C., & Schwartz, S. (1991). Writing and writing instruction for students with learning disabilities: Review of a research program. *Learning Disabilities Quarterly, 14*, 89–114.

Hart, T., Berninger, V., & Abbott, R. (in press). Comparison of teaching single or multiple orthographic-phonological connections for word recognition and spelling: Implications for instructional consultation. *School Psychology Review.*

Hart-Landsberg, S., & Reder, S. (1993, November). *Teamwork and literacy: Learning from a skills-poor position* (Tech. Rep. No. TR93-06). Philadelphia: National Center on Adult Literacy, University of Pennsylvania.

Henry, M. (1989). Children's word structure knowledge: Implications for decoding and spelling instruction. *Reading and Writing, 1*, 135–152.

Kolb, B., & Whishaw, I. (1990). *Fundamentals of human neuropsychology* (3rd ed.). New York: Freeman.

Levy, B., & Lysynchuk, L. (1995, April). *Segmentation versus whole word repetition: Optimal training methods for beginning and delayed readers.* Paper presented at the annual meeting of the Society for the Scientific Study of Reading, San Francisco, CA.

Lord, F. (1956). The measurement of growth. *Educational and Psychological Measurement, 16*, 421–437.

Lovett, M. (1987). A developmental approach to reading disability: Accuracy and speed criteria of normal and deficient reading skill. *Child Development, 58*, 234–260.

Lovett, M., Borden, S., DeLuca, T., Lacderenza, L., Benson, N., & Brackstone, D. (1994). Treating the core deficits of developmental dyslexia: Evidence of transfer of learning after phonologically- and strategy-based reading training programs. *Developmental Psychology, 30*, 805–822.

Lovett, M., Borden, S., Warren-Chaplin, P., Lacerenza, L., DeLuca, T., & Giovinazzo, R. (1996). Text comprehension training for disabled readers: An evaluation of reciprocal teaching and text analysis training programs. *Brain and Language, 54*, 447–480.

Luria, A. R. (1973). *The working brain.* New York: Basic Books.

Minsky, M. (1986). *The society of mind.* New York: Simon & Schuster.

Palinscar, A., & Brown, A. (1984). Reciprocal teaching of comprehension—fostering and comprehension-monitoring activity. *Cognition and Instruction, 2*, 117–175.

Perfetti, C. (1992). The representation problem in reading acquisition. In P. Gough, L. Ehri, & R. Treiman (Eds.), *Reading acquisition* (pp. 307–342). Hillsdale, NJ: Lawrence Erlbaum Associates.

Petersen, S., Fox, P., Posner, M., Mintun, M., & Raichle, M. (1989). Positron emission tomographic studies of the processing of single words. *Journal of Cognitive Neuroscience, 1*, 153–179.

Posner, M., Petersen, S., Fox, P., & Raichle, M. (1988). Localization of cognitive operations in the human brain. *Science, 240*, 1627–1631.

Rogosa, D., Brandt, D., & Zimowski, M. (1992). A growth curve approach to the measurement of change. *Psychological Bulletin, 92,* 726–748.

Rogosa, D., & Willett, J. (1985). Understanding correlates of change by modeling individual differences in growth. *Psychometrika, 50,* 203–228.

Rutberg, J., Abbott, R., & Berninger, V. (in preparation). *Comparison of combined neurodevelopmental and academic training with academic training only on handwriting growth.* Unpublished manuscript.

Stanovich, K. (1988). Explaining the differences between the dyslexic and the garden-variety poor reader: The phonological core variable difference model. *Journal of Learning Disabilities, 21,* 590–612.

Torgesen, J., & Hecht, S. (1996). Preventing and remediating reading disabilities: Instructional variables that make a difference for special students. In M. Graves, B. Taylor, & P. van den Broek (Eds.), *The first R: A right of all children* (pp. 133–159). Cambridge, MA: MIT Press.

Vellutino, F., & Scanlon, D. (1994, August). Presentation at conference on Treatment of Learning Disabilities, National Institute of Child Health and Human Development, Bethesda, MD.

Venezky, R. (1995). From orthography to psychology to reading. In V. W. Berninger (Ed.), *The varieties of orthographic knowledge II: Relationships to phonology, reading, and writing* (pp. 23–46). Dordrecht, The Netherlands: Kluwer Academic.

Venezky, R., Bristow, P., & Sabatini, J. (1994, April). *Measuring gain in adult literacy programs* (Tech. Rep. No. TR93–12). Philadelphia: National Center for Adult Literacy, University of Pennsylvania.

Wagner, R., Torgesen, J., & Rashotte, C. (1994). The development of reading-related phonological processing abilities: New evidence of bi-directional causality from a latent variable longitudinal study. *Developmental Psychology, 30,* 73–87.

Wikelund, K. (1993, November). *Motivations for learning: Voices of women welfare reform participants* (Tech. Rep. No. TR93–10). Philadelphia: National Center on Adult Literacy, University of Pennsylvania.

Willett, J. (1988). Questions and answers in the measurement of change. In E. Rothkopf (Ed.), *Review of research in education* (pp. 345–422). Washington, DC: AERA.

Wise, B., & Olson, R. (1995). Computer-based phonological awareness and reading instruction. *Annals of Dyslexia, 45,* 99–122.

Wolf, M. (1991). Naming-speed and reading: The contribution of the cognitive neurosciences. *Reading Research Quarterly, 26,* 123–141.

Wolf, M., Bally, H., & Morris, R. (1986). Automaticity, retrieval processes, and reading: A longitudinal study in average and impaired reading. *Child Development, 57,* 988–1000.

Wolf, M., Pfeil, C., Lotz, R., & Biddle, K. (1994). Towards a more universal understanding of the developmental dyslexias: The contribution of orthographic factors. In V. W. Berninger (Ed.), *The varieties of orthographic knowledge I: Theoretical and developmental issues* (pp. 137–171). Dordrecht, The Netherlands: Kluwer.

APPENDIX: LESSON PLAN 2

(Sample for Integrated Handwriting, Spelling, Composition Tutorial)

1. Begin every session by reading "I can learn to write. I can learn to spell. I can learn to compose."

2. HANDWRITING WARM-UP (about 5 minutes). Please copy each of the letters on this sheet. Copy them right below the model and be sure you follow the arrows which are cues to the direction for making each stroke. Pay attention to the proportionality (size of letter parts in relation to each other). (You can correct the child if he or she makes a mistake on this instructional part.)

Handwriting Probe 1: You will see the same letters on this sheet, but in a different order. Now I will time you as you copy each of the letters. Try to make the letters the same way as you did with the arrows on the other sheet. Pay attention to proportionality (size of letter parts in relation to each other). Be neat and accurate as well as quick.
Record the time here. _____

Handwriting Probe 2: On this sheet, write the letter that comes after A,F,P,K,U. Now write the letter that comes before B,G,L,O,V. Record time for this entire procedure here _____

3. Spelling (about 15 minutes)
There are 3 different ways to learn to spell words. The first way is imaging. Let's review the 5 steps of this strategy (read them in the Personal Dictionary). Now we will practice these steps with the second six words on the next page (kitchen, result, advice, purchase, brief, success). The probe for this is the number of words written correctly from memory with eyes open _____. The second way is using letter-sound relationships. Last time we reviewed the sounds that go with single consonant letters. This time we will review consonant combinations. Read the consonant combinations and example words (pp. 26, 27, 6, 9, 10, 11, and 12) with the child. Explain that sometimes the consonants blend and you hear the sound for each letter, like in bl, but that sometimes the consonants go together to make a completely new sound, like in th. The probe is the number of sounds the child can correctly produce for bl—, cl—, fl—, gl—, pl—, sl—, sp—, sto—, sw—, sm—, sn—, br—, cr—, dr—, fr—, gr—, pr—, tr—, sc—, sk—, tw—, ch—, ph—, sh—, th—, wh—, qu—, st—, sch—, scr—, shr—, spl—, spr—, squ—, str—, thr—. The third way is syllable patterns in words. Last time we learned about closed syllables (consonant, vowel, consonant and the vowel is short) and open syllables (consonant, vowel and the vowel is long). Today we will learn about vowel-consonant-silent e syllables which have a long vowel sound. Read examples at bottom of page 20. Practice reading the mixed syllables on p. 22. Talk about whether they are open, closed, or silent e syllables. Probes are the nonsense syllables on p. 23: dro—, tro—, deve—, sti—, grib—, blist—, tib—, shup—, mabe—, heb—, gli—bive—, chot—, pru—, ret—, blam—, sleme—, trast—, brun—, flot—.

4. Composition (about 15 minutes) Today we will write a composition about your house or apartment where you and your family live. We will use the PW2R strategy. What does the P stand for? What does the W stand for? What does the first R stand for? What does the second R stand for? I will model it again for you. First, I will plan. I will write the first paragraph about my house. I will tell what it looks like on the outside. I will tell what it looks like on the inside. I will tell what is in the backyard. I will write the second paragraph about my family. I will tell who is in my family. I will tell some of the things we do together. Now I will write

my composition: (Use this as a model, but personalize as you see fit for your situation. Misspell one or two words to correct.) I live in a yellow house (or 2 bedroom apartment). The outside is made of wood. Inside there is a living room, kitchen, and bedrooms. My favorite (misspell) room is the living room because that's where the tv is. Outside there is a garden. (Start a second paragraph). My family consists of my husband and myself. We have other family, too, but they do not live with us. We like to do many things together. We like to swim, hike, and picnic. Now I will review my composition (read it together). Now I will revise it. I will correct any misspellings. I will also decide if I should add or change any of my sentences. There are some other things we like to do together like take trips so I will add a sentence about that. Now, it is your turn to write your composition. First, I want you to plan out loud about what you will write. Provide cues (scaffolding) to help the child generate ideas. Now you have 5 minutes to write. When I say 5 minutes are up, you may review and revise. (The probe will be the number of words written in 5 minutes————). After 5 minutes let the child reread the composition and make any changes he or she wants, but indicate what those changes are so that the original number of words can be determined.

5. Practice or Individualization. (about 15 minutes)

a. For practice, write another composition. Or

b. Now we will work on some skills that should really help you with your writing. (coding activities)

Lesson Frame 7 (Sample from Integrated Reading-Writing Tutorial)

1. *First, we will review vowel and vowel combinations, key words, and sounds in our phonics pictionary. I will name the letter or letter combination, key word, and beginning or middle sounds that go with it or them. Then you name the letter or letter combination, key word, and beginning sound or sounds.* (Use the section of the Pictionary that begins with a. Present these combinations with a quick, rhythmic pace. Do not get involved in a lot of didactic teaching. The purpose is to teach paired associations and commit them to automatic recall. The time to teach analytic decoding is during the first oral reading of the story.) After you have gone through the whole list, test the child's memory by asking for the key word and sound(s) that goes (go) with each letter or letter combination. Score C for correct response and X for incorrect response for recall of the key word and sound separately. *If child misses item, tell the correct answer so testing also serves a teaching function. (Theoretical rationale:* Beginning readers need to learn correspondences between letter combinations and sounds.)

	Key word	Sound
short a		
a: long open syllable rule		

	Keyword	Sound
long a: final e rule		
ai: long a		
ay: long a		
al: broad o		
au: broad o		
aw: broad o		
ar: air sound		
ar: ar sound		
a: schwa		
e: short		
e: long open syllable rule		
e: silent		
ee: long e		
ea: long e		
ea: short e		
e: schwa		
er: r sound		
i: short		
i: long open		
i: long final e rule		
ir:		

PLEASE PRACTICE THESE LETTER-PICTURE COMBINATIONS AT HOME.

2. Next, we will do Reader's Warm-up (p. 1 of Reader 2). Use format, "i-n-k says "ink". Say "ink" Wait for child to repeat word and then move on. Point to each letter as you name it and make sure that child is attending. Sweep you finger in a left to right motion under the word as you pronounce it as a whole.

3. *Next, we will read a new story ("Hank's Nap in Reader 2). When you come to a word you do not know, try to sound it out. Think about the key words in your phonics pictionary to help you. If the first letter-sound combination does not work think of another sound that goes with that letter. It is also important to understand what you read. After we reread each page, I will ask you a question about what you read.* In this part of the lesson you should help the child sound out words he or she does not know and have child think about the Phonics Pictionary when doing so—point out single letters or letter combinations (spelling units) as appropriate. Record C is child answers question correctly and X if child does not..

page 2   Why is Hank sad? (He has to nap.)————

page 3   Why did Hank clap his hands? (He has a plan.)————

page 4   Where does Hank's dog nap? (In plants)————

page 5   Where did Hank skip to? (Flag Pond)————

page 6   What did Dan do that Hank did not do (do as his Dad said—take a nap)————

page 7   Where did Hank sit? (on a plank at Flag Pond)————

page 8   What did Hank do? (take a long nap)————

page 9   What is softer than a plank? (a cot)————

4. *After we have read a story to ourselves and thought about what it means, it is fun to go back and reread the whole story. Now I want you to start at the beginning and read this story to me.*

(By page number, make a tally mark by each page number each time a child cannot pronounce a word within 1 second or says the wrong word. If the child does not know the word or gives the wrong word, supply the correct word and move on. Also, time by stopwatch the amount of time it takes to read each page.) Theoretical rationale: to develop fluency and automatic whole word reading.

	Errors	Time (in seconds)
p. 2		
p. 3		
p. 4		
p. 5		
p. 6		
p. 7		
p. 8		
p. 9		

5. *To help us learn to recognize words, it helps us to play games that help us pay close attention to and remember letters in written words and to pay close attention to and remember sounds in spoken words.*

a. First, we will play a looking game to make sure we pay close attention to the letters in words. (Write the target words on the chalk board ahead of time. For each word, in the blank, put a C if the word is spelled correctly on the *first try* and an X if the word is not spelled correctly on the *first try*. If the first try does not result in a correct response, repeat up to 2 times until it does. Do not use these games to teach reading, but do teach strategies for looking at words more carefully. Do not make the sounds of the letters or say the name of the word. The purpose is simply to encourage careful looking at and memory for words.) (*Theoretical rationale:* Teaching orthographic awareness or letter patterns in written words)

1) Point to *spank*. Say, "*Look at this word carefully.*" After 1 second, cover it up with your hand. "*Now spell that word for me.*" If necessary repeat procedures until child spells word correctly. ——

2) Point to *sniff*. Say, "*Look at this word carefully.*" After 1 second, cover it up with your hand. "*Now spell that word for me.*" If necessary repeat procedures until child spells word correctly. ——

3) Point to *plank*. Say, "*Look at this word carefully.*" After 1 second, cover it up with your hand. "*Now spell that word for me.*" If necessary repeat procedures until child spells word correctly. ——

4) Point to *stops*. Say, "*Look at this word carefully.*" After 1 second, cover it up with your hand. "*Now spell that word for me.*" If necessary repeat procedures until child spells word correctly. ——

5) Point to *limps*. Say, "*Look at this word carefully.*" After 1 second, cover it up with your hand. "*Now spell that word for me.*" If necessary repeat procedures until child spells word correctly. ——

b. Now we will play a sound game. (Score for the first try. Then teach for up to 2 more trials to help child do sound segmentation successfully. Do not use this game to teach reading, that is, to relate sounds to letters. Use colored blocks to help make sound segmentation concrete on teaching trials only—not the first trial. Lay one block of a different color on the table for each phoneme as you pronounce word in left to right sequence. Then say whole word, remove the target phoneme to be deleted and ask child what is left.) (*theoretical rationale:* Teaching phonological awareness or sound patterns in spoken words)

1) Say flip. Now say it again, but don't say /f/.——
2) Say spot. Now say it again, but don't say /p/.——
3) Say sand. Now say it again, but don't say /s/.——
4) Say plan. Now say it again, but don't say /l/.——
5) Say flag. Now say it again, but don't say /f/.——

6. *Now we will do writers' warm-up.*

A. *Here is a sheet that has arrows to show the direction and order for making strokes to form each letter. I will name the letter. I want you to copy the letter following the arrows that show you how to make the strokes.* (Correct the child if he/she does not follow the arrows.) Avoid verbalizations other than naming the letter for the child.

——no. wrong requiring teaching assistance————total time for 26 letters

b. *Turn the sheet over. Write these letters from memory.* (C=correct, X=error) Help the child if nothing is written after 2 seconds or the letter is formed incorrectly. (If child has trouble with d, use this hint. It turns the opposite way from B. If child has trouble with p, use this rule, it is the only stick + ball letter that has the same shape for the lower case and capital letter.)

z———
b———
p———
f———
r———
c. Write the letter that comes before e———, f———, r———, j———,
m———.

D. Write the letter that comes after
c———, q———, h———, x———, f———.

7. *Now we will spell some words by sounding them out letter by letter. Say word. Ask child to spell it in writing on the lined paper provided.* (Help child by sounding it out if necessary) C = correct, X = incorrect on first trial. If child misspells word, teach how to spell it before moving on. (These are older 1 words from Venezky. Make sure that you point out spelling units, i.e., letter combinations, when teaching these.

ask———
best———
fast———
fish———
just———
last———
lunch———
much———
must———
ship———
stop———
than———
that———
then———
them———
wish———
with———

8. *Finally, we will compose. What I think, I can write. I will show you. I am thinking of a story called, "Pets". I have a pet cat. Her name is Snow White. Can you guess what color she is? I used to have a pet dog. His name was Spot? Can you guess what color he was? Now it is your turn to write a story called "Pets". First, think out loud what you want to write. We will use your Pictionary to help you make the sounds in your ideas into words. If you can't think how to spell a word, we will find the picture that begins with each sound in the word or has the sound in it. Let me show you how this works. Think of your first idea. Then try to write it down using the Pictionary if you need help with the spelling.* Then think of your second idea and try to write it down using the Pictionary to help with spelling. We will keep all your compositions and publish them in a book at the end of Readers/Writers Workshop.

7

Social Assessment of At-Risk Populations: Implications for Students With Learning Disabilities

Sharon Vaughn
Jane M. Sinagub
University of Miami

Since the mid-1970s, researchers addressed critical issues related to the social competence of children and adolescents. Today, the importance of social assessment and interventions for at-risk populations has been recognized (e.g., Parker & Asher, 1987). For example, studies examined the social development of individuals with learning disabilities (LD) relative to normal developmental patterns (e.g., Vaughn, Haager, Hogan, & Kouzekanani, 1992) and the extent to which within-individual differences occur over time (Vaughn & Hogan, 1994). The converging research showed that compared to typically achieving, nondisabled peers, students with LD exhibit greater social difficulties (for review, see Hazel & Schumaker, 1988; Pearl, Donahue, & Bryan, 1986).

Although academic difficulties, by definition, characterize students with LD, there is little question that many students with LD also demonstrate significant difficulties with social relationships or display inappropriate social behaviors (for review see, Hazel & Schumaker, 1988; Pearl et al., 1986). However, students with LD are also extremely heterogeneous and for a small subgroup of students with LD, social competence is an area of strength (Vaughn & Hogan, 1994).

As a result of the Interagency Committee on Learning Disabilities (1987) investigation of the state of knowledge regarding LD, several recommendations for assessment in the social domain were developed. These recommendations for the development of optimal measures for assessing social development include the following components: (a) they are based on empirically validated social skill problems of individuals with LD, (b) they are psychometrically sound, (c) they are useful in school settings, (d) they are able to assess individuals across the developmental age range from preschool through adulthood, and (e) they allow for the assessment of all social competence skills. Gresham and Elliott (1989) commented that it is unlikely that a single measurement instrument could adequately reflect all of these recommendations and that multiple measures are required.

This chapter provides a framework for understanding social competence, and applies this framework to the assessment and intervention of individuals with LD.

MODELS OF SOCIAL COMPETENCE

According to Killen (1989), social development is the ongoing, active social processes of interpretation, evaluation, and coordination of social events. The following three issues are central to understanding these social processes: context, conflict, and coordination. *Context* is important because of its influence on the nature and type of social interactions that occur. For example, children's behaviors are influenced by their setting. Thus, a child's behavior will be different at school than at home or in a community setting. The issue of context is particularly important when considering the social competence of individuals with LD. To illustrate, the school context is one in which these individuals have been unsuccessful, at least academically. When the social behavior of students with LD is assessed within the school context, the result may not be a typical representation of their behavior. Because access to youngsters for research purposes largely occurs in school or clinical settings, we know a great deal about their social functioning in these settings, but little about their social behavior in other settings. Further understanding of context as it relates to the social performance of all students, but particularly students with LD, is needed.

The second issue, *conflict*, provides an understanding of how an individual negotiates and interprets events and behaviors across settings. How children interpret events, solve problems, and negotiate interactions is fundamental to their social competence. Assessment in this area is largely dependent on observation and interpretation, self-reports, or reports from others (e.g., teachers, parents). The collection of observation data particularly in naturalistic settings is time-consuming and expensive; thus, structured observations, self-reports or reports from others are more frequently used. How a child interprets events and behaviors is perhaps the most difficult area to assess and interpret, particularly when observing students with LD who have information processing problems that interfere with their interpretation and communication. Many students with LD also display attention problems and memory problems (for review, see Lyon, 1994) that interfere with their interpretations of measurement items or their explanations of their perceptions. The third issue, *coordination*, or how one interacts with and responds to others, can be assessed through observations, self-reports, or reports from others (e.g., peers and teachers). A limited number of observational studies examined the interactions of students with LD as compared to students without LD (NLD). These studies have reported that students with LD engage in fewer positive interactions with peers as well as teachers (e.g., McIntosh, Vaughn, Schumm, Haager, & Lee, 1993). Overall, most of the social competence research related to individuals with LD examines how individuals with LD interpret, evaluate, or coordinate social events. Summarized elsewhere (e.g., Vaughn & Haager, 1994a), students with LD have difficulties in all three areas.

Vaughn and Hogan (1990) constructed a model of social competence that expands the three processes just outlined. According to this model, social competence is a multifaceted construct made up of the following constituent parts: positive relations with others, accurate and age-appropriate social cognition, absence of maladaptive behaviors, and effective social behaviors.

The first component, positive relations with others, refers to the existence of satisfying and healthy interpersonal relationships. The importance of positive peer relations is underscored by the negative correlation between peer relations and problems later in life (e.g., criminal behavior, premature termination of schooling, for review, see Parker & Asher, 1987). For children and adolescents, this feature is most commonly tapped into by examining peer relations with classmates. This is frequently accomplished through peer nominations and measures of peer acceptance, which reveal students' social status and the extent to which students are liked by their classmates, respectively. Students with LD are at greater risk than their NLD peers for being identified as rejected and unpopular by their classmates (see for review Pearl et al., 1986). Students with LD are also more likely to be perceived as undesirable partners for social interaction by their classmates, teachers, and parents (Vaughn & Hogan, 1990). Because we know that the presence of even one mutual friendship can offset some of the negative effects of low social status (Howes, 1987) future research needs to assess students' relationships outside of school (e.g., with neighborhood children who are not schoolmates, with family members).

The second component, accurate and age-appropriate social cognition, refers to an individual's ability to maneuver cognitively through interpersonal interactions. This would include evaluations of self and others, interpretations of social events (e.g., attributions of the motivations, feelings, and behaviors of others), and problem-solving abilities. As previously discussed, students with LD often demonstrate deficits in information processing that may interfere with their ability to accurately interpret and respond to social interactions.

The third element is the absence of maladaptive behaviors. Social competence requires that individuals not display socially noxious behavior (e.g., aggressive behavior). The assessment of child and adolescent behavior usually involves naturalistic observation or behavior rating scales completed by teachers, parents, and classmates. Students with LD have consistently been rated by their teachers as displaying greater problematic behavior (e.g., inappropriate talking, acting out) than their NLD peers in the classroom (McKinney & Feagans, 1983; McKinney & Speece, 1983). Specific difficulties were documented in the following areas: on-task behavior, conduct disorders, distractibility, and introverted behavior (Bender & Smith, 1990).

The fourth component is effective social behaviors. This area includes those specific skills that are necessary for the establishment and maintenance of positive interpersonal relationships. Frequently these skills are targeted for assessment and intervention. Because students with LD are perceived as displaying inappropriate behaviors that contribute to their poor social status, many interventions are aimed at increasing peer acceptance of these students (for review, see Zaragoza, Vaughn, & McIntosh, 1991). Opposing hypotheses were postulated to explain the social skill deficits exhibited by individuals with LD. According to the *causal* hypothesis, dysfunction in the central nervous system leads to social skills dysfunction. The *correlational* hypothesis asserts that academic and social skill difficulties are associated, but that a cause and effect relationship does not exist (Gresham, 1992).

Applications to Research

In the 1990s, we conducted a number of studies in which we applied the social competence model (Vaughn & Hogan, 1990) to school-age students with LD to better understand the nature and implications of their social difficulties (for review, see Haager & Vaughn, 1995). Through our research, we learned the importance of considering multiple factors of social competence (e.g., self-concept, relationships with others), multiple reporters (e.g., peers, parents, self), and multiple settings (e.g., home, school, play). Most of our studies revealed lower peer acceptance for students with LD than for NLD students (e.g., Haager & Vaughn, 1995; Vaughn et al., 1990). One study should be noted, however, in which subjects were selected from classrooms where teachers were highly accepting of students with LD. No significant differences in the peer acceptance of students with LD and typically achieving students across elementary and secondary grade levels were observed (Vaughn, McIntosh, Schumm, Haager, & Callwood, 1993). In a recent study (Vaughn, Elbaum, & Schumm, in press), students with LD were included full time in general education classrooms through a consultation–collaboration model with special education teachers. At one of the two school sites, all achievement groups (including students with LD) demonstrated increases from fall to spring in their peer acceptance. Teacher interviews from this school, as well as classroom observations, indicated high levels of acceptance and high expectations for students with LD in these classrooms. It appears that the classroom environment plays an important role in determining the acceptance of students with LD. Examinations of social competence across multiple settings (e.g., school and outside of school) are valuable in determining the extent to which behavior that is reported at school corresponds with behavior in other settings. In another study (Haager & Vaughn, 1995), teachers and parents were asked to rate children's social skills. Results indicated that teachers rated students with LD and other low achievers as less competent in terms of social skills than their typically achieving peers; however, parents' ratings did not differentiate between LD, low-achieving, and other students. Perhaps parents' perspectives outside of the school setting reveal different social behaviors by their children; or it may be that the social behaviors that are disturbing to teachers are not disturbing to parents. Also, parents, as compared to teachers, do not have access to as large a sample of same-age peers with whom to compare their child.

There are several correlates of social competence that are highly relevant to interpreting social outcomes. For example, athletic ability, physical appearance, and classroom behaviors are highly related to peer acceptance in school-age children (Dodge, 1983; Wiener, Harris, & Shirer, 1990). It is important to consider these factors when interpreting peer acceptance of target students. Students who are highly attractive or very good at sports are more likely to be accepted by their peers than students without these skills who display similar social behaviors.

An additional factor related to the social acceptance of students is their academic achievement. Because students with LD by definition are low achievers, the extent to which this factor influences the way they are perceived by others (e.g., teachers and students) is difficult to discern but important to consider when interpreting their low social ratings. One interpretation of the low social functioning of individuals with LD is that it is a function of their learning disability. That is, the learning process deficits that interfere with their ability to succeed academically also interfere with their ability to succeed socially. There is increasing evidence for the existence of a subgroup of students referred to as nonverbal learning disabled who display a pattern of behaviors that include low math functioning and poor social skills (Rourke, 1989). However, for many students with LD who display social difficulties there is compelling evidence that social difficulties may be concomitant with low achievement in general rather than causally related to LD (Gresham, 1992). Several of our studies demonstrated that for peer relations, behavioral adjustment, social skills, and self-perceptions, students with LD are similar to other low achievers who were not referred or identified as having LD (e.g., Haager & Vaughn, 1995; Vaughn et al., 1992; Vaughn, Zaragoza, Hogan, & Walker, 1993). Thus, there is accumulating evidence for the co-occurrence of achievement difficulties and social difficulties.

In the next section, methods for assessing the components of the Vaughn and Hogan (1990) model of social competence are addressed and examples from the authors' own research are provided.

INTERPERSONAL RELATIONSHIPS

Perhaps the single best indicator of overall social competence can be determined by examining an individual's relationships with others. For infants and very young children this frequently means their relationships with their parents, caregivers, and family. By the time children are 5 years old, most of them (75%) have a close relationship with another child (Howes, 1987). As children get older, parents play less of a role in influencing their relationships, and peers become increasingly important (Laursen, 1990). Most adolescents have a single best friend and fewer than 10% have no contact with friends outside of school (Crockett, Losoff, & Petersen, 1984). Making and maintaining friendships is of great importance to children and adolescents. Their friends are directly linked to their feelings of self-worth, social support, and satisfaction.

Because much research on children is conducted through the schools, most of what we know about the relationships of school-age children is through the eyes of their classmates. Measures that address the quality, nature, and number of friends provide perhaps the most relevant insight into an individual's overall social functioning. Why is this the case? Mostly, it is because we have a much larger research base on school-age children's peer relations than on any other relationships they have. Furthermore, the link between children's peer relations, particularly peer rejection, and later consequences (e.g., school dropout, adjustment problems) was made; thus, peer relations are often assessed as a predictor of later problems (for review, see Parker & Asher, 1987). Perceptions by peers also influence self-percep-tions and overall adjustment (Cowen, Pederson, Babigian, Izzo, & Trost, 1973). These implications are particularly relevant for individuals with LD who are more frequently rejected by their peers and are less well-accepted (e.g., Haager & Vaughn, 1995; Stone & La Greca, 1990; Wiener, 1987).

Sociometry is the most often used method of assessing social acceptance and status. Developed by Moreno (1934), sociometry is the study of peer rankings in a group. Most frequently, this is done with peer rating scales or nomination techniques. Peer rating scales yield a measure of a target student's likability within a peer group or peer acceptance, whereas peer nominations indicate social status within a peer group (i.e., peer rejection; Gresham, 1981). The number, network, type, and nature of peer friendships also provide insights into peer relations and overall social functioning.

Hartup (1992) indicated that children's friendships can be identified by applying one of the following four procedures:

1. Friendship nominations, in which someone (usually the child) is asked to identify who are his or her best friends.
2. Mutual liking, in which the child is asked to identify other children who are "especially liked."
3. Proximity, in which close relationships with the child are identified by observing which children remain in close proximity to the child.
4. Behavioral reciprocities, in which behaviors of children are used to identify friends from nonfriends.

Why is the assessment of friendships so critical? Hartup indicated that friendships serve four important functions: social skills are acquired or extended; friendships assist in acquiring self-knowledge, knowledge about others, and knowledge about the world; friendships provide emotional and cognitive support; and friendships provide opportunities to rehearse skills and self-knowledge in order to develop and maintain future intimate relationships.

Peer Acceptance

Rating scales are the most frequently used measures for identifying peer liking and acceptance. For research purposes, students from the class (most frequently those for whom parents provided permission to participate in the study) are asked to rate every other student on a designated criterion. Reliability increases with the number of raters (Asher & Hymel, 1981; Gresham & Elliott, 1989; Singleton & Asher, 1977), so obtaining ratings from as many students in the class as possible is desirable. When conducting research with individuals with LD, often 30 students in the class need to be permissioned even when only one student is the target of the research investigation. Because obtaining ratings from individual students' peer groups would be difficult outside the school setting, peer ratings are most frequently obtained within the classroom setting. Although various procedures for the conduct of peer ratings were used (e.g., an easel or card format), we found the use of a list of names of participating students from the class followed by rating indicators to be the most convenient.

In our own work, we use a 3-point scale with youngsters in preschool through first grade, then convert to a 4-point scale for youngsters in second grade and older, through high school (e.g., Vaughn et al., 1992; Vaughn, McIntosh, Schumm, Haager, & Callwood, 1993). We conduct peer ratings individually with children in second grade and younger. Children in third through fifth grade provide their peer ratings in small groups and we conduct whole class ratings after fifth grade. With children in second grade and younger, we use a visual prompt of three faces: a happy face, a neutral face, and an unhappy face, each represented on a separate card. We then provide some examples of items for the students to rate that are unrelated to rating their peers (e.g., how much they like to eat pizza, go swimming, clean their room). Each face is assigned a point value from 1 (least positive) to 3 (most positive). For older children in a group or class setting, we also use similar examples but use numbers instead of faces for the ratings, from 1 indicating (don't like at all) to 4 indicating (like a lot). When children are familiar with the procedure, we ask them to rate the youngsters on the roster, excluding themselves. It is important, even with older children, to assure that they can accurately read the names of all of the students on the roster.

The mean rating for each target student is calculated and scores are then used in a comparative analysis. The mean score is indicative of how well a student is liked or accepted by peers. Additionally, a list of all of the ratings for a target student will provide data about which students in the class like the target child a lot and which do not. This information can be used to assist the child in developing reciprocal friendships. Even for students who may not be liked by the class as a whole, if there are one or two students who rate the target child highly, the data provides a starting point for developing mutual friendships. We found the use of a grid to record peer acceptance choices to be a useful evaluation tool (see Fig. 7.1).

Sample Grid for Recording Peer Acceptance Choices

School_____

Teacher___ _____

Your name_____ Male ____ Female ____

Directions: Please circle the number that best represents each person listed below.
   Cross out your own name.

1 = not at all
2 = not much
3 = pretty much
4 = very much

Child's name	How well do you know				How much do you LIKE			
1.	1	2	3	4	1	2	3	4
2.	1	2	3	4	1	2	3	4
3.	1	2	3	4	1	2	3	4
4.	1	2	3	4	1	2	3	4
5.	1	2	3	4	1	2	3	4
6.	1	2	3	4	1	2	3	4
7.	1	2	3	4	1	2	3	4
8.	1	2	3	4	1	2	3	4
9.	1	2	3	4	1	2	3	4
10.	1	2	3	4	1	2	3	4
11.	1	2	3	4	1	2	3	4
12.	1	2	3	4	1	2	3	4
13.	1	2	3	4	1	2	3	4
14.	1	2	3	4	1	2	3	4
15.	1	2	3	4	1	2	3	4
16.	1	2	3	4	1	2	3	4
17.	1	2	3	4	1	2	3	4
18.	1	2	3	4	1	2	3	4
19.	1	2	3	4	1	2	3	4
20.	1	2	3	4	1	2	3	4

FIG. 7.1. Sample grid for recording peer acceptance choices. From: Social assessments of students with learning disabilities: Do they measure up? In S. Vaughn & C. Bos (Eds.), *Research issues in learning disabilities: Theory, methodology, assessment, and ethics* (pp. 276–311), by S. Vaughn & D. Haager, 1994, New York: Springer-Verlag. Copyright © 1994 by Springer-Verlag. Reprinted with permission.

Peer ratings are an effective procedure for assessing the acceptance and likability of target students. Despite the overall effectiveness of peer ratings, there are considerations for their use. First, the "stem" that is used for the ratings should be thoughtfully selected. The most frequently used stem is "How much do you like . . . (each name on the list)?" However, other possibilities include, "How much would you like to work with . . . ?" and, "How much would you like to play with . . . ?" or, "How much would you like to be friends with . . . ?" Each of these stems asks the rater to appraise the target student in a different way, thus we would not expect the ratings to be the same for all of these stems. This is particularly true for students with LD who demonstrate academic achievement difficulties and motor coordination problems. Stems that request appraisal on "work with" may be rated lower for students with LD because of their low achievement. Stems that request appraisal on "play with" may be rated lower for students with LD because of their motor problems. Gresham and Reschly (1986) conducted a study in which NLD students and students with LD were rated using both work with and play with stems. The largest statistically significant difference between the groups was obtained with the work with stem. If the interest is in assessing how well a student is liked by peers, the recommended stem to use is "How much do you like . . . ?" If other stems are used, they should be carefully selected to represent the desired attribute to be assessed.

Social Status

Social status refers to the student's overall standing with respect to peers. Previous research emphasized the importance of identifying peer **acceptance** and **rejection** as two separate dimensions in which children are viewed by peers (Coie, Dodge, & Coppotelli, 1982; Dodge, Coie, & Brakke, 1982). Social status is determined by the number of positive and negative nominations received from classmates. Nominations are obtained by asking students to identify three classmates who they like most or would consider to be their best friends in the class. These are referred to as positive nominations. Next, students are asked to write or name up to three classmates who they least like or would not want to be friends with. These are considered negative nominations. *Social impact scores*, indicative of influence in the group of the target student, are computed by adding the number of positive and negative nominations. *Social preference scores*, the extent to which a target child is highly liked by peers, are computed by subtracting the number of negative nominations from the number of positive nominations. Note that this could be a negative number if a student receives a high number of negative nominations. Scores are standardized by class by conversion to Z scores and yield social status categories using analysis procedures outlined by Coie et al. (1982). Using social preference and impact scores, students are categorized as popular (high positive social impact, high social preference), rejected (high negative social impact, low social preference), controversial (high positive and negative nominations), and neglected (low social impact). Behavior patterns associated with each social status category were identified (Coie & Kupersmidt, 1983; Dodge et al., 1982) and social status categories have demonstrated adequate test–retest reliability, with coefficients ranging from .59 to .78 (Bukowski & Newcomb, 1984; Wasik, 1987), and adequate criterion validity (Vosk, Forehand, Parker, & Richard, 1982).

Research established that students with LD are more likely to be rejected by their peers than are typically achieving students (Stone & La Greca, 1990; Vaughn et al., 1990). Peer rejection is associated with interpersonal difficulties, low levels of cooperation and friendliness, and high levels of aggression (e.g., Coie & Dodge, 1988; Coie, Dodge, & Kupersmidt, 1990). Peer rejection is also predictive of negative outcomes later in life such as poor adult adjustment, criminal involvement, and dropout (Parker & Asher, 1987). For this reason, considerable emphasis focused on better understanding the peer rejection of students with LD (e.g., Vaughn, McIntosh, & Spencer-Rowe, 1991).

Friendship Qualities.   Peer acceptance ratings and social status nominations provide information about students' social relationships from the perspective of the groups as a whole, usually classmates. However, these measures provide little information on the quality of the friendships, whether or not they have mutual friends, and the extent to which their friends provide social support for them. Little is known about the nature of friendships of students with LD (Vaughn & Haager, 1994a; Vaughn, McIntosh, Schumm, Haager, & Callwood, 1993). Because a single reciprocated best friend may serve as a buffer for the ill effects of low peer acceptance and rejection (La Greca & Fetter, 1995) a better understanding of children's reciprocal friendships is needed.

Bukowski and Hoza (1989) provided several orienting questions to assess the quality of children's friendships: Does the child have at least one mutual friend? How many mutual friends does the child have? What is or are the quality of that child's mutual friendships? One way of addressing these questions is through identifying *reciprocal* friendships. A reciprocal friendship occurs when two students nominate each other as best friends. We determine reciprocal friendships through the positive nomination procedures presented earlier. When two students nominate each other as best friends it is considered a hit, if not, then it is a miss.

Younger children are better able to handle peer group entry if they have a single reciprocal friend than if they do not (Howes, 1987). In a recent study examining the reciprocal friendships of students with LD in inclusion settings, overall peer acceptance of students with LD did not increase from fall to spring, however, the number of reciprocal friends did increase (Vaughn et al., in press). In a follow-up study (Vaughn et al., in press), students with LD who were in classes where teachers were both highly accepting and had high expectations experienced higher reciprocal friendship levels than did students with LD in other settings.

Self-reports and interviews were also developed to assess friendship quality. Bierman and McCauley (1987) developed a friendship questionnaire to specifically assess youngsters' peer relations and friendships outside of the school setting. This 32-item scale has three subscales: positive interactions, negative interactions, and extensive peer network.

The Friendship Survey (Berndt & Perry, 1986) is an 18-item questionnaire adapted from a structured interview designed to investigate dimensions of children's friendships (e.g., "Do you and your friends get together on weekends or after school?" to which children respond "yes," "sometimes," or "no"). Berndt and Perry identified six dimensions of friendship: play–association, prosocial behavior, intimacy, loyalty, attachment–self-esteem, and absence of conflicts. However, for second, fourth, and sixth graders studied, the ratings for all six dimensions loaded on a single factor. Although peer ratings and reciprocal friendship nominations address only those relationships that occur among classmates, the Friendship Survey gives an index of perceived support from friends irrespective of context and can provide information not tapped by classroom peer measures (Vaughn et al., in press).

SOCIAL SKILLS AND MALADAPTIVE BEHAVIORS

Social skills were defined as competencies that relate to initiation and maintenance of positive social relationships with others, promote adjustment with peers and at school, and provide for coping in the larger social environment (Walker et al., 1983).

Social skills refer to the prosocial and responding skills demonstrated by individuals across settings and persons. These skills include language, nonverbal reactions, and attitudes a person conveys to others. Some people demonstrate appropriate social skills across settings and persons; others demonstrate social skills that are more appropriate in particular settings and with selected others. A good example are the social skills demonstrated by many adolescents. These skills are frequently best suited for specific settings and with specific friends.

Maladaptive behaviors and social skills are not opposites on a continuum with maladaptive behaviors representing the absence or ineffective use of social skills. Maladaptive behaviors represent a type of behavior problem (e.g., conduct disorders, anxiety) rather than poor social skills. It is possible for individuals who display maladaptive behaviors to also demonstrate appropriate social skills. A student with conduct disorder may be able to display highly appropriate social behaviors in selected settings and also display acting out and aggressive behaviors in other settings. Table 7.1 provides a list of important social skills to consider.

The assessment of social skills is largely conducted through the use of rating scales completed by adults who have significant exposure to the target child's behavior (e.g., teacher, parent). These rating scale measures assess the extent to which the target youngster demonstrates age-appropri-

TABLE 7.1
Important Social Skills

Skill Area	Key Components
Enjoyment of Interactions	Smiling
	Laughing
Greeting	Looking at person
	Smiling
	Using the person's name
	Greeting Nicely
Joining	Standing near the child
	Asking to join nicely
	Acknowledging others when they join
	Handling refusals (e.g., Don't get mad)
Inviting	Asking other person to do something
	Accepting invitations nicely
	Handling refusals (e.g., Ask for another day)
Conversation	Asking conversational questions
	Talking more/sharing information about self
	Keeping a conversation going
	Taking turns in conversation
Sharing/Cooperation	Taking turns in peer activities
	Following game rules
	Being a "good sport" (good winner or good loser)
Complimenting/Giving	Looking at the person
Positive Feedback	Making a positive statement
	Accepting compliments from others positively
Conflict Resolution	Compromising
	Handling name-calling and teasing

Adapted from LaGreca and Mesibov 1979, Vaughn and La Greca 1993.

ate social behaviors with peers and adults across a range of settings (Vaughn & Haager, 1994b). Measures of social skills are most frequently completed by classroom teachers who are asked to rate the social behaviors of selected students in their classes. For this reason social skills measures were designed to include school-related social behaviors (e.g., completing homework, following teacher's directions) and other related social behaviors (e.g., greeting peers, solving one's own interpersonal problems). Social skills measures were also designed to assess parents' perceptions of their child's social skills (e.g., Gresham & Elliott, 1990).

There are many social skill rating scales available for use by teachers (for review, see Gresham & Elliott, 1989). The Social Skills Rating System (Gresham & Elliott, 1990) and the Walker–McConnell Scale of Social Competence and School Adjustment (Walker & McConnell, 1988, 1993) are two that have sound psychometric properties and national, normative databases. Social skills rating measures report better than adequate test–retest reliability with coefficients ranging from .75 to .88 (e.g., Gresham & Elliott, 1990; Matson, Rotatori, & Helsel, 1983; Walker & McConnell, 1988, 1993). Overall, teacher ratings of social skills provide an excellent resource for identifying students with social skills problems and selecting the skills for intervention that target students' needs (Walker, Colvin, & Ramsey, 1995).

There are several considerations regarding the use and interpretation of teacher rating scales of social skills for students with LD. First, most teacher rating scales address classroom-oriented behavior, which is a rather narrow, context-specific view of social skills. Although "following directions" is an important skill in the context of the classroom, it is questionable whether or not it is a social skill. The reason students with LD do not follow directions may be a result of difficulties other than social skills (e.g., they cannot remember the directions, they cannot process verbal commands in a large group setting). Second, the extent to which teacher bias for a student with LD in his or her classroom influences ratings of student social skills must be considered. In general, teachers do not value having students with LD placed into their classrooms (Garrett & Crump, 1980; Keogh, Tchir, & Windeguth-Behn, 1974). The extent to which teachers have a poor opinion about their students with LD may influence their ratings of their students' social skills. Third, as a researcher it is important to consider the extent to which the social behavior displayed in the school setting is representative of the youngster's behavior in other settings. Although this is true for other children as well, it is particularly problematic when conducting investigations with students with LD who demonstrate poorer academic performances than are expected for their level of intelligence. Thus, we would expect the classroom to be an environment in which students with LD experience frustration or anxiety, feelings that often lead to anger, aggression, or withdrawal.

For research purposes, it may be helpful to obtain ratings of students' behaviors both in and out of the classroom context, using multiple raters; thus, providing cross-validation of results. The Social Skills Rating System (SSRS–S; Gresham & Elliott, 1990), for example, includes parallel forms for both parent and teacher ratings and the items are specific to school and home contexts. When possible, the use of independent observations in addition to rating scales will minimize the bias inherent in rating scales. In one of our studies, parent and teacher ratings of the social skills of students with LD indicated fairly low levels of agreement (.22 for cooperation, .33 for self-control; Haager & Vaughn, 1995). According to Haager (1992), we might not expect teacher and parent ratings to converge because their knowledge of the child involves different settings and experiences.

Teacher and parent ratings of social skills are frequently used indices of the social behavior of youngsters, but what about peer and self-ratings? Although peer ratings are frequently used to assess peer acceptance and friendship (for review, see Landau & Milich, 1990), they are rarely used to assess social skills. We feel that peers' assessments of the social skills of their classmates present a promising area for several reasons. First, peers have an opportunity to see social behaviors not evident to teachers. Second, peers' perspectives on which social skills are acceptable and which are not are likely to be different from the perspectives of teachers or parents. Third, ratings by adults and peers are influenced by factors other than their unbiased views of the target student's social skills. Factors that bias teacher judgment are likely to be different from those factors that bias student judgment. Peers interact with their classmates across multiple settings and possess unique perspectives that are likely to influence their perspective of the social skills of the target students. Furthermore, peers' perceptions of the social skills of other students are likely to provide relevant information about their level of peer acceptance.

Walker (1991) developed a peer rating of prosocial behavior (PRPB) that was adapted from a teacher rating scale of social behavior (Gresham & Elliott, 1989; Vaughn & Hogan, 1990). The items on the PRPB reflect two factors: Outgoing–Initiating and Cooperating–Responding. This 6-item scale has a reported reliability of 0.85 (Walker, 1991). Much like peer ratings of acceptance, this measure provides an opportunity for each student to rate every other student on a 4-point Likert scale. Items on the scale are provided in Table 7.2.

TABLE 7.2
Peer Ratings of Prosocial Behavior

Directions: Children are to rate each target peer on the frequency with which they feel the target child demonstrates the prosocial behaviors that follow.

1 = never	2 = not very often
3 = pretty much	4 = all of the time

1. This child invites others to play with him/her.

2. This child makes friends easily.

3. This child plays/participates in games with other children.

4. This child can control his/her temper (doesn't get real angry) when he/she disagrees with others.

5. This child does something else instead of hitting when other children tease him/her.

6. This child can control himself/herself when other children tell lies about him/her.

Note. Items 1–3 correspond with Outgoing/Initiating. Items 4–6 correspond with Cooperating/Responding.
From: Vaughn, S., & Haager, D. (1994). Social assessments of students with learning disabilities: Do they measure up? In S. Vaughn & C. Bos (Eds.), *Research issues in learning disabilities: Theory, methodology, assessment, and ethics* (pp. 276–311), by S. Vaughn & D. Haager, 1994, New York: Springer-Verlag. Copyright © 1994 by Springer-Verlag. Reprinted with permission.

TABLE 7.3
Guess Who? Technique for Identifying Subtypes of Aggression

Provoked Physical Aggression

* This boy or girl will fight, but only if someone picks on him or her.
* This classmate will always fight back if you hit him or her.

Outburst Aggression

* This classmate gets very, very mad at times all of a sudden.
* This classmate gets so mad at times that he or she doesn't know what he or she is doing.

Unprovoked Physical Aggression

* This classmate starts a fight for no reason.
* This classmate gets mad while he or she is playing and ends up in a fight.
* This classmate is always looking for a fight.

Verbal Aggression

* This boy or girl often threatens other kids.
* This classmate always puts others down when playing a game with other kids.

Indirect Aggression

* This boy or girl tattles to the teacher about what other kids do.
* This classmate breaks things that belong to others on purpose.

From: Vaughn, S., & Haager, D. (1994). Social assessments of students with learning disabilities: Do they measure up? In S. Vaughn & C. Bos (Eds.), *Research issues in learning disabilities: Theory, methodology, assessment, and ethics* (pp. 276–311), by S. Vaughn & D. Haager, 1994, New York: Springer-Verlag. Copyright © 1994 by Springer-Verlag. Reprinted with permission.

In addition, a peer rating measure of aggression based on the Guess Who? technique was developed by Lesser (1959) and then used by Lancelotta and Vaughn (1989) to identify subtypes of aggressive children. Rather than rate every student in the class, students were asked to nominate individuals who represented each of the descriptors (see Table 7.3 for a list of items).

Teacher, parent, and peer reports of social skills provide important perspectives on the social functioning of target students. As with peer reports of social skills, there are relatively few self-reports of social skills. The Matson Evaluation of Social Skills with Youngsters (MESSY; Matson et al., 1983) provides a teacher rating form and a student self-report rating form (comprised of 62 items). Students evaluate themselves on each of the items using a 5-point Likert scale. The scale yields five factors: Appropriate Social Skills (23 items), Inappropriate Assertiveness (16 items), Impulsive–Recalcitrant (5 items), Overconfident (5 items), and Jealousy–Withdrawal (4 items) and 9 items that do not load on any of the factors.

Gresham and Elliott (1990) have a self-report version of their social skills rating scale, *SSRS-S* that provides a version for elementary age students (Grades 3-6) and for secondary school students (Grades 7-10). The self-rating has four dimensions: compliance, assertion, empathy, and self-control. Self-report measures of social skills are infrequently used with children for several reasons: response bias, reading difficulties, and making items understandable to youths (Gresham & Elliott, 1989; Webber, Scheuermann, & Wheeler, 1992).

Observations of Social Skills

For research purposes, observations provide several advantages for assessing social skills. First, observations offer an assessment of children's social behavior independent of teacher or parent bias, although observer bias is a potential risk (Repp, Nieminen, Olinger, & Brusca, 1988). Reliability is enhanced in observation studies by careful training of observers, interrater reliability checks, and the use of a well-defined data coding system in both qualitative and quantitative methods. Probably the greatest advantage is the opportunity to simultaneously observe the child's behavior and contextual factors such as the behaviors of teachers or peers and contextual events (Haager & Vaughn, 1995).

Although direct observation has been widely used in developmental research with NLD subjects, studies using observation techniques with LD subjects are limited (see for review Vaughn & Haager, 1994b). In the Vaughn and Haager review, eight studies that reported using observations of the social behavior of students with LD were summarized. The most recent study was conducted in 1982. Most of the studies addressed the communication behaviors of students with LD, peers' behaviors toward students with LD, children's displays of social skills in school settings, and problem solving. With the exception of work conducted by Schumaker and colleagues (Hazel, Schumaker, Sherman, & Sheldon, 1982; Schumaker, Hazel, Sherman, & Sheldon, 1982; Schumaker, Wildgen, & Sherman, 1982), observations were conducted on elementary age students.

Methods of observing include naturalistic observation, using either anecdotal recording, time sampling, frequency counting, checklists, or other recording techniques; and analogue or simulated situations designed to elicit specific responses or behaviors, often through role-playing techniques (see for review La Greca, 1990; Vaughn & Haager, 1994b). Naturalistic observation occurs when the focus is on a specific behavior(s) that occurs spontaneously in the environment (e.g., classroom, playground, or home setting; Vaughn & Haager, 1994b). This is contrasted with analogue or simulated situations in which a situation is constructed that will prompt a response from the child.

Although behavioral observations provide the best validity of all social measures (Asher & Hymel, 1981; Gresham, 1986; La Greca & Stark, 1986), the cost and time involved often prohibit their use. Naturalistic observation has the advantage of providing an assessment of a child in an environment in which the behavior occurs spontaneously, although when social behaviors infrequently occur it may be necessary to assess the behavior in a contrived setting. Observations in school settings are becoming increasingly more complicated, particularly when the researcher is interested in observing social behavior in a nondirected setting. Many school systems have replaced recess and free time with daily physical education, so there is no time during the school day when the student is involved in unguided social activities. It may be for this reason that much of the research examining the social behavior of individuals with disabilities was conducted with preschoolers (e.g., DeKlyen & Odom, 1989). Despite the need to use analogue or role-play methods of observation, these techniques have demonstrated low correlations with social status and with behaviors observed in the naturalistic setting (Asher & Hymel, 1981; Gresham, 1986). Gresham advised that the utilization of role-plays as a form of observational data may be useful in determining social skills deficits (e.g., inability to perform social tasks) rather than performance deficits (e.g., lack of use of social skills in natural environments).

In addition to observational data to assess social functioning of individuals in natural and analogue settings, there was interest in assessing the behavior of students with LD in classroom settings (Baker & Zigmond, 1990; McIntosh et al., 1993). For example, Slate and Saudargas (1986) conducted observations of fourth- and fifth-grade students with LD and average achievers and were not able to discriminate between the two groups based on their behavior. McIntosh et al. (1993) also indicated that students with LD in the general education classroom did not display more social difficulties than their peers but were less likely to respond to teachers' questions and to initiate requests for more information. This suggests that many of the social difficulties displayed by students with LD in the classroom are a result of their learning problems.

As stated elsewhere (Haager & Vaughn, 1995), there are several recurring themes regarding the assessment of social competence of individuals with LD and other at-risk groups.

Context

The setting in which the student is assessed is critical. Setting refers to where the assessment occurs, from what setting the raters are selected, and what the setting items refer to when ratings are requested. Consideration of setting is critical because most assessments of social competence occur in the school setting, a place where many at-risk students are unlikely to be successful. Thus, the extent to which the target student's behavior in the school setting is representative of his or her behavior in other settings must be considered. As a result, the use of multiple measures and raters that tap behavior in a range of settings is desirable.

Rater

Who rates the social competence of youngsters influences the outcome. Considerations about the amount of time and the setting in which the rater knows the child are important. Even when the same measure is used and ratings are completed by the special education teacher and the general education teacher, outcomes will differ (Haager & Vaughn, 1995). Multiple raters provide multiple perspectives; however, first consideration should be given to selecting a rater who matches the goals of the study or the purpose of the assessment.

Content

Consider the purpose of the measure, what it purports to assess, and what it actually assesses when selecting and interpreting the outcomes. Be sure to determine that the measure taps the dimension of interest and that items are worded appropriately.

Characteristics

Children's characteristics may interfere with their performance on social measures. For example, students with LD who have attention problems may incorrectly circle responses or write answers in the wrong place, thus altering their scores in significant ways that are not related to their social functioning. Memory and communication problems, frequently associated with students with LD, often interfere with students' performance on social measures and need to be considered when interpreting student responses.

CONCLUSION

The social functioning of at-risk youngsters is a developmental area that has yet to be thoroughly researched. Such social assessment, however, is vital to understanding the life course of these disorders and their accompanying symptomology, and is critical to the development and implementation of appropriate interventions. One explanation for this lag is the difficulty associated with assessing the social functioning of at-risk youngsters. This chapter provides an overview of the measures currently available and provides guidelines for their use. As indicated in the chapter, however, most of these measures have not been adequately tested and modified for at-risk populations. The development of adequate measures to assess self-concept, peer acceptance, social skills and behavior adjustment of at-risk youngsters progressed considerably since 1985, but is far from complete. The further development, implementation, and evaluation of reliable and valid assessment instruments would enhance and lead to greater confidence in the knowledge base.

REFERENCES

Asher, S. R., & Hymel, S. (1981). Children's social competence in peer relations: Sociometric and behavioral assessment. In J. D. Wine & M. D. Smye (Eds.), *Social competence* (pp. 124–159). New York: Guilford.

Baker J. M., & Zigmond, N. (1990). Are regular education classes equipped to accommodate students with learning disabilities? *Exceptional Children, 56*, 515–526.

Bender, W. N., & Smith, J. K. (1990). Classroom behavior of children and adolescents with learning disabilities: A meta-analysis. *Journal of Learning Disabilities, 23,* 298–306.

Berndt, T. J., & Perry, T. B. (1986). Children's perceptions of friendships as supportive relationships. *Developmental Psychology, 22,* 640–648.

Bierman, K. L., & McCauley, E. (1987). Children's descriptions of their peer interactions: Useful information for clinical child assessment. *Journal of Clinical Child Psychology, 55,* 194–200.

Bukowski, W. M., & Hoza, B. (1989). Popularity and friendship: Issues in theory, measurement, and outcome. In T. J. Berndt & G. W. Ladd (Eds.), *Peer relationships in child development* (pp. 15–45). New York: Wiley.

Bukowski, W. M., & Newcomb, A. F. (1984). Stability and determinants of sociometric status and friendship choice: A longitudinal perspective. *Developmental Psychology, 20,* 941–952.

Coie, J. D., & Dodge, K. A. (1988). Multiple sources of data on social behavior and social status. *Child Development, 59,* 815–829.

Coie, J. D., Dodge, K. A., & Coppotelli, H. (1982). Dimensions and types of social status: A cross-age perspective. *Developmental Psychology, 18,* 557–570.

Coie, J. D., Dodge, K. A., & Kupersmidt, J. B. (1990). Peer group behavior and social status. In S. R. Asher & J. D. Coie (Eds.), *Peer rejection in childhood* (pp. 17–59). Cambridge, England: Cambridge University Press.

Coie, J. D., & Kupersmidt, J. B. (1983). A behavioral analysis of emerging social status in boys' groups. *Child Development, 54,* 1400–1416.

Cowen, E. L., Pederson, A., Babigian, H., Izzo, L. D., & Trost, M. A. (1973). Long-term follow-up of early detected vulnerable children. *Journal of Consulting and Clinical Psychology, 41,* 438–446.

Crockett, L., Losoff, M., & Petersen, A. C. (1984). Perceptions of the peer group and friendship in early adolescence. *Journal of Early Adolescence, 4,* 155–181.

DeKlyen, M., & Odom, S. L. (1989). Activity structure and social interactions with peers in developmentally integrated play groups. *Journal of Early Intervention, 13,* 342–352.

Dodge, K. A. (1983). Behavioral antecedents of peer social status. *Child Development, 54,* 1386–1399.

Dodge, K. A., Coie, J. D., & Brakke, N. D. (1982). Behavior patterns of socially rejected and neglected preadolescents: The roles of social approach and aggression. *Journal of Abnormal Child Psychology, 10,* 389–409.

Garrett, M. K., & Crump, W. D. (1980). Peer acceptance, teacher preference and self-appraisal of social status among learning disabled students. *Learning Disability Quarterly, 3,* 42–48.

Gresham, F. M. (1981). Validity of social skills measures for assessing social competence in low-status children: A multivariate investigation. *Developmental Psychology, 17,* 390–398.

Gresham, F. M. (1986). Conceptual issues in the assessment of social competence in children. In P. S. Strain, M. J. Guralnick, & H. M. Walker (Eds.), *Children's social behavior: Development, assessment, and modification* (pp. 143–179). Orlando, FL: Academic Press.

Gresham, F. M. (1992). Social skills and learning disabilities: Causal, concomitant, or correlational? *School Psychology Review, 21,* 348–360.

Gresham, F. M., & Elliott, S. N. (1989). Social skills assessment technology for LD students. *Learning Disability Quarterly, 12,* 141–152.

Gresham, F. M., & Elliott, S. N. (1990). *Social skills rating system manual.* Circle Pines, MN: American Guidance Service.

Gresham, F. M., & Reschly, D. J. (1986). Social skills deficits and low peer acceptance of mainstreamed learning disabled children. *Learning Disability Quarterly, 9,* 23–32.

Haager, D. S. (1992). Multiple perspectives on the social functioning of students with learning disabilities: Teacher, parent, self, and peer reports. (Doctoral dissertation, University of Miami, 1992). *Dissertation Abstracts International, 92,* 27201.

Haager, D., & Vaughn, S. (1995). *Assessment of social competence.* Unpublished manuscript.

Hartup, W. W. (1992). Friendships and their developmental significance. In H. McGurk (Ed.), *Childhood social development: Contemporary perspectives* (pp. 175–205). Hillsdale, NJ: Lawrence Erlbaum Associates.

Hazel, J. S., & Schumaker, J. B. (1988). Social skills and learning disabilities: Current issues and recommendations for future research. In J. F. Kavanagh & T. J. Truss (Eds.), *Learning disabilities: Proceedings of the national conference* (pp. 293–344). Parkton, MD: York Press.

Hazel, J. S., Schumaker, J. B., Sherman, J. A., & Sheldon, J. (1982). Application of a group training program in social skills and problem solving to learning disabled and non-learning disabled youth. *Learning Disability Quarterly, 5,* 398–408.

Howes, C. (1987). Peer interaction of young children. *Monographs of the Society for Research in Child Development, 53* (1, Serial No. 217)

Interagency Committee on Learning Disabilities. (1987). *Learning disabilities: A report to the U.S. Congress.* Bethesda, MD: National Institutes of Health.

Keogh, B. K., Tchir, C., & Windeguth-Behn, A. (1974). Teachers' perceptions of educationally high risk children. *Journal of Learning Disabilities, 7,* 367–374.

Killen, M. (1989). Context, conflict, and coordination in social development. In L. T. Winegar (Ed.), *Social interaction and the development of children's understanding* (pp. 119–146). Norwood, NJ: Ablex.

La Greca, A. M. (Ed.). (1990). *Through the eyes of the child.* Needham Heights, MA: Allyn & Bacon.

La Greca, A. M., & Fetter, M. D. (1995). Peer relations. In A. R. Eisen, C. A. Kearney & C. E. Schaefer (Eds.), *Clinical handbook of anxiety disorders in children and adolescents* (pp. 82–130). Northvale, NJ: Aronson.

LaGreca, A. M. & Mesibov, G. B. (1979). Social skills intervention with learning disabled children: Selecting skills and implementing training. *Journal of Clinical Child Psychology, 8,* 234–241.

La Greca, A. M., & Stark, P. (1986). Naturalistic observations of children's social behavior. In P. S. Strain, M. J. Guralnick, & H. M. Walker (Eds.), *Children's social behavior: Development, assessment, and modification* (pp. 181–213). Orlando, FL: Academic Press.

Lancelotta, G. X., & Vaughn, S. (1989). Relation between types of aggression and sociometric status: Peer and teacher perceptions. *Journal of Educational Psychology, 81,* 86–90.

Landau, S., & Milich, R. (1990). Assessment of children's social status and peer relations. In A. M. La Greca (Ed.), *Through the eyes of the child* (pp. 259–291). Needham Heights, MA: Allyn & Bacon.

Laursen, B. P. (1990). Relationships and conflict during adolescence (Doctoral dissertation, University of Minnesota, 1989). *Dissertation Abstracts International, 90,* 05241.

Lesser, G. S. (1959). The relationship between various forms of aggression and popularity among lower class children. *Journal of Educational Psychology, 50,* 20–25.

Lyon, G. R. (1994). *Frames of reference for the assessment of learning disabilities: New views on measurement issues.* Baltimore: Brookes.

Matson, J. L., Rotatori, A. F., & Helsel, W. J. (1983). Development of a rating scale to measure social skills in children: The Matson evaluation of social skills with youngsters. *Behavioral Research and Therapy, 21,* 335–340.

McIntosh, R., Vaughn, S., Schumm, J. S., Haager, D., & Lee, O. (1993). Observations of students with learning disabilities in general education classrooms. *Exceptional Children, 60*(3), 249–261.

McKinney, J. D., & Feagans, L. (1983). Adaptive classroom behavior of learning disabled students. *Journal of Learning Disabilities, 16,* 360–367.

McKinney, J. D., & Speece, D. L. (1983). Classroom behavior and the academic progress of learning disabled students. *Journal of Applied Developmental Psychology, 4,* 149–161.

Moreno, J. L. (1934). *Who shall survive? A new approach to the problem of human interrelations.* Washington, DC: Nervous and Mental Disease Publishing.

Parker, J. G., & Asher, S. R. (1987). Peer relations and later personal adjustment: Are low-accepted children at risk? *Psychological Bulletin, 102,* 357–389.

Pearl, R., Donahue, M., & Bryan, T. (1986). Social relationships of learning-disabled children. In J. K. Torgesen & B. Y. L. Wong (Eds.), *Psychological and educational perspectives on learning disabilities* (pp. 193–224). Orlando, FL: Academic Press.

Repp, A. C., Nieminen, G. S., Olinger, E., & Brusca, R. (1988). Direct observation: Factors affecting the accuracy of observers. *Exceptional Children, 55,* 29–36.

Rourke, B. P. (1989). *Nonverbal learning disabilities: The syndrome and the model.* New York: Gulf

Schumaker, J. B., Hazel, J. S., Sherman, J. A., & Sheldon, J. (1982). Social skill performances of learning disabled, non-learning disabled, and delinquent adolescents. *Learning Disability Quarterly, 5,* 409–414.

Schumaker, J. B., Wildgen, J. S., & Sherman, J. A. (1982). Social interaction of learning disabled junior high students in their regular classrooms: An observational analysis. *Journal of Learning Disabilities, 15*(6), 355–358.

Singleton, L. C., & Asher, S. R. (1977). Peer preferences and social interaction among third-grade children in an integrated school district. *Journal of Educational Psychology, 69,* 330–336.

Slate, J. R., & Saudargas, R. A. (1986). Differences in learning disabled and average students' classroom behaviors. *Learning Disability Quarterly, 9,* 61–67.

Stone, W. L., & La Greca, A. M. (1990). The social status of children with LD: A reexamination. *Journal of Learning Disabilities, 23,* 32–37.

Vaughn, S., Elbaum, B., & Schumm, J. S. (in press). Are students with learning disabilities in inclusion classrooms better liked and less lonely? *Journal of Learning Disabilities.*

Vaughn, S., & Haager, D. (1994a). Social competence as a multifaceted construct: How do students with learning disabilities fare? *Learning Disability Quarterly, 17,* 253–266.

Vaughn, S., & Haager, D. (1994b). The measurement and assessment of social skills. In G. R. Lyon (Ed.), *Frames of reference for the assessment of learning disabilities: New views on measurement issues* (pp. 555–570). Baltimore: Brookes.

Vaughn, S., Haager, D., Hogan, A., & Kouzekanani, K. (1992). Self-concept and peer acceptance in students with learning disabilities: A four- to five-year prospective study. *Journal of Educational Psychology, 84,* 43–50.

Vaughn, S., & Hogan, A. (1990). Social competence and learning disabilities: A prospective study. In H. L. Swanson & B. K. Keogh (Eds.), *Learning disabilities: Theoretical and research issues* (pp. 175–191). Hillsdale, NJ: Lawrence Erlbaum Associates.

Vaughn, S., & Hogan, A. (1994). The social competence of students with learning disabilities over time: A within-individual examination. *Journal of Learning Disabilities, 27*(5), 292–303.

Vaughn, S., Hogan, A., Kouzekanani, K., & Shapiro, S. (1990). Peer acceptance, self-perceptions, and social skills of learning disabled students prior to identification. *Journal of Educational Psychology, 82,* 101–106.

Vaughn, S., & La Greca, A. (1993). Social skills training: Why, who, what, and how. In W. N. Bender (Ed.), *Learning disabilities: Best practices for professionals* (pp. 251–271). Stoneham, MA: Butterworth-Heinemann.

Vaughn, S., McIntosh, R., Schumm, J. S., Haager, D., & Callwood, D. (1993). Social status, peer acceptance, and reciprocal friendships revisited. *Learning Disabilities Research and Practice, 8,* 82–88.

Vaughn, S. R., McIntosh, R., & Spencer-Rowe, J. (1991). Peer rejection is a stubborn thing: Increasing peer acceptance of rejected students with learning disabilities. *Learning Disabilities Research and Practice, 6,* 83–88.

Vaughn, S., Zaragoza, N., Hogan, A., & Walker, J. (1993). A four-year longitudinal investigation of the social skills and behavior problems of students with learning disabilities. *Journal of Learning Disabilities, 26*(6), 404–412.

Vosk, B., Forehand, R., Parker, J. B., & Richard, K. (1982). A multimethod comparison of popular and unpopular children. *Developmental Psychology, 18,* 571–575.

Walker, J. J. (1991). Social desirability response tendencies in young children: Relation to teacher, peer, and self-ratings of social competence. (Doctoral dissertation, University of Miami, 1990). *Dissertation Abstracts International, 91,* 14822.

Walker, H. M., Colvin, G., & Ramsey, E. (1995). *Antisocial behavior in school: Strategies and best practices.* Pacific Grove, CA: Brooks/Cole.

Walker, H. M., & McConnell, S. R. (1988). *Walker–McConnell scale of social competence and school adjustment.* Austin, TX: PRO-ED.

Walker, H. M., & McConnell, S. R. (1993). *The Walker–McConnell scale of social competence and school adjustment.* Eugene: University of Oregon.

Walker, H. M., McConnell, S. R., Holmes, D., Todis, B., Walker, J., & Golden, N. (1983). *The Walker social skills curriculum: ACCEPTS program.* Austin, TX: PRO-ED.

Wasik, B. H. (1987). Sociometric measures and peer descriptors of kindergarten children: A study of reliability and validity. *Journal of Clinical Child Psychology, 16,* 218–224.

Webber, J., Scheuermann, B., & Wheeler, L. (1992). Relationships among student scores on four social skills measures. *Diagnostique, 17*(4), 244–254.

Wiener, J. (1987). Peer status of learning disabled children and adolescents: A review of the literature. *Learning Disabilities Research, 2*(2), 62–79.

Wiener, J., Harris, P., & Shirer, C. (1990). Achievement and social-behavioral correlates of peer status in LD children. *Learning Disability Quarterly, 13,* 114–127.

Zaragoza, N., Vaughn, S., & McIntosh, R. (1991). Social skills interventions and children with behavior problems: A review. *Behavioral Disorders, 16*(4), 260–275.

8

Tending the Social Ecology: Alternative Intervention Strategies for Violent Behavior

Alan Vaux
Southern Illinois University

The end of the 20th century is approaching, the American Psychological Association (APA) recently celebrated its first 100 years, and the country is in the throes of a debate about the proper role of government and the scope of public and private responsibility, not least as these issues concern the health and well-being of the citizenry. This seems an appropriate time to examine the contribution of psychology. How well have we identified, prioritized, and addressed major problems? What are the strengths and limitations of our principal intervention strategies? In the first section of this chapter, I describe the growth of applied psychology, discuss concerns about the nature of that growth (specifically, that dominance by clinical psychology has severely restricted the range of applied psychology interventions), and then briefly outline an alternative paradigm (i.e., community psychology). In the second section, I provide an overview of several forms of violence in order to make several key points: that these very serious problems have elicited a limited response from applied psychology and that the distribution of these problems indicates the need for ecological models of explanation and intervention—a shift from dominant intrapsychic clinical models. In the third and final section, I suggest some alternative intervention strategies for dealing with various forms of violence. Given the current state of relevant theory, research, and intervention, the illustration of these strategies is necessarily general: It is too early to provide a detailed description of demonstrably successful tactics; I merely argue for a shift in strategy—interventions designed to tend social ecologies.

APPLIED PSYCHOLOGY

Rise of Applied Psychology

There seems little question that psychology expanded dramatically during this century. In an APA centennial article, Sechrest (1992) noted that the number of psychologists had increased some twenty-fold since 1937, 10 times the growth rate of the population. By the early 1990s, APA boasts over 100,000 members, no small clan. Indeed, the majority of the world's psychologists work in the U.S.

There is less agreement about the character of this growth. Certainly, it has been predominantly in applied psychology—potentially an enormous benefit to the U.S. population. Sechrest (1992) estimated that, in the 10 years from 1975 to 1985, the number of **licensed** psychologists—presumably involved in practice of some kind—increased from 20,000 to 46,000, and that the number of clinically trained psychologists was about 23 per 100,000 (23/CK) of the population in 1989, almost double the rate of psychiatrists. Interestingly, the supply seems to be unevenly distributed around the country—presumably not a simple reflection of need—with almost four times the rate in the New England states as in the East South Central states (41 vs. 12/CK).

The disproportionate growth of applied psychology is very evident when we look at new PhD degrees, the vast majority of which are awarded in clinical and, to a lesser extent, counseling psychology. Clinical and counseling account for about 60% of the doctorates awarded by U.S. psychology departments in 1993. Of the other 25 subfields, only school and developmental psychology reach 5%, and 14 subfields fail to reach the 1% mark. Thus, about 12 PhDs were awarded in clinical or counseling for every 1 in school or in developmental psychology. Although some 1,200 doctorates were awarded in clinical or counseling in 1993, fewer than 10 were awarded in 9 subfields, including comparative, engineering, environmental, general, geropsychology, psycholinguistics, psychometrics, psychopharmacology, and systems–history–methods. In short, psychology has grown dramatically, especially applied psychology, and more specifically clinical psychology. As Sechrest (1992) neatly put it, "Clinical Psychology is Big."

Blessing or Curse?

The growth in clinical psychology—and in counseling psychology, which increasingly resembles it—might be seen as a great blessing, a tremendous contribution to the well-being of the population. Unfortunately, many take a less sanguine view and are critical of the field as it has developed. Let me briefly note some of these criticisms.

Many Human Problems and Potential Areas of Application Have Been Crowded out by Clinical Psychology.   In an early discussion of the future of clinical psychology, Woodworth (1937/1992) wrote "I do not believe that it [psychology] will split up into several disconnected specialties . . . The

scientific needs of these specialized groups will hold them together and will also hold them in close association with the general body of psychologists . . . This means that the profession of personal service psychology is going to be a large, highly varied but unified profession" (p. 16). Woodworth's predictions could hardly have been more wrong: Psychology is fragmented and "scientific needs" seem to divide rather than connect us. Yet, a more profound but often overlooked consequence of the dramatic growth of clinical psychology is that it has defined applied or professional psychology. As Fox (1994) and others noted, applied psychology is far from the "highly varied" profession Woodworth anticipated: Rather, psychopathology dominates problem identification and conceptualization, and psychotherapy dominates intervention. Problems and interventions not immediately recognizable within this framework are either transformed and absorbed or rejected as irrelevant—severely hampering the development of other approaches and domains of application.

Clinical Psychology Has Diverged From and, to a Large Degree, Functions Independently From the Core Discipline of Psychology. Certainly the growth of clinical research generated a high yield by bringing psychological theories and methods to bear on problems of human functioning. Yet, even within the research domain of clinical psychology, there is a disturbing lack of connection to the traditional and contemporary core of our field. Most clinical graduate programs provide training that is clinical in orientation, not integrative, and not optimal preparation for a research career. Students interested in becoming clinical scientists are hard-pressed to develop research proficiencies and substantive expertise while meeting clinical training requirements. Moreover, psychology's scientists and academics are increasingly clinical psychologists. Theories are lost, methods never learned, findings rediscovered, and so forth.

Much more critical, of course, is the separation of clinical practitioners from the academic discipline of psychology. In their study of APA-accredited clinical programs, Mayne, Norcross, and Sayette (1994) found that although the number of applicants was comparable across various types of program—PsyD, practice-oriented PhD, equal-emphasis PhD, and research-oriented PhD—the PsyD programs accepted two to three times as many students as the other programs and the research-oriented programs had the lowest acceptance rates: Add this to the large number of nonaccredited programs, and the trend is clear, "psychology " is becoming "psychological practice." Nor can we assume that graduate training is simply career-stage-appropriate specialization, building on a strong disciplinary foundation: Mayne et al. (1994) found that 10% of programs reported no specific course requirements, 10% required a psychology major or equivalent, but no more than three specific courses were required by more than 10% of the programs (paradoxically, these were statistics 65%, methods 48%, and psychopathology 29%). During graduate training, a practice-oriented student can limit his or her exposure to core psychological theory and research, need engage in only superficial synthesis of extant knowledge, and certainly need not incorporate it in practice. It is an open secret in the discipline—evident in program size, graduate admissions, faculty allocations, conferences, and identity—that the tail now wags the dog. The development of APS by research psychologists who felt that APA no longer represented the discipline is an indication of this split.

The Practice of Clinical Psychology Is Often Conducted Independently of, and Sometimes With Disdain for, an Empirical Knowledge Base. Almost everyone agrees that deriving practice from science is difficult. Even so, the commitment to use empirically based knowledge in conceptualizing problems and designing interventions often seems weak. When clinicians are asked about the usefulness of various sources of information for their practice, research publications are routinely rated at the bottom of the scale (Morrow-Bradley & Elliot, 1986). As Sechrest (1992) put it, "clinical psychologists do not even agree that clinical psychology should be scientific, many practitioners seeming to believe that art, intuition, literature, philosophy, and so on are the more dependable bases for practice" (p. 20). In a presidential address to APA Division 12 (Clinical Psychology) Section 3 (Society for a Science of Clinical Psychology), McFall (1991) presented a "manifesto for a science of clinical psychology." He decried the widespread tolerance for and promotion of practice distinct from science, and lamented the fact that advocates for a science of clinical psychology were relegated on the organizational chart to the level of a special interest group and that APA—in an effort to appease its scientist lobby—now devotes a portion of the national convention to "science weekend."

Clinical Psychology Has No Standards for Practice. In 1937, noting the potential demand for services, Woodworth wrote, "Will this vacuum be filled by an inrush of half-trained and semi-scientific practitioners, or are the leaders in the profession likely to be successful in their efforts to maintain and raise standards." (p. 16). Sechrest (1992) noted that although "enthusiasm for licensure, designation, and other professionally competitive maneuvers continues unabated" (p. 21), there is "little enthusiasm, even strong resistance, to close examination of the scientific basis for practice" (p. 21). There has been considerable jockeying among interest groups with related training (PsyDs, EdDs, MSWs, etc.) to gain access to professional turf, notably the private practice of psychotherapy. Sechrest noted that some colleagues have been developing a database of advertising used by psychologists regarding self-declared specialization. This and other sources yielded items that strain credulity, including APA members, PhDs, and licensed psychologists who claim to be specialists in such issues as "prenatal bonding," "abduction and abuse by extraterrestrials," and "treatment of the ambivalent archaic primitive liquid symbiotic transference" (this last in one state's psychology association newsletter advertisement). As Sechrest noted, clinical psychology seems to be unwilling to confront its "far side."

The Adoption of a Medical Paradigm Has Been a Prerequisite to the Growth of Clinical (and Counseling) Psychology.   A strong case can be made that applied psychology has won acceptance to the extent that it has adopted a medical paradigm, some key assumptions of which are that human problems are individual in nature, are analogous to somatic illnesses, involve pathology, can be effectively dealt with through office-based clinical treatment, and can be usefully described through a categorical diagnostic system. Professional and lay language are riddled with the terminology of this perspective. Yet, even within the more traditional areas of psychopathology difficulties are often social, bear little resemblance to illnesses in onset, course, or recovery, have no known pathological process, and often seem more like extremes of everyday functioning and adaptive processes, sometimes reflecting personality characteristics that by adulthood are highly resistant to change. The current reconceptualization of personality disorders in terms of the five-factor model of normal personality splendidly illustrates the potential benefits of escaping the medical view of pathological categories (Vaux, 1992; Widiger, 1994). A more radical shift would involve conceptualizing difficulties in terms of personal adaptive characteristics, niche-breadth, and habitat features.

The great flywheels of the medical paradigm are the successive diagnostic systems published by the American Psychiatric Association (1994). Historically, it took three attempts and several decades before diagnostic classification approached acceptable reliability. Despite recent progress made through a more empirical descriptive approach, many questions remain about the validity of the diagnostic system, because it is based as much on clinical lore as on empirical research. (Childhood problems are an exception: Having been ignored for decades, there was less clinical lore to hamper empirically based diagnostic criteria [Achenbach, 1985].) Further, the commitment to a categorical rather than dimensional system severely hampers the contributions research can make to the refinement of a descriptive system of diagnosis. As Mirowsky and Ross (1989) noted: Superimposing a diagnosis on a person's symptoms and situation does not add information; rather it removes information. Worse still, it entices us to think, talk, and act as if a hidden entity had been revealed. The mythical entity insinuates itself into the role of a named actor, and the symptoms and situation dissolve into mere signs of its presence. (p. 12).

The medical paradigm also led clinical psychology to focus treatment almost exclusively on those who seek help. Demand for services is economically important, but it is not equivalent to service need, nor is it the sole or most legitimate basis on which to set priorities for action by an applied discipline. To draw an analogy, people are quick to demand medical services when suffering, but slow to demand public health measures that may have less dramatic but more pervasive benefits. One manifestation of this problem is that many women currently receive treatment for "post-traumatic stress disorder" following rape (an important service, no less so for being a recent development), but a propensity to rape is not and (to my knowledge) never has been a diagnostic category, nor is it subject to extensive treatment services, let alone preventive interventions.

Conclusion.   Psychology has grown dramatically in the past century. This growth was disproportionately in the applied area, particularly clinical psychology. As the century approaches an end, clinical psychology seems ready to dominate the field—in numbers, paradigmatic assumptions, and disciplinary identity. On the surface, these developments might be seen as an enormous benefit to the U.S. population—the emergence from a solid scientific foundation of a mature profession. Yet, the emergent profession has been severely attacked as disconnected from its disciplinary foundation, unscientific, resistant to quality standards, and resting on questionable paradigmatic assumptions (Fox, 1994; McFall, 1991; Sechrest, 1992). These issues aside, the sheer size of clinical psychology raises concerns about how narrowly it represents the broad potential of applied psychology. In a distinguished career address, Fox (1994) was highly critical of the profession's primary focus on mental health issues. Reminiscent of Woodward (1937), he proposed a broad and diverse professional psychology concerned with enhancing the effectiveness of human behavior.

An Alternative Paradigm

I would like briefly to propose an alternative perspective on what applied psychology could and perhaps should be. Community psychology emerged from the civil and academic unrest of the 1960s, along with other nascent applied psychology areas. The major paradigmatic assumptions of community psychology are outlined briefly here and proposed as an alternative that would include but go far beyond a clinical approach.

Population Focus.   Although clinical psychology addresses the issues of those who seek out services, community psychology is concerned with the well-being of the population at large. In this sense, it is analogous to public health. Demand-based services may be disproportionately shaped by the resource-rich and by short-term need (e.g., cosmetic surgery and psychoanalysis may thrive, while inoculation and parent training wither). Arguably, conceptions of need should reflect problem prevalence, severity, impact on others, and epidemiological risk.

Breadth of Concern—Human Welfare.   Community psychology is concerned with human welfare, not just traditional psychopathology. This includes not only concern with a broader array of problems—transportation safety as well as head injury, "normal" as well as "psychopathological" criminality—but also with the promotion of adaptive functioning (civility, moral development, academic achievement, adult leisure, and so forth).

Social Criticism.   Community psychologists argue that the recognition of "problems," the priority they are given, and the solutions suggested are all social and political processes. The point can be made dramatically by imagining oneself being "well-adjusted" living in 1960 in a segregated South, in 1938 in an explicitly antiSemitic prewar Germany, or in 1920 when women did not have a vote. We cannot just innocently accept problems and priorities as given. The problem agenda, problem characterization, and existing interventions all need to be subjected to careful and ongoing social criticism.

Needs Assessment. Community psychology recognizes the importance of the empirical assessment of need for intervention. Once need is not equated with service demand, then we require epidemiological data on the incidence, prevalence, and distribution of problems, as well as comparable data on indicators of adaptive functioning (e.g., incidents of altruism, library circulation, school achievement, etc.). Obviously, the identification of need and the prioritizing of services will often require the synthesis of diverse data that, ideally, would inform the allocation of resources.

Social Ecological Perspective. From this point of view, human problems can rarely be understood, let alone resolved, independently of the social context within which they are embedded. Although an understanding of basic psychological processes might best be achieved through analysis of phenomena under highly controlled conditions, application of that knowledge must recognize extant conditions in relevant contexts. For example, poor parenting practices may reflect lack of skill, but also lack of support and limited resources that in turn reflect economic insecurity: The implication that parent training may be ineffective without changes in supporting conditions is an important one. Quite likely, it is no accident that the much decried "epidemic" of out-of-wedlock births is highest in that ethnic group with the highest rate of young male unemployment. Were the lack of stable material resources and poor prospects not the impediment to marriage that they are, critics would shift their moral outrage to those who have the gall to seek traditional family life without the means to do so! In short, the intrapsychic focus dominant in psychology may severely hamper understanding and resolution of many problems.

Diverse Interventions—Focus on Development and Prevention. Applied psychology, as conceived here, is likely to require a large and diverse tool kit of intervention techniques—far more diverse than those of classic psychotherapy. Such interventions often will involve an emphasis on prevention and development—that is, interventions designed to promote competence and resilience, to limit the effects of life disruptions, to redirect problematic life trajectories, and to facilitate the negotiation of developmental transitions. Moreover, it is important to consider the sustainability of those interventions. Programs that demand an unusual and unsustainable expenditure of financial or personnel resources have little social utility.

Program Evaluation. Community psychology recognizes the importance of the ongoing empirical evaluation of intervention efforts. Programs must be regularly monitored, subjected to critical review, and improved. Moreover, agencies, funding, and career structures need to be designed to facilitate rather than resist such ongoing adaptation. This is no easy task: Clinical psychology has strenuously resisted efforts to evaluate effectiveness and for the most part practice has blithely ignored or reinterpreted relevant empirical evidence—with some justification, although probably less than was exercised.

Conclusion. Community psychology represents an alternative paradigm for applied psychology—one that would include mental health as one domain of concern and psychotherapy as one strategy of intervention. My aim in the remainder of this chapter is to illustrate the limitations of clinical psychology and the potential of community psychology with respect to problems of violence.

ANTISOCIAL BEHAVIOR

This chapter is part of a larger effort to examine two broad areas of functioning, pro-and antisocial behavior, in terms of the limitations of extant applied psychology and the promise of the alternative paradigm just outlined. Obviously, these seem crucial to the well-being of the population and in many respects are complementary. By *prosocial behavior*, I mean both general civility (low rates of obnoxious public behavior, consideration for strangers, and trustworthiness) and capacity for friendship and intimacy (caring, respect, involvement, and secure attachment). By *violence*, I mean action knowingly undertaken by a person, group, or organization that is likely to result in substantial physical or psychological harm or suffering. Such actions are most likely to be recognized as violence when they violate recognized rights, deviate from established norms, or betray the trust of relationship.

In my view, neither of these general areas received the attention they deserve in applied psychology for several reasons: (a) clinical psychology focuses on problems, not prosocial behavior, (b) it focuses on psychopathology, not "normal" problems, (c) it focuses on those seeking services—victims rather than perpetrators of violence, and most important (d) social criticism and a shift in cultural perspective were necessary to reveal several of the problems of violence. In this chapter, I focus only on antisocial behavior, particularly select forms of violence. In this section, I provide data on incidence and social variation. My purpose is to show that these forms of violence are widespread enough to warrant the attention of applied psychologists, require ecological rather than intrapsychic explanations, and offer important opportunities for intervention.

Murder

Unlike many other kinds of violence, the definition of murder is relatively unproblematic. Moreover, it tends not to go undetected, so official statistics are quite reliable and valid (unless otherwise noted, data here are from

Holmes & DeBurger, 1988). In 1990, the overall U.S. murder rate was 9.5 per 100,000 (CK) of population, twice that in most large cities (Holmes & DeBurger, 1988; "Measuring Crime," 1994). This amounts to about 23,000 deaths per year, almost one half the U.S. battle deaths each year of World War II. With respect to age, most victims are young, about 60% younger than age 35. Most perpetrators are also young, an estimated one third between ages 15 and 24. With regard to gender, most victims (75%) and most perpetrators are male: Men kill 83% of male victims and 90% of female victims. Murder is almost entirely intraracial, but unevenly distributed by race. Thus, it is estimated that about 90% of murders involve a victim and perpetrator of the same race, yet 41% of victims and an estimated 45% of perpetrators are African American. Homicide is now the leading cause of death among young Black men. Indeed, between 1976 and 1992 the annual homicide victim rate (per CK) for Black teens (age 14–17) increased from about 30 to 75, and for young Black men (age 18–24) from about 120 to 190, whereas the rate for all groups of White men remained under 25 (data from the National Crime Analysis Program at Northeastern University and from the National Center for Health Statistics; cited in "Homicide," 1994).

Obviously, this is a very complicated and sensitive issue: Almost certainly, the distribution of murder has less to do with ethnicity per se than with the special place of African Americans in U.S. economy and culture. Contrary to the image of murder as a stranger-perpetrated instrumental act, only about 50% of murders involve strangers, whereas about 50% involve friends, relatives, or acquaintances: Indeed, 9% of murders are committed by a spouse. That is, although murders are committed for instrumental goals such as robbery, many take place in the context of arguments between people who know and care—sometimes too deeply—about one another. Another indicator of the intimacy of violence is that the leading cause of workplace fatalities among women is now homicide (43% of total), many a spillover from domestic violence (Bureau of Labor, cited by Dunkel, 1994).

Murder rates vary over time as well as across geographic and cultural areas. The U.S. murder rate rose steadily for decades, doubling from 4.8/CK in 1955 to a peak of over 10/CK in 1980, remaining at about that level today (Holmes & DeBurger, 1988). Rates of aggravated assault have also been rising steadily, from about 60/CK in 1955 to almost 300/CK in 1984 (Holmes & DeBurger, 1988). Although aggravated assault statistics are less reliable than those for murder, they are important because aggravated assault and murder may differ only in a perpetrator's strength or aim, a victim's vulnerability, the alacrity of an ambulance, or the distance to a hospital.

Violence also varies, sometimes dramatically, across social and cultural regions. Again, the murder rate is a valuable indicator because it tends to be reliable and less subject than other measures to variations in definition, detection, or recordkeeping. Dramatic differences are evident in murder rates across major cities in industrialized countries: for example, the rates (per CK) in 1990 were 1 in Tokyo, 2.5 in London, 29 in New York, and 81 in Washington, DC ("Does Death Work," 1994).

Within the United States, the murder rate varies markedly across cities. Thus, some cities have rates (per CK) around 10 (e.g., San Francisco, Indianapolis), others have rates around 25 (e.g., Chicago, New York, Los Angeles), whereas others have rates above 70 (e.g., Detroit, Washington, DC). Murder rates also vary by region of the country, being highest in the South (10/CK) and lowest in the Midwest and Northeast (6/CK), suggesting broad subnational cultural influences. Lester (1987) presented findings suggesting the importance of weapons as an explanation for the excess of violence in the South; thus, a "southerness" index correlated with homicide rates, gun suicide, and gun accidents. However, using archival, survey, and experimental data, Nisbett (1993) presented a strong case that Southern violence is related to a "culture of honor" linked to historic cultural factors shared by the people who settled the South, specifically dependence on a herding economy. White male homicide rates are two to three times higher in the South than North, especially in rural areas, but only for argument-related homicides. Southerners responding to surveys were no more likely than Northerners to endorse violent solutions to problems in general, but only when problems related to the protection of loved ones or a response to insult. Finally, Southerners were more likely than Northerners to respond to experimental insult with anger and to propose violent solutions in experimental scenarios afterward.

Murder is a serious problem that received little attention from applied psychologists. Of course, from the dominant perspective of clinical psychology, murder victims make poor clients. The epidemiology of murder strongly suggests that it cannot be understood through intrapsychic models alone. If we are to understand murder, let alone intervene to reduce it, we need social ecological models that synthesize knowledge about persons, relationships, social settings, and culture.

Rape

Rape is an extremely serious problem that until the 1980s was "hidden": narrowly defined in legal statutes, underestimated by official statistics, little studied by social scientists, and largely ignored by clinicians. This situation changed somewhat with the "uncovering" of the problem by feminist scholars (e.g., Brownmiller, 1976).

Rape incidence rates reported in the literature vary dramatically, perhaps more than any other form of violence (Koss & Harvey, 1991). A substantial portion of this inconsistency is explained by differences in definition (traditional or reform statutes) and in research method. Longstanding, oft-cited, and certainly wrong are the figures published in the Uniform Crime Reports (UCR), a collation of statistics reported by police forces around the country. According to the UCR figures, the national annual rape rate is less than 1 per 1,000 (0.73/K), only 6% of violent crime, although still a sobering total of 92,000 rapes in 1988. Beginning in 1966, the National Crime Survey (NCS)—a national, household, victimization survey—has been conducted. According to the NCS, the rape rate is 1.3/K, about twice the UCR estimate.

Moreover, compared to the UCR figures, a smaller proportion of rapes were completed and involved strangers. Both UCR and NCS data involve traditional, conservative definitions of rape, reported in the context of crime, and officially reported to police in the case of UCR data.

A dramatically different picture is obtained from community surveys of sexual behavior that use less restrictive, reform definitions of rape. For example, Russell (1982) conducted sensitive interviews with a large random sample of women residents in San Francisco. Using a California reform definition, Russell estimated the rape rate at 27/K. This is about 20 times the NCS and 40 times the UCR estimates. Moreover, these rapes differed from the "official" picture: Only 11% involved strangers, whereas 62% involved current–former husbands, lovers, or male relatives. Koss, Koss, and Woodruff (1990) conducted a large mail survey in Cleveland and estimated the rape rate as 28/K using the narrow UCR definition and 62/K using an Ohio reform definition. Definitional issues are clearly important, but data collection method is strikingly so: Official reports are merely the tip of the iceberg. The reluctance of women to report rape to the police (possibly lessening with advocacy efforts) is an important issue. It represents one of many instances in which the scope of a social problem greatly exceeds the portion that engages a formal response. Part of this reluctance lies in the nature of the rapes: Again, only about 17% of rapes involved strangers , whereas 39% involved husbands, partners, or relatives. (It should be noted that prior to state reforms during the 1980s, definitions of rape excluded marital rape as a legal possibility.) Koss, Gidycz, and Wisniewski (1987) conducted a survey of students at 32 colleges nationwide. In this group, rape rates were particularly high, 76/K using the UCR definition and 166/K using a reform definition. Again, the majority of rapes, 84%, involved a known perpetrator, with 57% occurring in the context of a date.

Rape, like murder, appears to vary across age, social group, and geography, and these differences are thought to only partly reflect differential reporting (Baron & Straus, 1987; Koss & Harvey, 1991). Most scholars now take a social ecological view: They recognize person, situational, relationship, institutional, and cultural influences as important (Koss & Harvey, 1991). The propensity to rape reflects—albeit in extreme form—widely held norms and beliefs, common interactional patterns, and cultural blueprints regarding the social position of men and women (Baron & Straus, 1987; Brownmiller, 1976; Koss & Harvey, 1991).

Violence Against Children

Violence within the family also remained a hidden problem until recently. Legal, social service, and research interest in child abuse was extremely limited until the 1960s, in spouse abuse until the 1970s, and in child sexual abuse until the 1980s. One can still read excellent scholarly reviews of the psychological research literature on aggression that barely mention these topics (e.g., Geen, 1990) and journals devoted to such violence are recent (e.g., the *Journal of Interpersonal Violence* was first published in 1986).

Extremely important work in estimating the extent of family violence—both between spouses and between parents and children—was
conducted by Straus and Gelles in their National Family Violence Surveys
of 1975 and 1985 (Straus, Gelles, & Steinmetz, 1980; Straus & Gelles, 1990),
and by Finkelhor in his surveys of child sexual abuse (Finkelhor, 1979;
Finkelhor, Hotaling, Lewis, & Smith, 1990). For brevity, I focus only on
violence against children here.

Finkelhor and Dziuba-Leatherman (1994) recently synthesized diverse
national estimates of child victimization. Although used to seeing these
estimates separately, I was stunned by the larger picture of child victimization presented by these collected data. It is clear that some serious forms of
violence occur infrequently but sufficiently often to be of major concern; for
instance, homicide (0.03/K), abduction by strangers (0.06/K) and family
(6/K), psychological maltreatment (3/K), and sexual abuse (6/K). Other
problems, such as neglect (20/K), physical abuse (23/K), and rape (118/K),
occur quite commonly. Yet other problems are extremely common, such as
assault (311/K), theft (497/K), physical punishment (499/K), and sibling
assault (800/K). The most common forms of child victimization, such as
peer or sibling assault, are often trivialized: a view that appears to reflect
an implicit sense of the limited rights of children rather than any solid
grounds for demonstrating that these incidents are less severe than is
assault between adults. Moreover, on the basis of data from the NCS and
UCR, teenagers appear to experience a higher rate of victimization than do
adults with respect to several crimes, including assault, rape, and robbery
(Finkelhor & Dziuba-Leatherman, 1994).

Victimization varies in a manner related to developmental and relationship factors, again highlighting the importance of ecological context. For
example, child homicide varies quite dramatically by age and by perpetrator, as a function of dependency and niche. Very young and highly dependent children are most often killed by parents or other family caretakers, who
kill them through neglect, abusive control efforts, or abusive expressive
violence (Goetting, 1988). For example, in Illinois in 1993, 74 children were
killed by parents in abuse–neglect cases. Infants and toddlers have been
drowned, shaken to death, even thrown off bridges and through windows,
sometimes by parents so ignorant of child development that they thought
an infant was soiling itself to spite them. Risk of homicide rises again in
adolescence, but perpetrators at this age tend to be acquaintances, and
deaths often involve guns used in social disputes, sometimes simply being
a bystander in a dangerous neighborhood. Homicide is the leading cause
of death among 15 to 19 year-olds in New York City. In Chicago, 61 children
under 15 were killed in 1993, and 29 under 10 in 1991 ("Year's toll," 1994),
whereas in St. Louis in 1993, 17 children under 14 were killed, 6% of all
homicides ("Silence protects killers," 1994). In a survey of New York City
public schools, 7% of 9th to 12th graders reported bringing a gun to school
within the previous month, and about 25% of urban high schools now
report utilizing metal detectors (cited in Dodell, 1993). Increasingly, youth
occupy dangerous habitats.

With respect to gender differences, girls and boys show similar rates of victimization in terms of abuse, homicide, and sexual abuse up to about age 5. After age 5, girls are more likely to experience sexual abuse (twice to three times more likely). Boys are more likely to experience physical abuse and homicide—five times more likely by age 17 (Finkelhor & Dziuba-Leatherman, 1994).

Space does not permit an examination of the literature on the consequences of violence against children, although these likely include detrimental effects to fundamental processes of attachment, trust, and social interaction. One interesting epidemiological study illustrates how profound and long term such effects might be. Sabotta and Davis (1992) conducted an elaborate archival study of mortality risk for children under age 18 in Washington State. Some 11,000 children whose cases were reported to the state child abuse registry were compared to carefully constructed control samples. Children previously reported to the child abuse registry had an elevated risk of death prior to age 18, three times higher overall and even higher for those who experienced early physical abuse. Remarkably, children reported to the registry were about 20 times more likely than peers to die of homicide.

Clearly violence against children is a serious problem. Again, the literature has shifted from individual pathology models to social ecological models that incorporate personal, interactional, situational, social, and cultural influences (Gelles & Loseke, 1993; Pagelow, 1984; Straus, Gelles, & Steinmetz, 1980).

Conduct Disorder

Even this brief overview of just a few forms of violence should make it clear that numerous contributing factors are involved. One approach to clarifying the puzzle and getting a lead on intervention options is to look at the development of violent behavior in childhood. Empirical studies of childhood problems routinely yield an important dimension of undercontrolled behavior—one aspect of which is termed *conduct disorder*. Achenbach (1985) and others described conduct problems in terms of behavior that overtly or covertly violates standards of honesty and respect for the rights of others. Such behavior includes aggression, conflict, noncompliance, dishonesty, and rule-breaking. It would be a grave error to assume that conduct disorder is a precursor to all the diverse forms of violent behavior briefly discussed here. Although conduct problems have been long recognized and there is empirical support for a general cluster of problem behavior, successive clinical diagnostic systems have created, collapsed, and modified various "disorder" subtypes and aggression is by no means a universal feature. Also, recall the point made earlier about categorical diagnostic systems: Conduct problems almost certainly differ in degree, so that research on disordered cases may involve an important loss of data. Nonetheless, empirical research on these problems is relevant to an understanding of the development of violent behavior. It is a useful starting point.

We have valuable prevalence data on conduct problems from several major epidemiological studies. Overall prevalence is thought to be in the 3% to 12% range, although estimates vary with definitions, criteria, measures, and sample age. For example, examination of a birth cohort from a small town in New Zealand yielded estimates of 3% for age 11, and 2% for age 13 (Anderson, Williams, McGee, & Silva, 1987; Frost, Moffitt, & McGee, 1989). A carefully selected sample of 2,000 households in Ontario yielded estimates of 4% for ages 4 to 11 and 7% for 12 to 16 (Offord et al., 1987, Offord, Boyle, & Racine, 1989; Thomas, Byrne, Offord, & Boyle, 1991). A sample of New York State children yielded higher estimates, 12% for both ages 9 to 12 and 13 to 18 (Velez, Johnson, & Cohen, 1989). Because these studies used *DSM–III* (or III–R) criteria, the higher New York rates may represent an actual variation in prevalence. Certainly, national differences of this size are not beyond the bounds of credibility, although they may simply reflect other differences in methodology.

With respect to age, rates of conduct disorder appear to rise to a peak in middle adolescence, then decline (Velez et al., 1989). With respect to gender, conduct disorder appears to be more prevalent among boys than girls: The male-to-female ratio of formal diagnosis is estimated at 3:1 (Anderson et al., 1987) or 4:1 for both children and adolescents (Offord et al., 1989), although the ratio may be as high as 10:1 for conduct problems defined by other-than-*DSM* criteria (Herbert, 1978). Generally, ratios are thought to increase with the seriousness of the conduct problems (e.g., violence vs. petty theft), although serious conduct problems among girls may be increasing.

The incidence of specific antisocial behaviors is high. For example, Feldman, Caplinger, and Wodarski (cited in Kazdin, 1987) estimated that, of teenagers aged 13 to 18, 35% report having engaged in assault, 50% in theft, and 45% in property damage. The financial costs of vandalism are estimated to be in the region of $600 million per year, and of fire setting $700 million per year (Kazdin, 1987). Conduct-disordered children comprise a large proportion of clinic referrals: 33% (Wiltz & Patterson, 1974), 33% to 50% (Robins, 1981). They are more likely than other children with problems to show continued involvement with various agencies: public aid, juvenile court, mental health, and criminal justice.

The prevalence of conduct disorder varies across social conditions. Epidemiological studies indicate that conduct problems meeting formal diagnostic criteria are significantly more likely among children living in families with low-income mothers, mother-only households, low-education fathers, minority ethnicity, life disruptions, and family dysfunction—with relative risk ratios ranging from two to four (Offord et al. 1989, Velez et al., 1989).

Continuity of Conduct Problems.   Children with conduct problems often continue to show problems in adolescence and adulthood. In the short term, McGee, Feehan, Williams, and Anderson (1992) observed continuity among boys but not girls in their study of New Zealand teenagers: For boys, conduct disorder at age 11 represented a fourfold risk for the disorder at age 15. Note that this continuity was observed despite the loss of data involved in categorical diagnostic measurement, whereby the severity and form of conduct problem are reduced to a simple dichotomy.

Stattin and Magnusson (1989) reported data from a large-sample longitudinal study in Sweden that avoided this problem. They used teacher ratings of aggressiveness at ages 10 and 13 to predict delinquency and the frequency, seriousness, and features of later crime up to age 26. For boys, high ratings of aggressiveness were predictive of more serious offenses, violent and property-damage offenses, and an unspecialized crime pattern (i.e., engaging in diverse crimes). For girls, only later aggressiveness (i.e., at age 13) was related to criminal activity. Although children rated as aggressive often showed other problems such as poor school achievement and social relationships, the association between aggressiveness ratings and later crime was largely independent of intelligence and family education for both sexes. Stattin and Magnusson (1989) also conducted a cluster analysis of criminal activity. Although only 20% of boys rated highly aggressive at age 10 fell into the conforming cluster, 65% fell into three multicategory crime clusters that included violent offenses.

Continuity was also found over longer developmental periods. In a classic study, Robins (1966) obtained files about to be destroyed from a child guidance clinic that had been closed. They drew a sample of children seen at the clinic during 1924 to 1929 for antisocial or emotional problems, selected a comparison sample of age and school peers, and interviewed these people of average age 43. Robins found that children seen for conduct problems at a clinic were more likely than children seen for emotional problems or than controls to show a variety of problems as adults, including to engage in major crime, be imprisoned, get divorced, or lose custody of their children. In their longitudinal study of a nonclinical sample, Huessmann, Eron, Lefkowitz, and Walder (1984) observed similar continuity in conduct problems: The number and seriousness of criminal convictions by age 30 were related to peer-nominated aggressiveness in school at age 8, for both sexes.

A variety of factors appear to influence, or at least predict, continuity of conduct problems. These include variables that reflect the robustness of the repertoire of antisocial behavior, including rate, intensity (e.g., hitting vs. torturing a peer or animal), diversity (i.e., showing few or many different behaviors), range (i.e., exhibiting problems in one or many settings), and early onset (Kazdin, 1987; Loeber, 1982). The robustness of a child's repertoire of antisocial behavior may reflect, in part, the influence of genetic factors. Yet, onset, rate, intensity, diversity, and range very likely represent the growth or decline of antisocial behavioral strategies in a favorable or unfavorable social context (Patterson, 1982). Other factors likely serve as detrimental influences (although they, too, may be a reaction to the behavior), including being placed away from parents, lacking adult role models, and growing up in poverty, such that continuity is all but universal among children experiencing all these risk factors (Robins, 1981).

Continuity is evident across lives as well as within them. Hetherington and Martin (1979), in their classic review of antisocial behavior and delinquency, made the important observation that "deviant parents have deviant children" (p. 257). For example, several studies found concordance of antisocial behavior among siblings, parents, and children, and even grandparents and grandchildren (e.g., Huesmann, Eron, Lefkowitz, & Walder, 1984). As DiLalla and Gottesman (1991) pointed out, this continuity is due in part to genetic factors. In the discussion here, I largely ignore biological influences for three reasons: the already broad scope of the chapter, the limited options for biological intervention, and the evidence of dramatic crossnational differences in violence that highlight the importance of social ecological factors. Hetherington and Martin (1979) discussed an array of family factors that were found to predict and possibly influence conduct problems and delinquency. These include (a) parental factors and interactions such as parental maladjustment, criminal activity, and marital discord; (b) parenting styles including extreme permissiveness or restrictiveness, power-assertive discipline, parental coldness, and inconsistent parenting; and (c) family system features such as large size, a chaotic household, and lax supervision.

Patterson, DeBaryshe, and Ramsey (1989) offered a developmental model of antisocial behavior. According to this model, conduct problems in early childhood lead to rejection by peers and academic failure in middle childhood, and to involvement with deviant peer groups and delinquency in late childhood and adolescence. The development and perpetuation of conduct problems lies in part with poor parental monitoring and discipline. Factors disrupting family management practices include a constellation of ecological conditions—limited personal, economic, and social resources, vulnerability to stressors, unemployment, marital conflict, neighborhood stressors, and so forth. We are not going to diminish antisocial behavior if we restrict our efforts to the clinical treatment of those seeking psychological services, not only because of the diversity of factors involved, but also because those most in need are least likely to seek services.

INTERVENTION AND PREVENTION

What general conclusions can be drawn from this brief overview of violence? First, many forms of violence are sufficiently prevalent and serious to warrant the attention of applied psychologists. Second, variations in problem rates across time, place, social groups, and culture suggest the need for social ecological models of these problems. Ecological models direct our attention not just to individual characteristics but to systems of socialization, support, and deviance control—not least the family, school, and community, as well as the systems that facilitate or disrupt their functioning including economic and cultural factors. Third, variation in the prevalence of violence also indicates its plasticity, suggesting that it can be managed.

Although space does not allow it, I believe that a similar (although currently weaker) case can be made for prosocial behavior—indeed, to a degree this is the other side of the coin.

Now, managing the forms of violence briefly discussed here no doubt seems like an awesome task—especially if we accept the need for a so-cial–ecological perspective. Yet, Lore and Schultz (1993) noted that a major obstacle to controlling aggression is the belief, widespread in our culture, that it cannot be controlled or at least not without terrible psychic cost. On the contrary they argued, humans, like other aggressive animals have evolved potent inhibitory mechanisms and are "exquisitely sensitive to subtle social controls" (p. 24) that might be used to reduce violence. As noted earlier, an applied psychology operating from a community para-digm might draw on a diverse tool kit of intervention techniques (Vaux, 1994). Optimally, these will involve sustainable programs built into the ecological context, designed to promote adaptive competence and resil-ience, to redirect problematic life trajectories, to facilitate the negotiation of developmental transitions, and to sustain stressor-resistant systems of so-cialization and deviance control. Before turning to a discussion of strategies for controlling violence, it might be useful to provide a brief overview of an ecological model that provides a framework for that discussion.

According to Bronfenbrenner (1979), development involves an individ-ual's changing capacity to understand and operate on the environment, which he characterized as a set of interrelated nested systems. *Microsystems* refer to ongoing settings in which the person occupies a role (e.g., family). *Exosystems* refer to settings that indirectly influence the operation of a microsystem (e.g., factory layoffs change family life). *Mesosystems* refer to the links between microsystems (e.g., work–family congruence or conflict). Finally, *macrosystems* are cultural blueprints for the conduct of social life: institutions, norms, and so forth that may have pervasive but subtle effects (e.g., gender relationships in many settings). This model provides one way of carving up the numerous interrelated influences on various forms of violence. As such, it will serve as a framework within which to examine intervention strategies. Through that discussion, it is important to keep in mind that some developmental periods may be critical intervention points for many types of violent behavior: for example, the development of warmth, trust, and empathy. Other periods may be particularly critical for different forms of violence. For example, the aggression, immaturity, non-compliance, or indifference that characterize conduct disorders may begin in early childhood, whereas sexual tastes that focus on children or that blend with the exertion of power may develop during adolescence.

Punishment and Treatment

Common sense strongly recommends a direct approach to changing per-petrators of violence, most commonly through legal sanction or clinical treatment. Such strategies should by no means be ruled out, but a few comments on their limitations seem warranted. Popular and political enthusiasm for punitive sanctions—longer and "truer" sentences, "three strikes and out" penalties, corporal punishment, capital punishment, and more prisons—is considerable and appears to be growing, even though the prison population has grown dramatically (60%-80% in eight states between 1988 and 1993) and now exceeds 1 million in the United States as a whole, a greater percentage of population than any other Western country (U.S. Department of Justice statistics, as cited in *World Almanac*, 1995). Retribution may be served, but not rehabilitation, perhaps not even deterrence (Currie, 1985). Comparisons across nations, U.S. states, and time all cast doubt on the effectiveness of even the most severe penalty, death ("Does death work," 1994). Many perpetrators are never caught or convicted ("Measuring crime," 1994). In the case of family violence or abuse, imprisonment or constraints on interaction necessarily restrict functional as well as dysfunctional family interaction: The family must be "broken" to be "fixed." Moreover, the moral and financial costs of punitive strategies are substantial. Alone in using capital punishment, the United States is subject to the moral approbation of other Western industrialized countries. To execute a convicted criminal costs an estimated $2 to $3 million and to keep one in prison costs approximately $20,000 per year ("Does death work," 1994). In short, popular support for punitive strategies greatly exceeds the evidence of their effectiveness, let alone their cost-effectiveness. A strong case might be made for alternative, less expensive forms of punishment and containment (e.g., education, community service, electronic monitoring) and for a reallocation of resources to preventive strategies (Currie, 1985).

Clinical treatment is rarely sought out by adult or adolescent perpetrators of violence and is of limited effectiveness when involuntary. Although children with conduct problems comprise as much as one half of clinical caseloads, many problem children including those most at risk are not treated. For example, parents who exhibit or approve of violent solutions to interpersonal conflict, or those whose family lives are in chaos, may be most likely to have violent children and least likely to seek clinical services for their child. Again, a strong case can be made for early intervention and prevention.

Microsystems

Individuals occupy many key microsystems during their lives. For developing children, home, school, and neighborhood probably are the most important conduits through which myriad influences operate and within which interventions to manage violence must be built. On an optimistic note, there appear to be many interrelated influences that seem, directly or indirectly, to be either beneficial or harmful across broad areas of development.

Family.   Not least of these influences are good parenting and the avoidance of stressors that disrupt it. Certainly there is much we need to learn, but there is also a good deal that we know already about family factors that lead to conduct problems and possibly the development of violence more generally (Hetherington & Martin, 1979; Patterson et al., 1989). Key influences are poor parental supervision, harsh or inconsistent discipline, and extended coercive exchanges. In their work over several decades at the Oregon Social Learning Center (OSLC), Patterson and colleagues identified coercion as a critical interactional pattern that often escalates, leading to an expanding repertoire of conduct problems and further breakdown in effective parenting (Patterson, 1982). A simplified account of the process follows. A child makes a request that is denied by a parent, the child engages in an aversive behavior (whining, aggression, etc.) and the parent gives in; when faced with a similar situation in future the child engages in aversive behavior at increasing rate, intensity, and diversity, to which the parent sometimes gives in. On each occasion that this happens, both child and parent are reinforced (the child gets what he or she wanted, the parent terminates the child's aversive behavior), but in the process the parent has shaped a growing repertoire of obnoxious behavior in the child, indeed, those very behaviors most aversive to the parent. This is a classic deviation amplification process, a positive feedback loop (Maruyama, 1963). Aggression often is a component of this growing repertoire of antisocial behavior, that generalizes beyond the family to school and other settings, and becomes very resistant to change. Consider the broader impact—the developing child loses a critical bond of affection, learns to defy authority, and learns to use coercion to achieve goals, whereas the parent develops ineffective parenting skills that may generalize to other interpersonal conflict situations (e.g., with a spouse). Moreover, the "provocation" of child coercive behavior sometimes may trigger a severe punitive response from the parent that may constitute a serious incident of child abuse or, given certain parent characteristics and history, develop into a pattern of child abuse (Wolfe, 1985). Although speculative, such a process might generalize to other relationships.

Another valuable model of parenting is that of Baumrind (1991), not least because it highlights fundamental issues in the socialization and deviance control process, not just in families but more generally. These issues have to do with freedom and control, responsibility and authority, agency and communion. Baumrind is conducting a longitudinal study of family socialization and developmental competence with a sample of primarily middle-class families. The scope of the project, some 50 hours of contact with each family at three time periods to date, makes it difficult to describe here. Baumrind identified important dimensions of parenting, developed family typologies, and related these to child development and adolescent competence, including resistance to one form of antisocial behavior, drug use. Parental demandingness refers to efforts to integrate the child into the family whole through supervision, making maturity demands, discipline, and willingness to confront noncompliance. Responsiveness refers to efforts to foster self-regulated individuality by being supportive, attuned, and acquiescent to a child's special needs.

Some of the most pertinent results follow. Adolescents from authoritative families, characterized by highly demanding and highly responsive parents, were found to show considerably greater competence than their peers. Adolescents from democratic families (highly responsive and moderately demanding) also showed high levels of competence. Compared to peers, both groups were more individuated, mature, resilient, and optimistic; they saw their parents as more loving and influential; they were more achievement oriented and scored higher on achievement tests; they showed greater self-regulation, social responsibility, self-esteem, and internal locus of control; they displayed fewer internalizing or externalizing problems and less alienation; finally, they showed less illicit drug use, alcohol use, and sexual acting out. Baumrind's study did not examine any form of violence directly. Yet, it is highly plausible that the relatively greater competence of the adolescents from authoritative and democratic families—especially in terms of loving relationship with parents, high achievement, resistance to antisocial behavior, and especially the absence of externalizing problems—all would counter violence. In contrast, adolescents from unengaged families—characterized by parents who were neither demanding nor responsive—were less competent than peers. They were relatively immature, showed underachievement, and displayed high rates of externalizing problems and of drug and alcohol use. Not only do adolescents from unengaged families show risk factors for violence, but their parents may show active rejection and an indifference to childrearing responsibility that constitute child neglect or abuse.

One strategy for controlling violence would focus on the family microsystem and particularly the quality of parenting. Although recognizing both endogenous and exogenous influences on parenting, the assumption is that quality parenting can be learned and that developmental trajectories of dysfunctional parenting can be altered. Parent education programs are not new, but whenever popular are often atheoretical, without a research foundation, and poorly evaluated. A striking exception has been the work of Patterson (1982) and his colleagues at the OSLC, who over many years have been refining an intervention targeting parental child-management skills. Based on the coercive exchange model outlined earlier, this intervention directly targets conduct problems including aggressive child behavior. The strategy involves helping parents to learn to identify coercive exchanges, to develop consistent patterns of discipline, not to reward aversive child behaviors, but to reward compliance and prosocial behavior, and to use nonphysical punishment. Other elements address both conduct and academic problems at school. Indirectly, it also may reduce abusive parental behavior. Evaluations of high quality parent training programs suggest that they are effective (Patterson, Chamberlain, & Reid, 1982).

A more radical version of the parent training strategy would seek to overcome the gap between the supply of and need for the intervention (exacerbated by our fee for service system of mental health delivery). Certainly, we need to increase the supply of such programs and, through more extensive screening, increase the chance of reaching those most in need. Yet, more radical approaches seem warranted. Although the right to freely marry and become a parent is held to be fundamental in our culture, more concerted efforts to prepare people for these roles seem necessary: Rates of family violence and levels of parenting-induced dysfunction make a mockery of any assumption that intimacy and parenting come "naturally." Programs based on Baumrind's (1991) work and other parenting models might be made compulsory prerequisites to parenthood or at least options with significant incentives.

Preschool. Hamblin (1973) and colleagues employed behavior analysis and social exchange models as the foundation for a fascinating series of carefully researched interventions, described in their book, *The Humanization Processes.* Although they addressed a variety of problems including academic achievement among children from low-income families, most pertinent here is their work with highly aggressive 4- to 5-year-old boys. Despite their age, these children had developed elaborate repertoires of noncompliance, defiance, tantrums, and aggression. One illustrative sportscaster-type log describes the project teacher's efforts to have these boys stop playing and switch to lessons. During 4 minutes of chaos and mayhem, the children quickly escalated from noncompliance to defiance, to destruction of property (turning over desks, smashing a phonograph), to outright aggression (kicking and throwing chairs at the teacher, hitting one child in the face). The teacher, too, becomes increasingly rough in her efforts to control the children (illustrating how coercion may provoke abuse) but eventually must "give in," allowing the boys to play while she takes care of the injured child. Building on Patterson's coercive exchange model, Hamblin's approach involves systematically training the teacher to extinguish defiant and aggressive behavior, to reward cooperation, and so forth. The evidence of effectiveness for these strategies was striking, strongly supporting the coercion model and highlighting the degree to which adults can be the architects either of obnoxious and aggressive behavior or of civil behavior in young children. By routinely screening for coercive behavior in preschool and implementing programs such as those described, we might limit the generalization of aggressive behavior from home to school and other settings.

Violence might be indirectly reduced by early school-based efforts to promote social competence. For example, Shure and Spivack (1988) built on their extensive research program and developed an intervention program designed to enhance interpersonal cognitive problem-solving skills. Having established that young children with behavior problems show deficits in thinking about alternative solutions to problems and about the consequences of actions, they developed and refined a training program to promote these skills. An elaborate curriculum was developed for urban poor preschool and kindergarten children (4 months of daily 20-min sessions). Evaluations of this program yielded evidence of improvements in targeted thinking, associated reduction in inhibited and impulsive problem behavior, enhancement of prosocial behavior, persistence of benefits over several years, and prevention of subsequent behavior problems. Many of these program effects were replicated when mothers, rather than teachers, implemented the program (Shure & Spivack, 1988). When implemented with older children (age 6 years and older), whose problem-solving strategies may be more established and less plastic, the program effects are less clear. At any rate, early implementation with young children is recommended. Finally, the success of this intervention was replicated by many studies, such that a meta-analysis of 27 studies yielded an effect size of 0.66 (Denham & Almeida, 1987).

Another strategy involves efforts to promote development more generally through early education programs, particularly those targeted at poor children and their families. The direct focus of such programs is rarely violence, but indirectly they may reduce violence by promoting social competence, academic achievement, and life skills. Although there appears to be substantial civic and political support for programs like Head Start, there is also powerful opposition from those who consider the benefits limited in light of program costs. However, Haskins (1989) recently reviewed evidence on Head Start and model preschool programs, such as the Perry Preschool Project. He concluded that both model programs and Head Start produce significant and meaningful gains in intellectual performance and socioemotional development by the end of the intervention year, but that these gains diminish postintervention as children enter regular school. In terms of special education placement and being held back a grade, Head Start overall shows modest positive effects, whereas strong effects are evident for model programs. On various measures of life success—avoiding teen pregnancy, delinquency, welfare participation, and unemployment—there is modest evidence of positive effects for the model programs, but little available research on Head Start. Finally, cost–benefit analyses of the best programs conclude that program expenditures may be as little as one fifth of the savings on child care, public special education, welfare, taxes lost from unemployment, and crime. In short, there are solid grounds for optimism: Evaluations to date did not assess violence as an outcome directly, but by promoting personal and family competence, these programs likely reduce risk for family and other forms of violence.

School. As a setting of formal educational activities and extensive social involvement, school constitutes an important microsystem in the development of children and later of some young adults. It also represents an important (although often controversial) conduit for interventions to limit violence.

An exemplary large intervention program designed to reduce violence in school was conducted by Olweus (1992). Since the 1970s, Olweus studied the problem of bullying among school children in Scandinavia. Such behavior received relatively little attention elsewhere, despite the likelihood that it plays an important role in the continuity of aggressive behavior. Data from a survey of over 700 schools in Norway indicated that 9% of students were bullied "now and then" or more often and 7% bullied other children. Generally, victims were relatively insecure, anxious, physically small (boys), and tended not to retaliate. Bullies tended to be relatively aggressive, defiant to adults, impulsive, dominant, physically strong (boys), and to hold positive attitudes toward violence. Some 60% of bullies in Grades 6 to 9 had a criminal conviction by age 24, and 35% to 40% had three or more convictions compared to only 10% of control children. Olweus also found that teachers in elementary and junior high schools tended to do little about bullying and parents tended not to know it was going on. Olweus wrote eloquently in describing the broader implications of this situation; that is, what both bullies and victims learn more generally about intimidation, authority, and civility.

Olweus adapted work on families discussed earlier (Baumrind, 1991; Patterson et al., 1989) to the school environment, in order to develop an intervention program to counteract bullying. The program involved new procedures at the school, class, and teacher–student level as well as written materials for teachers and parents. For the most part, the program was implemented by school staff and integrated into school procedures. The goal was to raise awareness about the problem and its seriousness and to promote a school atmosphere characterized essentially by both responsiveness (warmth and interest) and demandingness (clear limits to acceptable behavior), such that violations reliably elicited nonhostile, nonphysical sanctions. The program was implemented in 112 Grade 4 to 7 classes across 42 primary and junior high schools. Overall, the results of a careful evaluation indicated a substantial reduction after 8 and 20 months both in the prevalence of bullying and the incidence of new cases. The effect was observed for both sexes and there was no evidence that bullying simply shifted to outside school. Finally, there was a reduction in general antisocial behavior at school (i.e., vandalism, theft, truancy) and an increase in students' reported enjoyment of recess time. Clearly this program provides a model worthy of emulation.

Other school interventions might be useful in reducing violence indirectly. According to Patterson et al.'s (1989) developmental model of antisocial behavior, promoting academic achievement, school involvement, and social competence might decrease the likelihood of commitment to a deviant peer group and perpetuation of an antisocial developmental trajectory. One approach was to focus on what Bronfenbrenner (1979) termed *ecological transitions* during the school career: Changes in environmental demands may lead to successful adaptation with a growth in competence and resilience, or to adaptive failure sometimes prompting a downward spiral in functioning. Felner and Adan (1988) described a program to facilitate successful transition among low-income minority students into large schools that often are dramatically less responsive to individual students than their previous smaller schools. The program involves two principal elements: (a) a reduction in the complexity and flux of the physical and social environment (all primary subjects are taken with the same student group in a small set of proximal classrooms), and (b) changing the roles of homeroom teachers and guidance personnel (so that the homeroom teacher serves as the primary administrative and counseling link between students, parents, and school). Evaluations of this program indicate that it reduced negative transitional effects observed in nonparticipant controls, including more negative self-concept, decreased academic performance, and increased absenteeism. Moreover, a follow-up indicated a reduction in school dropout rate among participants (21%) compared to controls (43%). Again, this program involves redesigning the school ecology to promote adaptive success and to prevent young people from shifting their commitment to a deviant, possibly violent, peer group.

Another school-based strategy is emerging with the potential to reduce diverse forms of violence. Proposals that character or values education be (re)introduced to schools is causing considerable heated debate. Some (particularly, religious conservatives) fear the undermining of core beliefs in the face of a moral relativism, whereas others (particularly, secular liberals) fear the teaching of dogma and an end to free thought. Despite the fears, progress is being made on the development of curricula that might well incorporate elements relevant to violence: human dignity, respect for others, trust and betrayal, use and abuse of power, and so forth. It is difficult to imagine education of this sort having no impact on the likelihood of violence.

Moreover, mid- to late teenage years may be a particularly critical time to explore issues of sexual and relationship violence, because several high school surveys report violence in teenage dating relationships and some teenagers appear to equate anger and strong feelings with love (Pagelow, 1984). In a large survey of middle-school students, over one half of both boys and girls reported that it was acceptable for a man to force a woman to have sex if they were going steady (unpublished study cited in Koss & Harvey, 1991). Thus, discussion of topics such as the limits of seduction, honoring intimate trust, possessive love, and so forth might prove valuable. Finally, dangerous sexual tastes likely develop during adolescence. The possibility is real of detecting individuals for whom prepubertal children or violated adults are sexual targets, and the chances of changing them may be optimal. Yet, our punitive orientation may make intervention impossible: It is an issue worthy of further thought and research.

College.   College represents a pivotal point in the lives of many young people. Parental restraints on behavior are greatly reduced and most colleges encourage exploration not only of thought but also of values and behavior. One consequence is that college dating may be a very uncertain activity and the prevalence of nonconsensual sexual activity extremely high (Koss et al., 1987). In recent years, efforts to deal with this problem intensified largely at the instigation of campus women's groups. Yet, the majority of effort has been reactive: for example, crisis teams and advocacy for rape victims. Extremely valuable to those served, such efforts may engage only a small portion of those victimized. Preventive efforts are essentially what criminologists refer to as *target hardening*: brightway paths, companion services, self-defense training, and rape-awareness workshops. Some workshops are designed for and offered to both women and men, as such they are more primary preventive in design. Yet, informal reports indicate that these are often optional and do not "reach" men. Clearly there is a need for intervention programs (possibly compulsory ones) that challenge thinking about acceptable sexual behavior. At one college recently (Antioch), a code of conduct was developed by student government that placed great weight on explicit consensus prior to any escalation of sexual intimacy (a sort of "tell and kiss" rule).

Some situations (e.g., dates), settings (e.g., bars), and organizations (e.g., fraternities) appear to be particularly risky. For example, in a study of sorority women, Copenhaver and Grauerholz (1991) found that 24% reported being victims of attempted rape and 17% of completed rape since coming to college. Almost one half of the rapes occurred at a fraternity house and over one half at a fraternity function or involving a fraternity member. More research is needed on dangerous situations and settings and more interventions designed that target these specifically.

Neighborhood.   As noted earlier, most strikingly in the case of murder rates, some places are more violent than others. That this is so because of a concentration of certain kinds of people—for example, poor, unemployed, minority—is not trivial. Garbarino and Kostelny (1992) conducted an ecological study of child maltreatment in 77 community areas in Chicago. They replicated previous findings that community rates of child maltreatment are strongly linked to a set of ecological variables (e.g., percentage unemployed, in poverty, female-headed, in overcrowded housing, etc.). They further examined several pairs of high- and low-risk otherwise comparable communities (i.e., maltreatment rates were higher or lower than predicted from ecological conditions), plotting child maltreatment rates over a 6-year period. Surveys of community leaders revealed that areas that became relatively more dangerous for children over time were marked by social disorganization and lack of social coherence. Moreover, the downward spiral evident in some communities was reflected in relatively high child fatality rates. The key point is that ecological conditions in a neighborhood give it a positive or negative momentum that cannot be redressed solely by individual or family-level interventions.

Serious questions might be raised about the concentration of persons with limited resources into huge public housing projects. High-rise designs make it impossible for parents to supervise children once they are allowed outside and few of the public areas are what Newman (1972) termed *defensible space*, leaving it prone to vandalism and other antisocial behavior. Yancey (1971) documented the destructive process of social atomization in such housing: Pruitt–Igoe, a 3,000-apartment project that won architectural awards when it was built in the 1950s, became so inhospitable that it was demolished. Individuals living in such projects often face discrimination in job interviews, a social network high in dysfunction and low in conventional achievement, support networks with severely limited resources, and limited employment opportunities in a dead local economy. Given this bleak picture, loyalty to a gang that provides identity, social and material resources, organizational participation, and employment opportunities begins to look like a highly successful adaptation to the ecological conditions. Controlling gang-related violence will prove difficult until we can offer a more attractive set of options.

Exosystem and Mesosystem Influences

According to an ecological perspective, violence cannot be understood solely by examining microsystems. Rather, the functioning of systems like the family, school, and neighborhood are modified by their environments; that is, their links to one another (mesosystem influences) and to systems that indirectly alter them (exosystem influences). For example, Daniels and Moos (1989) found that fathers' work stressors and work support and mothers' extrafamilial social networks were associated with parental well-being (e.g., depression, esteem) and family functioning (e.g., arguments), and in turn, with children's problems. These processes are selectively examined here and some potential interventions outlined.

Home and School. In a general sense, home and school may operate as socialization systems that are complementary or contradictory, coordinated or independent. For example, a school's effort to promote educational achievement is likely undermined if parents denigrate academic pursuits. Parents employing an authoritative style may find it undermined and find themselves shifting to an authoritarian style if the school staff and teachers are unengaged, inconsistent, or arbitrarily intrusive. In general, socialization is enhanced when systems are coordinated, and interventions appear to be more effective when conducted in more than one system. Thus, Olweus (1992) found that neither schools nor parents initially dealt with school bullying, but he effectively mobilized both systems to counter this type of violence. Koretz and Lazar (1992) noted that interventions to reduce conduct problems, like those of Patterson and colleagues outlined previously, increasingly seek to link home and school through home note systems, daily report cards, telephone hotlines that parents can call to get information on their child's scheduled school activities, and changing extant norms about home–school separation. Interventions that involve a coordination of home and school socialization may offer benefits on many fronts—conduct, academics, vocational, and so forth. Moreover, agreement about goals may be easier to reach in the case of violence than in other areas. Of course, consistent and coordinated socialization may demand time and energy that some teachers and parents currently find difficult to provide.

Home, Work, and the Economy. The family may be construed as an open system that provides material and social resources to its members and civility and well-socialized citizens to the community (Foa & Foa, 1980; Vaux, Brownell, & Hill, 1982). Yet, smooth functioning depends not only on the inherent resources of family members (e.g., talent, skill, pathology, etc.) but also on the environment in which they operate, perhaps not least employment opportunities and government support programs. An example may help to illustrate: The drop in interest rates to a low in 1993 allowed recent home buyers with an average mortgage (say $100,000) to save enough through refinancing (about $200,000 in interest payments) to send several children to college. Certainly, job loss represents a radical change in a family's ability to provide resources to its members, quite likely involving disruptive effects on parenting and children's development. McLoyd (1989) proposed a model of the effects on children of paternal job loss, noting the importance of mediators such as paternal pessimism, punitiveness, and nurturance, maternal characteristics, and stressors secondary to the job loss. Brenner (1973, 1977), in a massive research program that examined archival historical data through time series analysis, demonstrated unemployment-related increases in diverse behavioral, psychological, and health problems: Most pertinent, an increase in unemployment in the 1970s predicted a sixfold increase in homicide. Steinberg, Catalano, and Dooley (1981) used sophisticated time-series analyses to demonstrate a relationship between economic downturns and child abuse reports in several California counties.

Some segments of the population experience chronic unemployment and underemployment. As Voydanoff (1989) noted, some minimum level of economic resources and security is essential for family formation and stability. Thus, high levels of unemployment among African Americans (12% vs. 6% among Whites), and especially among young Black men (over 60% vs. about 30% of Whites, among 18- to 19-year-olds in 1982), is certainly an important factor underlying the high percentage of Black families maintained by women (48% vs. 12% of White families in 1993), the high rate of out-of-wedlock births to Black women (55% vs. 12% of births to White women in 1986), and the high percentage of Black teenage mothers who are not married (80% vs. 20% of White teenage mothers; Chilman, 1988). Directly and indirectly these factors may contribute to disproportionate levels of violence in the Black communities, most dramatically homicide rates. Ethnicity aside, the family disruptions that arise in part from unemployment and low income do contribute directly and indirectly to various forms of violence. Children of teenage parents show diverse problems throughout childhood (Furstenberg, Brooks-Gunn, & Chase-Landsale, 1989) and are at relatively higher risk for abuse (Connelly & Straus, 1992). The risk of sexual abuse for girls is higher under any family circumstance other than living most of her childhood with two parents (Finkelhor, Hotaling, Lewis, & Smith, 1990). Conduct problems and delinquency are related to a variety of family instability factors that are exacerbated by low income and chronic unemployment (Hetherington & Martin, 1979).

Being employed, of course, is not always a benign influence on parenting or family functioning. The picture of family life that emerges from Engels' (1892/1969) description of work during England's industrial revolution is hardly a happy one. Closer to home, among those who work several jobs, long hours, night or weekend shifts, or for low wages, the costs of working may outweigh benefits in terms of parenting (Voydanoff, 1989). Although job satisfaction and rewards generally are associated with quality of family life, job involvement is related to work–family conflict and marital satisfaction among some groups, such as male professionals and managers (Voyandoff, 1989). Nor are the effects on academic commitment, social development, or family life of teenage employment during high school predominantly positive (Greenberger & Steinberg, 1986).

During the past several decades, the involvement of women in formal employment steadily increased. This increase is most dramatic among women with children under 6 years of age, from 20% to 54% between 1955 and 1985. Obviously, on moral grounds, the employment rights of women and men must be held to be equal. Yet, it is important to examine the impact on families. A large and complicated research literature has accumulated in an effort to document the benefits and costs of these changes to women, men, and families (Voyandoff, 1986). In general, women tend to benefit from multiple roles and from paid employment (Barnett & Baruch, 1987). However, the work role is typically added to women's homemaking responsibilities, and there is little evidence of a compensatory shift in home responsibilities including child care to men (if present): Thus, certain configurations of work and family roles—not least having young children—may lead to work–family conflict, job tension, and family disruption (Barnett & Baruch, 1987; Voyandoff, 1986). It is interesting to note that Baumrind's (1991) data suggest that in otherwise similar types of families, demandingness is less in those with greater maternal workplace involvement. Hoffman (1989) reviewed literature on maternal employment, noting various moderators—such as parental attitudes and role-shifts—that influence the nature and extent of beneficial or harmful effects on children. Of critical importance, any detriment in family well-being or quality of parenting might be due to the failure of partners, schools, and the workplace to accommodate through the widespread provision of high-quality accessible day care, parental leave, equitable homemaking, and so forth. Parenting is given a low priority in our culture if we judge by the practices and policies designed to support it. Most family-friendly employment practices are limited and we are only beginning to understand if and when they facilitate good parenting. For example, Clarke-Stewart (1989) reviewed literature on infant day care and some of its detrimental effects, noting that we need research to help us resolve potentially conflicting work and parenting demands.

A valuable role for applied psychologists with regard to these issues is to continue to conduct and synthesize relevant research, to highlight the danger of devaluing parenting, and to support family-friendly policies and practices. More specifically, programs worth further development and evaluation include extended parental leave, flexible working hours, job sharing, part-time work, flexible benefit packages, neighborhood or workplace day care, extended school hours, prior notification of job termination, income stabilization, and incentives for employment sector diversity within communities. From both a cultural and economic point of view, investment in raising civil, competent, and nonviolent children may have a far greater yield than the more immediate increases in output and consumption associated with expanded labor input.

Macrosystem

The macrosystem is comprised of broad cultural influences that, according to Bronfenbrenner (1979), serve as blueprints for the organization of social life in a society. As such, their influence is subtle but pervasive. A number of macrosystem elements are relevant to violence: Some involve broad strands of thought, others involve our use of technologies. Much of the previous discussion focused on how to improve systems of socialization and deviance control, but here questions are raised about how elements of our culture contribute to violence. These influences have considerable momentum, and intervention may take the rather nebulous form simply of engaging in the debates through which cultural changes come about.

Freedom and Constraint. In a recent television interview about malaise in the United States, (Chancie, 1995), social philosopher James Q. Wilson highlighted some important tensions in Western thought. He argued that, since the Enlightenment in the 18th century, people in most Western countries pushed the limits of individual freedom, shedding the constraints of dogma and authority. U.S. society emerged during this period, was founded on Enlightenment ideas, and had few indigenous constraining institutions to overcome. This press to individual freedom was amplified by the Western "youth movement" that emerged during the late 1960s, as the demographic swell of the postwar birth cohort went through adolescence—a developmental period marked by questioning of authority and by individuation. The level of social malaise (including violence) in the United States is, according to Wilson, simply the downside of our philosophy of unrestrained individual freedom: Harmdoing is likely, especially among those who can escape detection, are poorly socialized to civility, or have little to lose. He raised the question of whether or not we have reached the practical limits of this philosophy and are willing to accept some cultural constraints. This theme of freedom and responsibility is evident in other social commentaries and movements (e.g., Etzioni, 1993) and harkens back to issues noted earlier in discussing families: responsiveness and demandingness, agency and communion, individualism and collectivism. This is a debate to which applied psychologists might usefully contribute.

Men, Women, and Children. As with most of the world's cultures, the organization of social life in the United States historically involved the allocation of statuses, rights, and responsibilities according to gender and age (cf. history of voting and property rights). A number of scholars argued that this system promotes violence, by sustaining the right of men to exercise control over women and children (especially within their families) and by diminishing recognition of the harm that is done (Brownmiller, 1976; Dobash & Dobash, 1979; Pagelow, 1984). In short, patriarchy is seen as laying a foundation for spouse abuse, intimate homicide, rape, child abuse, and child sexual abuse; diverse forms of violence in which perpetrators are predominantly men and victims predominantly women or children. Evidence for this view comes from historical analysis, legal statutes and practices, norms expressed by ordinary folk in surveys, the demonstrable continuity between acceptable and unacceptable behavior, the prevalence of violence among intimates as opposed to strangers, and the distribution of violence across gender and age groups (Dobash & Dobash, 1979; Koss & Harvey, 1991; Pagelow, 1984).

Clearly our culture is changing such that the rights and status of women and children have grown in the 1900s, and especially since the 1960s. Yet, further change is by no means inevitable, it is quite likely to be resisted, and resistance may manifest itself as violence. Children, in particular, have limited power to claim access to resources and rights: They must rely on benevolent advocates. Applied psychologists can intervene by conducting and synthesizing relevant research and participating in a thoughtful debate about these issues, most directly as they arise in relation to gender- and age-related violence and policies and practices that deal with it.

Guns. No discussion of violence in the United States can ignore firearms. It is estimated that there are about 212 million guns in the United States, including about 67 million handguns, 75% of which are semiautomatic ("Guns in America," 1994). Although automatic weapons are illegal in the United States, restoring legal military-type weapons to their original automatic design is a simple procedure. Such weapons can fire 10 to 16 rounds per second, some are small enough to be concealed, and an early estimate suggested there may be as many as 500,000 in the country ("Machine Gun U.S.A.", 1985). Handgun murders are far more common in the United States (over 5/CK) than in other countries (Switzerland 1.4/CK; Canada and Sweden about 0.5/CK; Australia, Britain, and Japan less than 0.1/CK), and such homicides increased by 40% between 1985 and 1991 for those 15 to 24 years old ("Guns in America," 1994). Indeed, since 1900, more U.S. citizens were killed by private guns than in wars. Guns kept at home purportedly for protection are thought to increase the risk of suicide, accidental deaths to children, and homicide among intimates, the latter including women—twice as many of whom are killed by spouses or intimates as by strangers (Powell & Christoffel, 1994). Data on nonfatal firearm injuries are limited, but such injuries are estimated to occur at five times the rate of fatalities, and hospital and total costs are estimated at about $1 billion and $14 billion each year, respectively, about 80% of which is paid from public funds (Powell & Christoffel, 1994). The estimated hospital costs alone exceed 1993 expenditures on the Small Business Administration and amount to about 50% of expenditures on the FBI. In short, guns are extremely effective weapons that allow people with limited strength, skill, sense, or time to maim or kill others. There seems little doubt that we pay a high price for our right to bear arms.

Intervention in this domain is no simple matter: Opposition to gun control is extremely strong, although there is growing popular, police, and political support to control handguns and combat semiautomatics. Sports hunting (a predominantly long-gun activity) would be largely unaffected by a complete ban on handguns. Sport shooting of any kind might be permitted in controlled environments on a gun check-out basis. Even so, constraining handgun violence will take time, will require interventions that many see as intrusive, and will meet considerable resistance. A serious effort would involve a ban on production and importation of handguns, severe penalties for possession, and a systematic buy-back program to remove the stock of guns in the country. James Q. Wilson proposed that stopping gun-related violence may require that metal detectors or other forms of surveillance become a routine part of access to settings (e.g., shopping malls, high-rise housing). This may seem shocking but such detection is becoming more common in urban public high schools, and there are many settings people would be delighted to occupy with the confidence that they are free of guns. Obviously, these interventions are difficult, but the seriousness and scope of the problem may require them. Considerable political will, leadership, and effort to inform and influence public opinion will be required.

Media.   Another controversial area of potential macrosystem influence on violence is the media. The democratic tradition of free expression in the United States manifested itself in relatively unconstrained mass visual media. Concern over the possible role of television in promoting violence has been expressed since the 1960s, because in the United States, television is available in virtually every household, turned on an average of more than 6 hours each day, providing the viewer with about 1,000 murders per year (Huesmann & Malamuth, 1986). The emergence of cable television and VCRs raise further challenges in parental supervision and control of children's viewing. In their introduction to a special issue on the topic, veteran researchers Huesmann and Malamuth (1986) wrote: "the majority of researchers are now convinced that excessive violence in media increases the likelihood that at least some viewers will behave more violently" (p. 1). Decades of experimental and naturalistic research underlie this conclusion, clarifying an extremely complex set of processes linked through a cognitive neoassociationist model of aggression (Geen & Thomas, 1986). Media appear to promote violence through a variety of processes including modeling, cognitive scripts, arousal, desensitization of inhibitory emotional responses, and beliefs regarding the appropriateness of violence as a response to provocation or solution to interpersonal conflict (Geen & Thomas, 1986; Huesmann & Malamuth, 1986). Moreover, there is little evidence of a cathartic effect (Geen & Thomas, 1986), often a justification for media violence. Indeed, sophisticated time-series analysis of inflated homicide rates following prize fights, and of increased single-car accidents and teenage suicides following well-publicized suicides, led Lore and Schultz (1993) to conclude that media violence should be considered a form of natural advertisement. Huesmann (1986) emphasized the cumulative learning process during childhood, whereby aggressive behavior and preference for violent media are reciprocally related. In light of the long-term continuity of aggressive behavior noted earlier (Huesmann et al., 1984), he saw the contribution of violent media as extremely detrimental.

Intervening to control media violence is logistically straightforward but politically difficult. The commercial interests are substantial and have countered previous indictments of media violence by Surgeons General, the National Institute of Mental Health, politicians, and grassroots organizations like the National Coalition on Television Violence and the International Coalition Against Violent Entertainment. Yet, momentum is building and some progress in rating programs and movies has been made. Information and technology may at least allow parents to monitor and control viewing. Cable television generated some market segmentation, increasing the possibility of nonviolent channels. Jason (1987) demonstrated a program to help parents limit excessive television viewing by children. Yet, it is likely that children most at risk do not have parents who closely supervise their viewing. Abbott (1992) described a large-scale national effort by the Mental Health Foundation of New Zealand that over the course of 10 years showed some progress in changing public opinion and reducing television violence episodes by about one half. Again, broad interventions are difficult, but may yield broad benefits.

Grounds for Optimism

Lest the strategies outlined seem too vague, idealistic, or ambitious to have any pragmatic value in the face of serious problems of violence, there are grounds for optimism. There is substantial evidence—from meta-analytic studies—that we *can* design and implement interventions that bring about beneficial change in human functioning. Meta-analysis is a statistical procedure for synthesizing findings across studies. It allows researchers to make sense of studies that lack sufficient power to yield significant effects, to examine factors that account for variations in effect size, and to abstract an overall effect size for a given form of intervention. In contrast to traditional, qualitative literature reviews that typically result in confused, conflicting, or weak conclusions—Rossi and Wright (1984) described the results of evaluation research as a "parade of close-to-zero effects" (p. 342)—meta-analyses typically yield a fairly clear picture. Since its emergence in the 1970s, hundreds of meta-analyses have been conducted.

Marc Lipsey engaged in heroic and unprecedented efforts of research synthesis through meta-analysis procedures. Lipsey and Wilson (1993) published a second-order meta-analysis—that is, a meta-analysis of over 300 primary meta-analyses that, in turn, synthesized hundreds of research studies on numerous psychological, behavioral, organizational, and educational interventions. The distribution of mean effect sizes from the primary meta-analyses was positively skewed, with only 6 of 302 mean effect sizes being negative and the median mean effect size equal to .47. Several potential biases were examined, including study quality, study accessibility, and so forth, and a refined analysis was conducted including only "unbiased" estimated effect sizes. This analysis too yielded a positively skewed distribution of mean effects sizes, with a median mean effect size of .44. That is, interventions produced on average almost one half an *SD* gain for an intervention group relative to a comparison group.

Lipsey and Wilson (1993) concluded that:

> Well-developed psychological, educational, and behavioral treatments generally have meaningful positive effects on the intended outcome variables. The number and scope of effective treatments covered by this conclusion are impressive, and the magnitude of the effects for a substantial portion of those treatments is in a range of practical significance by almost any reasonable criterion. (p. 1199)

There are also reasons for caution. Lipsey and Wilson warned readers not to conclude that "anything works," and emphasized that meta-analyses tend to be conducted when a body of systematic research exists, usually reflecting promising interventions developed from established theory. Examining meta-analyses cited by Lipsey and Wilson on some interventions within the community psychology domain reveals programs that range from the immature or outright failures—13 prevention studies with an effect size of only .08—through to substantial successes—57 studies involving paraprofessionals with a respectable effect size of .60. In short, we need to keep developing and evaluating programs that are based on sound theory and research. Preventive interventions are especially difficult to evaluate. Powerful methodologies may be necessary to demonstrate that, possibly in the long-run, something did not happen that otherwise would have. Care must be taken not to maintain ineffective programs on ideological grounds, but also not to dismiss programs whose effects are substantial yet subtle and long term.

Another reason for concern relates to *program fidelity*. Once effective programs are developed, we must ensure they are carefully implemented. Weisz, Weiss, and Donenberg (1992), for example, raised disquieting concerns about the possible discrepancy between interventions conducted within research projects versus in the field. Four meta-analyses on psychotherapy for children and adolescents yielded effect sizes in the .70 to .80 range, whereas clinic studies yielded considerably smaller (sometimes negative) estimates of effects. They noted that research studies of interventions often involve carefully designed procedures, nonreferred targets, and specially trained therapists with small caseloads, factors that give them an advantage over their cousins in the field. In short, it is not sufficient that we design and demonstrate effective interventions; their implementation must be monitored to ensure fidelity and ongoing quality.

CONCLUSION

Psychology has grown dramatically during this century. This growth was predominantly within applied psychology, potentially an enormous benefit in terms of the well-being of the population. However, serious concerns have been raised about the nature of contemporary applied psychology and its underlying paradigmatic assumptions. Some of these problems are reflected in the limited attention paid to the broad areas of pro- and antisocial behavior. Data on selected forms of violence were reviewed in order to establish the prevalence and severity of these problems and to suggest the need for social ecological models, without which problems of violence can neither be understood nor resolved. Community psychology was proposed as a potentially valuable alternative to the clinical paradigm that dominates current applied psychology. Key assumptions of this alternative approach include a focus on the well-being of the population, a social–ecological perspective on problems, and a commitment to diverse interventions that emphasize prevention and a developmental perspective. General strategies for limiting violence were discussed within the framework of Bronfenbrenner's (1979) ecological theory. These interventions emphasized the importance of (a) promoting microsystems of socialization and deviance control, such as family and school; (b) facilitating the functioning of these systems by forging positive home–school and home–work mesosystems; (c) controlling exosystem factors such as economic insecurity that undermine microsystem function; and (d) addressing macrosystem influences that promote violence, such as sexism, media violence, and the availability of lethal weapons. Rather than providing treatment for victims of violence, or even attempting to change those with well-established problems, applied psychologists must shift their efforts to the myriad but interrelated factors that underpin the development of violence and prosocial behavior—they must tend the social ecology.

REFERENCES

Abbott, M. W. (1992). Television violence: A proactive prevention campaign. In G. W. Albee, L. A. Bond, & T. V. Cook Monsey (Eds.), *Improving children's lives: Global perspectives on prevention* (pp. 263–278). Newbury Park, CA: Sage.

Achenbach, T. M. (1985). *Assessment and taxonomy of child and adolescent psychopathology.* Beverly Hills, CA: Sage.

American Psychological Association. (1994). *Characteristics of 1993 doctorate recipients in psychology.* Unpublished manuscript.

Anderson, J. C., Williams, S., McGee, R., & Silva, P. A. (1987). DSM–III disorders in preadolescent children. *Archives of General Psychiatry, 44,* 69–76.

Barnett, R. C., & Baruch, G. K. (1987). Social roles, gender, and psychological distress. In R. C. Barnett, L. Biener, & G. K. Baruch (Eds.), *Gender and stress* (pp. 122–143). New York: The Free Press.

Baron, L., & Straus, M. A. (1987). Four theories of rape: A macrosociological analysis. *Social problems, 34,* 467–489.

Baumrind, D. (1991). The influence of parenting style on adolescent competence and substance abuse. *Journal of Early Adolescence, 11,* 56–95.

Brenner, M. H. (1973). *Mental illness and the economy.* Cambridge, MA: Harvard University Press.

Brenner, M. H. (1977). Personal stability and economic security. *Social Policy, 8,* 2–5.

Bronfenbrenner, U. (1979). *The ecology of human development.* Cambridge, MA: Harvard University Press.

Brownmiller, S. (1976). *Against our wills: Women and rape.* New York: Bantam.

Chancie, H., Jr. (Producer). (1995, February 24). *On values: Talk with Peggy Noonan.* Alexandria, VA: Public Broadcasting Service.

Chilman, C. S. (1988). Never-married, single, adolescent parents. In C. S. Chilman, E. W. Nunnally, & F. M. Cox (Eds.), *Variant family forms* (pp. 17–38). Newbury Park, CA: Sage.

Clarke-Stewart, K. A. (1989). Infant day-care: Maligned or malignant. *American Psychologist, 44,* 264–273.

Connelly, C. D., & Straus, M. A. (1992). Mother's age and risk for physical abuse. *Child Abuse and Neglect, 16,* 709–718.

Copenhaver, S., & Grauerholtz, E. (1991). Sexual victimization among sorority women: Exploring the link between sexual violence and institutional practices. *Sex Roles, 24,* 31–41.

Currie, E. (1985). *Confronting crime: An American challenge.* New York: Pantheon.

Daniels, D., & Moos, R. H. (1989). Exosystem influences on family and child functioning. In E. B. Goldsmith (Ed.), *Work and family: Theory, research, and applications* (pp. 113–133). Newbury Park, CA: Sage.

Denham, S. A., & Almeida, M. C. (1987). Children's social problem-solving skills, behavioral adjustment, and intervention. *Journal of Applied Developmental Psychology, 8,* 391–409.

DiLalla, L. F., & Gottesman, I. I. (1991). Biological and genetic contributors to violence—Widom's untold tale. *Psychological Bulletin, 109,* 125–129.

Dobash, R. E., & Dobash, R. P. (1979). *Violence against wives: A case against patriarchy.* New York: The Free Press.

Dodell, D. (1993, October 17). Violence-related attitudes and behaviors of high school students. *Health Info-Com Network: Medical Newsletter,* mednews@asuvm.inre.asu.edu.

Does death work? (1994, December 10). *Economist, 333,* p. 27.

Dunkel, T. (1994, Aug). Newest danger zone: Your office. *Working Women,* 38–74.

Engels, F. (1969). *The conditions of the English working class.* London: Panther. (Original work published in 1892).

Etzioni, A. (1993). *The spirit of community: The reinvention of American society.* New York: Touchstone.

Felner, R. D., & Adan, A. M. (1988). The school transition environment project: An ecological intervention and evaluation. In R. H. Price, E. L. Cowen, R. P. Lorion, & J. Ramos-McKay (Eds.), *Fourteen ounces of prevention* (pp. 111–122). Washington, DC: American Psychological Association.

Finkelhor, D. (1979). *Sexually victimized children.* New York: The Free Press.

Finkelhor, D., & Dziuba-Leatherman, J. (1994). Victimization of children. *American Psychologist, 49,* 174–183.

Finkelhor, D., Hotaling, G. T., Lewis, I. A., & Smith, C. (1990). Sexual abuse in a national survey of adult men and women: Prevalence, characteristics, and risk factors. *Child Abuse and Neglect, 14,* 19–28.

Foa, E. B., & Foa, U. G. (1980). Resource theory: Interpersonal behavior as exchange. In K. J. Gergens, M. S. Greenberg, & R. H. Wills (Eds.), *Social exchange: Advances in theory and research* (pp. 77–94). New York: Plenum.

Fox, R. E. (1994). Training professional psychologists for the 21st century. *American Psychologist, 49,* 200–210.

Frost, L. A., Moffitt, T. E., & McGee, R. (1989). Neurological correlates of psychopathology in an unselected cohort of young adolescents. *Journal of Abnormal Psychology, 98,* 307–313.

Furstenberg, F. F., Brooks-Gunn, J., & Chase-Lansdale, L. (1989). Teenaged pregnancy and childrearing. *American Psychologist, 44,* 313–320.

Garbarino, J., & Kostelny, K. (1992). Child maltreatment as a community problem. *Child Abuse and Neglect, 16,* 455–464.

Geen, R. G. (1990). *Human aggression.* Pacific Grove, CA: Brooks/Cole.

Geen, R. G., & Thomas, S. L. (1986). The immediate effects of media violence on behavior. *Journal of Social Issues, 42,* 7–28.

Gelles, R. J., & Loseke, D. R. (1993). *Current controversies on family violence.* Newbury Park, CA: Sage.

Greenberger, E., & Steinberg, L. (1986). *When teenagers work: The psychological and social costs of adolescent employment.* New York: Basic Books.

Goetting, A. (1988). When parents kill their young children: Detroit 1982–1986. *Journal of Family Violence, 4,* 339–346.

Guns in America: Home on the range. (1994, March 26), *Economist, 333,* pp. 23–28.

Hamblin, R. L. (1973). *The humanization processes.* New York: Wiley.

Haskings, R. (1989). Beyond metaphor: The efficacy of early childhood education. *American Psychologist, 44,* 274–282.

Herbert, M. (1978). *Conduct disorders of childhood and adolescence: A behavioral approach to assessment and treatment.* Chichester, England: Wiley.

Hetherington, E. M., & Martin, B. (1979). Family interaction. In H. C. Quay & J. S. Werry (Eds.), *Psychopathological disorders of childhood* (pp. 247–302). New York: Wiley.

Holmes, R. M., & DeBurger, J. (1988). *Serial murder.* Newbury Park, CA: Sage.

Hoffman, L. W. (1989). Effects of maternal employment in the two-parent family. *American Psychologist, 44,* 283–292.

Homicide. (1994, August 15). *Newsweek,* pp. 20–49.

Huesmann, L. R. (1986). Psychological processes promoting the relation between exposure to media violence and aggressive behavior by the viewer. *Journal of Social Issues, 42,* 125–140.

Huessman, L. R., Eron, L. D., Lefkowitz, M. M., & Walder, L. O. (1984). The stability of aggression over time and generations. *Developmental Psychology, 20,* 1120–1134.

Huesmann, L. R., & Malamuth, N. M. (1986). Media violence and antisocial behavior: An overview. *Journal of Social Issues, 42,* 1–7.

Jason, L. A. (1987). Reducing children's excessive television viewing and assessing secondary changes. *Journal of Consulting and Clinical Psychology, 16,* 245–250.

Kazdin, A. (1987). *Conduct disorder in children and adolescence.* Newbury Park, CA: Sage.

Koretz, D. S., & Lazar, J. B. (1992). New directions in research in the prevention of conduct disorder. In G. W. Albee, L. A. Bond, & T. V. Cook Monsey (Eds.), *Improving children's lives: Global perspectives on prevention* (pp. 296–308). Newbury Park, CA: Sage.

Koss, M. P., Gidycz, C. A., & Wisniewski, N. (1987). The scope of rape: Incidence and prevalence of sexual aggression and victimization in a national sample of higher education students. *Journal of Consulting and Clinical Psychology, 55,* 162–170.

Koss, M. P., & Harvey, M. R. (1991). *The rape victim: Clinical and community interventions.* Newbury Park, CA: Sage.

Koss, M. P., Koss, P. , & Woodruff, W. J. (1990). Relation of criminal victimization to health perceptions among women medical patients. *Journal of Consulting and Clinical Psychology, 58,* 147–152.

Lester, D. (1987). Southern subculture personal violence (suicide and homicide) and firearms. *Omega Journal of Death & Dying, 12,* 183–186.

Lipsey, M. W., & Wilson, D. B. (1993). The efficacy of psychological, educational, and behavioral treatment. *American Psychologist, 48,* 1181–1209.

Loeber, R. (1982). The stability of antisocial and delinquent child behavior: A review. *Child Development, 53,* 1431–1446.

Lore, R. K., & Schultz, L. A. (1993). Control of human aggression. *American Psychologist, 48,* 16–25.

Machine Gun U.S.A. (1985, October 14). *Newsweek,* pp. 46–51.

Mayne, T. J., Norcross, J. C., & Sayette, M. A. (1994). Admissions requirements, acceptance rates, and financial assistance in clinical psychology programs: Diversity across the practice-research continuum. *American Psychologist, 49,* 806–811.

Maruyama, M. (1963). The second cybernetics: Deviation amplifying mutual causal processes. *American Scientist, 51,* 164–179.

McFall, R. M. (1991). Manifesto for a science of clinical psychology. *The Clinical Psychologist, 44,* 75–88.

McFall, R. M. (1994). Clinical science in the 21st century. *American Psychological Society Observer, 7, 2,* 28–29.

McGee, R., Feehan, M., Williams, S., & Anderson, J. (1992). DSM–III disorders from age 11 to age 15 years. *Journal of the American Academy of Child and Adolescent Psychiatry, 31,* 50–59.

McLoyd, V. C. (1989). Socialization and development in a changing economy: The effects of paternal job and income loss on children. *American Psychologist, 44*, 293–302.

Measuring crime: A shadow on society. (1994, October 15). *Economist, 333*, pp. 21–23.

Mirowsky, J., & Ross, C. E. (1989). Psychiatric diagnosis as reified measurement. *Journal of Health and Social Behavior, 30*, 11–25.

Morrow-Bradley, C., & Elliott, R. (1986). Utilization of psychotherapy research by practicing psychotherapists. *American Psychologist, 41*, 188–197.

Newman, O. (1972). *Defensible space*. New York: Macmillan.

Nisbett, R. E. (1993). Violence and U.S. regional culture. *American Psychologist, 48*, 441–449.

Offord, D. R., Boyle, M. H., & Racine, Y. (1989). Ontario child health study: Correlates of disorder. *Journal of the American Academy of Child and Adolescent Psychiatry, 28*, 856–860.

Offord, D. R., Boyle, M. H., Szatmari, P., Rae-Grant, N. I., Links, P. S., Cadman, D. T., Byles, J. A., Crawford, J. W., Munroe Blum, H., Byrne, C., Thomas, H., & Woodward, C. A. (1987). Ontario Child Health Study: II Six-month prevalence of disorder and rates of service utilization. *Archives of General Psychiatry, 44*, 832–836.

Olweus, D. (1992). Victimization among schoolchildren. In G. W. Albee, L. A. Bond, & T. V. Cook Monsey (Eds.), *Improving children's lives: Global perspectives on prevention* (pp. 279–295). Newbury Park, CA: Sage.

Pagelow, M. D. (1984). *Family violence*. New York: Praeger.

Patterson, G. R. (1982). *A social learning approach: 3. Coercive family process*. Eugene, OR: Castalia.

Patterson, G. R., Chamberlain, P., & Reid, J. B. (1982). A comprehensive evaluation of a parent training program. *Behavior Therapy, 13*, 638–650.

Patterson, G. R., DeBaryshe, B. D., & Ramsey, E. (1989). A developmental perspective on antisocial behavior. *American Psychologist, 44*, 432–444.

Powell, E. C., & Christoffel, K. K. (1994). Firearms: A culture of violence. *The American Professional Society on the Abuse of Children Advisor, 7*, 8–10.

Robins, L. N. (1966). *Deviant children grown up: A sociological and psychiatric study of sociopathic personalities*. Baltimore: Williams & Wilkins.

Robins, L. N. (1981). Epidemiological approaches to natural history research: Antisocial disorders in children. *Journal of the American Academy of Child Psychiatry, 20*, 566–568.

Rossi, P. H., & Wright, J. D. (1984). Evaluation research: An assessment. *Annual Review of Sociology, 10*, 331–352.

Russell, D. E. H. (1982). *Rape in marriage*. New York: Macmillan.

Sabotta, E. E., & Davis, R. L. (1992). Fatalities after report to a child-abuse registry in Washington state, 1973–1986. *Child Abuse and Neglect, 16*, 627–635.

Sechrest, L. (1992). The past and future of clinical psychology: A reflection on Woodworth (1937). *Journal of Consulting and Clinical Psychology, 60*, 18–23.

Shure, M. B., & Spivack, B. (1988). Interpersonal problem solving. In R. H. Price, E. L. Cowen, R. P. Lorion, & J. Ramos-McKay (Eds.), *Fourteen ounces of prevention* (pp. 69–82). Washington, DC: American Psychological Association.

Silence protects killers. (1994, January 2). *St. Louis Post Dispatch, 116*, pp. 1A, 8A–11A.

Stattin, H., & Magnusson, D. (1989). The role of early aggressive behavior in the frequency, seriousness, and types of later crime. *Journal of Consulting and Clinical Psychology, 57*, 710–718.

Steinberg, L., Catalano, R., & Dooley, D. (1981). Economic antecedents of child abuse and neglect. *Child Abuse and Neglect, 52*, 264–267.

Straus, M. A., & Gelles, R. J. (1990). How violent are American families? Estimates from the National Family Violence Resurvey and other studies. In M. A. Straus & R. J. Gelles (Eds.), *Physical violence in American families: Risk factors and adaptations to violence in 8,145 families* (pp. 95–132). New Brunswick, NJ: Transaction.

Straus, M. A., Gelles, R. J., & Steinmetz, S. K. (1980). *Behind closed doors: Violence in the American family*. Garden City, NY: Anchor-Doubleday.

Thomas, B. H., Byrne, C., Offord, D. R., & Boyle, M. H. (1991). Prevalence of behavioral symptoms and the relationship of child, parent, and family variables in 4- and 5-year olds: Results from the Ontario Child Health Study. *Developmental and Behavioral Pediatrics, 12*, 177–184.

Vaux, A. (1992, May). *Disinhibited personality and social errors.* Paper presented at the Tenth International Nags Head Conference, Highland Beach, FL.

Vaux, A. (1994). Social intervention. In R. Corsini (Ed.), *Encyclopedia of psychology* (pp. 434–436). New York: Wiley.

Vaux, A., Brownell, A., & Hill, P. (1982). *Life stress and social support in the family system.* (Working Paper #158). Public Policy Research Organization, University of California, Irvine.

Velez, C. N., Johnson, J., & Cohen, P. (1989). A longitudinal analysis of selected risk factors in childhood psychopathology. *Journal of the American Academy of Child and Adolescent Psychiatry, 28*, 861–864.

Voydanoff, P. (1989). Work and family: A review and expanded conceptualization. In E. B. Goldsmith (Ed.), *Work and family: Theory, research, and applications* (pp. 1–22). Newbury Park, CA: Sage.

Weisz, J. R., Weiss, B., & Donenberg, G. R. (1992). The lab versus the clinic: Effects of child and adolescent psychotherapy. *American Psychologist, 47*, 1578–1585.

Widiger, T. A. (1994). Conceptualizing a disorder of personality from the five-factor model. In P. T. Costa & T. A. Widiger (Eds.), *Personality disorders and the five-factor model of personality* (pp. 311–317). Washington, DC: American Psychological Association.

Wiltz, N. A., & Patterson, G. R. (1974). An evaluation of parent training procedures designed to alter inappropriate aggressive behavior of boys. *Behavior Therapy, 5*, 205–211.

Wolfe, D. A. (1985). Child-abusive parents: An empirical review and analysis. *Psychological Bulletin, 97*, 462–482.

Woodworth, R. S. (1992). The future of clinical psychology. *Journal of Consulting and Clinical Psychology, 60*, 16–17. (Original work published 1937)

World Almanac and Book of Facts. (1995). Mahwah, NJ: Funk & Wagnalls.

Yancey, W. L. (1971). Architecture, interacton, and social control: The case of a large-scale public housing project. *Environment and Behavior, 3*, 3–18.

Year's toll: Our loss, our failures—killing our children. (1994, January 2). *Chicago Tribune*, 1, 6–7.

9

Culturally Relevant Intervention With Minority Adolescents:
Before the Beginning

Christina M. Mitchell
National Center for American Indian
and Alaska Native Mental Health Research
University of Colorado Health Sciences Center

> *In September of 1953, several of us left our second-grade class for morning recess and*
> *discovered a strange commotion out on the playground. Children were milling about*
> *in small groups, buzzing with excitement about the "Indian"—a real Indian—who*
> *was going to our school . . . Jerry Pete was a Navajo, and as he rocked back and forth*
> *on the playground swing he seemed a bit surprised about and perhaps suspicious of*
> *all the attention. I still remember thinking as I watched him that he was rather*
> *ordinary for a real Indian; he was not doing anything spectacular, at least not*
> *compared to television images of screaming warriors killing innocent pioneers.*

—Olson and Wilson (1984, p. 1)

When I began to write the talk on which this chapter is based, I realized I could have used an alternative subtitle—A journey from "lumper" toward "splitter." Painting with broad brush strokes, a lumper is someone who focuses on how people are the same; a splitter, on how people are different. The author in the quote was a lumper; his schoolmates, splitters. Many social science disciplines have factions organized along such a dividing line. Within anthropology, one hears of the etic (lumper) versus emic (splitter) approaches, or a universalistic (lumper) versus a relativistic (splitter) perspective (O'Nell, 1989). Within medical sociology, Pearlin referred to *structure* seeker (lumper) and *meaning* seeker (splitter) (Pearlin, 1992). Within psychology, we often talk about quantitative (lumper) versus qualitative (splitter) researchers (Cook & Reichhardt, 1979).

As a psychologist, I stay within the jargon of my discipline to make finer distinctions. A lumper (quantitative researcher) would tend to rely on large sample, survey data, using such analytic techniques as t tests (Hays, 1988), analyses of variance (Scheffe, 1959), or multisample comparisons of structural equation models (Bentler, 1992). A splitter (qualitative researcher) might utilize data such as case studies and interviews, and analytic approaches such as phenomenological analyses (Good, 1990), various narrative analyses (Mattingly, 1989), structural analyses (Turner, 1980), and stylistic analyses (Bakhtin, 1981). To a quantitative researcher, the error term of any analysis, coupled with the acknowledgment that inferences drawn from statistical tests are only probabilistic, carries with it (among other things) statistical noise—all of the unmeasured ways in which people might differ. In reality, though, the quantitative researcher's noise is the qualitative researcher's signal: one person's *error* term is the other's *main effect*.

Quantitative analyses, the powerful tools of lumpers, seem to provide reassurance that people are indeed more alike than they are different—at least in those ways that really matter. Yet, as my research moved toward understanding adolescent development within ethnic minority communities, statistical analyses began to raise as many questions for me as they answered. For instance, what might it mean if Black teenagers on average score higher on a hassles measure than do Latino teenagers? Perhaps the Black teenagers live in riskier neighborhoods; or they may be more willing to say something is a big hassle than Latinos are; or the measure may do a better job of tapping real hassles in a Black teenager's life. Even more troublesome is the practice of dummy coding group membership within multiple regression analyses (Cohen & Cohen, 1983), thereby statistically controlling for—perhaps actually removing—differences between groups. It is not uncommon in my experience to find different sets of predictors, depending on whether I ran regressions within group or across groups while controlling for group membership. Statistics as science, or as art?

Theoretically driven interventions try to build on existing theoretical and empirical literatures. Unfortunately, the vast amount of work in these literatures was conducted within mainstream, Euro-American samples. If we really want to be able to develop culturally relevant interventions to build on strengths of minority communities, we need to back up—to, in fact, before the beginning. In work with minority communities, we need to critically look at relationships between constructs reported in the literature, at our favorite measures of those constructs, and even at the very constructs themselves. If statistical associations are reported in the literature, what might they really mean in minority communities? Are measures asking questions that are valid in these cultures? Are these constructs the most important ones in that culture—representing the true epicenter of successful life in that community? The scant literature that deals with minority populations must be utilized thoughtfully. Most work focused on Black and Hispanic–Latino populations (Kazdin, 1993); those working with other minority populations such as Asian American or American Indian have even less to draw from and must generalize from extant minority literature with caution.

I was thoroughly schooled, long practicing, and proudly training younger generations in the broad basics and fine points of the lumper tradition, while conducting large-scale research with paper-and-pencil measures trying to understand key risk and mediating processes underlying development among minority adolescents primarily living in poverty. However, in the recent past, I slowly began to realize some of the limitations that accompany this tradition. Within this chapter, I highlight some of the lessons I learned as I started to wander a bit from my vigilant lumper outpost to consider the strengths the splitter outlook can offer to adolescence research. As such, this chapter is uncharacteristically nonquantitative. I begin the tale of my journey with a few early experiences in my professional life that set me on my course toward research with ethnic minority groups. Four broad areas are discussed that present challenges for me in learning about the lives of ethnic minority adolescents: general research issues, general measurement concerns, concerns arising within adolescent development, and community issues that demand attention. I close the chapter revisiting implications of these issues for designing and implementing interventions with minority adolescents.

EARLY EXPERIENCES

I spent the first 30 years of my life, including both my undergraduate and graduate educations, as a member of mainstream, middle-class, Midwestern White United States. From such a life, I developed little awareness of culture as a powerful ingredient in understanding how people move through the world. As a matter of fact, I was so engulfed by my majority culture that I used to think I did not really have a culture at all—only other people had cultures. As unbelievable as that might sound, Kelly (1955) referred to this as a *dichotomy corollary*: All constructs are bipolar or dichotomous, made up of at least two elements that are similar, and a third element different from those two. For instance, to know happy, you must also know sad; to know hot, you must also know cold; to know beautiful, ugly. To understand mainstream–minority culture, I needed to have some experience outside my own culture.

With almost no real exposure to cultures other than my own, I took my first postgraduate job on the faculty at the University of Virginia. Moving at last outside of the Midwest, I had my first serious interactions with a different culture—"Southerners." The experience was quite a dramatic one for me. For example, I grew up as a dutiful student of public schools in Illinois—"the Land of Lincoln." There, I was taught that the Civil War was about such issues as slavery and economics and national unity. Suddenly, I found myself in the midst of people who referred to that period as "the War of Northern Aggression." I had neighbors whose conversations—which I was certain were in English—I really couldn't understand. For instance, I slowly realized that what sounded to me like *ha ha yoo* was actually, "Hi. How are you?" The supermarkets seemed to sell every part of a pig in the meat department—feet, ears, even heads! My eyes were beginning to open—just a bit—and that was only the beginning.

Leaving Virginia, I next found myself at New York University. There, I was Project Director of the Adolescent Pathways Project (Seidman, Aber, Allen, & Mitchell, 1994), a research project to explore the developmental pathways of adolescents living in poor neighborhoods—predominantly African- or Caribbean-American Black and Puerto Rican or Dominican youth. There, I was adopted by two Latina graduate students and a Black colleague, who all believed I was at least trainable on issues of culture. These three women set out to help me gain glimpses about life in minority cultures; in the process, I learned a lot about myself. I now find myself involved in research among American Indian nations—not just one more ethnic minority group, but in reality over 500 different culture groups. Who would have thought, from such humble, naive, and Eurocentric roots, my journey would bring me here?

GENERAL CONCERNS IN RESEARCH
WITH ETHNIC MINORITY GROUPS

One of the earliest things I learned in trying to conduct research with ethnic minority teenagers was that determining a person's ethnicity was much like a set of Russian tea dolls. (Some may know them as nested santas or matreshkas.) You have probably seen such things: You start with one large doll, open that one up and find a second, smaller doll; opening the second, you find an even smaller, third doll; inside the third, a tinier fourth, and so on. I began my research among ethnic minority teenagers with the mentality of the Census Bureau—a person is simply White, Black, Hispanic, or Other. The fact I realized these groups could be different at all, and different in important ways, was certainly a huge leap from my early years. Yet, the more I listened, the more I began to understand that such broad strokes were just about as useless as making no distinctions at all. For instance, Black families can come from very different culture groups: African-American and Caribbean heritages represented many of the families in the New York area. Customs and experiences were likely to be very different for a youth, depending on which culture was experienced. Moreover, let us say a youth's family had Caribbean roots. Which island? Families from Haiti are likely to be quite different from families from Jamaica or Trinidad. Once you have discerned this, you need also to know whether or not the youth was born in the United States or not. Compared to a youth born in the United States, one born outside could have quite a different childhood—one perhaps filled with greater mobility and movement between family living on the islands and family living on the U.S. mainland. If the youth was born in the United States, was he or she the first generation born here? If so, that youth may play an important role in his or her family—one of navigator of service systems for the family, or translator for nonenglish-speaking family members. A parallel set of matreshka exists for latino youth. What culture group? Puerto Rican families have many different customs and experiences than do Dominican families, or than those from countries in Central or South America. In fact, many Hispanic families in the southwest have lived in the United States for a number of centuries, predating Euro-American settlement. U.S.-born or not? First generation or not? The groupings and subgroupings can continue well beyond even these.

American Indian cultures have a different set of parameters that represent cultural groupings, but they serve a similar function for understanding how a youth grew up. Membership within a tribe is generally determined by *blood quantum*—a proxy for a person's genetic makeup, or how much American Indian ancestry a person has. For instance, .75 blood quantum would represent someone who had three grandparents who were full-blooded members of a tribe, and one grandparent who was non-Indian.[1] In many tribes, level of blood quantum—especially full-blood versus mixed-blood—translates into important differences in daily life for youth. Tribe of origin is another important piece of information. Although most tribes have had similar—and stormy—relationships to the U.S. government, each tribe has a number of important cultural differences from other tribes. Further-more, in some tribes, knowledge about the band, or the clan, or even the family can carry with it powerful information about key cultural differences. For example, members of the Navajo nation may introduce themselves to each other by saying what clan they are born "for" (meaning the mother's clan) and what clan they are born "to" (the father's clan). With this information, others who are familiar with these clans immediately gain important information about the customs, beliefs, and lineage of that person. Furthermore, the "traditionality" of a person's family is an important concern. Some families follow customs that changed little from times before Whites appeared, whereas other families follow more modern (i.e., mainstream) customs. These distinctions can represent important differences in how a youth was raised. Still another aspect is whether or not a youth was raised on or near his or her tribe's reservation, or at least has had some connection with others on that reservation. Those with stronger connections to the reservation are likely to have more exposure to and experience with tribal customs in ways that may powerfully influence development.

---

[1]Although it functions as a way to determine who has the right to Federal programs and monies, this widely accepted practice continues to make me uneasy. Such genetic proxies bring to mind similar, although generally disparaging, labels applied to Blacks in the 19th century, such as "quadroon" (one-fourth Black, or one of four grandparents who was Black) and "octoroon" (one-eighth Black, or 2 of 16 great-grandparents who were Black).

Where on earth do we stop? If we do not draw the line somewhere, we (of the lumper tradition) may end up with one person in each cell. In effect, we would have become splitters. As I struggled with the issue of where to stop, I was continually reminded of the (grossly paraphrased) Chinese proverb—"Be careful what you ask for; you just might get it." As I began to care about measuring more specific aspects of ethnic group membership, I learned that you can't really stop there. Ironically, I also developed greater sympathy for the Census Bureau mentality. The extreme simplicity of a forced-choice White–Black–Hispanic–Other classification system certainly holds a powerful allure—although in my most honest moments, I realize that such information is just too lumped to be really meaningful.

MEASUREMENT ISSUES

Many of the examples to follow are drawn from the project I currently run—the Voices of Indian Teens Project, or VOICES. Funded by the National Institute of Alcohol Abuse and Alcoholism, that project is following more than 2,000 adolescents in 10 high schools within five indian communities in the west. Twice a year, youth fill out a survey asking about risk–protective factors (e.g., stressful life events, poverty) and underlying mediating processes (e.g., social support, coping, self-esteem) leading to adaptive and maladaptive outcomes, including alcohol and other substance use, behavioral symptomatology, and educational achievement. To date, analyses focused on the multidimensionality of alcohol use (Mitchell et al., 1996), culturally specific definitions of pathological drinking (O'Nell & Mitchell, 1996), and the latent structure of problem-behavior syndrome (Mitchell & O'Nell, 1995). The project has a number of goals: An explication of processes leading adolescents to choose either to drink or not to drink; an understanding of broad issues in development among American Indian adolescents; the empirical testing and refinement of theories that can be used to guide subsequent creation and implementation of innovative programs to prevent mental health problems and promote strengths within Indian communities.

During pilot work for VOICES, we wanted to question as many of our most fundamental measurement assumptions as we possibly could, in order to devise measures that were not only psychometrically sound, but also culturally relevant. We tried to start before the beginning. For example, one basic concern focused on the common Likert scales so typical in survey research: You assign your thoughts, feelings, or experiences to a number between, say, 1 (*not at all*) and 5 (*very often*). American Indian cultures have been described as less linear and more holistic in relating concepts to one another than are Euro-American cultures (Bryde, 1971). If this is truly the case, perhaps asking Indian teenagers to quantify their feelings and life experiences so arbitrarily would be too foreign and meaningless a task. However, we quickly realized that this task presented no problem—the teenagers handled this task without a hitch. Looking back, we should not have been surprised. These teens were operating in close contact with mainstream culture for much of their lives, through schools funded by the Bureau of Indian Affairs, or dealings with White businesses on the reservations, or simply watching omnipresent television. As a result, internal consistency estimates of a number of scales commonly utilized in mainstream adolescent research demonstrated that Indian youth were indeed answering questions in meaningful and consistent ways.

With VOICES, we wanted to be conversant with the mainstream adolescent development literature and culturally relevant in our operationalizations of our constructs. We drew most of the constructs from those commonly discussed as theoretically important for mainstream adolescents; however, we deliberately chose measures that were used with at least one ethnic minority group. We then attempted to determine the cultural relevance and meaningfulness of the measures we intended to use. Center staff conducted a series of focus groups with adolescents, parents, and youth-serving adults (e.g., teachers, dorm aides, counselors) in several of the participating communities—a south-central boarding school, a Northern Plains reservation, and a southwestern Pueblo community. In groups of six to eight, focus group participants become the "teachers," and the Center staff members facilitating the discussion become the "learners." Reviewing every question and response, the participants discussed what each might mean within their communities, whether or not the responses were appropriate, and whether or not other responses might better elucidate a youth's experiences. In addition, we asked about constructs that might be important within the community, but that we had not included.

This process helped to alert us to several important issues. For example, social support questions contained phrases such as "support from friends who are not your relatives." However, in Indian communities, family typically are friends; moreover, friends who were not related but who are important members of a person's network are often actually given family names, such as "auntie." To force a distinction between family and friends seemed confusing, arbitrary, and meaningless to the participants. In another instance, participants were discussing a response set that ranged from *not at all satisfactory* to *very satisfactory*. It came to light that in that community's language, the closest translation to *satisfactory* was *just enough to keep my heart beating*. It quickly became clear that gradations of such a construct were nonsensical: *not at all enough to keep my heart beating, sort of enough to keep my heart beating* . . . We knew we needed to find a different term.

We also discovered that some constructs were difficult for youth to report. For instance, within many minority communities, poverty is likely to be an important risk factor. However, within American Indian communities, values of generosity and reciprocity may actually act as important buffers against traditionally defined lower levels of socioeconomic status (SES) or resources. To look at such a possibility, we needed some measure of socioeconomic resources from the youth. However, adolescents often do not have access to the information needed for the more commonly utilized measures of SES or occupational prestige, such as a precise description of what the primary caretaker's job is, or how many hours a week that person works, or how much money that person makes. Youth often cannot even report accurately the most common proxy for SES—parents' education levels. (Although middle- and upper-class families may spend time discussing parents' education, such conversations simply are not common among poorer families.) Furthermore, within American Indian communities, such measures also miss a large part of the wage-earning economy, such as making jewelry or weaving rugs. Finally, we found that the American Indian teenagers were typically willing to give us information about themselves, but they were reluctant to report much about other members of their families. In general, they felt such questions should be addressed to those people themselves; any such information was not theirs to share with outsiders.

ADOLESCENT DEVELOPMENT

Developmental tasks define the transition of adolescents from children to adults. This transition differs considerably across cultural, age, and gender groups. By mainstream Euro-American norms, a person becomes an adult as he or she progresses toward a number of markers: completion of high school, occupational identity, marriage, and parenthood. Successfully navigating these transitions can be especially problematic for minority youth, due to the poverty and discrimination that many face. Furthermore, the expectations for minority adolescents and young adults within their own culture groups may conflict with those of mainstream Euro-American society, both in the nature and meanings of the developmental tasks and their timing. For example, mainstream norms emphasize a young person's increasing autonomy, with decreasing dependence on his or her family of origin. Yet, American Indian communities, for instance, value as a sign of maturity a youth's increasing responsibility in contributing to, honoring, and caring for the family. In general, minority youth must weigh the expectations of their home communities against the values of the dominant society. Resolutions of these struggles are likely to be related to issues of psychological competence in important ways. For example, finding a well-paying job may mean that the youth has to leave his or her home community; yet much spiritual strength and self-esteem is deeply rooted in that community and land. Moreover, we anticipate that family and community judgments concerning the "pathology" of a teen's behavior is tied to whether or not that behavior markedly interferes with his or her ability to progress toward markers of growing maturity that matter to that community. Without a thorough explication of family and community expectations for adolescents moving into adulthood, adaptive and maladaptive psychosocial development cannot be fully understood. Let us look at the three commonly discussed developmental markers for adolescence in a bit more detail.

Completion of High School

Among mainstream groups, the completion of high school (and for many, undergraduate and postgraduate studies, as well) is generally considered a necessary step toward adulthood. Yet ethnic minority students are at high risk educationally: Black, Latino, and American Indian youth drop out of high school at rates well above those for mainstream youth.[2] Minority students share many characteristics and motivations for leaving school prematurely with their mainstream counterparts (Chavez, Edwards, & Oetting, 1989). In addition, though, culture-specific factors may fuel the problem of premature school leaving. For example, many American Indian families function on the basis of mutual obligation and reciprocity, in which family needs exert greater influence on individual members than do personal desires or the demands of the mainstream economy. Consequently, many American Indian school dropouts cite a variety of family-related problems such as family mobility, residential instability, and loneliness as reasons for leaving school (Brown, 1973; Shore & Nicholls, 1975; Wax, 1963). Moreover, American Indian girls are more likely to leave than are boys—the reverse of the pattern found among many other populations (Peng, 1983). Also responsible for minority students' dropout rates is the lack of congruity between the content and nature of the educational process and a minority teenager's traditional values (Dehyle, 1992). For instance, mainstream classrooms rely heavily on learning by reading and memorizing facts and figures; many American Indian families and communities emphasize learning through oral storytelling and allegory.

Moreover, leaving school prematurely may not carry the same stigma as in the mainstream groups. In cultures with subsistence economies, leaving school might actually have a positive economic impact on the youth and his or her family. A teen may be able to bring in some extra money, or provide child care so that others can work. Thus, rather than feeling rootless and alienated and, therefore, more likely to evidence psychosocial problems, these young adults may actually be very well adjusted.

Occupational Identity

Developmental scholars studying mainstream Euro-American cultures argued that deciding one's occupation and the pursuit of this goal (*occupational identity*) are critical tasks of early adulthood. In the general population, youth unemployment is linked to drug and alcohol use, violence, delinquency, and suicide (Levine, 1982). Changes in employment status were shown to affect psychological distress; however, this relationship may be moderated by commitment to work. In other words, those who want to work and are unable to find employment report greater distress

---

[2]In fact, *all* attrition rates must be considered with some caution. Our experience with 10 high schools in the VOICES project demonstrated repeatedly that schools in these communities tend to overreport their enrollment figures in order to obtain the maximum funding possible; they also make very little distinction among "school leavers." For instance, a youth dropping out of school and one simply moving to another school are often both classified as dropouts. Such is likely to be the case within overcrowded urban schools serving other minority youth, as well. In view of high mobility among many ethnic minority groups, this distinction is a critical one.

and report poor family and social relationships (Donovan, Oddy, Pardo, & Ades, 1992; Jackson, Stafford, Banks, & Warr, 1983).

Indeed, employment and, conversely, poverty, are serious concerns within minority communities. The causes of high unemployment within minority communities tend to be largely structural in nature: there are simply few wage-earning opportunities in either isolated urban ghettos or barrios (Wilson, 1987) or in remote, rural American Indian communities. Considering the scarce employment opportunities in these areas, why don't young people simply move out to other areas with more employment opportunities? Once again, cultural factors must be considered to understand the effect unemployment may have on these youth. The issue is perhaps most salient within American Indian communities. The preeminence of the extended family and strong ties to the land in many of these communities often outweigh or even preclude such considerations. Alternative sources of commerce are common. Barter is an accepted form of financial transaction, as is earning money through craftwork. Occupational prestige, or even status as a wage earner, may have little to do with one's identity, or even status, within these communities (O'Nell, 1992).

Working from mainstream Euro-American norms, one group of authors stated, "Occupation and identity are inextricably linked in modern society and identity-formation may be seriously affected by the failure to find work" (Donovan et al., 1992, p. 65) The negative impact of unemployment allegedly results not only in a lack of income, but also in continued (and, assumed deleterious) dependence on one's family, difficulty in forming intimate relationships, and a lack of structured activity (Jahoda, 1979). Although such outcomes may present problems within mainstream youth, the assumption that they are universally detrimental is culturally suspect. Instead, a more useful variation of this developmental marker, at least in American Indian communities, would be becoming a wage earner capable of contributing money and other resources to the needs of the family and community. For example, as a youth assumes more responsibility within the family, he or she might be expected to use his or her own earned income to purchase extra food for a dinner honoring a family member. Thus, although appearing to remain dependent on the family, he or she is actually enacting a more mature, developmentally appropriate, and highly valued role. Clearly, this developmental marker highlights the importance of culturally grounded ethnographic work in determining the relevance, importance, and precise form of such a marker.

Marriage and Parenthood

Along with completion of education and the development of an occupational identity, the development of intimate relationships (usually culminating in marriage) and the decision to become a parent are typically considered the final developmental marker for movement into mainstream Euro-American young adulthood. In such research, teenage motherhood was shown to be associated with marital instability, economic problems, and difficulty in family size regulation, whereas adolescent fatherhood was shown to be related to academic, drug, and conduct problems (Dryfoos, 1990). With minority communities, data did not definitively shown that marriage and parenthood are necessarily linked in meaningful ways. For example, much attention was paid to the disintegration of the American Indian family in the face of assimilation pressures, including forced boarding school attendance (Hauswald, 1987; Medicine, 1979). However, early parenthood may not necessarily be discouraged, and the presence of extended family networks in minority communities may lessen the economic hardships faced by young, single mothers (Shomaker, 1989). As with employment and occupational issues, this developmental marker needs much more ethnographic work in order to elucidate the importance, relevance, and countenance of intimate romantic relationships and parenthood. For example, formal marriage may not be as important an "achievement" as is the establishment of intimate, romantic relationships. Moreover, marriage and parenthood are likely to be two related, but still distinct, markers of development—with different meanings for males and females.

Additional Important Developmental Markers

To this point, I have focused on markers defined as important within mainstream communities. Yet, other developmental markers appear central within minority communities but play a less important role in mainstream societies. For instance, in some cultures, increasing participation in spiritual and community events may be important to becoming an adult. American Indian children, for instance, are often permitted to come and go freely during community events and spiritual ceremonies; however, as they mature, youth are expected to attend fully to such events, and even to participate actively—perhaps by doing dishes following a meal or helping to serve food at a ceremony. In addition, rituals of manhood and womanhood assist youth in seeking spiritual helpers to increase his or her potency or ability to perform required adult roles appropriately and respectfully.

A second arena of importance not typically given much weight in the research literature revolves around community entertainment—most commonly, sporting events. Games among young children are certainly acknowledged and supported; however, in some communities, teenagers and young adults are responsible for many of the organized settings of excitement, such as softball and football competitions. Such activities are extremely important to, and attended in great numbers by, community members. Indeed, successful young adults and teenagers in many minority communities are involved in sports, either through school activities or tribal teams.[3]

---

[3]This marker is not likely unique to minority communities, but one that may be important for many youth growing up in rural areas, as well.

Little is known about the transitions from adolescence to adulthood in minority populations—whether or not mainstream markers mean the same things, whether or not they are as important, or whether or not other tasks are equally important, but overlooked. To add even more confusion, Topper (1974) suggested that the actual time frame of adolescence may differ among communities, and by gender within communities: Males in some cultures may not actually participate in more adult roles in the family until they are much older—often until they enter a grandparent role.

COMMUNITY CONCERNS

When communities are a researcher's laboratory, a number of important concerns need serious attention. In the following discussion, five issues encountered are presented. Although attention to these concerns is potentially important in any research laboratory setting, ignoring them in community settings puts the researcher in the likely position of being refused cooperation—basically closing that setting to any and all research efforts.

Outsiders Versus Insiders

Many minority communities are wary of the intrusion of Euro-American researchers into their communities in the name of science, and rightfully so. Academic researchers unfortunately developed a reputation of bustling into minority communities, collecting data, and then vanishing to their ivory towers to further their own careers through scientific publications and academic promotion. American Indian communities are among those most mistreated. First came repeated broken promises experienced through treaties between American Indian nations and the U.S. government; next came early anthropologists, who often lived in the communities, studied the members, and then left—never to return with information or findings for the community (Maynard, 1974). Vine Deloria (1969) noted:

> Into each life, it is said, some rain must fall. Some people have had horoscopes, others take tips on the stock market . . . But Indians have been cursed above all other people. Indians have anthropologists. The origin of the anthropologist is hidden in the historical mists. Indians are certain all societies of the Near East had anthropologists at one time because all those societies are now defunct. (p. 83)

Within minority communities, the image of the lone wolf researcher—riding into town, doing his or her work independent of the town members, and then riding off into the sunset—will no longer be tolerated. Many communities are aware that important information can be gained using the culture of Western science. For instance, baseline data can help in preparing more compelling and competitive data-based grant applications, program planning efforts, and requests for continuing and additional services. However, communities now are also demanding an equal share in the selection of the problems to study, precisely how those problems will be defined and measured, and what will be done with results.

Who "Owns" the Data?

Who has the right to interpret and disseminate information from a community-based study should never be in question—the participating community has *at least* one half ownership of anything that comes from a study in which their members participated. A stunning example of this right's having been overlooked became a classic among researchers working in American Indian communities. In 1979, a nonlocal research group, in conjunction with a local public office, conducted a survey of the use of alcohol among the Inupiat in Barrow, Alaska (Klausner & Foulks, 1982):

> Using a 1972 demographic survey of the community, they drew a 10% representative sample of everyone over the age of 15—a total of 88 Inupiat. Results indicated that 41% considered themselves to be excessive drinkers, and 60% reported that drinking ultimately created severe problems with family and spouse . . . Drinking in this community was described primarily as a social event; only five individuals in our sample reported drinking alone. (Foulks, 1989, pp. 7–8)

The researchers released this information at a press conference in New York City. Within a week, the *New York Times* printed an article headlined "Alcohol plagues Eskimos (1980)." The newspaper reported a 72% alcoholism rate, as well as a quote by one of the other researchers that characterized "the Eskimos . . . {as} not a collection of individual alcoholics but a society which is alcoholic, and therefore facing extinction" (p. C1). Other wire services followed suit, reporting that alcoholism and violence had overtaken Eskimo society after the sudden burst of development in response to the oil industry had resulted in epidemics of alcoholism in the native societies. Foulks (1989) noted, "In reporting the study, the press confirmed the stereotype of the drunken Alaska Native, whose traditional culture had been plundered. The public exposure had brought shame on the community, and the people were now angry and defensive" (p. 13).

Although it is simple to state that the community owns the data, it can be complicated to hear one single voice from any community. Foulks (1989) noted:

> The community of Barrow was complex and multifaceted, containing many opinions and factions—non-Native and Inupiat alike. Our research team was sponsored by only a few of these factions, including Intersect and the Department of Public Safety. Methods were not developed to ensure more community participation because we wrongly believed that the Steering Committee and the Technical Advisory Committee reflected general public opinion. (p. 16)

Furthermore, to the extent to which researchers feel the pressures to publish or perish, they are likely to be inclined to try to hurry or even ignore critical community-level processes and the multitude of voices so crucial to develop an understanding and acceptance of research findings in order to expedite personal agenda and gains.

Researchers also have a responsibility to ensure that they give back the information in ways that are accessible and usable by the community members. Yet, few community researchers have any training or experience in writing for such audiences, using clear formats and jargon-free language written at a reasonably accessible reading level of sixth or seventh grade. For instance, with the VOICES data, we create site-specific reports twice a year for each school that participates; we also produce a semiannual youth newsletter twice a year, dealing with the same issues as the site report. Although extremely important from a community relationship perspective, these activities take a considerable amount of time and accomplish little of importance in the eyes of my home academic institution. Does the fact that I spent several weeks each time writing—and re-and re-rewriting—these documents move me closer to promotion within a medical school? I can assure you it does not. Moreover, these reports so far have been what we think the communities might find interesting from our data set. We create the reports and hold meetings inviting the people who might be interested, but the information flow too often seems to stop there. We believe the communities could use these data—which we have gathered with their kindness, cooperation, and consent from their youth—in many ways. However, how strongly can we demand that they drop their current tasks and think with us about what else we could offer them? Although it is an altruistic request, it also presents extra burdens for already overworked professionals in the community. In a few of the VOICES sites, a key person or two—an Assistant Superintendent, or a substance use counselor—has been able to frame a question or two important to them that we were able to use the data from their youth to address further. However, such discussions take their own time—not only for us, but for those in the communities. Perhaps the best we can do is to continue to keep our routine streams of communications open, and hope that should an opportunity arise in which we can provide more useful information, we will make appropriate note of it and be in a position to respond in a timely fashion.

Community Confidentiality

Psychologists are well trained to protect confidentiality of individual clients and research participants. But community confidentiality can raise important concerns, as well. Within densely populated communities such as urban neighborhoods, keeping the community's exact identity confidential may not be quite so pressing (although I am not all that certain, even then). For instance, in New York City, naming participating neighborhoods such as Bedford–Stuyvesant or Harlem may result in little harm to individuals, given the population density of these communities. However, within very small communities, confidentiality of both the participants and the community are powerfully intertwined. Worries run especially high if the research deals with extreme behaviors. If a community is identified, and behaviors such as extensive alcohol use or physical abuse are described, simple deduction alone may identify actual individuals. Thus, even if the researcher is careful to render each individual's data anonymous, those who know the members of the community may be able to circumvent that anonymity.

In the VOICES project, we refer to participating communities by generic pseudonyms such as "Northern Plains" or "South Central" culture groups. In this way, we hope to avoid inadvertently identifying individuals and to avoid creating or perpetuating negative stereotypes about individual tribes or culture groups. For instance, if we found that one group of youth consistently reported lower educational achievement and higher levels of drinking, we would be loathe to be even the most minute players in a process that could eventually label that particular group as "permitting" youth to drink excessively and contribute to poor school performance. Yet, this cultural anonymity creates an important dilemma. We speak of the heterogeneity among American Indian nations; in fact, the communities of the VOICES project were deliberately selected to represent groups from quite different cultural and historical backgrounds. How can we meaningfully discuss important cultural differences potentially playing a role in developmental processes, without describing key aspects of these cultural groups in such detail that we risk destroying their anonymity? It is a tension that haunts everything we write.

Styles of Communication and Organization

In conducting field research, researchers often have to develop a keen—some might say, obsessive—eye for detail, order, procedure, and control. For instance, in preparing for a major data collection effort, I typically make lists and prioritize tasks by weeks, carefully crossing off tasks as they are completed. In VOICES, though, we operate primarily through community field offices, staffed by community members, and supervised long-distance by staff at the Denver office. As a result, I cannot control data collection directly, but must rely on staff in the field office to do so. During my first experience in overseeing data collection through VOICES Field Offices, I found myself diligently prioritizing tasks and making lists not only for myself, but for the field staff as well. As data collection dates neared, I would fax more and more lists of tasks and target dates for completion. At one site in particular, I would fax my lists, and then call the field office Director to make sure he had received and understood the lists. He would calmly acknowledge that he had indeed received and understood the lists. I would call back later to see what had been accomplished, and he would simply say, "It'll get done." Never "Oh, yes. I've done that," or "I'll be working on that tomorrow and I expect to have it finished by next week." Simply, "It'll get done." I tried hard not to express my exasperation, but I am sure he could sense it—and I am even surer that he found it quite amusing. However, he was absolutely correct—whatever it was, it always did get done, and it got done in a manner and at a pace consonant with the community. As we continued to work together, he and I were able to create a trusting relationship, wherein I could make fun of myself and my need for sending him lists. He, too, could laugh at himself (and me) by reiterating, "It'll get done"—and then set about to accomplish all of the tasks that needed to get done in a community-appropriate fashion and pace.

Unexpected Rewards and Responsibilities

Working carefully and caringly within a different culture brings with it marvelous opportunities and rewards and important responsibilities. The rewards are probably obvious to most community researchers. For instance, I was graciously invited to and warmly received at community pow-wows, honoring ceremonies, and funerals. Each time, I marvel at this unique opportunity for someone raised as I was—middle-class, mainstream, Midwestern. I am continually amazed by the generosity and trust members of the community offer. At the same time, though, that giving must go both ways. I cannot only receive, but must also try to think of ways I can give back, as well—however small that giving might be. The extent to which I simply accept generosity with no reciprocity, I risk being just another variation of the lone wolf researcher, using yet another native community for my own gains.

Perhaps my clearest opportunity to participate truly as a community member—both giving and receiving—came with a local ceremony to honor our field site Director, who had died the previous year. His widow was planning a community giveaway, and she was gathering articles to be given away. Among the most cherished items were blankets—traditionally, in this community, handmade quilts. As we talked at the Center about the coming ceremony, we began to realize that we could actually contribute—in a very real and concrete way—to honoring our coworker's memory. So, a group of us set about to knit, and then donate, afghans. They were not as elegant as hand-stitched quilts, to be sure, but nevertheless, a clear statement of the importance of and our connections with the members of that community. When his widow heard of our efforts, she was deeply moved. As I participated in the ceremony and saw our afghans among all the other items, I felt almost unspeakably proud and honored to have been able to offer something so meaningful and concrete back to that community.

SUMMARY

Although this story was one of journey, it was a journey not without serious tensions. If lumpers carry their adopting of splitter mindsets to their extremes, we could all end up as amateur cultural anthropologists. Clearly, this is not my intention. If we look only for how people differ, we may end up immobilized. For instance, we will be able to devise no broad-based interventions; we will be unable to tap funding sources that are indeed interested in a number of the questions quantitative researchers are equipped to answer. Simply because there are alternative ways to approach the same question does not mean we should all race to become ethnographers. Both traditions bring important strengths as well as weaknesses in addressing important research questions needed to guide interventions with ethnic minority adolescents.

Instead, I think of this as akin to the optical illusion typically presented in discussions of perception in introductory psychology texts: Do you see two profiles facing each other, or a goblet? My hope is for more fluid movement between opposing, but complementary, view of figure and ground: quantitative and qualitative research approaches; community and research office cultures; mainstream and minority values. In each pairing, neither one nor the other is the right view. Depending on what is useful at the moment, one brings that view to the fore.

Basic developmental research is merely a promissory note given to us by the communities within which we work. In basic, nonapplied research, we try to understand the current, naturalistic unfolding of development; we gather information from the community members over a period of years, possibly offering little back to the communities during that period. However, as we near completion of these studies, we owe it to the participants and their communities to return to begin to figure out ways to make life better for people in those communities. In designing interventions for and with minority communities, we must start before the beginning. We must never assume that research conducted within mainstream groups is indeed the gold standard. Instead, we should raise questions at every stage of designing a research or intervention program. This list below is a mere beginning:

Are the constructs those the community feels are the most important to understand?

Are the instruments used to measure those constructs valid within that community?

How much confidence can we put into patterns of relationships that are currently present in the research literature?

And what about relationships that have not been reported—can we confidently believe they might not exist in minority communities? In fact, nonsignificant findings may actually represent problems with the first two areas—poor construct selection or invalid operationalizations.

Finally, we need to be perpetually alert to the power inherent in problem definition. How a problem is defined immediately determines what we can and will do to intervene with that problem (Humphreys & Rappaport, 1993). Tesh (1988) offered a public health example of the power of problem definition. If we define smoking as the cause of lung cancer, individual-level interventions to cut down on cigarette intake immediately make sense. However, if we define tobacco as the cause, environmental interventions such as analyzing the continuing presence of tobacco in our society come to the fore.

One of the soundest ways to ensure that we define problems in ways that are consonant with the community is simply to include the community at all levels. For instance, in the VOICES project, key informants such as educational, health, and spiritual leaders offered crucial insights into important processes and competencies. These people were especially important in helping us determine constructs, such as community-mindedness and spirituality, that are important for healthy development from the community's point of view, but were widely discussed in mainstream research literature. Focus groups, consisting of youth-serving professionals, dorm aides, and teenagers themselves, were pivotal in examining every measure—word by word—to highlight questions that might be misunderstood or response categories that were missing or difficult to use. Each time we return to the community to collect the next wave of data, we bring site-specific reports for school personnel and others in youth-serving positions, and newsletters for the youth that explain some of the findings from the previous date collection. We continually work with youth-serving agencies in the communities to use VOICES data as baseline data to justify new programs or gauge the impact of existing programs. As we write manuscripts, key informants again help, reading drafts and commenting to help us understand how communities might react to findings or to offer alternative interpretations. Only by including the community in such ways as a collaborator—before the beginning, as well as after the end—can we hope to bring research to bear on critical aspects of development.

ACKNOWLEDGMENTS

The preparation of this chapter was supported by the National Institute of Alcohol Abuse and Alcoholism, #R01–AA08474.

REFERENCES

Alcohol plagues Eskimos. (1980, January 22). *New York Times*, p. C1.

Bakhtin, M. (1981). *The dialogic imagination: Four essays*. Austin: University of Texas Press.

Bentler, P. M. (1992). *EQS: Structural equations program manual*. Los Angeles: BMDP Statistical Software.

Brown, C. C. (1973). Identification of selected problems of Indians residing in Klamath cuonty, Oregon—An examination of data generated since termination of the Klamath reservation. *Dissertation Abstract International, Education, Guidance and Counseling*, 7532-A.

Bryde, J. F. (1971). *Modern Indian psychology*. Vermillion, SD: Institute of Indian Studies.

Chavez, E. L., Edwards, R., & Oetting, E. R. (1989). Mexican American and White American school dropouts' drug use, health status, and involvement in violence. *Public Health Reports, 104*, 594–604.

Cohen, J., & Cohen, P. (1983). *Applied multiple regression/correlation analysis for the behavioral sciences*. Hillsdale, NJ: Lawrence Erlbaum Associates.

Cook, T. D., & Reichhardt, C. S. (1979). *Quantitative and qualitative methods in evaluation research*. Beverly Hills, CA: Sage.

Dehyle, D. (1992). Constructing failure and maintaining cultural identity: Navajo and Ute school leavers. *Journal of American Indian Education, 31*, 24–47.

Deloria, V. (1969). *Custer died for your sins: An Indian manifesto*. New York: Macmillan.

Donovan, A., Oddy, M., Pardoe, R., & Ades, A. (1992). Employment status and psychological well-being: A longitudinal study of 16-year-old school-leavers. *Journal of Child Psychology and Psychiatry, 27*, 65–76.

Dryfoos, J. G. (1990). *Adolescents at risk: Prevalence and prevention*. New York: Oxford University Press.

Foulks, E. F. (1989). Misalliances in the Barrow Alcohol Study. *American Indian and Alaska Native Mental Health Research, 2*, 7–17.

Good, B. (1990, August). *Illness, narrative, and experience*. Paper presented at the Lewis Henry Morgan Lectures, University of Rochester, Rochester, NY.

Hauswald, L. (1987). External pressure/internal change: Child neglect on the Navajo reservation. In N. Scheper-Hughes (Ed.), *Child survival: Anthropological perspectives in the treatment and maltreatment of children* (pp. 145–164). Boston: D. Reidel.

Hays, W. L. (1988). *Statistics*. Fort Worth, TX: Holt, Rinehart & Winston.

Humphreys, K., & Rappaport, J. (1993). From the community mental health movement to the war on drugs. *American Psychologist, 48*, 892–901.

Jackson, P. R., Stafford, E. M., Banks, M. H., & Warr, P. B. (1983). Unemployment and psychological disoress in young people: The moderating role of employment commitment. *Journal of Applied Psychology, 68*, 525–535.

Jahoda, M. (1979). The impact of unemployment in the 1930s and 1970s. *Journal of the British Psychological Society, 32*, 34–44.

Kazdin, A. E. (1993). Adolescent mental health: Prevention and tratment programs. *American Psychologist, 48*, 127–141.

Kelly, G. A. (1955). *The psychology of personal constructs: A theory of personality*. New York: Norton.

Klausner, S., & Foulks, E. (1982). *Eskimo capitalists: Oil, alcohol and social change*. Montclair, NJ: Allenheld & Osmun.

Levine, S. V. (1982). *The psychological and social effects of youth unemployment*. Chicago: University of Chicago Press.

Mattingly, C. (1989). *Thinking with stories: Story and experience in a clinical practice*. Unpublished doctoral dissertation, Massachusetts Institute of Technology, Cambridge, MA.

Maynard, E. (1974). The growing negative image of the anthropologist among American Indians. *Human Organization, 33*, 402–404.

Medicine, B. (1979). American Indian family: Cultural change and adaptive strategies. *The Journal of Ethnic Studies, 8*, 13–23.

Mitchell, C. M., & O'Nell, T. D. (1995). *Problem behaviors among American Indian adolescents: Structure and validity*. Unpublished manuscript.

Mitchell, C. M., O'Nell, T. D., Beals, J., Dick, R. W., Keane, E., & Manson, S. M. (1996). Dimensionality of alcohol use among American Indian adolescents: Latent structure, construct validity, and implications for developmental research. *Journal of Research on Adolescence, 6*, 151–180.

Olson, J. S., & Wilson, R. (1984). *Native Americans in the twentieth century*. Chicago: University of Illinois Press.

O'Nell, T. D. (1989). Psychiatric investigations among American Indians and Alaska Natives: A critical review. *Culture, Medicine and Psychiatry, 13*, 51–87.

O'Nell, T. D. (1992, July). *PTSD among American Indian Vietnam veterans: Cultural consideration in epidemiological research*. Paper presented at the Eighth Annual Meeting of the International Social for Traumatic Stress Studies, Los Angeles, CA.

O'Nell, T. D., & Mitchell, C. M. (1996). Alcohol use among American Indian adolescents: The role of culture in pathological drinking. *Social Science and Medicine, 42*, 565–578.

Pearlin, L. I. (1992). Structure and meaning in medical sociology. *Journal of Health and Social Behavior, 33,* 1–9.

Peng, S. S. (1983). *High school dropouts: Descriptive information from high school and beyond* (NCES 83022b). Washington, DC: National Center for Health Statistics.

Scheffe, H. (1959). *Analysis of variance.* New York: Wiley.

Seidman, E., Aber, J. L., Allen, L., & Mitchell, C. M. (1994). School transitions among poor urban adolescents: Impact on the self-system and perceived social context. *Child Development, 65,* 507–522.

Shomaker, D. (1989). Transfer of children and the importance of grandmothers among the Navajo Indians. *Journal of Cross-Cultural Gerontology, 4,* 1–8.

Shore, J. H., & Nicholls, W. M. (1975). Indian children and tribal group homes: New interpretation of the Whipper Man. *American Journal of Psychiatry, 132,* 454–456.

Tesh, S. N. (1988). *Hidden arguments: Political ideology and disease prevention policy.* New Brunswick, NJ: Rutgers University Press.

Topper, M. D. (1974). Drinking patterns, culture change, sociability and Navajo "adolescents." *Addictive Disorders, 1,* 97–116.

Turner, V. (1980). Social dramas and stories about them. In W. Mitchell (Ed.), *On narrative.* (pp. 137–164). Chicago: University of Chicago Press.

Wax, M. L. (1963). American Indian education as a cultural transaction. *Teacher's College Record, 64,* 696–704.

Wilson, W. J. (1987). *The truly disadvantaged.* Chicago: University of Chicago Press.

10

Perspectives on Biological, Social, and Psychological Phenomena in Middle- and Old-Age Women:
Interference or Intervention?

Linda Gannon
Southern Illinois University–Carbondale

Improved health care and a diminishing birth rate resulted in an increasing aged population with the consequent focus of the helping professions on the social, psychological, cultural, and biological development that characterizes middle and old age. Due to culturally defined gender roles, aging is a particular disadvantage for women. Aging is associated with worthlessness and loss because women are traditionally biologically defined and valued for their youthful beauty and fertility (Dickson, 1993). Thus, for women, the lifelong experience of diminished economic, political, and social power is exaggerated with biological aging. Theoretical conceptualizations of these developmental changes vary considerably and have wide-ranging effects, which include shaping societal attitudes, influencing research funding priorities, and determining intervention (or nonintervention) strategies. This discussion compares and contrasts several theoretical approaches to biological, social, and psychological phenomena in middle- and old-age women.

CONTRASTING PARADIGMATIC VIEWS OF AGING IN WOMEN

Numerous paradigms have been presented and delineated within which researchers have attempted to study and understand the phenomenon of aging. Two major paradigms within which aging has been studied in women are "medical" and "feminist." These are, perhaps, not the most precise labels. I use these terms as brief descriptions of my observations rather than as labels of logically consistent and ideologically pure philosophical constructs.

The medical paradigm of aging in women is essentially limited to biology; that is, menopause and the hormonal changes that accompany menopause. In this paradigm, the study of menopause was designed and interpreted within a theoretical context in which the menopause is viewed as a disease. The "medicalization of menopause" began in the 1940s with the production of inexpensive estrogens and continues today as is evidenced by the Merck Manual of Geriatrics (Abrams & Berkow, 1990), which lists menopause under metabolic and endocrine disorders, and the 21st Edition of the Physician's Handbook (Krupp, Tierney, Jawetz, Roe, & Camargo, 1985) describing menopause as a "clinical disorder" of the ovary (p. 274) characterized by estrogen deficiency. Current medical opinion recommends that all women, when suspecting the beginning of menopause, be evaluated by their physician, and be treated with estrogen for the rest of their lives (Mishell, 1989; Studd, 1989).

Social scientists frequently described the medicalization of menopause as an instance of medical imperialism: The motivation is profit and power and women and the elderly are easy targets because they lack status and influence in our society (Reissman, 1983; Strong, 1979). Feminists (e.g., Logothetis, 1988; McCrea, 1983) lament the ultimate consequences. In addition to the obvious negative connotations associated with the disease label and the fostering of dependency on physicians, the medical paradigm of menopause encourages women to ascribe gender inequality to biology rather than to the social, economic, and political arenas (Kaufert, 1982; Strong, 1979). Reissman (1983) noted that some women, believing that medical intervention would free them of their biological destinies, may endorse the medical model of menopause only to find that physicians, rather than themselves, are in control of their experience.

Feminists proposed an alternative paradigm (e.g., Hunter, 1990c; Kahn & Holt, 1987) in which aging is viewed as a natural, developmental process. Menopause is only part of the aging process and represents a life transition in much the same way as puberty. Puberty may be associated with skin problems and emotional distress but these problems are not viewed as symptoms of an underlying clinical disorder nor are attempts made to prevent puberty by suppressing hormone production. Similarly, according to this model, menopause may be accompanied by hot flashes and the emotional turmoil associated with identity and role issues, but these are dealt with as problems associated with a normal and expected transition rather than as indicative of a disease process. The focus is not on deficiency and artificially maintaining a particular hormonal state, but rather on viewing menopause as only one of many biological, social, and psychological changes accompanying aging and as an inevitable life stage associated with new challenges and freedoms. This is my paradigm.

In the last several decades, various models of aging were advanced that loosely fit either the medical or the feminist paradigms (Gannon, 1985). One such model conforms precisely to the medical paradigm in that the study of aging in women focuses exclusively on menopause as the event of crucial importance and attributes all physical and psychological changes associated with aging to diminishing levels of estrogen. The "nonmedical" models include: (a) the *"domino" theory*, which postulates that hormonal factors are responsible for hot flashes, whereas other "symptoms," such as insomnia, depression, and irritability, result from the discomfort associated with hot flashes; (b) the *premorbid personality theory*, which hypothesizes that psychological symptoms are an exacerbation of or a simple continuation of previously existing symptoms; (c) the *coincidental stress model*, which suggests that the particular stresses that occur during middle and old age, such as children leaving home or illness or death of parents, predispose women to psychological problems; and finally, (d) the *cultural relativism model*, which posits, as causal, particular cultural, societal, or historical factors, such as the influence of individual attitudes and cultural stereotypes on aging.

Although definitive empirical support favoring one model over the others is lacking, information relevant to the evaluation of these models has been published. Selected findings include (for a thorough review, see Gannon, 1985): (a) the relationship between overall symptom severity and hormonal levels was not significant (Abe, Furuhashi, Yamaya, Hashiai, & Suzuki, 1977; Aksel, Schomberg, Tyrey, & Hammond, 1976); (b) women experiencing hot flashes had significantly lower levels of estrogen than those not experiencing hot flashes (Hutton, Jacobs, Murray, & James, 1978); (c) exogenous estrogen effectively treated hot flashes and atrophic vaginitis but not depression, irritability, insomnia, and palpitations (Poller, Thomson, & Coope, 1980; Utian, 1972); (d) 38% and 43% of the variance in psychological and somatic symptoms, respectively, was accounted for by life stress, whereas the contribution of menopausal status was small and nonsignificant (Greene & Cooke, 1980); (e) attitudes, beliefs, and expectations concerning menopause and aging were found to be predictive of reported distress during middle and old age (Bart, 1969). In general, results of investigations across models and disciplines were surprisingly consistent in supporting the view that hot flashes and atrophic vaginitis are primarily caused by the changing hormonal environment of menopause, whereas other somatic and psychological changes are the result of aging, historical, cultural, and stress factors.

Although both hot flashes and atrophic vaginitis were empirically linked to hormonal levels, neither symptom should be construed as solely a medical problem amenable to only medical solutions. Hot flash frequency and severity were found to be significantly related to stress in some women (Gannon, Hansel, & Goodwin, 1987) and stress reduction techniques were found to be effective in alleviating the problem (Freedman & Woodward, 1992). The most common complaint associated with atrophic vaginitis has been diminished lubrication during sexual arousal. The medical community assumed that this is related to sexual behavior during menopause; that is, diminished lubrication results in diminished interest in sex (e.g., Sarrel, 1982). However, the empirical research is not supportive of such a simple and straightforward pattern. For example, quantity and quality of lubrication during sexual arousal seems to be unrelated to menopausal status, hormonal levels, and frequency and satisfaction of sexual activity (Gannon, 1994, Hunter, 1990a).

Paradigmatic Assumptions

The highly disparate perspectives on aging reflect equally disparate underlying beliefs, values, and assumptions. A basic assumption of the medical paradigm in the context of women's health is biological determinism. Thus, the only relevant events for aging women are menopause and the related lowered levels of estrogen and progesterone. The application of biological determinism to women, but not to men, is a mainstay of patriarchy: Women are at the mercy of their biology, rendering them helpless to change, grow, or develop; their roles are limited to wife, sex partner, and mother. Aging and menopause thus leave women with few roles—roles of little importance to society. This same ideology is evident in the emphasis placed on the menstrual cycle in determining mood and behavior in menstruating women. Estrogen levels, the assumed determinant of women's moods and behaviors, are inferred by phase of menstrual cycle in premenopausal women and by menopausal status in postmenopausal women. The variability in men's moods and behaviors equals or exceeds the variability found linked to estrogen levels in women (Parlee, 1980; Swandby, 1981), and testosterone levels diminish with aging in men (Davidson, 1980). Yet, aging men's moods and behaviors are attributed to their intellect, coping abilities, performance, and success—not to their declining levels of testosterone.

Within the feminist paradigm, women's and men's moods and behaviors are influenced by the same determinants—the social, economic, and political milieu. Biology plays a minor role in the lives of persons of both sexes. Roles are determined by the individuals' social, familial, and achievement history as well as their talents, skills, desires, and perceptions. In our present society, the patriarchal ideology and structure forces women and men to experience different social, economic and political realities; the consequences of these different realities are the gender differences of everyday life—gender differences that are perceived, within the context of other paradigms, as biologically driven.

Paradigmatic Consequences

The influence of these paradigms on everyday life and attitudes toward women and aging is not trivial. Consider, for example, a recent description of menopause that appeared in a newspaper:

"I think of the menopause as a deficiency disease, like diabetes," a San Francisco gynecologist told the New York Times . . . "Most women develop some symptoms whether they are aware of them or not, so I prescribe estrogens for virtually all menopausal women for an indefinite period." (Seaman & Seaman, 1977, p. 293).

Contrast this with a hypothetical feminist version of menopause:

After approximately 30 years of menstrual cycles in order to provide transitory fertility, normality is restored, estrogen levels return to normal, menstruation ceases. The woman is able to participate fully in her career, social, family activities as she need no longer be concerned about the problems associated with menstruation, birth control and pregnancy and is no longer at a heightened risk for endometriosis, uterine fibroids, and breast cancer.

Consider how different our attitudes would be toward women and aging if we repeatedly heard and read versions of the feminist definition rather than, as is currently the case, versions of the medical definition.

The language of the medical paradigm became the language of everyday life with little awareness of the implications of particular terms and phrases. Consider the following medical terms (on the left) and alternative terms consistent with a feminist ideology (on the right):

Medical	*Feminist*
Menopause	Reproductive release
Ovarian failure	Ovarian serenity
Estrogen deficiency	Estrogen stability

The terms and phrases of the medical paradigm clearly construe menopause as a failure or a disability or a loss and the terms and phrases of the feminist paradigm convey a life transition of potential growth and development and comfort. The language of the medical paradigm conveys the idea that help or treatment or prevention is desirable, whereas the feminist paradigm portrays menopause as positive and welcome and normal. Although the biological determinism inherent in the medical model is obvious, the sexist nature of this model is not apparent in the absence of parallel language for men. Although men experience diminishing levels of testosterone as they age, there is no medical term to describe this loss because men are not viewed as products of their biology. To appreciate the difference, consider the phrase "she's premenstrual" to dismiss or trivialize a woman who is angry. In contrast, a man who is angry or aggressive is assumed to have a legitimate cause for his emotions; he is not described as having too much testosterone.

The medical profession argues for acceptance of their paradigm on the grounds that it is "scientific"—that there exist objective, empirical data for the medical conceptualization of aging in women. There is a tremendous increase in public interest in menopause as evidenced by media attention and popular books. The medical community has participated in the form of pronouncements, advice on treatments and claims of cures but not in the form of making menopause a research priority.

In a recent study (Gannon, Stevens, & Stecker, unpublished manuscript), the three major obstetrics and gynecology journals were examined; the content, focus, purpose, and funding source of all articles for the years 1975, 1980, 1985, 1990, and 1993 were analyzed. The results indicated that articles with a focus on reproductive issues far outnumbered those on women's health at a ratio of 4:1, that the percentage of articles on menopause and sexually transmitted disorders did not change over the years and remained at a low 1% to 2%. The authors concluded:

> ... rather than responding to current medical needs based on changing social needs and life-styles, the obstetrics/gynecology specialty has continued to emphasize the reproductive nature of women and has ignored the health and well-being requirements of non-pregnant and non-fertile women. The social values and attitudes toward women inferred from the priorities evident in these data are ideologically consistent with the view that women's primary role is that of reproduction. (p. 2)

In contrast to the claim of "objective science," the medical model seems based on opinion, stereotype, politics, and profit, not on reliable and valid data.

Within the closed system of the medical paradigm, the path from biological determinism to defining menopause as a disease is logical and justifiable. If we assume women are essentially biologically determined and driven, then their roles will be limited to those of wife, sex partner, and mother. Continuing with this logic, the standard, normal, optimal biology for women is that which allows and facilitates these roles—menstruation (evidence of fertility) and pregnancy (proof of fertility); the nonmenstruating–nonpregnancy states are seen as abnormal, diseased, and deficient.

Although the only universal consequence of menopause is the absence of fertility, patriarchal ideology provides a set of "logical" correlates for this state—fat, sagging breasts, wrinkles, depression, anxiety, cognitive deterioration—and then provides a "cure" for this loss of fertility interpreted as a loss of femininity. (Indeed, a recent advertisement for HRT by a pharmaceutical company described their product as "The Essence of Womanhood in Tablet Form.") Only within the joint influence of biological determinism and cultural sexism could aging be defined as menopause and menopause as the loss of womanhood. Only in this system of beliefs and values could the development of a method for postmenopausal women to conceive and bear children take priority over universal basic health care.

Thus, the medical paradigm of aging in women redefines women's normal developmental transitions and experiences as medical problems that require medical interventions. Not only does the medical community benefit by increased profits and status, but defining an experience that is universal to all women as a disease, as is currently the practice with menopause, reinforces women's inferior status. Within the feminist paradigm, woman's standard, normal, optimal biology is individually and environmentally determined. For some women, childhood, for others, puberty, and for still others, menopause may be the best time of their lives. Only for those women who valued above all else their ability to conceive and bear children would menopause be considered a sad loss. Menopause, for all women, is a symbol of aging and impending death but no more so than becoming a grandparent or retirement. Within the feminist paradigm, menopause is only one of many symbols that is associated with aging and not necessarily the most essential or the most important.

PARADIGMATIC CRITIQUES OF SELECTED PHENOMENA OF AGING

Changes, symptoms or diseases that are attributed to the aging process in women are many and varied. They include hot flashes, profuse sweating, headaches, increased weight, dryness and thinning of the vaginal walls, increased incidence of vaginal infections, depression, insomnia, anxiety, loss of breast firmness, dizziness, sensations of cold in the hands and feet, irritability, pruritus of the sexual organs, loss of libido, constipation, atherosclerosis, osteoporosis, coronary artery disease, and Alzheimer's disease, among others. Within the medical model, all changes associated with aging in women are viewed as due to menopause and to a diminishing production of estrogen. The medical response to any of these difficulties occurring in middle and old-age women is to recommend exogenous estrogen.

Estrogens became readily available in the 1950's and were commonly prescribed for menopausal women as a method of treating hot flashes. Wilson's (1966) famous book, *Feminine Forever*, claimed estrogen to be a cure for wrinkles, sagging breasts, depression, anxiety, marital problems, sexual problems, a cackle-type laugh, and alienation of one's children. Although many physicians prescribed estrogen for these purposes, the primary reason women sought medical help remained hot flashes. Through the early 1970s, hormone replacement therapy (HRT) contained only estrogen. In the mid-1970s, the link between exogenous estrogens and uterine cancer became clear and physicians were unwilling to prescribe it and women unwilling to take it. However, within a few years, the pharmaceutical companies began to market a new product with both estrogen and progesterone—the goal being to provide the hormones without the increased risk of uterine cancer (e.g., Sturdee, Wade-Evans, Paterson, Thom, & Studd, 1978). The addition of progesterone was found to eliminate the increased risk of uterine cancer but there is a strong possibility that this regimen is associated with numerous negative side effects, including an increased risk of breast cancer (e.g., Bergkvist, Adami, Persson, Hoover, & Schairer, 1989).

Women were not so ready to trust the new HRT or, perhaps, they did not feel that hot flashes, an uncomfortable but not dangerous or life-threatening problem, justified the regular use of a strong drug. Regardless of their reasons, women did not readily comply with medical recommendations with regard to HRT. This lack of compliance may have provided the motivation for the medical profession and pharmaceutical companies to "discover" other, more life-threatening, reasons for women to take HRT. Because there is no direct evidence that HRT cures osteoporosis or cardio-vascular disease (MacPherson, 1993), the FDA did not approve it as a form of treatment. However, HRT is advertised as a method of prevention for both. To follow are critiques of opposing paradigmatic views of particular phenomena that are modified during the aging process—sexuality, depression, osteoporosis, and cardiovascular health. These were selected for the following reasons: (a) problems in these areas are viewed, within the medical paradigm, as "menopausal symptoms," but, within the feminist paradigm, as related to stress, environment, and lifestyle; (b) they are used by physicians as justifications for the recommendation of HRT; and, (c) sexual politics are apparent in the definition and treatment of these problems.

Sexuality

Stereotypes of middle and old-age woman in our society—that of grand-mother or crone—explicitly exclude sexuality. However, numerous surveys of elderly woman from the 1950s to the present indicate that changes in sexuality with aging vary considerably in direction and size (e.g., Kinsey, Pomeroy, Martin, & Gebhard, 1953; Leiblum & Swartzman, 1986). In a survey of 967 women, Kahn and Holt (1987) concluded that, "While some women say there is also reduced intensity of their sexual response, others say it is better than ever. Those who enjoyed satisfying sexual experiences before menopause continue to do so, some with heightened responses because of the absence of fear of pregnancy and the lack of interruption by children" (p. 167). Hunter (1990a) found some evidence for reduced sexual activity in postmenopausal women as did Hallstrom and Samuelsoon (1990) who found 29% of women aged 60 reporting the absence of sexual desire. However, the authors of both of these recent surveys noted that sexual activity in postmenopausal women was more strongly correlated with factors other than menopausal status, most notably the availability of a partner, adequate emotional support from spouse, alcoholism in spouse, and psychological problems.

In spite of evidence to the contrary, stereotypes are buried deep and historically in culture and continue to be viewed by both lay and professional persons as factual if they support and reinforce societal values. Assuming that, throughout a woman's life, her sexuality is directed, determined, and governed by hormones, particularly estrogen, is consistent with the biological determinism of patriarchy. One way in which the relationship between hormones and sexuality was researched was by studying the change in sexuality across the menstrual cycle. Schreiner-Engel, Schiani, Smith, and White (1981) reviewed 32 studies that reported significant findings on sexual arousability and the menstrual cycle: Sexual arousal peaked at ovulation in 8 studies, premenstrually in 17 studies, postmenstrually in 18 studies, and during menstruation in 4 studies. In their own study, they determined menstrual cycle phase by hormonal analysis and measured both subjective and physiological measures. Sexual arousal and hormonal levels were found to be unrelated. A study similar in design was published 1 year later (Hoon, Bruce, & Kinchloe, 1982), with phase determined by basal temperature and arousal measured both subjectively and physiologically; no significant phase effects were found. Bancroft, Sanders, Davidson, and Warner (1983), after conducting a similar study, reported similar results. Again, in 1991, Slob, Ernste, and van der Werfften Bosch conducted a similar study. This one included a comparison between those women using and those not using oral contraceptives; the results did not support the hypothesized relationship between sexuality and either endogenous or exogenous hormones. Finally, Meuwissen and Over (1992) reported the results of three studies: There were no menstrual cycle phase effects for subjective or physiological sexual arousal nor for processes believed to mediate sexual arousal including mood state, recency of sexual experience, and vividness of imagery. How many times does this type of study have to be replicated and published before the results are accepted?

In spite of a clear lack of support for congruence between hormonal levels and sexuality during the menstrual cycle, and in spite of evidence that in only a minority of women does sexuality decrease with menopause, many professionals continue to recommend some form of hormone therapy in order to increase sexual activity in menopausal and postmenopausal women. Numerous studies evaluating the impact of hormone supplements on sexual parameters in aging women have been published. Walling, Andersen, and Johnson (1990) reviewed studies testing the effects of HRT on sexual outcomes in postmenopausal women. Their review can be summarized as follows: (a) Estrogen supplements were superior to placebo for problems with vaginal lubrication but estrogen was not effective for increasing sexual frequency, satisfaction or desire; (b) estrogen combined with progesterone was associated with no improvement in any measure of sexuality; (c) studies evaluating estrogen combined with androgens found these drugs to effectively treat "loss of desire" and dysparneuia, but none of these studies utilized placebo–control groups, so essentially they cannot be construed as evidence for effectiveness.

The feminist version of sexuality in aging women questions the validity of an hormonal explanation and focuses on social, economic, and political causes. Why is it recommended that middle-age and elderly women take estrogen supplements in order to remain sexual, whereas it is not recommended that men of similar age take androgens? Both women and men produce less of their respective hormones as they age and experience similar changes in sexuality (Gannon, 1994). Why is "biology is destiny" only applied to women? It has never been argued (at least by men in power) that men are unqualified to be president because of their raging testosterone. A patriarchy, in order to survive as such, must keep women as separate, as other, and the easiest way to achieve this is to emphasize the most obvious differences—those that are biological. Not only are women defined throughout their reproductive years as sources of sexual gratification and as mothers, but at menopause, when they are finally relieved of these demands, and perhaps have the opportunity for new challenges, they are told they have a deficiency disease, and are encouraged to take hormones in order to retain their beauty and sexuality—neither of which is there evidence that they have lost nor that hormones provide. As early as 1948, Ruth Herschberger wrote: "Physicians are so preoccupied with explaining the reasons for the disappearance of sexual feeling in women of fifty that not many of them have stopped to ask: 'by the way, madam, sexual feeling *has* disappeared, hasn't it?'" (p. 55).

Diminishing levels of estrogen were empirically linked to less vaginal lubrication during sexual arousal, and, within the medical paradigm, estrogen is the primary determinant of vaginal lubrication and, in turn, of sexual activity. Within a feminist paradigm of aging, determinants of vaginal lubrication, other than hormone levels, were identified. "Women who engaged in regular masturbation . . . reported increased lubrication with a partner and the disappearance of vaginal pain due to dryness (Reitz, 1977, p. 146); "the fact is that we can maintain and improve our ability to lubricate through any type of arousing sexual activity" (Boston Women's Health Book Collective, 1984, p. 452). Furthermore, in the Reitz (1977) survey, some women reported that the appearance of lubrication was affected by their feelings toward their partner. Hunter (1990c) adds: "Anxiety, anger, insufficient stimulation, tiredness, relationship problems and lack of communication can all reduce sexual arousal, and hence lubrication" (p. 43). And, finally, all of these factors are obvious determinants of a woman's inclination to engage in sexual activity, in general or with a specific partner, regardless of the amount of lubrication.

The idea that infrequent or absent sexual activity may cause a woman to lubricate less or less quickly during sexual arousal is consistent with other information reported by menopausal and postmenopausal women such as: (a) the best predictor of sexuality in later life is sexuality in early life, that is, those who have been sexually active are likely to remain so (Pfeiffer, 1978; Weg, 1983); and (b) " . . . boredom and habit are a common [problem] . . . Women who embark on a new relationship in their fifties and sixties tend to enjoy more lively and active sex lives than those approaching their thirtieth wedding anniversary" (Hunter, 1990c, p. 42). Vaginal lubrication and sexual activity are multiply determined and the relationship appears to be interactive rather than causal.

Medicine, as part of the larger scientific enterprise, claims that the medical paradigm is based on empirical evidence, whereas alternative paradigms are based on opinion, prejudice, and politics. Consider, however, the changing views of sexuality in middle and old-age women from the 19th century to the present. From the 19th century: "Whenever sexual impulse is first felt at the change of life, some morbid ovario-uterine condition will be found to explain it . . . It, therefore, is most imprudent for women to marry at this epoch without having obtained the sanction of a medical man" (Smith-Rosenberg, 1985, p. 192); and from the 20th century: "Most women after the menopause, if they're reasonably healthy and happy, do not experience a diminution in sex drive" (Sheehy, 1992, p. 82). Are these drastically different medical views based on empirical evidence? Three of the 1,700 pages of the two Kinsey reports are concerned with sexuality in older people; there were eight entries in Index Medicus on sexuality and menopause between 1988 and 1992; there were 1,424 entries in Psychological Abstracts between 1986 and 1992 on sexuality, and only 4 of these were concerned with menopause or aging. One could argue that it is the medical view of sexuality in aging women that is based on opinion, prejudice, and politics.

Depression

The belief that menopause is a major cause of psychological problems has been popular for at least the last century. According to Formanek (1990), the 1888 Surgeon General's Catalogue directs readers interested in menopause to "See also: insanity in women"; in 1909, the German psychiatrist Kraepelin coined the term *involutional melancholia*: "Its onset was gradual during the climacterium; it was marked by hypochondriasis, pessimism, and irritability and led to a full-blown depressive syndrome. Prominent symptoms included agitation, restlessness, anxiety and apprehension, occasionally bizarre guilt and worthlessness" (Formanek, 1990, p. 28). This view continues today: "Anxiety, depression, irritability, and fatigue increase after menopause" (Marshburn & Carr, 1992, p. 145).

The empirical research offers little support for this perspective. Data from large surveys of women of menopausal age indicate that depression does not vary predictably with menopausal status (Ballinger, 1975, 1976; Kaufert & Gilbert, 1986; Leiblum & Swartzman, 1986; Lennon, 1987; McKinlay & Jeffreys, 1974; McKinlay, McKinlay, & Brambilla, 1987). Studies aimed at demonstrating relationships between hormonal levels and psychological states have consistently failed. An early study by Abe et al. (1977) found no significant relationships between the severity of psychological symptoms and serum level of estrogen, progesterone, FSH, and LH in menopausal women. Castrogiovianni et al. (1982), in a study evaluating plasma levels of hormones and various mood and personality variables in menopausal women, reported no significant associations; the hormonal profile of those who were depressed was identical to that of those not depressed. Finally, surveys of psychological problems, including depression, in women across the life span have found the ages associated with childbearing and childrearing, rather than menopause, to have the highest incidence (Steiner, 1992).

Consistent with a lack of association between levels of hormones and psychological symptoms is research failing to demonstrate the effectiveness of hormonal therapy. As early as 1950, Fessler noted that although hormonal treatment was effective in reducing hot flashes, it did not relieve irritability and depression. A later study, which satisfied the strict methodological requirements of double-blind and placebo control, was reported by Utian (1972). He compared the effectiveness of exogenous estrogen to placebo treatment in women experiencing natural and surgical menopause. Only hot flashes and atrophic vaginitis were relieved by estrogen, but not by placebos, although symptoms of depression, irritability, insomnia, and palpitations responded significantly both to estrogen and placebo therapies. These results were replicated (George, Utian, Beumont, & Beardwood, 1973; Gerdes, EtPhil, Sonnendecker, & Polakow, 1982; Poller, Thomson, & Coope, 1980).

In spite of such clear and consistent evidence, studies are still being published (at least one per year) that do not use a placebo control, and conclude that HRT does significantly elevate mood (e.g., Best, Rees, Marlow, & Cowan, 1992). The results of this inadequate and misleading research are passed on to medical consumers. For example, Ettinger (1988) wrote: " . . . estrogen therapy can alleviate menopause-related sleep disorders, psychological problems, and sexual dysfunction" (p. 31S), but neglects to cite supporting research. Brenner (1988) stated: "Estrogen replacement therapy enables postmenopausal women to sleep better, wake rested, perform better, and feel less irritable and depressed" (p. 7S), and cited early research by Thomson and Oswald (1977) who did, indeed, find estrogen to relieve depression, but not as effectively as did a placebo. In the context of maintaining the stereotype in the face of evidence to the contrary, Schmidt and Rubinow published in 1991 an article titled "Menopause-related Affective Disorders: A Justification for Further Study." They argued that mood-related symptoms occur with declining levels of estrogen citing one study on surgical menopause and then suggested that HRT alleviates the symptoms citing only studies that did not employ placebo controls. They claimed that " . . . the evidence is far from conclusive in refuting the existence of a menopause-related affective syndrome" (p. 846) and recommended continued research to scientifically document a stereotype the authors believe to be real. Given the overwhelming number of mental disorders catalogued by *DSM–IV*, society is not best served by channelling resources into the attempt to establish the existence of yet another mental disorder—particularly one for which there is considerable evidence that it does not exist.

Feminists do not deny that some middle and old-age women experience depression, but the focus is on causal factors other than biology. Middle and old-age women are likely to experience traumatic stress, such as death of a family member or friend, as well as chronic stress, such as poverty, loneliness, and declining health (McKinlay et al., 1987). In a society in which women have traditionally been valued for their roles as lovers and mothers, menopause is likely to diminish self-esteem. Researchers (e.g., Bart, 1969; Flint, 1975) have suggested that in cultures where menopause is associated with a loss of significant roles and a reduction in power and freedom, the primary societal attitude toward aging women is negative and aging women experience adverse psychological consequences. On the other hand, in societies where aging increases one's status and perceived wisdom, where the desexualization associated with menopause makes women less threatening to men, or where women's freedom increases with menopause, there is little evidence of psychological and emotional difficulties associated with menopause.

Ballinger (1990) placed a portion of the blame for our ignorance and neglect of the menopausal and postmenopausal woman on the "experts": "Professional preoccupation with the active reproductive years and lack of interest in the past-reproductive years may well influence women's attitudes and self-esteem at this time" (p. 779). To illustrate, pregnancy, a less "universal" experience than menopause, and one accompanied by clear discomfort and pain, is viewed with understanding and indulgence and has been the focus of much research. On the other hand, menopause has been of little interest in both the professional and lay arenas. The recent and dramatic increase in popular publications on menopause is unparalleled in the medical research where the percentage of articles on menopause has remained at virtually the same low rate of 1% to 2% since the 1970s (Gannon et al., unpublished manuscript).

Finally, the medical paradigm of menopause in action may render menopausal women vulnerable to depression. Consider the psychological consequences of being informed at age 50 that one has a chronic disease that is incurable but can be "controlled" with powerful and potentially dangerous drugs and will require regular medical visits for the rest of one's life. The laboratory and clinical research documenting the importance of perceived control on psychological health (e.g., Seligman, 1975) is abundant and thorough. Although most people will experience a diminished sense of control as they age, those who have chronic physical problems necessitating a strong dependence on medical help will experience a particularly intense loss of control. Rodin (1986) proposed that the strength of the relation between health and control increases with aging—perhaps because the elderly have, in reality, less control as they age so they may be more sensitive to the loss of what they have.

To summarize, the medical paradigm of aging in women predicts psychological problems, especially depression, at and after menopause due to declining levels of estrogen. The empirical research does not support a meaningful relationship between hormones and depression or between menopausal status and depression, nor does the empirical research indicate that the incidence of depression in women increases during the ages when women typically experience menopause. On the other hand, middle and old-age women do experience environmental, social, economic, political, and physical stressors—stressors known to precipitate psychological distress.

Osteoporosis

Throughout life, new bone is continually formed and existing bone continually reabsorbed or lost. In the young, particularly during the years of growth, more bone is made than is lost. Peak bone mass is reached at about age 35, after which time reabsorption exceeds formation, and all persons lose bone with advancing age. If the bone loss is excessive or if the peak bone mass was inadequate, then bone density decreases to such an extent that bones break easily; this proclivity to fractures due to low bone density is referred to as *osteoporosis*. Osteoporotic fractures most commonly occur in the vertebra, the forearm, and the hips. Within the medical paradigm, osteoporosis is viewed as primarily a problem associated with menopause and appropriately treated with HRT: "Bone loss with aging (osteoporosis) is very largely a female problem resulting from loss of gonadal function" (Gordon, 1990, p. 225). Within the feminist paradigm, osteoporosis is not a female problem but a lifestyle problem and is primarily related to aging, genetics, and lifestyle factors such as diet, weight, and exercise.

Although statements such as the one given by Gordon sound clear and decisive, the medical research on osteoporosis is confusing and contradictory. Because the medical community defined osteoporosis as a menopausal problem and because the pharmaceutical companies fund research likely to support the treatment of menopausal women with HRT, there is far more research on women's aging bones than on men's. Furthermore, this research tends to ignore the impact of variables other than hormone levels. The resulting body of research is restricted, biased, and highly inadequate. Consider the following quotes from medical journals published in the last 5 years:

> It is possible to prevent bone loss and estrogen is the only established means of achieving this (Fogelman, 1991, p. 276).

> . . . estrogens do not restore lost bone . . . (Genant, Baylink, & Gallagher, 1989, p. 1843).

> Hormone replacement therapy is without question the established treatment for osteoporosis and is the main means of its prevention (Stevenson, 1990, p. 40S).

> Five years after discontinuing hormone treatment, there is likely to be little difference in bone density between treated and untreated women . . . (Nordin, Need, Chatterton, Horowitz, & Morris, 1990, p. 87).

My interpretation of the research that has been published on osteoporosis as a menopausal symptom follows, but the reader should note that the validity of this interpretation is limited by the poor quality and limited quantity of research. In women, the rate of bone loss does increase at menopause, over and above the loss due to aging. This increase is transient and lasts approximately 5 years; the rate of loss then returns to the lower, age-related loss. These two causes of bone loss in women, age and menopause, respond to different treatments. HRT slows or stops the menopause-related bone loss if treatment is initiated concurrently with the beginning of menopause, and this bone loss is prevented only as long as the woman remains on HRT. If she stops taking the hormones, the bone loss will occur to the same extent and at the same rate as it would have had the hormones never been taken. If HRT is begun after the menopause-related bone loss occurred, it will have no effect—it will not restore lost bone nor will HRT have an effect on age-related bone loss. The woman considering HRT to reduce vulnerability to osteoporosis should also take into account her risk of developing osteoporosis. If the risk is small, she may choose not to take hormones that often have negative side effects.

The feminist paradigm views osteoporosis as multiply determined—menopause is one of many factors relevant to osteoporosis. Consider the following:

1. If it were solely a menopausal disorder, all older women would suffer from it, yet only 25% do so (Notelovitz, 1989).
2. African American women, in general, do not suffer from osteoporosis but experience menopause, and some men suffer from osteoporosis, yet do not experience menopause (Iskrant, 1968).
3. Among the Chinese in Singapore, the rate of osteoporosis is greater for men than for women (Brown, 1988).
4. In the last 20 years, osteoporotic fractures increased in urban areas of Scandanavia to an incidence rate that is the highest in the world (Johansson, Mellstrom, Lerner, & Osterberg, 1992).
5. Fig. 10.1 (Iskrant, 1968) breaks down the annual death rates by falls for women and men, African American and Caucasian.

These data emphasize the absurdity of labeling osteoporosis a menopausal symptom. The characteristics of those who suffer from osteoporosis are White, thin, have a sedentary lifestyle, low lifetime calcium intake, high consumption of alcohol or caffeine, smoke, and chronically use corticosteroids (Brown, 1988).

Because the two primary determinants of osteoporosis are peak bone mass and rate of bone loss, either or both can contribute to an eventual problem. Peak bone mass is determined by genetics, diet, weight-bearing load, and exercise, whereas the rate of bone loss is determined by weight, exercise, diet, and sex hormones in both men and women. The body makes bone in response to need, so if the bone needs to support weight in the form of fat or in the form of muscle, the bone will be stronger. Gravity-bearing exercise places stress on bones and causes the bone to increase in density. Diet contributes by supplying the necessary bone-making ingredients of calcium, magnesium, and vitamin D.

Cultural values and practices provide a partial, but important, explanation for the differences in the incidence of osteoporosis between women and men in the United States. Men are less likely to be concerned about their weight and are, therefore, heavier than are women. The heavier weight of men requires stronger bones and, because men tend to eat more to maintain their heavier weight, they are more likely to have adequate calcium intake. Until recently, it was been more socially acceptable for men to exercise than for women and the extra demand of exercise leads to greater bone density and the sunlight from outdoor exercise increases vitamin D. Furthermore, bone loss is accelerated by decreased estrogen in women and by decreased testosterone in men. Although both women and men experience diminished levels of their respective sex hormones as they age, women are far more likely to have had their ovaries surgically removed than are men to

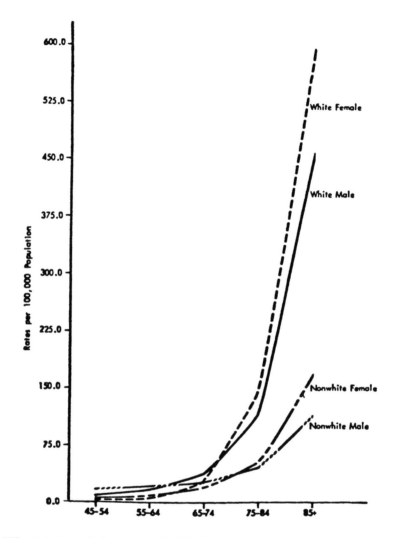

FIG. 10.1. Annual death rates for falls by age, color, and sex, United States, 1959–1961, persons age 45 and over. From "The Etiology of Fractured Hips in Females," by A. P. Iskrant, 1968, *Journal of Public Health, 58,* pp. 485–491. Copyright © 1968 by American Public Health Association. Reprinted with permission.

have had their testicles surgically removed. Women are, therefore, more likely than men to experience a sudden and drastic reduction in hormones. Finally, women apparently begin to lose bone in their 40s whereas men do so in their 60s. Although this was attributed to differences in diminishing rates of sex hormones, the reason could be related to the traditional gender-related activities and careers promoted by our society—that of housewife for the woman and wage earner for the man. For those who conformed to these roles, a woman's career diminishes considerably when her children leave home, usually occurring when the woman is in her 40s, and a man's career when he retires, usually in his 60s. Both of these events may be accompanied by a drastic reduction in physical activity leading to increased vulnerability of osteoporosis.

The intensity and type of exercise of the average woman changed dramatically during this century and could well explain the changing incidence of osteoporosis. Prior to the 1950s, many women were required to exercise in order to survive—they were farmers, factory workers, or housewives who lived without modern appliances. When the role of women became more housewifely and the home became mechanized, the U.S. woman became the "little woman" and feminine was defined as frail and small—someone who did not exercise. Also, the undeniable expectation that all women be mothers may have placed women of this generation at risk. One study found a strong association between bone strength in elderly women and the number of children they had had—women who had not had children lost virtually no bone over a 10-year study period (Abdulla, Hart, Lindsay, & Aitken, 1984). Pregnant and lactating women have higher calcium needs due to the demands of the fetus–infant and, if these needs are not met with diet or supplements, the woman's bones will be depleted of calcium in order to supply the need. This demand apparently has long-term negative consequences and predisposes the woman to osteoporosis as she ages. Women who were 20 to 30 years of age in the 1950s are today 60 to 70 years of age and their bones may be suffering the consequences of poor exercise, poor diet, and too many children. Since the 1970s, with much help from the women's movement, women athletes are recognized, aerobics are not only socially acceptable but desirable, and the cultural demand to produce children has lessened. Perhaps the current generation of women will not suffer similar consequences with regard to osteoporosis.

Although the research on the impact of HRT on osteoporosis yielded contradictory and confusing results, the research on the benefits of calcium supplements and weight-bearing exercise is fairly conclusive. Numerous studies (e.g., Albanese, Edelson, Lorenze, Woodhull, & Wein, 1975; Dawson-Hughes et al., 1990, 1991; Sinaki, Wahner, Offord, & Hodgson, 1989; Smith, Gilligan, Smith, & Sempos, 1989) documented the benefits of calcium supplements on bone in elderly women. The studies by Dawson-Hughes showed that calcium helps all women but is particularly effective in women who are more than 5 years past menopause and who have low dietary calcium.

The beneficial effects of weight-bearing exercise on bone density and size as well as the detrimental effects of immobility were known for decades; they are certainly known by anyone who broke a bone and was dismayed at the emaciated limb that emerged from the cast. Perhaps this information was not applied to osteoporosis in the elderly because it was assumed that, to be effective, the exercise had to be strenuous and prolonged and beyond the capabilities of elderly persons. Research in the last decade (Dalsky et al., 1988; Gerber & Rey, 1991; Lane et al., 1986; Rikli & MacManis, 1990; Sazy

& Horstmann, 1991; Shangold, 1990; Shephard, 1989; Simkin, Ayalon, & Leichter, 1987) proved without any doubt that exercise is an effective method of preventing and even reversing age-related bone loss. For example, Dalsky et al. (1988) recruited 35 women between the ages of 55 and 70 who led sedentary lifestyles. Seventeen of these began an exercise program consisting of walking and jogging, with treadmill and stair climbing added later as they became more fit. They exercised three times per week for about 1 hour each time. At the end of 9 months, the exercisers increased their bone mineral content by 5.2%, whereas the nonexercisers lost 1.4%. Some of the exercisers continued for 13 more months; these women showed an increase of 6.1%, whereas the nonexercisers lost 1.1%, and those in the exercise group who stopped exercising at 9 months lost 4.8%. The differences are even more remarkable when comparing different life exercise patterns. One study (Lane et al., 1986) found runners, aged 50 to 72, had 40% higher bone density than did sedentary persons of the same age and weight; another (Sazy & Horstmann, 1991) found cross-country runners aged 50 to 59 to have 20% greater bone mineral density than did nonexercisers of similar age and weight.

The medical community has been slow to advocate exercise as a treatment for osteoporosis:

> On the basis of these initial studies, it is unwise to make confident recommendations for the prophylactic use of exercise. We must first establish which types of exercise programs will have the greatest benefit to the skeleton, and then undertake more rigorously designed studies to determine their specific role in building and maintaining bone mass prospectively . . . Research in this area is sorely needed. But until the results of these and other studies are made available, we must refrain from indiscriminately counseling individuals to undertake programs of exercise with the hope of preventing osteoporosis. (Block, Smith, Black & Genant, 1987, p. 3116)

Physicians are ready and willing to prescribe HRT for osteoporosis in the absence of consistent research support and with minimal information on the specific mechanisms by which hormones impact the skeletal system and in spite of evidence of negative sideeffects from long-term HRT. Yet, they are unwilling to advocate exercise that research consistently supports as being beneficial. Osteoporosis is not a disorder associated with menopause in women but a disorder affecting persons of all ages, both genders, and all races whose lifestyle precludes healthy bone. Medical and sexual politics create the ideological milieu in which physicians prescribe HRT, with its attendant risks of endometrial and breast cancer, but caution against exercise, with its attendant benefits on the heart, the lungs, cholesterol, and mood.

Cardiovascular Disorders

Since the 1980s, advocates of HRT have, promoted the idea that menopause causes women to have an increased risk for cardiovascular disorders.

Consequently, many of the medical profession view HRT as a cardiovascular panacea: "I believe in the years ahead, protection against heart disease will become a compelling indication for hormone replacement therapy in most, if not all, postmenopausal women" (Whitehead, 1988, p. 1661). The idea that HRT will protect women from cardiovascular disorder is based on the assumption that estrogen, present in abundance prior to menopause, is beneficial to the coronary system, and, when estrogen diminishes, women's cardiovascular system suffers. Direct evidence for any of these assumptions is conspicuously lacking. Indirect evidence that is typically cited is the difference in cardiovascular disorders between women and men and the inferred causes of this difference. Prior to middle age, men suffer from significantly more cardiovascular disorders than do women. Beginning at 40 to 50 years of age, the gap between men and women decreases, although men continue to experience more cardiovascular problems than do women throughout life. The narrowing of the gap between women and men in midlife was attributed by gynecologists to diminished estrogen in women (Whitehead, 1988).

Cardiologists, on the other hand, attribute the narrowing of this gap to lowered levels of testosterone in men, testosterone having negative effects on the cardiovascular system. As evidence, cardiologists Godsland, Wynn, Path, Crook; and Miller (1987) presented Fig. 10.2. The gap between men and women does decrease in midlife. However, close inspection of the figure suggests that the slope of the line for women remains the same throughout life, whereas the slope of the line for men decreases in midlife. This would suggest that, throughout life, women experience the gradual, age-related deterioration of the cardiovascular system in a linear manner. On the other hand, the rate of cardiovascular deterioration in men tends to slow down in midlife and this change in the linear function was attributed to lowered levels of testosterone (Godsland et al., 1987). Thus, the only empirical support for the assumptions on which HRT is recommended for cardiovascular disorders is indirect, and even this is interpreted differently depending on the medical specialty.

The evidence cited to support the use of HRT to treat aging women's cardiovascular systems comes from epidemiological studies that find that women taking HRT have healthier cardiovascular systems than women not taking HRT (Hemminki & Sihvo, 1993). Epidemiological studies compare a group of women who have been taking HRT for a number of years to a group of women who have not taken HRT. The women are not randomly assigned to HRT, there is no comparison group of women taking placebos, and the groups are not matched on any variable that might influence their group membership. Gynecologists have, in error, interpreted these data as conclusive proof that HRT improves one's cardiovascular health, but this is only one of many possible interpretations of these data. Another interpretation is that women taking HRT have healthier cardiovascular systems because these women had healthier cardiovascular systems prior to taking HRT than those who chose not to take it. Indeed, Derby et al. (1993) studied over 2,000 women in New England and found HRT users, compared to

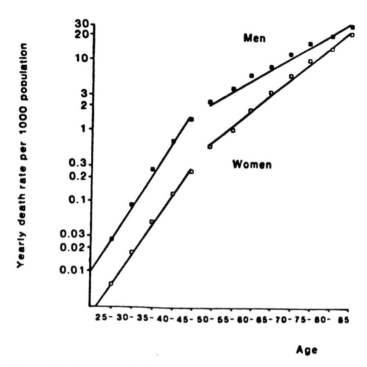

FIG. 10.2. Death rates from ischemic heart disease (plotted logarithmically) in men and women according to age (England and Wales, 1970, 1974). From "Sex, Plasma, Lipoproteins, and Atherosclerosis: Prevailing Assumptions and Outstanding Questions," by I. F. Godsland, V. Wynn, F. R. C. Path, D. Crook, and N. E. Miller, 1987, *American Heart Journal, 114*, pp. 1467–1501. Copyright © 1987 by Mosby Year-Book, Inc. Reprinted with permission.

nonusers, were more likely to not smoke, to exercise, to have had their cholesterol measured in the last year, to have higher incomes and more education, to have lower BMI (an index of body fat), and higher HDL ("good" cholesterol). Such data seriously compromise the recommendation for HRT based on epidemiological research. The effect of HRT on the cardiovascular system remains unknown in the absence of controlled studies.

A second difficulty with the research on the effects of HRT is that almost all of the research published prior to 1990 evaluated estrogen-only types of HRT. There has not been sufficient time to adequately study the risks and benefits of today's version of HRT. Progesterone has been added to HRT in order to avoid the increased risk of uterine cancer, but this combination could actually cause cardiovascular difficulties. The potential significance of this difference between the two forms of HRT is not acknowledged by the medical community. After reviewing the epidemiological evidence for the benefits of estrogen on the cardiovasuclar system, Knopp (1988) said: "A reasonable hope exists that natural progesterone, given in combination with postmenopausal ERT, will have a minimal effect on lipoprotein concentrations" (p. 1641). Hope?

Oral contraceptives, drugs with similar ingredients to HRT, were found to significantly increase one's risk of blood clots, stroke, and heart attack (Seaman & Seaman, 1977). Because of these hazardous side effects, pharmaceutical companies were encouraged to develop low-dose pills. However, seven studies published in 1990 indicate that, although the adverse effects on the cardiovascular system are lessened with lower doses of current oral contraceptives, they are still substantial and include harmful changes in cholesterol levels (Clarkson et al, 1990; Leuven et al., 1990; Simon et al., 1990) and increased risk of thrombosis (Daly & Bonner, 1990; Hirvonen & Idanpaan-Heikkila, 1990; Kelleher, 1990).

Given the documented negative effects of oral contraceptives on the cardiovascular system, it is somewhat paradoxical that HRT, with the same ingredients, is claimed to be beneficial to the cardiovascular system. The published medical literature rarely addresses this issue and, when it is mentioned, the dilemma is dismissed as "irrelevant" or explained away by pointing out that women at an age when they take oral contraceptives have different body chemistry than those at an age appropriate for HRT, that the dosages of the hormones in oral contraceptives differ from those in HRT, and that the type of estrogen in the two is different. Although these points indicate that it would be inappropriate to assume that HRT is associated with the same risks as oral contraceptives, they do not demonstrate that HRT is safe for the cardiovascular system. If HRT is beneficial, or even safe, to the cardiovascular system, why does one gynecologist advise that women on HRT also take aspirin everyday to prevent clotting problems (Notelovitz, 1989)? And why does the British National Formulary recommend HRT be discontinued 4 to 6 weeks prior to major surgery because of concerns over postoperative venous thromboembolism?

The media tends to focus on those "experts" who make definitive and positive claims for cures. Consequently, lay persons seldom are exposed to the inconsistencies, the doubts, the "other side," and the potential negative side effects. Newspapers, magazines, radio, and television promote HRT as a cure for cardiovascular problems in women whereas medical opinion varies widely:

Epidemiologic evidence . . . clearly showed a marked increase in the incidence of cardiovascular disease after menopause (L'Hermite, 1990, p. 222).

The reality is that there is no clear change in female mortality from ischemic heart disease as women enter menopause (Notelovitz, 1989, p. 411).

. . . after adjustment for age and other risk factors, women with a natural menopause had a 3.4 times greater risk of atherosclerosis than premenopausal women (L'Hermite, 1990, p. 223).

. . . it thus appears that menopause per se is not affecting the rate of death from atherosclerotic heart disease (Godsland et al., 1987, p. 1479).

The claim that oestrogens prevent heart attacks is nonsensical (Grant, 1994, p. 67).

As with osteoporosis, feminists view causes of cardiovascular disorder in women as due to similar causes as cardiovascular disorders in men, that is, as primarily related to lifestyle variables, such as diet and exercise, and to environmental, social, and career stress. The rate of CHD mortality declined 37% between 1963 and 1983. This decline was similar for women and for men and is usually attributed to cultural changes resulting in healthier lifestyles—better diet, more exercise, and less use of alcohol, nicotine, and caffeine.

There are well-documented differences between women and men in cholesterol level and in CHD. These differences were assumed to be biological, usually hormonal. However, there are several tantalizing bits of information that argue against this. Godsland et al. (1987) pointed out that, in societies where CHD is rare, there are no sex differences in lipoproteins; these authors interpret this finding to mean that the sex differences in cholesterol found in our society, are due to sex differences in lifestyle, that is, diet, exercise, and stress. Supporting this interpretation, Strickland (1988) reported that, in the United States, the wives of men who develop CHD are twice as likely to suffer from CHD than women whose husbands are free of the disease. Unless CHD is contagious, this suggests powerful environmental influences: " . . . the leading causes of death in this country are linked to dysfunctional life styles and behaviors" (Strickland, 1988, p. 387) and lifestyles are likely to be similar in persons who live together.

The sexual politics of medicine is perhaps nowhere more apparent than in the differential medical treatment of cardiovascular disease in women and men. We have yet to see a well-controlled study on the benefits of HRT for women's cardiovascular system, yet, physicians are currently prescribing HRT for this reason. In contrast, 22,000 men took an aspirin a day for 5 years prior to the medical community recommending aspirin as a method of preventing cardiovascular problems in men (Steering Committee of the Physicians' Health Study Research Group, 1989). Similarly, in a large survey of men and women hospitalized with severe heart attacks, the men were twice as likely to have had coronary angiography and twice as likely to undergo coronary bypass surgery than were the women (Aburdene & Naisbitt, 1992).

INTERFERENCE OR INTERVENTION?

Medical interventions specifically designed "for" women do not have a good reputation. Diethylstilbestrol (DES), oral contraceptives, breast implants, intrauterine devices, and ERT were widely prescribed for women at various points in history. What do these "treatments" have in common? First, they are aggressive, dramatic, and heroic. Ehrenreich and English (1979) discussed the history of heroic medicine that developed throughout the 18th and 19th centuries. In order to increase both the perceptive and financial value of their services, physicians recognized the necessity of producing a dramatic effect, beneficial or not, on the patient so " . . . there could be no question but that the doctor was doing something: something visible, tangible, and roughly measurable" (p. 45). Second, none of these treatments was designed to treat an illness that impairs health but to change women in such a way as to be more in line with patriarchal values; all are aids in becoming stereotypically attractive, pregnant, spontaneous sexual partners, and feminine forever. Third, none were tested adequately prior to being introduced to the public. For example, oral contraceptives were approved in 1960 on the basis of clinical trials of 132 women who had taken the drugs for 1 year (Seaman & Seaman, 1977). Fourth, all were eventually found to be associated with some form of life-threatening danger such as cardiovascular problems related to oral contraceptive use and immune deficiencies experienced after breast implants. And, fifth, there was an "unexplained" time span between suspicions of and evidence for danger and informing the public of the danger; for example, ERT was suspected to cause uterine cancer as early as the 1950s but this information was not provided to the public until 1975 (see Seaman & Seaman, 1977, for a complete discussion).

Given this history, suspicion and reluctance in women whose physicians recommend that they take HRT for the rest of their lives seems appropriate, logical, intelligent, and justified. However, women's reluctance is taken as further evidence by the medical profession that women are weak and stupid. Ettinger (1988), in documenting problems associated with ERT other than uterine cancer, noted that women on ERT are five to seven times more likely to suffer from abnormal bleeding and that more than one fourth of ERT users required a hysterectomy. He then comments: "[women] need special reassurance to overcome *irrational* fears . . . women need to know that estrogen is 'natural' and that living 30 or more years without it may be less so" (italics added, p. 34S). Medicine developed within and remains an active participant of patriarchy—an ideology that does not recognize and value women.

Finally, what is the effect on women of accepting the deficiency disease concept of their aging? Several years ago, we conducted a study (Gannon & Ekstrom, 1993) designed to evaluate paradigmatic influences on attitudes toward menopause in a large sample of both women and men between ages 17 and 88. Participants were assigned to one of three groups distinguished by the context within which they expressed their attitudes toward menopause. One group described their attitudes toward three medical problems, including menopause; a second group described their attitudes toward three life transitions, including menopause; and a third group described their attitudes toward three symbols of aging, including menopause. The results indicated that the medical context elicited significantly more negative and fewer positive attitudes than did the other two contexts, particularly among the older participants. And, importantly, previous research indicated that attitudes have an impact on experience. Meltzer (1974), utilizing a cross-sectional design, and Hunter (1990a) and Avis and McKinlay (1991), utilizing prospective designs, found that attitudes, beliefs, and expectations were predictive of reported distress at the time of menopause.

Negative attitudes were associated with negative experiences, whereas positive attitudes were associated with positive experiences. Thus, accepting the deficiency disease concept of menopause and focusing on menopause as the most relevant aspect of aging in women could well increase the likelihood of a middle and old age characterized by pessimism and discomfort, whereas accepting the treatment recommendations could result in life-threatening side effects.

The medical paradigm of aging in women focuses on the reproductive and sexual nature of women rather than on their health. Labeling breast implants, oral contraceptives, and HRT as "interventions" or "treatment" or "solutions" implies that there is a problem that needs fixing. Convincing women that their normal and natural development is flawed and requires intervention—that they should have large breasts, be safe sex partners, and have premenopausal levels of estrogen at the age of 70—engenders feelings of inadequacy and low self-esteem. When women internalize this negative self-image, they become vulnerable to promises of a quick fix or fountain of youth. They are made to feel desperate and then offered a panacea for their desperation. The medical paradigm of aging in women is not about improving physical health but about interfering with normal and natural development.

REFERENCES

Abdulla, H. I., Hart, D. M., Lindsay, R., & Aiken, M (1984, June). *Determinants of bone mass and bone loss response to oestrogen therapy in oophorectomized women.* Paper presented at the Fourth International Congress on the Menopause, Orlando, FL.

Abe, T., Furuhashi, N., Yamaya, Y., Hoshiai, A., & Suzuki, M. (1977). Correlation between climacteric symptoms and serum levels of estradiol, progesterone, follicle-stimulating hormone, and luteinizing hormone. *American Journal of Obstetrics and Gynecology, 129,* 63–67.

Abrams, W. B., & Berkow, R. (Eds). (1990). *The Merck manual of geriatrics.* Rahway, NJ: Merck, Sharp, & Dohme Research Laboratories.

Aburdene, P., & Naisbitt, J. (1992). *Megatrends for women.* New York: Villard Books.

Aksel, S., Schomberg, D. W., Tyrey, L., & Hammond, C. B. (1976). Vasomotor symptoms, serum estrogens and gonadotropin levels in surgical menopause. *American Journal of Obstetrics and Gynecology, 126,* 165–169.

Albanese, A., Edelson, A. H., Lorenze, E. J., Woodhull, M. L., & Wein, E. (1975). Problems with bone health in elderly. *New York State Journal of Medicine, 35,* 326–336.

Avis, N. E., & McKinlay, S. M. (1991). A longitudinal analysis of women's attitudes toward the menopause: Results from the Massachusetts Women's Health Study. *Maturitas, 13,* 65–79.

Ballinger, C. B. (1975). Psychiatric morbidity and the menopause: Screening of general population sample. *British Medical Journal, 3,* 344–346.

Ballinger, C. B. (1990). Psychiatric aspects of the menopause. *British Journal of Psychiatry, 156,* 773–787.

Bancroft, J., Sanders, D., Davidson, D. & Warner, P. (1983). Mood, sexuality, hormones, and the menstrual cycle: III. Sexuality and the role of androgens. *Psychosomatic Medicine, 45,* 509–516.

Bart, P. (1969, Fall). Why women's status changes in middle age: The turns of the social ferris wheel. *Sociological Symposium,* 1–14.

Bergkvist, L., Adami, H-O., Persson, J., Hoover, R., & Schairer, C. (1989). The risk of breast cancer after estrogen and estrogen-progestin replacement. *New England Journal of Medicine, 321,* 293–297.

Best, N. R., Rees, M. P. Barlow, D. H., & Cowen, P. J. (1992). Effect of estradiol implant on noradrenergic function and mood in menopausal subjects. *Psychoneuroendocrinology, 17,* 87–93.

Block, J. E., Smith, R., Black, D., & Genant, H. K. (1987). Does exercise prevent osteoporosis? *Journal of the American Medical Association, 257,* 3115–3117.

Boston Women's Health Book Collective. (1984). *The new ourbodies ourselves.* New York: Simon & Schuster.

Brenner, P. F. (1988). The menopausal syndrome. *Obstetrics and Gynecology, 72,* 6S–11S.

Brown, S. (1988, July–August). Osteoporosis: Sorting fact from fallacy. *The Network News: National Women's Health Network,* 1–2.

Castrogiovanni, P., de Luca, I. B., Teti, G., Corradi, I., Moggi, G., Zecca, R., Murru, S., Silvestri, D., & Fioretti, P. (1982). Depressive states during the menopause: A preliminary study of endocrinological, socioenvironmental and personality factors. In P. Fioretti, L. Martini, G. B. Milis, & S. S. C. Yen (Eds.), *The menopause: Clinical, endocrinological, and pathophysiological aspects* (pp. 425–436). New York: Academic Press.

Clarkson, T. B., Shivley, C. A., Morgan, T. M., Koritnik, D. R., Adams, M. R., & Kaplan, J. R. (1990). Oral contraceptives and coronary artery artherosclerosiss of cynomolgus monkeys. *Obstetrics and Gynecology, 75,* 217–222.

Dalsky, G. P., Stocke, K. S., Ehsani, A. A., Slatopolsky, E., Lee, W. C., & Birge, S. I. (1988). Weight-bearing exercise training and lumbar bone mineral content in postmenopausal women. *Annals of Internal Medicine, 108,* 824–828.

Daly, L., & Bonnar, J. (1990). Comparative studies of 30 ug ethinyl estradiol combine with gestodene and desogestrel on blood coagulation, fibrinolysis, and platelets. *American Journal of Obstetrics and Gynecology, 163,* 430–437.

Davidson, J. M. (1980). Hormones and sexual behavior in the male. In D. T. Krieger & J. C. Hughes (Eds.), *Neuroendocrinology,* (pp. 232–238). Sunderland, MA: Sinauer Associates.

Dawson-Hughes, B., Dallal, G. E., Krall, E. A., Sadowski, L., Sahyoun, N., & Tannenbaum, S. (1990). A controlled trial of the effect of calcium supplementation on bone density in postmenopausal women. *New England Journal of Medicine, 323,* 878–883.

Derby, C. A., Hume, A. L., Barbour, M. M., McPhillip, J. B., Lasater, T. M., & Carleton, R. A. (1993). Correlates of postmenopausal estrogen use and trends through 1980's in two southeastern New England communities. *American Journal of Epidemiology, 137,* 1125–1135.

Dickson, G. L. (1993). Metaphors of menopause: The metalanguage of menopause research. In J. C. Callahan (Ed.), *Menopause: A midlife passage.* (pp. 36–58). Bloomington: Indiana University Press.

Ehrenreich, B., & English, D. (1979). *For her own good: 150 years of the experts' advice to women.* Garden City, NY: Anchor.

Ettinger, B. (1988). Optimal use of postmenopausal hormone replacement. *Obstetrics and Gynecology, 72,* 31S–36S.

Flint, M. (1975). The menopause: Reward or punishment? *Psychosomatics, 16,* 161–163.

Fogelman, I. (1991). Oestrogen, the prevention of bone loss and osteoporosis. *British Journal of Rheumatology, 30,* 276–281.

Formanek, R. (1990). Continuity and change and 'the change of life': Premodern views of the menopause. In R. Formanek (Ed.), *The meanings of menopause* (pp. 3–42). Hillsdale, NJ: The Analytic Press.

Freedman, R., & Woodward, S. (1992). Behavioral treatment of menopausal hot flushes: Evaluation by ambulatory monitoring. *American Journal of Obstetrics and Gynecology, 167,* 439–449.

Gannon, L. R. (1985). *Menstrual disorders and menopause.* New York: Praeger.

Gannon, L. R. (1994). Sexuality and menopause. In P. Y. L. Choi & P. Nicolson (Eds.), *Female sexuality: psychology, biology, and social context* (pp. 100–124). London: Harvester Wheatsheaf.

Gannon, L. R., & Ekstrom, B. (1993). Attitudes toward menopause: The influence of sociocultural paradigms. *Psychology of Women Quarterly, 17,* 275–288.

Gannon, L. R., Hansel, S., & Goodwin, J. (1987). Correlates of menopausal hot flashes. *Journal of Behavioral Medicine, 10,* 277–285.

Gannon, L. R., Stevens, J., & Stecker, T. (Unpublished manuscript). A content analysis of obstetrics/gynecology scholarship: Implications for women's health.

Genant, H. K., Baylink, D. J., & Gallagher, J. C. (1989). Estrogens in the prevention of osteoporosis in postmenopausal women. *American Journal of Obstetrics and Gynecology, 161,*1842–1846.

Gerber, N. J., & Rey, B. (1991). Can exercise prevent osteoporosis? *British Journal of Rheumatology, 30,* 2–3.

Godsland, I. F., Wynn, V., Path, F. R. C., Crook, D., & Miller, N. E. (1987). Sex, plasma lipoproteins, and atherosclerosis: Prevailing assumptions and outstanding questions. *American Heart Journal, 114,* 1467–1501.

Gordon, G. S. (1990). Prevention of bone loss and fractures in women. *Maturitas, 6,* 225–242.

Grant, E. (1994). *Sexual chemistry: Understanding our hormones, the pill, and HRT.* London: Cedar.

Greene, J. G., & Cooke, D. J. (1980). Life stress and symptoms at the climacterium. *British Journal of Psychiatry, 136,* 486–491.

Hallstrom, T., & Samuelsoon, S. (1990). Changes in women's sexual desire in middle age: The longitudinal study of women in Gothenburg. *Archives of Sexual Behavior, 19,* 259–268.

Hemminki, E., & Sihvo, S. (1993). A review of postmenopausal hormone therapy recommendation: Potential for selection bias. *Obstetrics and Gynecology, 82,* 1021–1028

Herschberger, R. (1948). *Adam's rib.* New York: Pellegrini & Cudahy.

Hirvonen, E., & Idanpaan-Heikkila, J. (1990). Cardiovascular death among women under 40 years of age using low-estrogen oral contraceptives and intrauterine devices in Finland from 1975 to 1984. *American Journal of Obstetrics and Gynecology, 163,* 281–284.

Hunter, M. S. (1990b). Psychological and somatic experience of the menopause: A prospective study. *Psychosomatic Medicine, 52,* 357–367.

Hunter, M. S. (1990c). *Your menopause: Prepare now for a positive future.* London: Pandora Press.

Hutton, J. D., Jacobs, H. S., Murray, M. A. F., & James, V. H. T. (1978, April). Relation between plasma oestrone and oestradiol and climacteric symptoms. *Lancet,* 678–681.

Iskrant, A. P. (1968). The etiology of fractured hips in females. *American Journal of Public Health, 58,* 485–491.

Johansson, C., Mellstrom, D., Lerner, U., & Osterberg, T. (1992). Coffee drinking: A minor risk factor for bone loss and fractures. *Age and Aging, 21,* 20–26.

Kahn, A., & Holt, L. H. (1987). *Menopause: The best years of your life?* London: Bloomsbury.

Kaufert, P. (1982). Anthropology and the menopause: The development of a theoretical framework. *Maturitas, 4,* 181–193.

Kaufert, P., & Gilbert, P. (1986). The context of menopause: Psychotropic drug use and menopausal status. *Social Science and Medicine, 23,* 747–755.

Kelleher, C. C. (1990). Clinical aspects of the relationship between oral contraceptives and abnormalities of the hemostatic system: Relation to the development of cardiovascular disease. *American Journal of Obstetrics and Gynecology, 163,* 392–395.

Kinsey, A. C., Pomeroy, W. B., Martin, C. E., & Gebhard, P. H. (1953). *Sexual behavior in the human female.* Philadelphia: Saunders.

Knopp, R. H. (1988). The effects of postmenopausal estrogen therapy on the incidence of arteriosclerotic vascular disease. *Obstetrics and Gynecology, 72,* 23S–30S.

Krupp, M. A., Tierney, L. M., Jawetz, E., Roe, R. L., & Camargo, C. A. (Eds.) (1985). *21st Edition of Physician's Handbook.* Los Altos, CA: Lange Medical Publications.

Lane, N. E., Bloch, D. A., Jones, H. H., Marshall, W. H., Wood, P. O., & Fries, J. F. (1986). Long-distance running, bone density, and osteoarthritis. *Journal of the American Medical Association, 255,* 1147–1151.

Leiblum, S. R., & Swartzman, L. C. (1986). Women's attitudes toward the menopause: An update. *Maturitas, 8,* 47–56.

Lennon, M. C. (1987). Is menopause depressing? An investigation of the perspectives. *Sex Roles, 17,* 1–16.

L'Hermite, M. (1990). Risks of estrogens and progestogens. *Maturitas, 12,* 215–246.

Logothetis, M. L. (1988, November–December). The medicalization of menopause. *Women's Studies Newsletter: University of Indiana, 14*, 1–2.

MacPherson, K. I. (1993). The false promises of hormone replacement therapy and current dilemmas. In J. C. Callahan (Ed.), *Menopause: A midlife passage* (pp. 145–159). Bloomington: Indiana University Press.

Marshburn, P. B., & Carr, B. R. (1992). Hormone replacement therapy: Protection against the consequences of menopause. *Postgraduate Medicine, 92*, 145–159.

McCrea, F. B. (1983). The politics of menopause: The "discovery" of a deficiency disease. *Social Problems, 31*, 111–123.

McKinlay, J. B., McKinlay, S. M., & Brambilla, D. (1987). The relative contributions of endocrine changes and social circumstances to depression in mid-aged women. *Journal of Health and Social Behavior, 28*, 345–363.

McKinlay, S. M., & Jeffreys, M. (1974). The menopausal syndrome. *British Journal of Preventative and Social Medicine, 28*, 108–115.

Meltzer, L. J. (1974). The aging female: A study of attitudes toward aging and self-concept held by pre-menopausal, menopausal, and post-menopausal women. *Dissertation Abstracts International, 35B*, 1055.

Meuwissen, I., & Over, R. (1992). Sexual arousal phases of the human menstrual cycle. *Archives of Sexual Behavior, 21*, 101–120.

Mishell, D. R. (1989). Estrogen replacement therapy: An overview. *American Journal of Obstetrics and Gynecology, 161*, 1825–1827.

Nordin, B. E. C., Need, A. G., Chatterton, B. E., Horowitz, M., & Morris, H. A. (1990). The relative contributions of age and years since menopause to postmenopausal bone loss. *Journal of Clinical Endocrinology and Metabolism, 70*, 83–88.

Notelovitz, M. (1989). An opposing view. *Journal of Family Practice, 29*, 410–415.

Parlee, M. B. (1980). Positive changes in moods and activation levels during the menstrual cycle in experimentally naive subjects. In A. J. Dan, E. A. Graham, & C. P. Beecher (Eds.), *The menstrual cycle, Vol. 1: A synthesis of interdisciplinary research* (pp. 151–174). New York: Springer.

Pfeiffer, E. (1978). Sexuality in the aging individual. In R. L. Solnick (Ed), *Sexuality and aging* (pp. 5–35). Los Angeles: Southern California Press.

Poller, L., Thomson, J. M., & Coope, J. (1980). A double-blind cross-over study of piperazine oestrone sulphate and placebo with coagulation studies. *British Journal of Obstetrics and Gynecology, 87*, 718–725.

Reissman, C. K. (1983, summer). Women and medicalization: A new perspective. *Social Policy, 14*, 3–18.

Reitz, R. (1977). *Menopause: A positive approach.* New York: Penguin.

Rikli, R., & McManis, B. (1990). Effects of exercise on bone mineral content in postmenopausal women. *Research Quarterly for Exercise and Sport, 61*, 243–249.

Rodin, J. (1986). Aging and health: Effects of the sense of control. *Science, 233*, 1271–1275.

Sarrel, P. M. (1982). Sex problems after menopause: A study of fifty married couples treated in a sex counseling programme. *Maturitas, 4*, 231–237.

Sazy, J. A., & Horstmann, H. M. (1991). Exercise participation after menopause. *Clinics in Sports Medicine, 10*, 359–369.

Schmidt, P. J., & Rubinow, D. R. (1991). Menopause-related affective disorders: A justification for further study. *American Journal of Psychiatry, 148*, 844–852.

Schreiner-Engel, P., Schiani, R. C., Smith, H. & White, D. (1981). Sexual arousability and the menstrual cycle. *Psychosomatic Medicine, 43*, 199–213.

Seaman, B., & Seaman, G. (1977). *Women and the crisis in sex hormones.* New York: Rawson Associates.

Seligman, M. E. P. (1975). *Helplessness.* San Francisco: Freeman.

Shangold, M. (1990). Exercise in the menopausal woman. *Obstetrics and Gynecology, 75*, 53S–58S.

Sheehy, G. (1992). *Menopause: The silent passage.* New York: Random House.

Shephard, R. J. (1989). Nutritional benefits of exercise. *Journal of Sports Medicine and Physical Fitness, 29*, 83–90.

Simkin, A., Ayalon, J., & Leichter, I. (1987). Increased trabecular bone density due to bone-loading exercises in postmenopausal osteoporotic women. *Calcified Tissue International, 40,* 59–63.

Simon, D., Senan, C., Garnier, P., Saint-Paul, M., Garat, E., Thibult, N., & Papoz, L. (1990). Effects of oral contraceptives on carbohydrate and lipid metabolism in a health population: The Telecom Study. *American Journal of Obstetrics and Gynecology, 163,* 382–387.

Sinaki, M., Wahner, H. W., Offord, K. P., & Hodgson, S. F. (1989). Efficacy of nonloading exercises in prevention of vertebral bone loss in postmenopausal women: C controlled trial. *Mayo Clinical Proceedings, 64,* 762–769.

Smith, E. L., Gilligan, C., Smith, P. E., & Sempos, C. T. (1989). Calcium supplementation and bone loss in middle-aged women. *American Journal of Clinical Nutrition, 50,* 833–842.

Smith-Rosenberg, C. (1985). Puberty to menopause: The cycle of femininity in nineteenth-century America. In C. Smith-Rosenberg (Ed.), *Disorderly conduct* (pp. 183–196). New York: Knopf.

Steering Committee of the Physicians' Health Study Research Group. (1989). Final report on the aspirin component of the ongoing physicians' health study. *New England Journal of Medicine, 321,* 129–135.

Steiner, M. (1992). Female-specific mood disorders. *Clinical Obstetrics and Gynecology, 35,* 599–611.

Stevenson, J. C. (1990). Pathogenesis, prevention, and treatment of osteoporosis. *Obstetrics and Gynecology, 75,* 36S–41S.

Strickland, B. (1988). Sex-related differences in health and illness. *Psychology of Women Quarterly, 12,* 381–399.

Strong, P. M. (1979). Sociological imperialism and the progression of medicine. *Social Science and Medicine, 13A,* 199–215.

Studd, J. (1989). Prophylactic oophorectomy. *British Journal of Obstetrics and Gynecology, 96,* 506–509.

Sturdee, D. W., Wade-Evans, T., Paterson, M. E. L., Thom, M., & Studd, J. W. W. (1978). Relations between bleeding pattern, endometrial histology, and oestrogen treatment in menopausal women. *British Medical Journal, 1,* 1575–1577.

Swandby, J. R. (1981). A longitudinal study of daily mood self-reports and their relationship to the menstrual cycle. In P. Komnenish, M. McSweeney, J. A. Noack, & N. Elder (Eds.), *The menstrual cycle, Vol. 2: Research and implications for women's health* (pp. 68–90). New York: Springer.

Thomson, J., & Oswald, I. (1977). Effect of oestrogen on the sleep, mood, and anxiety of menopausal women. *British Medical Journal, 2,* 317–319.

Utian, W. H. (1972). The mental tonic effect of oestrogens administered to oophorectomized females. *South African Medical Journal, 46,* 1079–1082.

Walling, M., Andersen, B. L., & Johnson, S. R. (1990). Hormonal replacement therapy for postmenopausal women: A review of sexual outcomes and related gynecologic effects. *Archives of Sexual Behavior, 19,* 119–137.

Weg, R. B. (1983). The physiological perspective. In R. B. Weg (Ed.), *Sexuality in the later years: Roles and behavior.* (pp. 3–42). New York: Academic Press.

Whitehead, M. I. (1988). Effects of hormone replacement therapy on cardiovascular disease: An interview. *American Journal of Obstetrics and Gynecology, 158,* 1658–1659.

Wilson, R. (1966). *Feminine forever.* New York: Evans.

11

Enhancing Mobility in the Elderly:
Attentional Interventions for Driving

Karlene Ball
The University of Alabama at Birmingham

It is intuitively obvious to most individuals that we can attend to only a very small percentage of the many stimuli around us at any given time. It is also obvious that some objects are easily noticed (i.e., are conspicuous), whereas other inconspicuous objects may require considerable time and effort to locate. These common experiences capture the basic distinction between the two processes proposed in many models of attentional processing. Although they go by different names in different models (ambient vs. focal, automatic vs. effortful, parallel vs. serial), we adopt the terms *preattentive and attentive systems of processing* as used by Neisser (1967, 1976) and Julesz (1981).

In most previous descriptions, the preattentive system functions as a guide for the attentive system. In the visual domain, it makes use of rapid parallel processing over large spatial areas to alert or orient the attentive system to locations in space where there is relevant or changing information. Once the preattentive system has alerted the attentive system about where to look, the attentive system can then be used to discern detail, identify, or recognize stimuli. The attentive system thus represents a concentration of attentional resources within a small visual area, whereas the preattentive system represents a diffuse allocation of resources to a much larger spatial extent (considered by some to have no capacity limitations other than sensory).

One research technique that was extensively used to investigate attention and these two systems of information processing is visual search. In this technique observers must search for one item, or target, amid varying numbers of other items, or distracters, presented simultaneously (Ball, Owsley, Sloane, Roenker, & Bruni, 1993; Treisman & Gelade, 1980). Under some conditions, the entire stimulus array is processed simultaneously (i.e., preattentively) and the relevant target is conspicuous, or "pops out," regardless of the number of elements in the display. In other conditions, however, it appears that items must be processed sequentially (i.e., attentively) such that the number of other items in the display becomes a critical factor in the time required to locate or identify the target.

ATTENTION IN A TECHNICAL SOCIETY

Situations in which an individual must localize relevant information or objects in a visually cluttered environment are numerous and range from simply locating a certain restaurant sign on a busy section of highway, to detecting defects in products on a production line, to detecting enemy tanks on an active battlefield. In such environments, the observer must search for an object, make a decision about the relevance of the object to the search, release the object from attention if appropriate, and locate (attend to) additional objects. Key elements of this process are the ability of the observer to have his or her attention attracted to relevant objects (preattentive search) and the ability to switch attention voluntarily between objects (attentive search). The technological changes since the 1980s have made such searches more, rather than less demanding. For example, with the advent of stealth aircraft and sophisticated camouflage in the military, it has become almost impossible to visually detect the presence of relevant targets. Automobile manufacturers are considering the production of vehicles with "heads up displays" (HUD) in which traffic and other types of information may be displayed on the windshield, thus demanding dual attention to this information as well as the highway. Car phones can result in an additional attentional demand while navigating a vehicle. More and more people are driving, resulting in congestion in most large cities with resultant increases in attentional demand. It is unlikely that many such situations can be changed in ways to make the observer's task less difficult (the enemy is unlikely to paint his or her tanks pink). Rather, it seems more prudent to attempt to understand the capabilities and limitations of the observer, with an eye to increasing or expanding these abilities.

The difficulties associated with localizing a target in a cluttered environment are exacerbated by decreases in viewing time. Finding a sign becomes even more difficult when traveling rapidly down the road. The world of the pilot is one filled with multiple sources of information and rapidly presented stimuli requiring detection, attention , and the release of attention to new objects. Professional athletes must also be constantly aware of the location and movements of other players on the field.

Some individuals function more effectively in high-demand environments than others. For example, those individuals with exceptional attentional skills will function more effectively as air traffic controllers than will those with minimal skills. These individual differences become extremely relevant where ineffective function can result in injury. Safety is a particularly important issue for attentionally demanding activities or occupations for two populations of individuals: special populations with diminished function (e.g., due to head injury, stroke, dementia, attentional deficit disorders, or age-related declines), or special occupations that require exceptional performance (e.g., fighter pilots or tankers; air traffic controllers; power plant operators; emergency vehicle operators of firetrucks, ambulances, or police cars; and professional athletes). These populations fall at the two extremes of the continuum of attentional function where assessment of functional abilities becomes relevant for a determination of fitness for duty or competence to continue an everyday activity such as driving.

Whereas most people agree that attention is critical for the performance of many daily activities, there is not widespread agreement on how to measure it. The Useful Field of View (UFOV)® paradigm is a new approach developed to assess the functional attentional skills required for daily activities such as driving and attentionally demanding occupations, and to train those skills when they are lacking or when exceptional performance is required. The following studies describe the validation of this new technique with respect to crash risk among older drivers.

ATTENTION AND DRIVING

There is little doubt that under most circumstances driving is an attentionally demanding task, especially if one's attentional capabilities have declined. Over the past several years, we found that the likelihood of a decline in attentional ability increases with age (Ball, et al., 1993). For example, although approximately 7% of individuals between the ages of 55 and 60 experience attentional decline, close to 50% of those over age 85 have diminished attentional function. Furthermore, throughout the transportation literature since the mid-1970s, researchers found that most older drivers have excellent driving records, but those who crash do so because of an inability to attend to relevant cues in the driving environment (Barrett, Mihal, Panek, Sterns, & Alexander, 1977; Kahneman, Ben-Ishai, & Lotan, 1973; Mihal & Barrett, 1976; Shinar, 1978). Thus, older individuals who drive represent an ideal population for evaluating new attentional measures and understanding individual differences in attentional capabilities in an everyday context. Furthermore, such studies provide an opportunity for investigating the amenability of attentional skills to training.

Although the understanding of attention may be a worthwhile goal in and of itself, understanding the older driver's limitations addresses a larger social issue. Several years ago, we began a program of research whose ultimate goal was to enhance the mobility of older adults without sacrificing safety concerns (Ball et al., 1993; Ball & Owsley, 1991, 1993; Owsley & Ball, 1993; Owsley, Ball, Sloane, Overley, & White, 1994; Owsley, Ball,

Sloane, Roenker, & Bruni, 1991). The need to solve the problems of older drivers has appeared at the top of many national agendas (Barr, 1991; Federal Highway Administration, 1989; National Highway Traffic Safety Administration, 1989; National Research Council, 1985; Transportation Research Board, 1988), and thus our research on mobility problems in the elderly began by focusing on driving. A number of trends referenced in these reports document the need for research in this area. For example, the elderly represent the most rapidly growing segment of the driving population, both in the total number of drivers on the road, and the number of miles driven annually per driver. It is estimated that by the year 2024, one out of four drivers will be over age 65. Older drivers as a group have more traffic convictions and crashes and incur more fatalities per mile driven than most other age groups. For every 100,000 miles driven, crash rates for older drivers are double those of younger drivers. Vehicle crashes are the second most common reason for an emergency room visit by the elderly. Finally, like other age groups in our society, older adults rely on the personal automobile for transportation. Although the stereotype of the impaired older driver may be true for some older adults, there are many older drivers who have excellent driving skills. We viewed our research task as determining what factors place some older drivers at risk for crash involvement, and then to use this information to develop interventions that could be use to minimize their crash risk.

Our research to date has three implications. First, tests of higher order visual abilities, such as the assessment of useful field of view size, are better predictors of driving problems in the elderly than are tests of visual sensory abilities, such as measures of acuity and peripheral vision. The size of the useful field of view depends on several types of visual skills, such as spatial resolution, light sensitivity, contrast sensitivity, divided attention, selective attention, and the speed by which visual input is processed, and thus is a more global or "encompassing" measure of visual ability. A breakdown in one or more of these skills will negatively impact performance in the useful field of view task.

The second implication of our research is that it generates suggestions for possible interventions to be evaluated in terms of their ability to minimize driving problems in the elderly. For example, if poor vision (e.g., acuity, contrast sensitivity) and poor visual attentional skills are associated with an increased risk for crashes, then improving vision and attentional skills should reduce risk. Evaluating these types of interventions is an important step in our research program. Because identifying the mechanisms underlying older adults' visual performance problems is not enough, we must also develop feasible solutions. Although work is ongoing in this area across multiple sites, we have preliminary evidence for transfer of improved visual attentional skills to better driving performance.

The third implication is broader in scope and relevant to older adults' visual performance problems in general, not just driving problems. In our efforts to understand the basis of older adults' difficulties with everyday tasks, vision scientists tended to dwell almost exclusively on visual sensory mechanisms. Yet most visual tasks depend on much more than visual sensory skills, such as resolution and contrast sensitivity. Most daily tasks are performed in a visually cluttered environment with auditory distraction, involve the simultaneous use of central and peripheral vision, and require the execution of primary and secondary tasks. Performance is not only limited by visual and cognitive factors but can be influenced by musculoskeletal problems, medication usage, cardiovascular problems, and other systemic conditions such as diabetes, all of which are relatively prevalent in the elderly population. Thus, it is important for us to realize at the outset that the causes of older adults' performance problems in complex visual tasks, driving or otherwise, are likely to be multifactorial in origin.

Because driving is a highly visual task, the conventional wisdom was that the increased prevalence of vision impairment and eye disease in the elderly is the primary cause of their driving difficulty. However, previous studies showed only weak correlations between visual sensory function and the number of crashes incurred over some period of time (Henderson & Burg, 1974; Hills & Burg, 1977; Shinar, 1977). These correlations are typically statistically significant, documenting that there is an association between, for example, acuity and crashes, but they account for only a small amount of the crash variance in the sample. There are undoubtedly many reasons why the earlier studies failed to find a visual factor that strongly differentiates crash-involved drivers from those who are crash-free, and we and others have discussed these reasons at length elsewhere (Ball & Owsley, 1991; National Highway Traffic Safety Administration, 1989; Shinar & Schieber, 1991).

One aspect of the earlier work we thought was particularly troublesome was the failure to include reliable assessments of higher order visual skills, such as visual attention abilities. Previous studies on older drivers focused on primarily one potential correlate at a time (e.g., visual sensory variables, cognitive variables, diseases, or higher order variables such as decision time). Only rarely was a measure of visual attention measured, yet visual attentional skills seemed to be highly relevant in a complex visual task such as driving. Furthermore, previous work was consistent with this notion. Several studies on commercial drivers found an association between selective attention problems and increased number of crashes (Mihal & Barrett, 1976). In another study of police accident reports, most crashes by older drivers were caused by alleged driver inattention (Shinar, 1978). Therefore, in our own studies, we assessed visual attentional skills in older drivers, but we also included visual sensory tests because the ability of the visual system to adequately register visual stimulation had to be a necessary starting point. Finally, it is well-known in the gerontological literature that deficits in visual sensory and visual attentional skills are prevalent in the older adult population (Ball, Roenker, & Bruni, 1990; Owsley & Sloane, 1990; Parasuraman & Nestor, 1991; Plude & Hoyer, 1985). One advantage of examining both visual sensory and higher order skills within the same sample is that it permits one to assess the impact of these deficits, both separately and in combination on crash risk.

Methods

Our sample consisted of 294 older drivers (range 56–90 years, M = 71 years) who were recruited from the population of drivers age 55 and over in Jefferson County, Alabama. The sample was age stratified, in that it included approximately equal numbers of individuals in each 5 years of life, between 55 and 90 years. We wanted to make sure the sample included the "oldest old." The sample was also stratified with respect to the number of crashes on record with the state over the previous 5-year period. This was important because we wanted to ensure that the sample included problem drivers (i.e., drivers who had a history of multiple crashes), as well as drivers with good records (i.e., drivers with no crashes on record). The details of our sampling procedures and rationale were previously discussed (Ball et al., 1993).

All subjects participated in the following protocol during a single visit to the laboratory in 1990. The main elements of this protocol are listed in Table 11.1. The protocol consisted of tests that evaluated different aspects of the visual information processing system including visual sensory func-

TABLE 11.1
Main Evaluations Included in the Protocol

Category	Functional Ability	Test
Visual sensory function	Acuity	ETDRS chart
	Contrast sensitivity	Pelli–Robson chart
	Color discrimination	D–15
	Disability glare	VisTech MCT–8000
	Night acuity	VisTech MCT–8000
	Stereoacuity	Randot
		Frisby
		TNO
	Central field sensitivity	HFA Program 30–2
	Peripheral field sensitivity	HFA Program 60–2
Cognitive function	General mental status	MOMSSE
		Rey–Osterreith
		Trailmaking test
		Block Design (WAIS-R)
Visual attention/speed of processing	Useful field of view size	Visual attention
		Analyzer
Eye health	Central retinal health	Sum of 3-pt. rating
	Peripheral retinal health	of each category:
	Ocular media	0 = no problem
		1 = mod. problem
		2 = severe problem

tion, cognitive status using a test specifically designed to measure cognitive deficits in the elderly, eye health examination, which assessed the presence or absence of ocular disease on a 3-point scale, and a measure of the size of the useful field of view.

The visual sensory function tests consisted of visual acuity (both day and night), contrast sensitivity, disability glare, stereopsis, color discrimination, and visual field sensitivity. Visual acuity was measured with the Bailey–Lovie Chart (Ferris, Kassoff, Bresnick, & Bailey, 1982), and expressed as log minimum angle resolvable (log MAR). Contrast sensitivity was measured with the Pelli–Robson Contrast Sensitivity Chart (Pelli, Robson, & Wilkins, 1988), and expressed as log contrast sensitivity. Disability glare was measured with the MCT–8000 (Vistech Consultants), and defined as the difference in letter acuity (logMAR) under conditions of glare versus no glare. Stereopsis was measured with three clinical tests (Randot, TNO, and Frisby, described in Simons, 1981). Color discrimination was measured with the enlarged D-15 test (Farnsworth, 1947). Visual field sensitivity was measured with the Humphrey Field Analyzer using the screening program for the central 60 degrees with the quantify defects option (Haley, 1987).

All tests were binocular except the visual field test, in which each eye was tested separately (Humphrey Prog. 30–2, 0–60 deg). For most tests, subjects wore their own habitual optical correction because their everyday visual performance was of interest. However, if a test of visual function specifically called for a near-correction in the standard instructions for administering the test, we followed those instructions (e.g., Humphrey Field Analyzer, Pelli–Robson chart). These specific tests were chosen because they represent major aspects of visual sensory function and have good test–retest reliability.

Mental status was assessed by the Mattis Organic Mental Status Syndrome Examination (MOMSSE), specifically designed to assess cognitive status in the elderly (Mattis, 1976). This test provides a composite score of cognitive function that reflects performance in several categories such as abstraction, digit span, verbal and visual memory, and block design. Additional cognitive tests were carried out to evaluate visuospatial abilities (Lezak, 1983) and included the Rey–Osterreith test, the Trailmaking test, and the block design of the Wechsler Adult Intelligence Scale (Revised).

A questionnaire was administered that asked about the subject's driving habits such as: (a) driving exposure (e.g., how many miles per year, how many days per week, how many trips per day), (b) avoidance of potentially challenging driving situations (e.g., left-hand turns across traffic, driving alone), and (c) number of crashes incurred during the previous 5-year period where the police came to the scene. In addition to this self-report crash information, crash frequency during the previous 5-year period was obtained for each subject from the state computer of the Alabama Department of Public Safety. Following completion of data collection, the written accident reports (filed by the officer at the scene) for all subjects were obtained from the State, which detailed the circumstances surrounding each crash.

All subjects received a detailed eye health examination by an ophthalmologist, which included direct and indirect ophthalmoscopy after dilation, biomicroscopy, applanation tonometry, a refraction for distance, and an assessment of external eye health. A 3-point rating scale, as described in our earlier study (Owsley et al., 1991), was used to determine to what extent clinical changes in the eye would be expected to cause a functional problem in each of three broad categories—central vision problem, peripheral vision problem, and ocular media problem. In addition, each subject was assigned to a primary diagnostic category (e.g., normal, cataract, macular disease).

The protocol included a measure of the size of the useful field of view, which assesses the visual field area over which one can rapidly use visual information (Ball et al., 1993). Ball and colleagues developed a rapid and reliable method for evaluating the useful field of view size (Ball & Owsley, 1993; Ball, Roenker, & Bruni, 1990), and is particularly useful in clinical studies. To summarize, the paradigm consists of a radial localization task in which a person must identify the radial direction of a target presented up to 30 degrees in the periphery, simultaneously discriminating two targets presented in central vision. By varying the eccentricity of the peripheral target, the visual field area over which a subject can rapidly use information can be estimated. In some trials the peripheral target is embedded in distracting stimuli. Thus the task has both divided attention components (i.e., the subject must perform a central discrimination task at fixation while localizing the simultaneously presented peripheral target) and a selective attention component (i.e., the subject must indicate the radial direction of the peripheral target even though it is embedded in other distracting stimuli in the periphery). An additional variable that is manipulated is the duration of the display, which is varied from 40 to 240 ms. A subject's overall performance across trials is evaluated in terms of his or her ability to localize the peripheral target at various eccentricities as a function of three variables: (a) their ability to successfully divide their attention between central and peripheral tasks (divided attention), (b) their ability to localize the peripheral target when it is embedded in distracters (selective attention), and (c) the minimum duration by which they can perform these tasks (speed of processing). Performance in the useful field of view task is expressed in terms of percent reduction of a maximum 30 degree field size; a 30 degree field was considered as the maimum field size for baseline purposes because this was the largest field size allowable by the screen size and viewing distance in our apparatus.

We were interested in how visual sensory function, cognitive function, useful field of view size, and eye health status—as assessed in the protocol—are related to the number of vehicle crashes incurred by our older drivers. Crash data on all subjects were obtained from the Alabama Department of Public Safety, which compiles records on all drivers licensed by the State. This data included the written accident report, filed by the officer at the scene, which detailed the circumstances surrounding each crash. For the purposes of our study, we defined crashes as including only "at-fault" crashes and eliminated those crashes from the database where our driver was clearly not at fault. Fault was determined by three independent raters. Although the raters did not always agree on the degree of fault (concordance = 83%), the three raters always agreed that our driver was at least partially at fault (Ball et al., 1993).

There was a retrospective portion to our study and a prospective portion to the study. The retrospective study consisted of relating performance in the protocol in 1990 to the number of crashes incurred by our drivers in the previous 5-year period. In this aspect of the study, the goal was to predict older drivers with a *history* of crash problems (Ball et al., 1993). The prospective component of the study focused on relating performance in the protocol in 1990 to the number of crashes incurred in the subsequent 3-year period (Owsley, 1994; Owsley et al., 1994). The goal in the prospective study was to predict which older drivers are at risk for *future* crashes.

Results

The goal of this study was to evaluate a battery of measures relative to their usefulness in predicting crash frequency in older drivers. The results of the retrospective study are discussed first. As a first step in data analysis, we examined how our various independent variables correlated with each other, the dependent variable, and the number of at-fault crashes in the previous 5-year period (see Table 11.2). As discussed in the previous section, the independent variables to be evaluated in model development were various aspects of central vision, peripheral vision, eye health, useful field of view size, and mental status. Because the protocol included more than one type of assessment of central vision and peripheral vision (which were highly intercorrelated), we chose for inclusion in model development that measure of central vision and of peripheral vision with the highest zero-order correlation with number of crashes.

The variables used in model development and their intercorrelations are listed in Table 11.3. Eye health, central and peripheral vision, UFOV® size, and cognitive function were all significantly and positively related to crashes. The useful field of view test was the most strongly correlated with crashes, $r = 0.52$, as compared with Pearson correlation coefficients in the .2s and .3s for the other visual and cognitive variables. These data were used to construct a LISREL model (Byrne, 1989; Joreskog & Sorbom, 1989) for predicting crash frequency. This modeling program analyzes the covariance matrix among the variables to arrive at a system of simultaneous linear equations that allows the dependent variable (number of crashes) to be expressed in terms of the structural relationships among the independent variables. An important advantage of LISREL over approaches such as multiple regression is that it allows one to evaluate whether each independent variable has a direct versus indirect effect on the dependent variable. The details of the LISREL model development were described elsewhere (Ball et al., 1993). The best fitting model is pictured in Fig. 11.1. The only variables that had direct effects on the number of crashes incurred during the previous 5 years were the size of the UFOV® and to a lesser

TABLE 11.2
Correlations Among the Protocol Variables and Number of Prior Crashes

	CS	CD	DG	NG	CVF	PVF	MS	UFOV®	CRH	PRH	OM	Prior Crashes
Visual Acuity (VA)	-.73	-.35	.15	.19	.48	.47	.18	.41	.62	.61	.46	.23
Contr Sensitivity (CS)		.36	-.11	-.23	-.58	-.57	-.21	-.47	-.66	-.66	-.49	-.24
Color Discr (CD)			-.02	-.04	-.24	-.22	-.10	-.18	-.31	-.35	-.27	-.11
Day Glare (DG)				.06	.13	.13	.09	.08	.08	.02	-.02	.10
Night Glare (NG)					.14	.17	.16	.28	.23	.19	.26	.16
Central VF (CVF)						.84	.23	.46	.52	.50	.38	.28
Periph VF (PVF)							.29	.47	.50	.50	.35	.26
Mental Status (MS)								.48	.22	.21	.19	.34
UFOV®									.42	.39	.27	.52
Cent Ret Health (CRH)										.76	.80	.24
Periph Ret Health (PRH)											.62	.18
Ocular Media (OM)												.17

Note: Critical $r = 0.12$, $df = 294$, $p < .05$, two-tailed.

TABLE 11.3
Correlations Among Variables Used in the LISREL
Model for Predicting Prior Crashes

	Central Vision	Peripheral Vision	Mental Status	UFOV®	Prior Crashes
Eye Health	-.67	.50	.24	.40	.23
Central Vision		-.57	-.20	-.47	-.24
Peripheral Vision			.29	.48	.26
Mental Status				.48	.34
UFOV®					.52

Note: Critical $r = 0.12$, $df = 294$, $p < .05$, two-tailed.

extent, mental status. The measures of central and peripheral vision and eye health were related to crashes; however, their effects on the number of crashes were indirect and mediated by the size of the useful field of view. Although the overall model accounted for 74% of the variance in the sample data, it was also of interest to determine the R^2 associated with crash prediction alone. Only two variables, UFOV® and mental status, had direct effects on crash frequency, jointly accounting for 28% of the crash variance. Alternative models were evaluated, but none were superior to the model in Fig. 11.1 in that they did not improve the percentage of crash variance accounted for. For example, when the LISREL model was respecified so that central and peripheral vision were forced to have direct effects on crash frequency (in addition to their indirect effect through UFOV®), there was no increase in R^2. The main role of central and peripheral vision in the model is their significant direct effect on the size of UFOV®; together they accounted for 30% of the UFOV® variance. Not surprisingly, visual attentional skills like those used in the UFOV® task crucially depend on the integrity of information entering the visual sensory channel. In other respecifications of the model, we entirely removed UFOV®. Because central and peripheral vision were correlated with UFOV®, perhaps UFOV® provided redundant information to the model. However, with UFOV® omitted, the visual variables (central vision, peripheral vision, and eye health) jointly accounted for only 5% of the crash variance, and with the introduction of mental status to the model, R^2 only increased to 16%. Therefore, the model presented in Figure 11.1, which includes UFOV® and accounts for 28% of the crash variance, clearly maximizes the prediction of crash frequency during the prior 5-year period.

In summary, vision is a necessary but not sufficient predictor of crash frequency. Eye health and visual function do not contribute any unique variance to crash frequency in addition to their indirect effect through UFOV®. Mental status also had a significant direct effect on UFOV®, and a statistically significant direct effect on crash frequency. However, the effect of mental status on crash frequency was primarily indirect, because removal of its direct effect in the LISREL model only slightly reduced the amount of crash frequency variance accounted for (from 28% to 27%). These

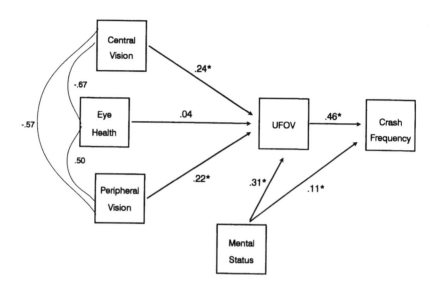

FIG. 11.1. LISREL model for predicting the number of crashes incurred over 5-year period prior to the test date (from Ball et al., 1993). The solid arrows represent the hypothesized direct effects, and each is labeled with a standardized path coefficient. Significant direct effects are indicated with an asterisk. Curvilinear lines on the left side of Fig. 11.1 indicate that central vision, peripheral vision, and eye health are intercorrelated, and the r labels each curve. UFOV® and mental status were the only variables that had direct effects on crash frequency. The overall LISREL model accounted for 74% of the variance in the data, and 28% of the crash variance. Other models were considered (see text), but the model portrayed here maximizes the prediction of number of prior crashes.

results supported our hypothesis that UFOV® is a mediating variable between crash frequency on the one hand, and eye health, visual function, and mental status on the other.

Another way to look at this data is to determine how well the main independent variables identify older drivers who were crash-involved in the prior 5 years versus those older drivers who were crash-free. Recall that most of the independent variables were performance-based tests evaluating various aspects of the visual processing system. For the purpose of generating an ROC curve for each independent variable, the definition of good performance on each variable was varied. Then, for this set of definitions, the probability of a hit was plotted against the probability of a false alarm. A false alarm was defined as a driver who performed poorly on the independent variable (e.g., poor acuity) but who nevertheless had no crashes on record. Figure 11.2 displays these ROC curves. Values on the diagonal indicate an equal probability of hits and false alarms, that is, an inability to classify drivers appropriately. Greater distance between an ROC curve and the diagonal corresponds to higher sensitivity in correctly identifying drivers at risk for crashes. Note that the UFOV® test is clearly superior to acuity, contrast sensitivity, peripheral field sensitivity, and mental status in identifying older drivers with a history of at least one crash in the previous 5 years.

Figure 11.3 illustrates that the average number of crashes increases with increasing severity of UFOV® reduction. Given the UFOV® test's superior predictability as illustrated in the ROC analysis, it is useful to consider its utility as a "diagnostic" test using a 2 × 2 contingency table, perhaps a more typical way to look at the issue from a clinical standpoint. The reader is referred to Table 11.4. In this context, *sensitivity* refers to the probability that an older driver with a greater than 40% reduction in UFOV® has one or more crashes during the prior 5 years. *Specificity* refers to the probability that an older driver with no crashes on record in the prior 5 years has a UFOV® reduction 40% or less. The UFOV® test had both high sensitivity (89%) and high specificity (81%) in classifying older drivers as crash involved. This level of predictability is unprecedented in the research literature on crash-risk in older drivers.

Furthermore, the information in Fig. 11.3 was also used to calculate an odds ratio, indicating that individuals with UFOV® reduction greater than

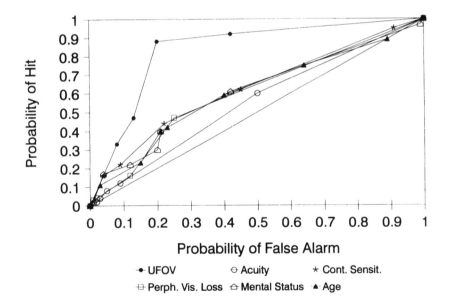

FIG. 11.2. ROC curves (probability of hits plotted against probability of false alarms) for major independent variables. These curves provide information about the ability of each independent variable to identify drivers who have a history of crash problems. The d' values for each of the ROC curve are: acuity (d' = 0.24), contrast sensitivity (d'= 0.67), peripheral field sensitivity (d' = 0.60), mental status (d' = 0.50), UFOV® (d' = 2.27), age (d' = 0.58). It is clear that UFOV® is superior to all other variables in identifying older drivers with a history of crash problems.

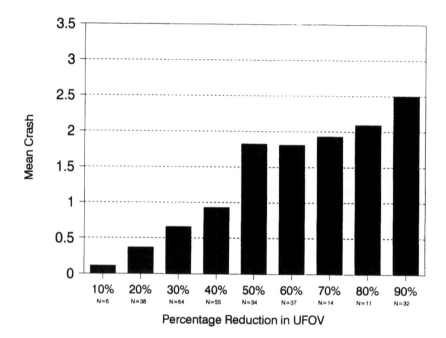

FIG. 11.3. Mean crash frequency as a function of UFOV® reduction for drivers with "good" mental status versus those with "poor" mental status. For the purposes of our analysis, good mental status is defined as a MOMSSE composite score of < 9, and poor mental status as a score > 9. Note that the relationship between crash frequency and UFOV® reduction is very similar within each mental status subgroup. Our analysis indicates that although UFOV® reduction is correlated with poor mental status, the two are not identical constructs. An older subject can have decreased mental status, yet have a normal UFOV®.

TABLE 11.4
Number of Subjects in Each UFOV and Crash Category
in the Retrospective Study

| | Prior Crash Category | |
UFOV® Category	≥ 1 Crashes	0 Crashes
UFOV® reduction ≥ 40%	142	25
UFOV® reduction < 40%	18	109

Sensitivity = 89%
Specificity = 81%

40% were six times more likely to be at least partially responsible for a crash than those with reduction of 40% or less. Of the 25 false-positive predictions, 19 were subjects who reported that they avoided driving in general, avoided driving alone, or avoided left-hand turns, which thus minimized their driving exposure. In fact, if we exclude those individuals who specified on the driving habits questionnaire that they avoided these particular aspects of driving, the correlation between UFOV® and crash frequency increased from $r = .52$ to $r = .62$. Although avoidance is a somewhat difficult construct to measure, it appears that some older drivers are effectively compensating for visual or attentional decline and that some valid measure of exposure or avoidance behavior would be an appropriate addition to a predictive model of crash frequency.

Figure 11.4 illustrates how restrictions in the UFOV® may increase the probability of crashes. Panel A displays the average size of the "attentional window" for those individuals with little to no restriction of the UFOV® (< 10% as shown in Fig. 11.3). Panel B displays this window for those individuals with approximately 40% decline. Panel C displays this window for those individuals with approximately 80% reduction. Finally, the most extreme case of UFOV® restriction is illustrated in Panel D (90% reduction). The areas depicted in this figure do not represent the size of the visual field, but are scaled to represent relative reductions in the size of the UFOV® for different groups of individuals.

Another question that arises is whether UFOV® reduction is predictive of only certain categories of at-fault crashes (e.g. failure to notice a traffic signal, merging), or whether the prediction applies to many crash types. In order to evaluate this question, 364 at-fault crashes incurred by our sample were classified into six types: failure to notice a traffic control device ($n = 35$), failure to notice another vehicle ($n = 174$), merging ($n = 51$), hitting the rear of another vehicle ($n = 54$), backing up into another vehicle or object ($n = 26$), other ($n = 24$). The correlation between UFOV® and crash frequency was similarly high for each crash type ($r = .45$ to $.48$), and the slight reduction in the strength of these correlation coefficients (compared to the analysis on all crash types) was due to decreased sample size for each type of crash, and to a lower total accident frequency for a given subject. An alternative breakdown of crashes into intersection ($n = 220$) and nonintersection crashes ($n = 144$) also revealed that the UFOV® was a good predictor of both types ($r = .41$ for nonintersection, and $r = .49$ for intersection accidents). These analyses imply that the UFOV® task assesses some critical visual attentional factor common to many types of at-fault crashes.

Thus far, the discussion has been directed at the retrospective study in which the relationship between visual–cognitive factors and crashes previous to our test date was examined. The more crucial question might be whether or not visual and cognitive abilities can predict which older drivers are at risk for future crashes. In our prospective study (Owsley, 1994), the number of future crashes for each subject was defined as the total number of at-fault crashes incurred by that subject between the 1990 test date and October 1993, approximately a 3-year period. Our approach to data analysis

FIG. 11.4. An illustration of how restrictions in the UFOV® may increase the probability of crashes. Panel A displays the average size of the attentional window for those individuals with no restriction of the UFOV. Panel B displays this window for those individuals who have experienced a significant decline in the speed of visual information processing. Panel C displays this window for those individuals who have experienced both a slowing and an extreme sensitivity to distraction. Finally, the most extreme cases of UFOV® restriction is illustrated in Panel D for those individuals who have experienced slowing, sensitivity to distraction, and the inability to divide their attention between central and peripheral tasks. Note that the areas depicted do not represent the size of the visual field, but are scaled to represent relative reductions in the size of the UFOV® for different groups of individuals.

was similar to that used for the retrospective study (Ball et al., 1993). We wanted to determine whether or not the LISREL model developed on the basis of our retrospective data (see Fig. 11.1) was also applicable to the prediction of future crashes.

Before proceeding with the data analysis, however, it was important to take into consideration those subjects who stopped driving or died during the 3-year prospective period. If a subject was not driving during this time period, then they could not incur vehicle crashes, that is, their crash risk would be zero by definition. Thirty-nine subjects stopped driving and 32 subjects died during the first 36 months of the prospective period, leaving a sample of 223 older drivers, which served as the basis of the prospective data analysis. Table 11.5 lists the correlation matrix among the main independent variables to be used in model development and the number of future crashes. Also included in Table 11.5 are the correlations between number of at-fault prior crashes and the other variables. The rationale for including this variable is that the number of previous crashes is typically a good predictor of the number of future crashes, as is well-known in the automobile insurance industry. Thus, we thought it important to include prior crashes as a variable in the attempt to predict future crashes.

Looking at the last column of Table 11.5, the pattern of correlations among the visual and cognitive variables and the number of future crashes is similar to that from the retrospective study (see Table 11.3). More specifically, the strongest correlate of future crashes is UFOV® with $r = .46$. Central vision, peripheral vision, and mental status were also significantly correlated with future crashes; however, the strength of these relationships was weaker than that between UFOV® and future crashes. The relationship between eye health status and future crashes was not significant, unlike the retrospective study analysis on prior crashes. The strength of the correlation coefficients was generally lower in the prospective study (Table 11.5) compared to the retrospective study (Table 11.3). Two factors that may be contributing to this trend are that crash data were averaged over a shorter period in the prospective study (3 years) than in the retrospective study (5 years), and subjects who dropped out of the sample (because they died or stopped driving) tended to be those with serious visual or cognitive impairment. Both of these factors could reduce the magnitude of correlations. The number of prior crashes was significantly correlated with the number of future crashes ($r = .40$), but was not as strong as the relationship between UFOV® and future crashes ($r = .46$).

Using the covariance matrix of the independent variables and future crash data, we evaluated how well the original LISREL model (see Fig. 11.1), which optimized the prediction of prior crashes, predicted future crashes. Figure 11.5 displays the model from Figure 11.1, but this time the dependent

TABLE 11.5
Correlations Among Variables Used in the LISREL
Model for Predicting Future Crashes

	Central Vision	Peripheral Vision	Mental Status	UFOV®	Future Crashes
Eye health	-.60	.47	.16	.34	.10
Central vision		.41	.09	.30	.15
Peripheral vision			.26	.44	.21
Mental status				.43	.16
UFOV					.46

Note: Critical $r = .13$, $df = 223$, $p < .05$, two-tailed.

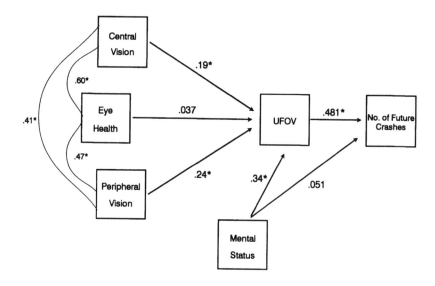

FIG. 11.5. LISREL model for predicting the number of future crashes incurred over
the next 3 years after the test date. This model maximized the prediction of future
crashes. The overall LISREL model accounted for 56% of the variance in the data,
and 22% of the crash variance. Note that the general structure of the model is
identical to that in Fig. 11.1, where the independent variable was the number of
prior crashes. UFOV® (but not mental status) was the only variable that had a direct
effect on the number of future crashes.

variable is the number of future crashes and the standardized path coefficients and other labels are based on the prospective data set. Unlike the
retrospective model, only one variable, UFOV®, but not mental status, has
a significant direct effect on the number of future crashes. This model
accounts for 22% of the crash variance. Other alternative models were
considered in order to determine if the model pictured in Figure 11.5 is
actually the best fitting model. Because central vision and peripheral vision
were both correlated with UFOV®, we considered the possibility that
UFOV® was providing redundant information in the model, given that
central and peripheral vision were already entered. If UFOV® and mental
status are omitted, then the percentage of crash variance accounted for is
4.6%. This is drastically less than the 22% of the variance accounted for
when UFOV® is in the model. In another respecification of the model, we
included the number of prior crashes as an independent variable, as illustrated in Fig. 11.6, as Table 11.5 indicated that it was correlated with the
number of future crashes. It was included in the same position in the model
as in the retrospective model (to the right of UFOV®, see Fig. 11.1). This
model accounted for 21% of the crash variance. This was not an improvement over the percentage of variance accounted for by the model in Fig.
11.5 (22%), which did not include prior crashes. Thus, information about

prior crashes, although significantly correlated with future crashes, does not appear to provide critical information to the model not already provided by the visual and cognitive variables.

The sensitivity and specificity of the UFOV® test were computed in the same way as discussed earlier, in terms of its ability to identify older drivers at risk for one or more crashes over the next 3 years. Table 11.6 presents the 2 × 2 table, analogous to Table 11.4, but this time for future crashes. The sensitivity and the specificity of the UFOV® test are still relatively high (94% and 65%, respectively). The information in Table 11.6 was used to compute an odds ratio, which indicated that older drivers with greater than 40% reduction in UFOV® were 16 times more likely to incur one or more crashes than were those with no or minimal UFOV® reduction. Individuals with UFOV® reduction greater than 40% (top line of Table 11.6) were heavily represented in both the crash-involved and crash-free categories. This result might be due to the fact that individuals with severe UFOV® reduction (> 40%) were more likely to drop out of the study during the prospective period than were those with no or minimal reduction (≥40%). Specifically, 37% of the > 40% reduction category dropped out of the study, compared to only 8% of the ≤40% UFOV® reduction category. These dropouts were either due to death or to stopping driving. This association between UFOV® reduction and death or mobility restriction is interesting in and of itself.

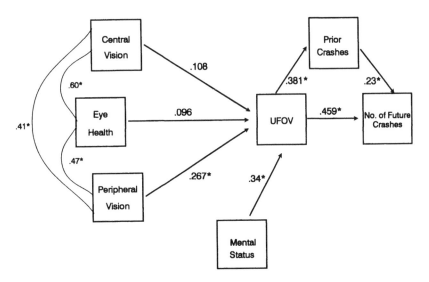

FIG. 11.6. LISREL model for predicting the number of future crashes incurred over the next 3 years after the test date, but in this model, the number of prior crashes is also included as an independent variable in the model. This model accounted for 21% of the crash variance, less variance than in the future crash model—which did not include prior crashes (see Fig. 11.5). Thus, the inclusion of information about the number of prior crashes did not improve Fig. 11.5.

TABLE 11.6
Number of Subjects in Each UFOV
and Crash Category in the Prospective Study

UFOV® Category	Future Crash Category	
	1 Crashes	0 Crashes
UFOV® Reduction ≥ 40%	44	62
UFOV® Reduction < 40%	3	114
Sensitivity = 94%		
Specificity = 65%		

Discussion

This program of research suggests that older drivers in poor eye health, with visual sensory impairment, cognitive impairment, and/or visual attentional deficits are at greater risk for crashes than are those without these problems. The UFOV test, which is a measure of visual attention skills and visual processing speed, was more useful, compared to other visual–cognitive measures, in identifying older drivers who are likely to have one or more crashes. It had a relatively high sensitivity and specificity in identifying crash-involved drivers.

Older drivers with a severe restriction in the spatial area over which they could rapidly use visual information were six times more likely to have incurred one or more crashes in the previous 5-year period than were those with minimal or no restriction. There are several types of mechanisms that could potentially underlie a restriction in the size of the useful field of view in older adults. Earlier research demonstrated that many older adults have deficits in selective attention and divided attention (Parasuraman & Nestor, 1991; Plude & Hoyer, 1986), as well as a slowing in the rate of visual information processing (Hoyer & Plude, 1982). These types of deficits could contribute to a narrowing of the perceptual window. Another potential cause of UFOV® constrictions is visual sensory impairment, such as severe loss in central or peripheral vision; an observer cannot attend to a visual event that is not adequately registered. Visual sensory and attentional deficits in older adults can occur separately or together. For example, we previously showed that useful field of view shrinkage can occur even in older adults with excellent visual field sensitivity (Ball, Owsley, & Beard, 1990). In fact, 41% of our subjects in the present study having a UFOV® reduction greater than 40% had an average loss of visual field sensitivity of less than 2.5 dB. Furthermore, 43% of our subjects with acuity better than 20/20 had a UFOV® reduction of greater than 40%. Thus although visual status is related to the size of the UFOV®, good visual status alone is not a sufficient condition for a normal UFOV®. Because the UFOV® test relies on both visual sensory and cognitive skills, it provides a more global measure of visual functional status than either sensory or cognitive tests alone, thus improving its sensitivity and specificity in identifying older drivers at risk for crashes. We are currently examining these visual and cognitive mechanisms in order to sort out their relative contributions to UFOV® restrictions, as well as their interactions.

This research has several implications. It suggests that policies that restrict driving privileges based solely on age or on common stereotypes of age-related declines in vision and cognition are scientifically unfounded, as others also argued (Drachman, 1988). Our data also imply that current visual screening techniques, such as tests of acuity and peripheral vision as used at driver licensing sites, are not adequate in identifying which elderly drivers are likely to be involved in crashes. Screening tests of acuity and peripheral vision administered at licensing offices may have other benefits for the older adult population, such as screening out those with profound vision loss and designating those in need of referral for eye care. But our analysis indicates they do not successfully identify elderly drivers who have a recent history of crash involvement, thus posing a safety risk to themselves and other road users. We identified a composite measure of visual attention and visual processing speed highly predictive of crash problems in the elderly. With the identification of this or similar tests, this study points to a way in which the suitability of licensure in the older driver can be based on objective, performance-based criteria.

ATTENTIONAL TRAINING
AND OTHER INTERVENTIONS

In general, medical diagnoses and sensory tests are inadequate for prediction of everyday abilities, or for competency in industrial or military settings. There is a need, therefore, for functional measures, such as the UFOV®, which are predictive of job or task performance. In addition, there is a need to explore ways in which performance can be improved. It is likely that some older adults will have to be restricted from driving because of serious and irreversible deterioration in skills crucial to driving. However, it may be the case that many older adults with driving problems can improve their driving skills through treatment of ocular conditions impairing visual function (e.g., cataract, glaucoma) or through training or educational programs. We previously showed that a reduction in UFOV® size in some older adults can be at least partially reversed through a training program (Ball, Beard, Roenker, Miller, & Griggs, 1988; Ball, Roenker, & Bruni, 1990). This training targeted the individual's specific attentional deficit(s) (e.g., processing speed or the ability to divide attention between two targets in either an uncluttered or cluttered visual field). Training progressed by gradually decreasing presentation time in order to increase processing speed and, in the case of multiple targets, successively increasing the eccentricity of peripheral targets. The training required only a modest investment in time, and the resulting field expansion was maintained 1 year after completion of the program.

The intriguing question remaining is, given that UFOV® shrinkage is associated with increased crash frequency, would expansions in UFOV® size through a laboratory training program lead to improved driving performance and decreased crashes? Our study also indicated that some older adults, who are at risk for crashes because they have serious visual impairment, modify their driving behavior by avoiding exposure to challenging driving situations (e.g., driving alone, turning left across traffi, driving at night). This self-regulation of driving behavior was associated with a lower crash frequency. Therefore, if older adults were better educated about their visual information processing problems including visual attentional deficits, some might voluntarily impose restrictions on their driving behavior that could lower their crash risk. Research to evaluate these potential interventions should be given high priority, given society's need to enhance the mobility and personal independence of older adults without sacrificing safety concerns.

Given these statements, a logical step in the research is to evaluate potential interventions for reducing crash risk. Our model in Figs. 11.1 or 11.5 suggests there are at least two ways in which one could intervene to lower crash risk—to improve visual sensory function, or to expand the size of the useful field of view. We are examining these two ways of intervening in our ongoing research. First, patients who are candidates for cataract surgery will be evaluated with respect to visual and cognitive abilities before and after surgery and intraocular lens insertion in terms of how this ophthalmic intervention reduces crash risk and expands driving habits. Cataract surgery is the most common surgical procedure covered by Medicare in the elderly population, accounting for 12% of the entire Medicare budget (Stark, Sommer & Smith, 1989), and is also a highly successful intervention. Studies reported that 90% of patients achieve at least 20/40 acuity or better following surgery (Straatsma, Foos, Horwitz, Gardner, & Petit, 1985). This is a common and effective way that vision is improved in the elderly, and is thus an ideal scenario for evaluating to what extent improvement in visual sensory function reduces crash risk and improves other aspects of mobility.

For our second intervention, which is currently under evaluation, there is some preliminary evidence that expansion of the UFOV® improves driving performance. Mature drivers (55+ years, N = 317) were screened on acuity, contrast sensitivity, and UFOV®. From this pool, 87 individuals were identified for potential inclusion in a training study (primarily based on the extent of UFOV® reduction), and 68 agreed to participate. Thirty-three of these subjects completed a UFOV® training program, 24 completed a simulator training program, and 11 served as controls. Subjects in the UFOV® training group received individualized training until a UFOV® size of less than 30% loss was achieved. Subjects in the simulator training group received 3 hours of training in a Doron Driving Simulator and 1 additional hour in an open road demonstration of the skills discussed while in the simulator. Control subjects received no training. All subjects were assessed pre- and posttraining on (a) the size of the UFOV®, (b) simple and complex RT as well as the detection of threatening driving situations in a Doron

Driving Simulator, and (c) a detailed evaluation with a driving instructor during an on-the-road driving test.

The results of UFOV® training were successful in that those in the UFOV® training group showed a significant decrease in UFOV® loss. UFOV® size did not change significantly during the training phase for those in the simulator or control groups. Both simple RT measures and the probability of detecting a threatening event did not differ between the three groups initially, and was not altered by training. Performance in the complex RT task, however, did reveal a significant improvement for the UFOV® training group only. In this task, subjects were required to scan a display covering an area of 8' × 10' and containing three to six targets. Unpredictably, one of the targets would change and the subject was required to respond to the change. Given a car moving at 55 miles per hour, subjects in the UFOV® training group responded by stopping or maneuvering their vehicle 26 feet earlier following training relative to their pretest measure. This corresponds to a 14% improvement in stopping time.

Several measures were evaluated from the open road driving test: (a) a global rating of driving skill by an experienced driving instructor, (b) a global rating by two back seat evaluators, (c) six composite scores generated from 455 behaviorally anchored specific driving maneuvers, and (d) the number of hazardous maneuvers during the drive as determined by the driving instructor. For all subjects, regardless of group, there was a significant improvement in global ratings of their driving skills during the testing period as rated by both the experienced driving instructor and the back seat evaluators. All six composites generated from the 455 items also showed significant improvement from pre- to posttraining regardless of group. The number of hazardous maneuvers during the drive showed a different pattern, however. For this measure, the number of hazardous maneuvers was significantly reduced for only the UFOV® training group (by 50%). The number of hazardous maneuvers did not differ for the simulator and control groups pre- and posttraining.

Thus, study data demonstrate that UFOV® training transfers to driving tasks, such as reduced stopping time to an unexpected perceptual event, and to a reduction in the number of dangerous maneuvers in an on-the-road driving evaluation. Although the occurrence of hazardous maneuvers is relatively infrequent while driving, a 50% reduction in such maneuvers has potential safety benefits.

Other types of interventions must also be considered. Older drivers with visual impairment were more likely to avoid difficult driving situations than were those without these deficits (Ball et al., 1993). That is, some older drivers may self-regulate their driving (i.e., exercise certain self-imposed limitations if they became aware of their visual deficits). Thus, a mechanism for educating older drivers about how their visual processing problems impact their driving ability under challenging driving situations may minimize crash risk. These types of interventions underwent some preliminary evaluations (Janke, 1994), but a clear-cut answer as to the utility of this type of intervention is not yet available.

APPLICATIONS FOR ATTENTION
ASSESSMENT-TRAINING

As stated earlier, the ability to pay attention is a functional ability we cannot do without, and yet this ability is something most adults take for granted. Everyone experiences diminished attentional function at some time due to fatigue, stress, illness, or alcohol consumption. However, it is only when this ability is lost, such as following traumatic brain injury, stroke, dementia, or age-related decline, that the full range of everyday activities affected by attentional function become apparent. At the other end of the continuum, occupations that require above-average attentional skills are becoming more prevalent in industry and the military as society continues to become more technical. Thus, the applications for new technology to evaluate and train attentional function include not only older drivers, but also older pilots, older workers, and younger individuals who must meet the requirements for exceptional performance. Our research showed that although attentional function can be regained in some individuals following traumatic brain injury, this type of rehabilitation is both time consuming and costly. Thus the benefits of using new technology for prevention of injury on the road or in the workplace could significantly reduce the cost of health care in the future.

ACKNOWLEDGMENTS

The research program described in this chapter is a collaborative effort between the author and Cynthia Owsley, University of Alabama at Birmingham, and is performed under the auspices of the Center for Mobility Enhancement in the Elderly, an Edward R. Roybal Center for Research in Applied Gerontology, funded by the National Institute on Aging/NIH (P5O AG11684). Additional support was provided by NIH grants R01 AG04212, R01 AG05739, R44 AG09727, EY08084, the AARP Andrus Foundation, and Research to Prevent Blindness, Inc. I would like to thank the following collaborators who participated in various aspects of the research: Michael Sloane, Daniel Roenker, John Bruni, Milton White, Mark Graves, Dewanna Keeton, Todd Overley, Arren Graf, Beth Thomas, Lynn Tyndall, Gayla Cissel, and Pat Roenker. I would also like to thank the Alabama Department of Public Safety and the Kentucky Deptartment of Transportation for their cooperation.

REFERENCES

Ball, K., Beard, B., Roenker, D. L., Miller, R., & Griggs, D. (1988). Age and visual search: Expanding the useful field of view. *Journal of the Optical Society of America, 5*, 2210–2219.
Ball, K., & Owsley, C. (1991). Identifying correlates of accident involvement for the older driver. *Human Factors, 33*, 583–595.

Ball, K., & Owsley, C. (1993). The useful field of view test: A new technique for evaluating age-related declines in visual function. *Journal of the American Optometric Association, 64,* 71–79.

Ball, K., Owsley, C., & Beard, B. (1990). Clinical visual perimetry underestimates peripheral field problems in older adults. *Clinical Vision Science, 5,* 113–125.

Ball, K., Owsley, C., Sloane, M. E., Roenker, D. L., & Bruni, J. R. (1993). Visual attention problems as a predictor of vehicle crashes in older drivers. *Investigative Ophthalmology and Visual Science, 34,* 3110–3123.

Ball, K., Roenker, D. L., & Bruni, J. R. (1990). Developmental changes in attention and visual search throughout adulthood. In J. Enns (Ed.), *Advances in psychology* (Vol. 69, pp. 489–508). Amsterdam: Elsevier.

Barr, R. A. (1991). Recent changes in driving among older adults. *Human Factors, 33,* 597–600.

Barrett, B. V., Mihal, W. L., Panek, P. E., Sterns, H. L., & Alexander, R. A. (1977). Information-processing skills predictive of accident involvement for younger and older commercial drivers. *Ind Gerontol, 4,* 173–182.

Byrne, B. (Ed.). (1989). *A primer of LISREL VII.* New York: Springer-Verlag.

Drachman, D. A. (1988). Who may drive? Who may not? Who shall decide? *Annals of Neurology, 24,* 787–788.

Farnsworth, D. (1947). *The Farnsworth Dichotomous Test for Color Blindness, Panel D-15 Manual.* New York: Psychological Corporation.

Federal Highway Administration. (1989). *The Federal Highway Administration's action plan for older persons.* Washington, DC: U.S. Department of Transportation.

Ferris, III, F. L., Kassoff, A., Bresnick, G. H., & Bailey, I. (1982). New visual acuity charts for clinical research. *American Journal of Ophthalmology, 94,* 91–96.

Haley, M. J., (Ed.). (1987). *The Humphrey Field Analyzer primer.* San Leandro, CA: Allergan Humphrey.

Henderson, R., & Burg, A. (1974). *Vision and audition in driving* (Tech. Rep. No. TM(L)–5297–000–000). Crawthorne, England: U.S. Department of Transportation.

Hills, B. L., & Burg, A. (1977). *A Re-analysis of California driver vision data: General findings* (Rep. No. 768). Crowthorne, England: Transport and Road Research Laboratory.

Hoyer, W., & Plude, D. (1982). Aging and the allocation of attentional resources in visual information processing. In R. Sekuler, D. Kline & K. Dismukes (Eds.), *Aging and human visual function.* (pp. 245–263). New York: Liss.

Janke, M. (1994). *Age-related disabilities that may impair driving and their assessment.* California Dept. Of Motor Vehicles.

Joreskog, K. G., & Sorbom, D. (1989). *LISREL VII: A guide to the program and application* (2nd ed.). Chicago: SPSS, Inc.

Julesz, B. (1981). Textons, the elements of texture perception and their interactions. *Nature, 290,* 91–97.

Kahneman, D., Ben-Ishai, R., & Lotan, M. (1973). Relation of a test of attention to road accidents. *Journal of Applied Psychology, 58,* 113–115.

Lezak, M. D. (1983). *Neuropsychological assessment* (2nd ed.). New York: Oxford University Press.

Mattis, S. (1976). Mental status examination for organic mental syndrome in the elderly patient. L. Bella & T. B. Karasu (Eds.), *Geriatric psychiatry* (2nd ed., pp. 77–121). New York: Oxford University Press.

Mihal, W. L. & Barrett, G. V. (1976). Individual differences in perceptual information processing and their relation to automobile accident involvement. *Journal of Applied Psychology, 61,* 229–233.

National Highway Traffic Safety Administration. (1989). *Conference on research and development needed to improve safety and mobility of older drivers* (Rep. No. DOT–807–554). Washington, DC: U.S. Department of Transportation.

National Research Council. (1985). *Injury in America: A continuing public health problem.* Washington DC: National Academy Press.

Neisser, U. (1967). *Cognitive psychology.* New York: Appleton-Century-Crofts.

Neisser, U. (1976). *Cognition and reality.* San Francisco: Freeman.

Owsley, C. (1994). Vision and driving in the elderly. *Optometry and Vision Science, 71*, 727–735.

Owsley, C., & Ball, K. (1993). Assessing visual function in the older driver . In S. Retchin (Ed.), *Clinics in geriatric medicine: Medical considerations in the older driver* (pp. 389–401). Philadelphia: Saunders.

Owsley, C., Ball, K., Sloane, M. E., Overley, E. T., & White, M. F. (1994). Predicting vehicle crashes in the elderly: Who is at risk? *The Gerontologist, 34*, 61.

Owsley, C., Ball, K., Sloane, M., Roenker, D. L., & Bruni, J. R. (1991). Visual/cognitive correlates of vehicle accidents in older drivers. *Psychology of Aging, 6*, 403–415.

Owsley, C., & Sloane, M. E. (1990). Vision and aging. In F. Boller & J. Grafman (Eds.), *Handbook of neuropsychology* (pp. 229–249). Amsterdam: Elsevier.

Parasuraman, R., & Nestor, P. G. (1991). Attention and driving skills in aging and Alzheimer's Disease. *Human Factors, 33*, 539–557.

Pelli, D. G., Robson, J. G., & Wilkins, A. J. (1988). The design of a new letter chart for measuring contrast sensitivity. *Clinical Visual Science, 2*, 187–199.

Plude, D. J., & Hoyer, W. J. (1985). Attention and performance: Identifying and localizing age deficits. In N. Charness (Eds.), *Aging and performance* (pp. 47–99). London: Wiley.

Plude, D. J., & Hoyer, W. J. (1986). Age and selectivity of visual information processing. *Journal of Psychology and Aging, 1*, 4–10.

Shinar, D. (1977). *Driver visual limitations: Diagnosis and treatment.* (Contract No. DOT–HS–5–1275). Washington, DC: U.S. Department of Transportation.

Shinar, D. (1978). *Driver performance and individual differences in attention and information processing: Vol. 1. Driver inattention* (Rep. No. DOT–HS–8–801819). Washington, DC: U.S. Department of Transportation.

Shinar, D., & Schieber, F. (1991). Visual requirements for safety and mobility of older drivers. *Human Factors, 33*, 507–519.

Simons, K. (1981). A comparison of the Frisby, Random-Dot E, TNO, and Randot Circles Stereotests in screening and office use. *Archaological Ophthalmology, 99*, 446–452.

Stark, W. J., Sommer, A., & Smith, R. E. (1989). Changing trends in introcular lens implantation. *Archives of Ophthalmology, 107*, 1441.

Straatsma, B. R., Foos, R. X., Horwitz, J., Gardner, K. M., & Petit, T. H. (1985). Aging related cataract: Laboratory investigating and clinical management. *Annals of Internal Medicine, 107*, 82–92

Transportation Research Board. (1988). *Transportation in an aging society.* Washington, DC: National Research Council.

Treisman, A., & Gelade, G. (1980). A feature-integration theory of attention. *Cognitive Psychology, 12*, 97–136.

Verriest, G., Barca, L., Calbria, E., et al. (1983). The occupational visual field: II. Practical aspects: The functional visual field in abnormal conditions and its relationship to visual ergonomics, visual impairment and job fitness. In G. Verriest (Ed.), *Sixth International Visual Field Symposium* (pp. 281–326). Junk, The Netherlands: Kluwer Academic.

Author Index

A

Abbott, M. W., 212, *214*
Abbott, R., 105, *119*, 127, 128, 130, 133, 134, 136, 137, 138, 142, *149, 150, 151*
Abdulla, H. I., 255, *262*
Abe, T., 241, 249, *262*
Aber, J. L., 222, *238*
Abrams, W. B., 240, *262*
Aburdene, P., 261, *262*
Achenbach, T. M., 185, 193, *214*
Adami, H-O, 245, *263*
Adams, M. R., 259, *263*
Adan, A. M., 203, *215*
Ades, A., 228, *237*
Adler, A., 106, *118*
Aiken, M., 255, *262*
Ainsworth, M. D. S., 42, *74*
Aksel, S., 241, *262*
Albanese, A., 255, *262*
Alegria, J., 90, 91, *98, 100*
Alexander, R. A., 269, *291*
Allen, L., 222, *238*
Almeida, M. C., 202, *215*
American Psychological Association, 185, *214*
Andersen, B. L., 247, *266*
Anderson, J., 194, *216*
Anderson, J. C., 194, *214*
Applebaum, M., 133, *150*
Arter, J., 127, *149*
Asher, S. R., 159, 161, 164, 165, 168, 174, 175, *176, 178, 179*
Astone, N. M., 21, 22, 24, 27, *32*
Avis, N. E., *262*
Ayalon, J., 256, *266*
Aylward, G. P., 9, 10, 11, 12, 15, 16, 17, 18, 19, 22, 23, *31*

B

Babigian, H., 164, *177*
Backman, J., 81, 90, 94, *98*
Baddeley, A. D., 78, *98*
Baerts, W., 9, 11, *34*
Bailey, I., 273, *291*
Bakeman, R., 9, 16, *31*
Baker, J. M., 175, *176*
Bakhtin, M., 220, *236*
Baldwin, C. D., 15, *33*
Ball, K., 268, 269, 271, 272, 274, 275, 278, 282, 286, 287, 289, 290, 291, *292*
Ballinger, C. B., 249, 251, *262*
Bally, H., 138, *152*
Bancroft, J., 247, *262*
Bandler, R., 72, *74*
Banks, M. H., 228, *237*
Barbour, M. M., 257, *263*
Barder, T., 105, *122*
Barken, T., 106, *118*
Barlow, D. H., 250, *263*
Barnard, K., 106, 112, *119*
Barnard, K. E., 11, 12, 13, 16, 18, *31*
Barnett, R. C., 208, *214*
Barocas, R., 12, *34,* 112, *121*
Baron, J., 82, *98*
Baron, L., 191, *214*
Barr, R. A., 270, *291*
Barrett, B. V., 269, 271, *291*
Barrett, K., 112, *118*
Bart, P., 241, 250, *262*
Baruch, G. K., 208, *214*
Bates, E., 127, *149*
Bauer, C. R., 29, *32*
Baumrind, D., 199, 201, 203, 208, *214*
Bayley, N., 108, *118*

293

Subject Index

305